ISBN 978-1-5281-7699-6
PIBN 10927949

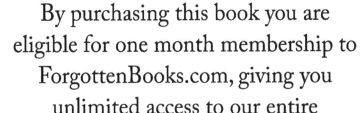

English
Français
Deutsche
Italiano
Español
Português

www.forgottenbooks.com

Mythology Photography **Fiction**
Fishing Christianity **Art** Cooking
Essays Buddhism Freemasonry
Medicine **Biology** Music **Ancient**
Egypt Evolution Carpentry Physics
Dance Geology **Mathematics** Fitness
Shakespeare **Folklore** Yoga Marketing
Confidence Immortality Biographies
Poetry **Psychology** Witchcraft
Electronics Chemistry History **Law**
Accounting **Philosophy** Anthropology
Alchemy Drama Quantum Mechanics
Atheism Sexual Health **Ancient History**
Entrepreneurship Languages Sport
Paleontology Needlework Islam
Metaphysics Investment Archaeology
Parenting Statistics Criminology
Motivational

EXTRACTS

FROM THE

INFORMATION RECEIVED

BY

HIS MAJESTY'S COMMISSIONERS,

AS TO THE

ADMINISTRATION AND OPERATION

OF THE

POOR-LAWS.

PUBLISHED BY AUTHORITY.

LONDON:

B. FELLOWES, LUDGATE STREET.

MDCCCXXXIII.

TO THE

RIGHT HON. LORD VISCOUNT MELBOURNE,

His Majesty's Principal Secretary of State for the Home Department.

MY LORD,

On the receipt of the letter with which we were honoured by your Lordship, " requesting us to transmit, in detail, the information which we have received as to the administration and operation of the poor-laws, in some of the parishes in which those laws have been administered in various modes, and particularly any returns to our inquiries, which show the results of the various modes adopted in those parishes," we applied to the gentlemen who have had the kindness to act as our assistant commissioners, and requested them to furnish us with such extracts from the evidence collected by them as they thought most instructive. The following pages contain answers to our applications, and we have appended to them a copy of the instructions given by us to the assistant commissioners at the commencement of their inquiries in order to show the specific points to which their attention was directed.

The length to which this collection has extended is much greater than we at first expected it to be. But it appeared to us on consideration, that evidence from which any practical conclusions could be drawn, must consist of many instances spread over a considerable extent of country. The modes in which the poor-laws are administered, the motives to their mal-administration, and the results of each form of mal-administration, are so numerous and so diversified, that a complete statement of them, even without comment, would fill a much larger volume than that which we now present to your Lordship. We believe, however, that this volume, though a small portion of the evidence, which we are preparing to report to His Majesty, contains more information on the subject to which it relates than has ever yet been afforded to the country. The most important, and certainly the most painful parts of its contents are,—the proof that the mal-administration, which was supposed to be principally confined to some of the agricultural districts, appears to have spread over almost every part of the country, and into the manufacturing towns—the proof that actual intimidation, directed against those who are, or are supposed to be unfavourable to profuse relief, is one of the most extensive sources of mal-administration,—and the proof that the evil, though checked in some places by extraordinary energy and talents, is, on the whole, steadily and rapidly progressive.

We have the honour to be,

My Lord,

Your Lordship's obedient Servants,

C. J. LONDON.

J. B. CHESTER.

W. STURGES BOURNE.

NASSAU W. SENIOR.

HENRY BISHOP.

HENRY GAWLER.

W. COULSON.

Poor-Law Commission, 19th March, 1833.

CONTENTS.

b

CONTENTS.

OVERSEERS AND PAROCHIAL OFFICERS

ERRATA.

Note in Mr. Majendie's reports,—the returns of expenditure for 1832 include county-rate, &c.

Page 4, note, for ' expense of collection,' read ' expense of cultivation.'

—— 32, for ' Hill ' read ' Hele.'

—— 196, line 19,—sum granted to Board of Health should be ' 1000*l*.,' not ' 100*l*.'

—— 200, line 12, for ' silk-clubs,' read sick-clubs.'

—— 230, line 22, amount of deposits should be ' 8753*l*. 17*s*. 2*d*. ;' or the average should be ' 38*l*.' not ' 88*l*.'

—— 282, line 32, for ' 14,500,' read ' 14,640.'

—— 332, line 22, for ' Mr. Burns,' read ' Mr. Bunn.'

Communication to the Poor-Law Commissioners from Ashhurst Majendie, Esq.

My Lords and Gentlemen,

In the following selections from the important district which has been assigned to me, my object has been to show, first, from the example of Lenham, in Kent, the effects of a local redundancy of population, a lavish scale of relief, and a general want of control, in forcing land from the occupation of the tenant, and partially out of cultivation. The present condition of Eastbourn seems to prove the absolute necessity of some general superintendence; and that, under the present system, there is no security for the continuance of any temporary improvement, which the exertions of individuals may have effected. Seaford offers an instance of abuse, by the application of Poor-Rates to borough influence. The inadequate wages paid to single men, the harsh treatment of the unemployed, and the payment of wages and relief by tickets on the shops, produced a degree of irritation among the labourers, which led to the riots in East Sussex. The consequence has been, the establishment of a compulsory rate of wages and relief, which is rapidly exhausting the funds on which the labourers depend for subsistence. The first step to amendment is, the protection of property by an effective police. The introduction of Mr. Becher's improved workhouse system at Stanford Rivers, in Essex, has nearly banished pauperism from that place. It is most satisfactory to observe, in this and all cases where the " allowance " system has been abolished, that the condition of the labourers has been materially improved. The benefit of Cottage Allotments is strongly shown at Saffron Walden. Of all remedies for pauperism, this offers the most cheering prospect: it affords to the labourers the means of increasing the funds for their maintenance by their own exertions; it calls into action industry, the source of all capital, under the influence of the best feelings of our nature.

I have the honour to be,
My Lords and Gentlemen,
Your very obedient and very humble servant,
ASHHURST MAJENDIE.

B

LENHAM, KENT.

Expended on Poor.

£.	£.	£.	£.
In 1816..1468	1820..2154	1824..3041	1828..2482
1817..1598	1821..2348	1825..3438	1829..2611
1818..2150	1822..2618	1826..2531	1830..3040
1819..2016	1823..2786	1827..2731	1831..2679
			1832..4299

POPULATION.

In 1801	In 1811	In 1821	In 1831
1434	1509	1959	2197

Acres.	Rental.	Value.	Rates in the £	Expenditure, March, 1832.
6523	6423*l.*	⅔	12*s.* expected to rise to 14*s.*	Casual relief, 1992*l.* 6*s.* Weekly pay, 1033*l.* 17*s.* Various bills, 1273*l.* 9*s.* Total 4299*l.* 12*s.*

Labour and bills for work on the highways . 561*l.*
Deduct money repaid by the commissioners . 147*l.*
                                          414*l.*

Total Expenditure of Poor and Surveyor's Rates   4713*l.* 12*s.*

This is an extensive agricultural parish; much of the land is of poor quality, still there is a considerable quantity of land of a fair average; some is out of cultivation; a large estate has been several years in the hands of the proprietor, and a farm of 420 acres of good land, tithe free, well situated, has been just thrown up by the tenant of another landowner: the poor-rate on this farm amounts to nearly 300*l.* per annum. Wages in summer are 2*s.* 3*d.* When labourers are out of employ, or only in partial employ, their wages are made up according to the following scale :—

		£.	*s.*	*d.*
Single man, from . . .		3*s.* 6*d.* to	7*s.*	0*d.*
Man and wife			10	0
Do. with 1 or 2 children . . .			12	0
Do.	3 do.		13	0
Do.	4 do.		14	0
Do.	5 do.		15	6
Do.	6 do.		17	0
Do.	7 do.		18	6
Do.	8 do.		20	0

The labourers are sent to work on the roads if there is anything to do, but they are paid according to this scale whether they work or not. On Saturday the 13th of October last, 27 men were paid from 12*s.* upwards each, though no work whatever had been done. There have been 70 men on the roads in one week, paid according to scale: the greater part of the work is unnecessary; besides the wages, tools are provided, and it is calculated that the value of the labour does not exceed the expense of the tools and carting. The average number unemployed from November to May is from 60 to 70. During the harvest they are mostly in employ, but if a man loses a day's work, he comes to the parish to have it made up. Nearly 100 out-parishioners, living at Maidstone, receive occasional, or constant relief. There is a man who hires two cows and keeps several pigs, who, when out of work, receives from the parish 18s. per week. The population of this parish is beyond the demand for labour; but early marriages are constantly taking place without any consideration on that score: of six of these marriages contracted last October, it was expected that most of the parties would be on the parish pay-list in the month of November. A man lately married a girl, who left her place for that purpose on Wednesday, they applied for relief on the Saturday. It will appear from the scale that, on marriage, there is an immediate increase of 3s. per week*. The administering relief to from 70 to 100 men on the pay night, in a district near the place where the riots first broke out, and where one of the causes of dissatisfaction was the reduction of " allowances," is a duty requiring more firmness than belongs to many overseers; nor is the present state of the rural police adequate to the requisite protection. Relief is given in money. There is no fixed salary to the surgeon ; the average medical expense is about 70*l*.

The Select Vestry is not well attended, and there is a great division among the parishioners. The assistant-overseer has a salary of 60*l*. The system of accounts is not satisfactory. Four principal farmers were lately appointed auditors, who found many overcharges. After this statement, it is not surprising that the parish has been forced this summer to borrow 100*l*. from the Maidstone Bank, for the purpose of paying the paupers. Among the modes devised for improvement has been a Labour Rate†.

* In the workhouse are 35 inmates. Young men have been sometimes sent there, but they have said, " You put us in to punish us ; we will only marry the sooner."

† This has been attempted under the late Act of Parliament. According to the following plan, there are in the parish 115 married men, 75 single men, and 40 boys above the age of 12. The wages of these, calculating the married at 13s. 6d. per week, single at 8s., boys at 3s., would amount to about 500*l*. per month. This sum has been assessed on the respective occupiers, according to the different value of the land.

	s.	d.	
The poor arable, at	1	6	per acre, per month.
The superior arable	2	0	
Hops	5	0	
Meadow, pasture, and wood	0	10	
Great tithes, 9 men, at	9	6	} 5*l*. 14s. per week.
Small tithes, 3 men	9	6	

The amount is either to be worked out, or paid to the overseer at the end of the month. The plan has been in operation three weeks, during which

Emigration has been carried to some extent last spring. It having appeared that of a population of 2200 persons, 1200 received relief, 450*l.* was borrowed on the bond of some principal occupiers, to be repaid by yearly instalments, according to the expense which would have been incurred for the maintenance of the families had they remained: 50 persons were sent to Quebec. It was found, on their arrival, that there was not that demand for labour which was expected; they went forward to York, in Upper Canada, and found the same state of things: the letters which have been received represent that the land is not good; that the farmers are not able to employ the labourers; that in several places the influx of emigrants has been too great; that many could not get work; and the letters are so unfavourable, that it is thought that no more will go to Canada. The only letter which I saw, however, was one lately arrived, which was of a favourable description, for the man had obtained a situation, where he was boarded, and received 35*l.* per annum as wages. It unfortunately happens in the parish of Lenham, that there has not always been a good understanding between the Magistrates and the Select Vestry. Four labourers of bad character, receiving constant parish pay, applied for linen and other clothing, and were refused by the Select Vestry. On application to the Bench, an order was made on the overseer to give money to the men; the Vestry directed the overseer not to obey; the Magistrates threatened to issue a distress warrant; but a deputation from the Vestry proceeded to the Magistrates' meeting, pointed out the clause, respecting relief, in Mr. Sturges Bourne's Act, and the order was rescinded. There is only a monthly sitting, and no acting Magistrate near; so that the overseer is forced to go 10 miles to Maidstone, when a summons is required.

time there have been eight or nine men on the roads; whereas, at a corresponding period in preceding years, there have been from 60 to 80 men out of employ, nor would these few have been out of work, but that it is thought the Act is not so worded as to make agreements compulsory. The farmers now seem to think there are not too many hands in the parish to cultivate the land properly. The parish, consisting of 6500 acres, the sum of 500*l.* per month, amounts to about 1*l.* per acre per annum; and according to general information, the labour required in fair farming must be equal to that expenditure. The experiment is but just commenced, and must be continued for a length of time before it can be ascertained whether it may ultimately succeed. The effect of a Labour Rate can hardly be brought to a fairer test, as respects its effects on the parish adopting it. How far the parish will be affected by other parishes following its example and returning to Lenham all the Lenham men in their employ, is another question. It is obvious too that giving to the tithe owner, who is entitled to his tithe free from the expense of collection, and consequently has a very small demand for labour, the alternative of either employing 12 men or paying 5*l.* 14*s.* a week, is, in fact, a mode of relieving the rate-payers by confiscating the tithes; which indeed is the usual motive to a labour-rate.

Answers from the Vicar, Churchwarden, and Assistant-Overseer of the Parish of Lenham, in the County of Kent, to the Queries of the Commissioners.

ANSWERS BY THE VICAR, CHURCHWARDEN, AND
QUERIES CIRCULATED BY

Queries.	Vicar.
1. Is it less common than formerly for labourers to live under their employers' roofs, and to what do you attribute the change?	It is less common than formerly; the change, I conceive, is to be attributed to the allowance system; married men, whom it would be impossible to lodge, are employed in preference to single, as the latter can be maintained at less expense by the parish.
2. What class of persons are the usual proprietors of cottages?	Tradesmen principally, who find it a certain and productive investment of capital.
3. Are cottages frequently exempted from rates? and is their rent often paid by the parish?	Always. In many instances rent paid, indirectly, by the parish.
4. Is the industry of the labourers in your neighbourhood supposed to be increasing or diminishing; that is, are your labourers supposed to be better or worse workmen than they formerly were?	Decidedly diminishing: nor is it to be wondered at, when a man maintained in idleness (nominally at work) on the road receives the same as a man regularly at work on the land.
5. Is piece-work general in your neighbourhood?	Not at all.
6. What might an average labourer obtaining an average amount of employment expect to earn during the year, including harvest work?	His wages, independent of his allowance according to the number of his family, would amount to 35*l*., and he might expect to earn, in addition, 1*l*. or 2*l*. at harvest.
7. What might his wife and four children, aged 14, 11, 8, and 5 years, respectively expect to earn?	From 3*l*. to 5*l*.
8. Could the family subsist on these earnings? And if so, on what food?	I think they might. On bread, cheese, or butter; tea, and occasionally salt pork.

ASSISTANT-OVERSEER OF LENHAM KENT, TO THE THE COMMISSIONERS.

Churchwarden.	Assistant Overseer.
Yes. Because a married man has more from the poor books than a single one.	It is not usual for farm-servants in this parish to live under the roofs of the masters.
Persons that are making a small income rather larger, instead of embarking it in business, where it is sure to be taxed.	Landed proprietors, professional men, and tradesmen.
Always exempted from the rate, if the labourer belongs to the parish. The rents are much paid by the parish.	They are exempt from rates, except when possessed by persons chargeable to other parishes, and the rent in all cases paid by the parish.
Very much diminishing: one-third of our labourers do not work at all; the greater number of the remainder are much contaminated; the rising population learn nothing; the others are forgetting what they knew, for want of practice.	They are decidedly less industrious, and worse workmen.
Not much.	No.
A good labourer in constant employment will earn 2s. 3d. per day, wet day excepted. With a little task-work, which he will have at harvest and hopping, he will average 2s. 6d. per day: he must not be sick during the year.	An industrious labourer might earn 40l. or 45l.
They may earn in harvest and hopping two or three pounds: there is no employment at any other time.	They might collectively earn 5l.
They can buy more food now wheat is about 8s. per bushel for 2s. 6d., than they could for 3s. 6d., when wheat was about 15s.	I think they could. They could subsist on bread, cheese, bacon, suet-puddings, and potatoes.

Queries.	Vicar.
9. Could it lay by any thing? and how much?	The present system inculcates such improvidence, that saving is utterly out of the question. Our carpenters and bricklayers, though earning a guinea a week in summer, always fall on the parish during the winter months.
10. Is there any and what difference between the wages of the married and unmarried?	On the road, man and wife, 10s.; single, 7s. 6d. On the land, I believe, there is no difference.
11. Have you many able-bodied labourers receiving allowance or regular relief from your parish?	In a population of 2100 souls, during the year, we have from 40 to 90, *entirely* subsistent on the parish funds; in addition, and all those with more than 3 children, receive weekly sums proportionate to the number of their family. Last winter, a very mild one, our weekly pays amounted to nearly 90l. a week for many weeks; they are now 50l.
12. Is that relief or allowance generally given in consequence of the advice or order of the magistrates? or under the opinion that the magistrates would make an order for it if application were made to them?	Certainly; under the impression that an order would be made, should we refuse.
13. Is any and what attention paid to the character of the applicant, or the causes of his distress?	None whatever.
14. Is relief or allowance given according to any, and what scale?	Man and wife, with 1 or 2 children, 12s.; 3, 13s.; 4, 14s.; 5, 15s. 6d.; 6, 17s.; 7, 18s. 6d.; 8, 20s
15. What do you think would be the effects, both immediate and ultimate, of an enactment forbidding such allowance? And should families of more than a certain, and	As nothing can be more ruinous than the present system, I should conceive such an enactment beneficial; and though its immediate effects might be attended with some inconvenience to the poor, I should

Churchwarden.	Assistant Overseer.
They do not attempt; for immediately they are out of work, or ill, they apply for their parish allowance.	Certainly not.
There are but few single men get employment; some give them 1s. per day, others 1s. 6d.: when they employ them, a married man gets 2s. 3d.	A very great difference. A married man has 2s. 3d. per day, and a single man 1s. 6d.
Yes; a very great number: we have about 180 able-bodied workmen, and we average about 60 of them entirely on the parish the whole of the year.	There are 140 who receive regular relief during winter, and 70 during summer. There are 70 unemployed on the average during the year.
We do generally relieve them without the order of the magistrates; but we are certain they would make us, " from experience:" we do so to save expense, which the magistrates are not very particular in running the parish and county to.	Relief is occasionally given at the recommendation of the magistrates, but most frequently under the conviction that if a pauper would apply to them, an order would follow for whatever sum they thought proper.
The greatest thief in the parish has the magistrates' allowance; the honest but unfortunate get no more.	None whatever. The idle and dissolute are paid equally with the industrious and prudent.
Yes. The single man 5s.; man and wife 10s.; ditto, 1 child, 12s.; 2, 12s.; 3, 13s.; 4, 14s.; 5, 15s.; 6, 17s.; 7, 18s. 6d.; 8, 1l.; to lay about in the roads.	It is given according to an arbitrary scale adopted by the magistrates; viz., two children, 12s.; three, 13s.; four, 14s.; five, 15s. 6d.; six, 17s.; seven, 18s. 6d.; eight, 1l.
I cannot see any benefit we should derive from it.	Such a legislative enactment would be attended with the most beneficial consequences. It would immediately prevent the formation of improvident marriages, which are weekly taking place here in

what number of children, be excepted out of the enactment? And do you think that such an enactment could be successfully evaded in any, and what manner?

apprehend, the occupier h that money in hand which is paid as rate, would expend additional labour, thereby g increased employment; and bringing his land into a hi state of cultivation, increasin own means at the same Very large families ought, per to be exempt, or, at least, prov made for their assistance.

16. What do you think would be the effect, immediate and ultimate, of an enactment giving no appeal from the vestry respecting relief, except to the Quarter Sessions?

I am inclined to think enactment would be desirable, vestry in general is the best j of the nature and measure of : to be granted; whilst the m trates, when appealed to, migh haps feel themselves obliged t here to a prescribed and general

17. Is the amount of agricultural capital in your neighbourhood · increasing or diminishing? And do you attribute such increase or diminution to any cause connected with the administration of the poor laws?

Diminishing: in this parish than 2000*l.* a year is expend unproductive labour, whilst a same time the land is becor daily in a worse state of cultiva and consequently the mean raising this sum daily diminish thus the farmer is compelle employ fewer hands, or sac his capital : by the former mea he increases the rate, alread much as he can pay; by the l he ruins himself.

18. What do you think would be the effects, immediate and ultimate, of an enactment abolishing settlement by hiring and service, apprenticeship, renting or purchasing a tenement, and serving a parish office?

Anything that would sim the manner of acquiring a se ment would be productive of g er benefit.

consequence of the premium held out by the foregoing scale, and ultimately save the parties from that wretchedness and misery which always attend early pauper unions. Relief only to commence when the family increased to three children. I am not aware how the enactment could be evaded.

s little law as possible.

It would immediately save the expenses monthly incurred before the magistrates by the paupers applying for further relief, and ultimately render them more satisfied with the gentlemen composing the Select Vestry, who are generally well acquainted with their characters, their earnings, and wants.

ecreasing. We are compelled eep an increased population. e are but few men that can ibly exist without employment; will invest their capital in ing, to be subject to keep that lation. If they are put on the , the titheman conscientiously s his seventh, and escapes ing them by his rate diminish-

The capital is rapidly diminishing, and is wholly to be ascribed to the heavy poor rates.

would be an inestimable beto this parish.

It would enable this parish immediately to dispose of many young men in towns as apprentices, who are prevented at present from obtaining such situations from an apprehension of their becoming parishioners, as well as give employment to agricultural labourers in neighbouring parishes not oppressed like this with a redundant population, and ultimately save those annual law expenses incurred for appeals to Quarter Sessions on trifling disputed cases.

Queries.	Vicar.
9. Can you give the Commissioners any information respecting the causes and consequences of the agricultural riots and burning of 1830 and 1831?	I conceive the present system of Poor Laws tends to alienate the lower classes from those they have been in the habit of looking up to; renders them idle and improvident, and congregating them in large bodies on the roads, without the wholesome restraint of a master, affords an unchecked opportunity to a few bad characters of inciting others to indulge in wanton mischief, and often more serious crimes.
0. What is the name and county of your parish or township?	Parish of Lenham, county of Kent.

CHARLES PARKIN,
Vicar.

Churchwarden.	Assistant-Overseer.
a. The want of employment ar labourers, and their know- of the abuse which causes the to be left to run to waste.	In the Eastern Division of Kent, where they first commenced, no doubt inadequate wages produced discontent and riot. Many dissatis- fied persons here imagined this a favourable opportunity to extort a more liberal scale of payment, and entered for such purpose into a combination to enforce it. They succeeded in their demands. It did not arise from distress here, as the people were paid much more liberally than in East Kent.
Parish of Lenham, county of Kent.	Lenham, Kent.
GEORGE POWELL, *Churchwarden.*	JOHN PAYNE, *Assistant Overseer.*

EASTBOURN, SUSSEX.

Expended on Poor.

£.	£.	£.	£.
In 1816..3768	1820..2627	1824..2515	1828..2411
1817..3715	1821..3510	1825..2319	1829..2814
1818..3131	1822..2998	1826..2411	1830..3991
1819..3030	1823..2441	1827..2367	1831..3551
			1832..4250

POPULATION.

In 1801	In 1811	In 1821	In 1831
1668	2623	2607	2726

Acres.	Present Rental.	Value.	Rates in the £.	Present Expenditure.
4597	6288l.	said to be near the rack.	13s.	4250l.

Rental, 1815, 8866l.

Weekly Wages, 12s.

EASTBOURNE possesses very great advantages : there is down land of excellent quality for sheep, marsh for cattle, first-rate arable land, producing most abundant crops; chalk cliffs, afford- ing a great source of labour, both in burning lime, and in quarry- ing chalk for export to Rye, and other places on the coast; it is a watering-place, much frequented during the summer; the fishery is in some seasons very productive; and the sea-shore affords boulders for building, and shingle for the repair of roads. With all these sources of employment, the rates have lately nearly doubled. Some years ago, a Select Vestry was established; the cavalry barrack, a building admirably adapted for the purpose, was purchased by the two landowners, to whom the principal property in the parish belongs, for a workhouse; a retired serjeant of militia placed in it as master, and a manufactory of coarse woollens and linens established. Where families were large, some of the children were taken into the house by day, and there earned something for their support, instead of their parents receiving the usual allowance for them; and by constant attention of some of the proprietors and principal occupiers the rates were much reduced. After a time, the master of the workhouse was worn out by the fatigue of the different occupations thrown on him; the manufactory got considerably in debt, and the parish relapsed into a worse state than before; the rates increased to a greater extent than ever, and in the last year, the sum of 150*l.* was borrowed from the Lewes Bank, for the purpose of paying the paupers. With the sole exception of the tickets on shops, all the evils attendant on the administration of the Poor Laws in Sussex are here combined. Cottage rents paid by the parish—allowance according to the number of children—vast sums * expended on unproductive labour, paid at the highest rate of wages, equal to and even exceeding those paid by farmers to their industrious labourers; so that women have been heard to lament that their husbands were not on parish employ, alleging that they would be better off. In the year 1830, a considerable reduction of wages had taken place, many men were out of work, and the wages to single men on the parish did not exceed 7*d.* per day. A general spirit of discontent broke out. Incendiarism prevailed to a frightful extent; an eye-witness informed me, that on one night there were three fires burning at once, in the stack-yards of farmers within the parish; and that for nearly a month, hardly a night passed without conflagrations in the neighbourhood, and tumultuous assemblies of labourers demanding a rise of wages. Under these alarming circumstances, a meeting was called, and an agreement made that the wages should be 2*s.* per day, for an able-bodied married man, 1*s.* 6*d.* for a single man of 18, and from 3*s.* 6*d.* to 5*s.* per week, for boys from 15 to 18. That the surplus labourers on the parish should be paid according to the following scale :—

* These amounted in the year ending March, 1832, to 947*l.*; and the value of the work to the parish is less than 140*l.*

Single man, 18 years of age . 6s. per week.
Man and wife . . . . . 9s. do.
Do. with 1 child . 10s. do.
Do. 2 children 12s. do.
Do. 3 do. . . 12s. do. and a gall. of flour, or 13s. 4d.
Do. 4 ditto . 12s. do. and 2 gall. of flour.

And so on till, for 10 children, the pay might amount to 18s. 8d. per week. A discretion was given to the overseers to grant the flour, or place the children in the poor-house; the latter measure is so unpopular that they dare not put it in practice. The effect of this forced rise of parish pay was soon apparent: the sale of the farmer's produce could not suffice for both wages and rates; a most injurious transfer took place of a portion of the sum expended on labour to the account of rates. The principal occupier in the parish states the relative proportion on his farm to stand thus in round numbers:—

1830.			1831.		
Labour	. .	900l.	Labour	. .	700l.
Rates	.	300l.	Rates	.	500l.

This scale of wages has been continued to those on parish pay to the present day. Being secure of good wages for mere nominal work, the ill-disposed and idle throw themselves wilfully on the parish; the effect is most ruinous on the small householders, who being already on the verge of pauperism, may be converted, by a slight addition to their burthens, from payers to receivers of rates. They have no means of protection, but by uniting for the purpose of an expensive litigation; and have not the opportunity, like the farmers who constitute the Select Vestry, and are principally tenants at will, to throw part of their burthen on their landlords. From a printed statement of the expenditure of the parish, are taken the following items of sums received by families of paupers:—

John Carter, bricklayer, aged 43, wife, and 5
   children, at an allowance of 14s. 8d. per week,
   cost the parish last year . . . £42 12 4
Joseph Carter, 34, wife, and 7 children, 16s. 8d.
   per week £49 11 8
J. Mitchell, 46, wife, and 2 children, 12s. do. 35 4 0
G. Paul, 50, fisherman, do. do. 15s. 6d. do. 25 8 9½

This lavish expenditure, which has been extorted by the violence of the able bodied, is not extended to the aged and infirm, the proper objects of the Poor-Laws, as may be seen by the following items—

Mary Carter, widow, aged 76, at 2s. 6d. per week £6 10 0
Lydia Collins, do. 90 2s. do. 5 4 0
Ann Chapman, do. 75 1s. 6d. do. 3 18 0

In the month of December, 1832, four healthy young men, receiving from 12*s.* to 14*s.* per week from the parish, refused to work at threshing for a farmer at 2*s.* 6*d.* and a quart of ale per day, and the only punishment inflicted on them by the parish officers, was taking off half a day's pay, 1*s.*; at the same time, a poor widow, aged 75, could obtain but 1*s.* per week for her support from the Vestry. The fishermen being secure of pay without labour, refuse to go out to sea in winter: one has said, " Why should I expose myself to fatigue and danger, when the parish supports my family and pays my rent?" The masters in the fishery have in consequence been forced to send to Hastings for hands requisite to man their boats. Rent of cottages is generally paid for families of three children, to the annual amount of 307*l.* Since the time of the riots, and the establishment of the present scale of parish wages, the Vestries held every fortnight for determining relief are very ill attended,—the parishioners seeming to despair of any improvement; and anxious hopes are expressed of the interference of Government.

It is obvious, while such a system of management prevails, that any attempt on the part of proprietors to reduce the rates, or improve the condition of the labourers, must be mere palliatives. Allotments of land, however, have been introduced by Mrs. Davies Gilbert, commencing in 1830 with 35, and increasing the number since to 117. The tenants pay their rent with punctuality; and such is the conviction of the benefit derived, that some other labourers have made a voluntary offer to give up a part of the parish allowance, if allotments were let to them. A remarkable experiment has also been made by Mrs. Gilbert, following a hint given by the Archbishop of Dublin:—a portion of the shingle on the sea-shore has been covered with clay dug from an adjoining marsh, and some good soil afterwards spread on the surface; this land was hired by labourers at 3*d.* per rod, *i. e.* at the rate of 40*s.* per acre, which exceeds the rent of the best arable land in the parish, and a crop of potatoes was raised in the autumn from that which in the spring was unproductive beach.

LIST OF PAUPERS receiving Parochial Relief in the Parish of Eastbourn, Statement of Weekly Allowance to Paupers, and Total Allowance from Lady-day, 1831, to Lady-day, 1832.

Widows, Infirm, and Sick.

Paupers' Names.	Age.	Description.	Residence.	Children under 12 Years.	Weekly Allowance.	Allowance from Lady-day 1831 to Lady-day 1832.
					s. d.	*£. s. d.*
Baker, Ann	68	Widow	Town		2 6	6 10 0
Baulcomb, Ann	70	Ditto	Meads		2 6	6 10 0
Betts, Elizabeth	46	Ditto	Sea-side	1	4 0	9 10 0
Bradford, Nicholas}	69	Labourer	Town			2 11 6
Breden, Thomas		Fisherman	Ditto			6 10 0
Carter, Mary	76	Widow	South		2 6	6 10 0
Collins, Lydia	90	Ditto	Meads		2 0	5 4 0
Chapman, Ann	75	Ditto	Ditto		1 6	3 18 0
Criss, Susan	75	Ditto	South		2 6	6 10 0
Crunden, Mary	67	Ditto	Ditto		2 0	5 4 6
French, Mary	78	Ditto	Since dead		2 6	4 17 0
Fraser, Jane		Ditto	Ditto		2 6	4 15 0
Harrington, Mary	78	Ditto	Sea-side		2 6	6 10 0
Head, Charlotte	61	Ditto	Ditto		1 6	3 18 0
Holter, Charlotte	45	Ditto	Meads	6	9 0	27 8 0
Hollands, Lydia	67	Ditto	Town		2 6	1 5 0
Marchant, Henry	59	Sawyer	South			1 0 0
Mewett, Frances	43		London	2		3 10 0
King, Sarah	63	Widow	Town		1 0	2 12 0
Kenyon, Mary	78	Ditto	Ditto		2 6	6 10 0
Luxford, Mary	28	Ditto	London			3 18 0
Luxford, Jeremiah	66		South			0 15 0
Paul, Ann	75	Ditto	Ditto		1 0	2 12 0
Prodger, Ann	67	Ditto	Since dead		2 6	6 16 0
Reed, Edw. and Elizabeth	64 64	Fisherman	Town			3 0 0
Richardson, Matthew	81	Bricklayer	Hastings		2 6	6 10 0
Rollason, Wm. and Susan	66 63	Shepherd	Town		5 0	13 0 0
Rich, Sarah	64	Widow	Ditto		1 6	3 18 0
Sinden, Wm. and Mary	72 71	Mason	Ditto		4 0	11 10 0
Sutton, Mary	70	Widow	Ditto		1 6	3 18 0
Snatt, Keturah	61	Ditto	Since dead		2 6	7 15 6
Ticehurst, Ann	26	Ditto	Meads			1 4 0
Tutt, Mary	87	Ditto	Ditto		4 0	10 8 0
Tourle, John and Martha	70 65		Town		2 6	9 6 6
Vine, Elizabeth	64	Ditto	Ditto		2 6	6 10 0
Verrall, Lucy	16	Ditto	Meads		1 6	3 18 0
Ward, Wm. and Mary	70 76		Town		7 6	19 10 0
Waymark, Mary	73	Ditto	South		2 6	6 10 0
Wood, Elizabeth	56	Ditto	Town		2 0	5 4 0
Wood, Sarah	60	Ditto	Prentice-st.		2 6	6 10 0
Wilkins, Charles	57	Shoemaker	Town		2 6	6 10 0
Yielding, Sarah	72	Widow	Meads		2 6	6 10 0
Young, Lucy	58	Ditto	South		2 0	5 4 0

Paupers not coming under the description of Infirm or Sick.

Paupers' Names.	Age.	Description.	Residence.	Children under 12 Years.	Weekly Allowance.	Allowance from Lady-day 1831 to Lady-day 1832.
Adams, Rich. and Charity	53 55	Carpenter	South			18 19 6
Aldridge, John and Ann		Labourer	Town		15 4	23 10 8
Alce, Wm. and Mary		Ditto	Ditto			4 4 0
Aucock, Thos. and Elis.		Bricklayer	Ditto		7 6	7 16 3
Aucock, James and Susan		Labourer	Ditto		13 4	16 1 4
Aucock, Wm. and Ann		Ditto	Ditto		13 4	31 12 6
Aucock, William		Ditto	Ditto			0 11 0

Paupers not coming under the description of Infirm or Sick.

Paupers' Names.	Age.	Description.	Residence.	Children under 12 Years.	Weekly Allowance.		Allowance from Lady-day 1831, to Lady-day 1832.		
					s.	*d.*	£.	*s.*	*d.*
Banister, Joseph and Mary	70 75	Ditto	Ditto		7	6	20	10	0
Bartholomew, John .	78	Ditto	South		4	0	10	15	6
Bignell, William . . .	46	Ditto	Town		9	0	14	1	0
Bignell, Elizabeth . .	16		Town				0	7	0
Boniface, Henry . . .	27	Labourer	Meads				1	16	0
Bottle, John	56	Ditto	Boxley, Kt.				1	0	0
Boniface, Wm. and Mary	45 40	Ditto	Town	3	13	4	10	4	3
Bridger, Wm. and Martha	26 21	Baker	Ditto				0	15	0
Bridger, Edw. and Harriet	23 23	Ditto	Ditto	3			8	17	0
Bridger, Wm. and Mary	36 34	Carpenter	South	2	12	0	7	8	0
Breden, Thomas . . .	44	Labourer	Town	2	13	4	8	19	0
Brook, Thos. and Mary	68 64	Fisherman	South				2		1½
Brook, Jane			Ditto		6	0	15	10	0
Bradford, Fr. and Sarah	41 38	Labourer	Ditto	2	13	6	15	12	9
Breach, Thomas . . .	42	Ditto	Meads				6	15	4
Breach, Wm. and Ann .	31 28	Ditto	Ditto	4	14	8	4	13	0
Breach, John	55	Ditto	Steyning				3	0	0
Bruce, Chas. and Susannah	28	Shoemaker	Brighton				3	0	0
Burchfield, Thomas .	62		Kingston, T.	1			8	5	0
Bridger, John and Phillis	27 20	Tailor	Town	1			17		3½
•Carter, John and Sarah	43 44	Bricklayer	Sea-side	5	14	8	42	12	4
Carter, Joseph and Eliz.	34 37	Constable	South	7	16	8	49	11	8
Carter, William . . .	20	Labourer	Town				3	7	6
Carter, Edward . . .	18	Ditto	Ditto				1	18	6
Carter, John	16	Ditto	Ditto				1	14	0
Carpenter, John and Mary	2 3	Ditto	Ditto	4	14	0	15	9	0
Chapman, William . .	53	Ditto	Meads				5	0	3
Collins, Reuben and Mary	0 3	Ditto	Prentice-st.	3			1	2	10
Collins, John and Ann .	4 6	Ditto	Ditto		7	6	14	14	1
Collins, Thomas . . .	18	Ditto	Ditto				1	9	0
Coppard, William . .	48	Ditto	Ditto		6	0	16	17	8
Crunden, Thos. and Eliz.		Ditto	South	2	12	0	13	18	0
Crunden, Sam. and Susan	39 21	Ditto	Ditto	2	14	0	5	11	0
Cramp, Robert and Mary	40 36	Ditto	Town	3	2	6	10	10	0
Cummins, Rich. and Reb.	50 51	Fisherman	Sea-side	2	12	0	10	0	6
Cummins, Joseph . .		Ditto	Ditto	1	10	0	8	11	8
Cummins, Henry . . .		Ditto	Ditto				2	8	0
Davis, John and Ann .	73 72	Labourer	Town		7	6	0		7½
Deadman, Jas. and Mary		Ditto	Ditto	2	12	0			
Diplock, Wm. and Ann .	38 36	Ditto	Meads	3	16	0	9	8	0
Dore, James and Mary	57 54	Ditto	Town	1	1	0	2	12	0
Douch, David and Mary	35 37	Tailor	Ditto	3			15	14	11
Dunstan, Wm. and Han.		Labourer	Wish		9	0	10	5	6
Elphick, Charles . .			Brighton				1	3	0
Erridge, Wm. and Lydia	38 39	Fisherman	Prentice-st.	2			4	4	0
French, George and Ann		Ditto	South	3	12	0	9	16	0
Fraser, John and Esther	40 38	Labourer	Meads	3	12	0	24	13	1½
French, John and Jemima	45 50		Hastings				1	0	0
Gatland, Rich. and Han.	75 65	Ditto	Prentice-st.		7	6	9	12	4
Gatland, James and Eliz.	20 19	Ditto	Town	1	9	0	8	2	0
Gosden, Wm. and Jane .	30 34	Ditto	Ditto	1	10	0	14	5	10
Gosden, Wm. and Mary	67 65	Ditto	Ditto		6	0	9	9	6
Godden, Michael and Lucy	65 53	Ditto	Meads		9	0	13	5	6
Godden, George and Ann	29 29	Ditto	Ditto	3			3	15	8
Godden, Thomas and Ann	32 32	Ditto	Ditto	3			2	1	0
Gower, Samuel, and Wife	62 51	Ditto	Ditto		12	0	5	18	0
Gower, Walter, and Wife	69 68	Ditto	Ditto		4	0	5	1	0

Paupers' Names.	Age.	Description.	Residence.	Children under 12 Years.	Weekly Allowance.		Allowance from Lady-day 1831, to Lady-day 1832.		
Gower, Reuben . . .	23	Labourer	Meads				1	7	0
Gower, Levi	19	Ditto	Ditto				0	8	0
Gosden, Thomas . .	54	Ditto	Ditto				1	16	0
Gower, Charity . . .	16		Ditto				2	12	0
Hart, Thomas and Lucy	34 32	Bricklayer	Brighton	2			2	0	0
Hart, William . . .	42				6	6	16	18	0
Head, Thomas and Mary	37 40	Labourer	Sea-side	2	12	0	18	12	0
Hollands, John and Lydia	74 67	Ditto	Since dead		7	6	15	5	0
Huggett, Benj. and Han.	63 65	Constable	Town		8	0	24	16	0
Huggett, Benjamin . .	18	Labourer	Ditto				1	10	0
Huggett, Henry and Ann	43 44	Shoemaker	Sea-side	5	6	0	14	1	4
Huggett, Henry . . .	20	Fisherman	Ditto				0	14	0
Huggett, Edw. and Mary	28 27	Labourer	Town	3	12	0	14	19	0
Hunt, Abram and Ann	69 69	Ditto	South		9	0	9	7	6
Hunt, Wm. and Mary .	28 28	Ditto	Ditto	1	9	0	9	0	0
Hunter, John and Lucy .	79 75	Ditto	Meads		7	6	19	10	0
Hutchins, Jas. and Char.	44 46	Fisherman	Sea-side	2	13	6	15	6	2½
Hurst, Sam. and Eliz.	57 66	Labourer	Town				1	11	6
Knight, Samuel . .	50	Ditto	Ditto				8	7	0
Lane, Sam. and Rebecca	32 30	Ditto	Meads	2			4	0	0
Lamport, John and Eliz. .	45 42	Ditto	Bath	1			3	0	0
Lewis, Thos. and Eliz. .	26 23	Ditto	Town	2	12	0	10	16	0
Lewis, George . . .	18	Ditto	Ditto				0	5	0
Maynard, William . .	31	Fishmonger	Ditto				1	5	0
Maynard, Rob. and Harriet	29 31	Ditto	Ditto				0	10	0
Maynard, George . .	22	Flyman	Brighton				1	0	0
Maynard, James . . .	24	Ditto	Ditto				1	10	0
Markwick, Edw. and Mary	35 35	Labourer	Meads	3	2	8	7	8	8
Mewett, Rob. and Lucy .	26 24	Ditto	Town	3	13	4	22	14	8
Mewett, Thomas . .	43	Ditto	Ditto				3	10	0
Mitchell, Thos. and Eliz.	45	Fisherman	Sea-side	1	6	0	12	1	6
Mitchell, Jas. and Hannah	46 26	Labourer	Town	2	12	0	35	4	0
Mitchell, Geo. and Eliz.	72 69	Ditto	Ditto		7	6	18	17	11
Mitchell, Thomas . .	33	Ditto	Ditto				0	5	0
Mitchell, Thos. and Eliz.	76 67	Ditto	Prentice-st.		7	6	22	2	0
Mitchell, Thomas . .		Ditto	Croydon				2	0	0
Morris, Thos. and Sarah	37 38	Ditto	Town	3	13	4	24	2	6
Morris, Sam. and Mary .	68 67	Ditto	Ditto		7	6	16	8	3
Morris, Henry and Sarah	30 29	Ditto	Ditto	1			1	18	4
Morris, John and Sarah	32 39	Ditto	Sea-side		9	0	11	11	9
Morris, Edward and Eliz.	28 27	Ditto	Ditto	2	12	0	9	6	0
Morris, Richard and Mary	45 44	Ditto	Prentice-st.	1			5	6	11
Morris, Richard . . .	18	Ditto	Ditto				1	6	6
Morris, Elizabeth . .	46		Sea-side				5	10	0
Miller, Henry and Lucy .	26 28	Ditto	Town	3	14	4	21	13	2
Miller, Wm. and Lucy .	55 49	Ditto	South	3	13	4	8	4	8
Newman, John . . .	21	Ditto	Town				1	13	0
Paul, George and Eliz. .	50 46	Fisherman	South	2	15	6	25	8	9½
Paul, Jonathan . . .	26	Ditto	Ditto				1	11	9
Paul, William . . .	24	Ditto	Ditto				3	17	0
Parsons, Jas. and Harriet	48 41	Labourer	Town	2	2	6	9	13	1½
Payn, George and Mary	68 65	Ditto	South		9	0	3	1	6
Pankhurst, Thos. and Maria	56 53	Fisherman	Prentice-st.		5	0	7	10	0
Pearson, Alan and Char.	36 36	Labourer	Town	3	10	0	18	12	0
Prodger, Thomas and Ann	46 45	Painter	South	3	13	4	23	14	1
Prodger, John and Ann	52 50	Ditto	Ditto		12	0	10	16	0
Prodger, John . . .	20	Fisherman	Ditto				3	9	0

Paupers' Names.	Age.	Description.	Residence.	Children under 12 Years.	Weekly Allowance.		Allowance from Lady-day 1831, to Lady-day 1832		
Pickering, William . .	60		Dunkingfield				2	0	0
Pumphry, Thomas . .	56	Labourer	Willingdon	2			4	0	0
Reed, William . . .	19	Ditto	Town				1	14	0
Reed, James and Eliz. .	36 35	Ditto	South	3	12	0	20	6	0
Reed, Thomas . . .	28	Ditto	Sea-side				2	15	0
Riddle, Alex. and Eliz. .	73 70	Ditto	South		7	6	19	10	0
Riddle, Wm. and Mary .	52 50	Ditto	Ditto	3	15	0	29	9	0
Robbins, John and Mary	52 40	Ditto	Meads	2	12	0	13	14	0
Rollason, Fran. and Mary	33 32	Shepherd	Hastings				5	4	0
Rollason, William . .	46	Shepherd	Town	4			3	0	0
Sinden, Wm. and Sarah .	45 41	Mason	Ditto		10	0	11	10	0
Sinden, John and Ann .	39 35	Bricklayer	Ditto	2	14	8	15	4	0
Sinden, Job and Susan .	28 32	Ditto	Ditto	2	12	0	15	0	0
Sinden, Thomas . . .	24	Ditto	Ditto				1	4	0
Sinden, John . . .	19	Ditto	Ditto				1	3	0
Sinden, George and Mary	31 29	Ditto	Lewes	1			1	0	0
Smith, Charlotte . . .	33		Sea-side	2	2	0	5	4	0
Sharp, Thomas and Mary	40 26	Tailor	Town	4	13	4	3	15	0
Stevens, John and Frances	37 37	Shoemaker	Ditto	5			3	10	0
Stevens, George . . .	35	Ditto	Framfield	4			3	0	0
Stevens, Samuel and Sarah	66 67	Ditto	Town				5	0	0
Stevens, George and Mary	36 38	Labourer	Meads	4	17	6	20	19	6
Snatt, John and Harriet	32 31	Ditto	Town	3	2	6	6	0	6
Stevens, John and Eliz. .	25 25	Ditto	South	2	12	0	9	6	2
Taylor, Elizabeth . .	17		Town				5	8	0
Ticehurst, John and Ann	28 26	Ditto	Since dead				2	0	0
Ticehurst, Richard . .	45	Ditto	Meads	2	3	0	12	6	4
Ticehurst, Samuel · .	19	Ditto	Ditto				1	19	0
Ticehurst, James . .	17	Ditto	Ditto	3			1	0	0
Todman, Wm. and Susan	47 45	Ditto	London				3	0	0
Tutt, Timothy and Eliz. .	33	Ditto	Meads	3	13	4	16	13	4
Tourle, Thomas and Ann	35 42	Shepherd	Town	3			8	11	10
Tourle, James and Ann .	36 43	Labourer	Ditto	3	14	8	18	10	4
Tourle, Richard . . .	39 40	Bricklayer	Brighton	2			10	0	0
Trigwell, Henry . . .	45	Ditto	Ditto				3	0	0
Tutt, William . . .	58	Ditto	Ditto				2	10	0
Varnham, Henry and Lucy	53 43	Labourer	Town	4			16	2	1
Varnham, Rich. and Har.	33 37	Ditto	Meads	2	13	4	16	8	8
Verrall, Sam. and Caroline	24	Ditto	Ditto	2	12	0	12	6	6
Verrall, Henry . . .	48	Ditto	Ditto				3	18	0
Verrall, Samuel and Jane	42 41	Ditto	Ditto	1	14	8	20	10	8
Verrall, Wm. and Elizabeth	57 59	Ditto	Ditto		10	0	4	9	4
Verrall, John and Lucy .	44 38	Ditto	Goffs		2	0	4	15	0
Verrall, Edward and Mary	51 53	Ditto	Brighton				1	0	0
Verrall, Thomas and Mary	19 19	Ditto	Meads		9	0	4	16	6
Ward, William . . .	49	Ditto	Ditto	1	12	0	15	9	0
Ward, James . . .	24	Ditto	Ditto				5	11	6
Waymark, Isaac and Sarah	36	Fisherman	Sea-side	4	15	4	29	15	8
Waymark, Jona. and Lucy	37	Ditto	South	4	16	0	27	18	6
Wilkins, Wm. and Sarah	32 30	Labourer	Town	4	15	0	10	14	3
Wood, Wm. and Winifred	34 31	Fisherman	Ditto	3	13	4	17	19	0
Wood, John and Elizabeth	40 41	Ditto	Sea-side	2	12	0	12	12	0
Wood, Thomas and Mary	37 39	Ditto	Prentice St.	4	15	6	14	16	2
Wood, Edward . . .	19	Ditto	Sea-side				2	9	8
Wood, Richard and Ann	34 32	Labourer	Wish	3	6	0	9	12	0
Young, John and Sarah	36 38	Ditto	Prentice St.	4			1	11	0
‾ . John . . .	15	Ditto	Hasti				0	19	6

Illegitimate Children receiving Pay from the Parish of Eastbourn.

Child's Name.	Age.	Mother's Name.	Mother's Residence.	Weekly Allow-ance.	Allowance from Lady-day 1831, to Lady-day 1832.
				s. d.	£. s. d.
Avery, Keziah .	¾	Avery, Elizabeth.	House of Industry	2 0	5 4 0
Baker, Mary Ann	9	Baker, Jane . .	Town . . .	3 6	9 2 0
Baker, William .	6	Baker, Susan .	South . . .	2 6	6 10 0
Betts, Charles .	5	Betts, Ann . .	Sea-side . .	2 0	5 4 0
Brook, Elizabeth	1	Brook, Elizabeth	Brighton . .	2 0	5 4 0
Brook, Louisa . .	8	Brook, Catherine	South . . .	3 0	7 16 0
Chapman, Jane .	6	Chapman, Harriet	Meads . . .	3 0	7 16 0
Collins, Catherine	7	Collins, Mary .	Prentice Street .	3 0	7 16 0
Duly, Thomas .	1½	Duly, Elizabeth .	South . . .	2 0	5 4 0
Dyer, Eve . . .	4	Dyer, Eve . .	. . . . .	2 0	5 4 0
Gosden, Luther	8	Gosden, Sarah .	Town. . . .	2 6	6 10 0
Geering, Harriet	2	Geering, Harriet .	Willingdon . .	2 0	5 4 0
Gignell, Elizabeth	7	Muggridge, Ann	Brighton . .	2 0	5 4 0
Logan, Charles	¾	Logan, Mary .	House of Industry	2 0	5 4 0
Mac Dold, Louisa	15	Mac Dold, Ket. .	Willingdon . .	2 6	6 10 0
Markwick, Eliz. .	3	Markwick, Eliz. .	Meads . . .	4 0	10 8 0
Pelling, Francis .	9	Pelling, Frances .	. . . . .	2 6	6 10 0
Prodger, Samuel	14	Prodger, Hannah	Meads . . .	2 6	6 10 0
Quaif, Edward .	1½	Quaif, Jane .	Ashburnham .	2 0	5 4 0
Reed, William .	8	Reed, Mary .	. . . . .	3 0	7 16 0
Todman, John .	4	Todman, Sophia .	. . . . .	2 0	5 4 0
Ward, Ann . .	8	Ward, Mary . .	Sea-side . .	3 0	7 16 0
Wickham, Susan.	3	Wickham, Susan.	Meads . . .	4 0	10 8 0
Wilkins, Charles	9	Wilkins, Mary .	Town . . .	2 0	5 4 0
Verrall, George .	1	Verrall, Jane .	South . . .	2 6	6 10 0
Verrall, Charlotte		Verrall, Jane .	Ditto . . .	2 6	6 10 0
Verrall, Agnes .	2	Verrall, Agnes .	Ditto . . .	2 0	5 4 0

List of Paupers in the House of Industry, belonging to the Parish of Eastbourn.*

Name.	Age.	Name.	Age.	Name.	Age.	Name.	Age.
Aucock, Thos.	18	Bridger, Har. .	27	Hart, Elizabeth	49	Rollason, Fan.	½
Baker, Samuel	25	Breden, Thos.	11	Hollands, Hetty	44	Reed, Thomas.	24
Baker, Eliza	22	Brown, Edw. .	8	Hollands, Thos.	39	Reed, George	21
Baker, Martha	12	Brown, Ben. .	10	Hilton, William	87	Snatt, Mary .	51
Baker, Susan .	9	Constable, J. .	7	Luxford, Wm. .	77	Simmons, Geo.	18
Bennet, Harriet	44	Collins, Henry	11	Logan, Mary .	28	Smith, John .	11
Betts, Maria .	20	Crunden, Sam.	37	Logan, Charles	¾	Tuppen, Nicho.	67
Betts, William	9	Crunden, Sus. .	20	Mitchell, John.	44	Tourle, William	36
Bennett, Thos.	2	Crunden, Mary	3	Morris, Jane .	19	Tourle, Mary .	34
Bennett, George	15	Crunden, Eliz.	1	Morris, Ann .	¼	Tourle, Susan .	11
Bingham, Edw.	85	Collins, Samuel	9	Morris, James .	24	Vine, George .	40
Bignell, Rich.	12	Douch, James	8	Morris, Samuel	16	Vine, Caroline	10
Bignell, Eliza .	16	Duly, William .	18	Morris, Edward	10	Vine, Thomas .	6
Breach, Wm. .	50	Dyer, William .	16	Morris, Mary .	13	Waymark, Geo.	13
Bridger, Wm. .	24	Dyer, John .	14	Muett, Henry .	28	Waymark, Ed.	9
Bridger, M. .	23	Earl, Charlotte	21	Nicolas, Mary .	17	Young, Lucy .	30
Bridger, M. A.	3	Erridge, Jane .	77	Page, Leonard .	18	Young, John .	10
Bridger, Eliz. .	1½	Fowler, John .	17	Peckham, Jas. .	64	Young, William	½
Bradford, Mary	17	Francisco, Ann	16	Pearson, Mary .	11	Young, Jane .	52
Bradford, Fran.	7	Gilbert, James	24	Reed, Mary .	16	Young, Chris. .	13
Brook, James	19	Gilbert, Eliz. .	18	Reed, Matilda .	11	Young, George	11
Brook, Ann .	17	Gosden, Jane .	10	Rollason, Sus. .	23		

* Average Weekly number of Paupers in the House of Industry between 25th March 1831, and 25th March 1832.

Dr. INCOME, 1831-2.	£.	s.	d.
To Balance of Old Rate	45	6	4¼
Midsummer Rate at 3s. in the pound.			
Collected	978	17	5¾
Michaelmas Rate at 2s. 6d. in the pound.			
Collected	806	8	4¾
Christmas Rate at 3s. 6d. in the pound.			
Collected	1078	3	10¾
Rate to Lady-day, 1832, at 4s. in the pound.			
Collected	963	17	9½
Cash borrowed of Messrs Gill & Co.	150	0	0
Ditto for Illegitimate Children	103	19	0
Ditto for Building Materials	12	3	4½
Rent of J. J. Lanyon, Esq. and Mr. J. P. Gorringe	18	0	0
Cash from Manufactory	30	0	0
Ditto for Labour from Workhouse	35	16	0¼
Ditto for Lead sold from ditto	1	19	2
Ditto from other Parishes	3	12	0
Ditto repaid for Weekly Relief	21	19	0
Ditto received back for Summonses	0	10	0
	£4250	12	5¾

EXPENDITURE, 1831-2. Cr.	First Quarter. £.	s.	d.	Second Quarter. £.	s.	d.	Third Quarter. £.	s.	d.	Fourth Quarter. £.	s.	d.	Total. £.	s.	d.
By Cash paid for Permanent and Casual Relief to Paupers, Widows, Infirm, and Sick	438	5	7	385	12	11	706	9	2	657	4	0	2187	11	8
At the Workhouse	158	8	2	130	1	0	161	6	7¼	121	17	1¼	571	12	10½
Allowance for Children at Service	21	17	0	6	2	0	11	3	4	6	17	0	45	19	4
Illegitimate Children, by order of Justices	15	4	6	22	0	6	24	7	0	18	3	6	79	15	6
Letters 4*l.* 12*s.* 7*d*, Stamps 4*s.* 7*d.*	4	17	2	0	0	0	0	0	0	0	0	0	4	17	2
Premiums for Apprentices	0	0	0	5	0	0	0	0	0	0	0	0	5	0	0
Journeys	2	10	9	3	6	8	0	13	4	2	12	4	9	2	9
Constables	12	18	6	0	0	0	0	2	6	0	0	0	13	1	0
County Rate	0	0	0	0	0	0	76	12	0	0	0	0	76	12	0
Law Expenses	2	17	6	13	17	10	0	0	0	0	0	0	16	15	4
Funerals	5	0	0	12	6	0	0	4	0	0	0	0	17	10	0
Coroner's Inquest	0	0	0	0	0	0	0	0	0	0	18	6	0	18	6
New Tools and Repairs	30	9	4½	0	0	0	17	3	4	9	7	5	57	0	1½
Surgeon's Salary	25	0	0	0	0	0	0	0	0	25	0	0	50	0	0
Extra attendance	0	9	6	0	0	0	2	2	4	0	0	0	2	11	10
Repairs to old Workhouse, &c.	10	2	11	0	0	0	0	0	0	4	12	3	14	15	2
Money borrowed and paid, with Interest	237	1	0	152	8	0	0	0	0	0	0	0	389	9	0
Bills	51	15	9	34	9	2	69	0	5½	54	12	10¼	209	18	2¾
Insurance	0	0	0	1	7	6	0	0	0	0	0	0	1	7	6
Workhouse Rent	0	0	0	0	0	0	45	0	0	45	0	0	90	0	0
Cottage Rents	181	1	0	14	1	0	49	17	0	62	3	0	307	2	0
Wool, Straw, and Corn	13	8	0	15	14	6	0	0	0	0	0	0	29	12	6
Vestry Clerk	15	0	0	15	0	0	15	0	0	15	0	0	60	0	0
Miscellaneous Services	0	0	0	0	0	0	5	0	0	5	0	0	10	0	0
	£1226	16	8½	816	7	1	1179	1	0¾	1028	7	7½	4250	12	5¾

THE CHURCHWARDENS IN A WITH THE PARISH.

Dr.	£.	*s.*	*d.*	*Cr.*	
Amount of Church-Rate at 2*d.* in the Pound	43	8	7¾	Bills . . .	4

SEAFORD.

Population.	Rates in the £.	Value.	Average Expenditure.
1098	12s.	¾	1800l.

SEAFORD is a liberty of itself.

This is rather a strong instance of the effect of a town in crushing the land.

Of the above sum one-third is paid by the town; the remaining two-thirds by the land.

From one of the principal farms, of the value of something more than 1000l. per annum, and assessed at 878l., the average annual payment of rates for the last three years has been 577l.

There is another reason, however, for the high rates of this place: being a borough, the various mysterious modes of keeping up the patron's interest were in full operation; and the rates on houses not called for from accommodating voters, but kept suspended over their heads, in case of *misconduct*, were among the engines put in force; and of course it could not be expedient to examine too strictly the applications for relief made by freemen and their relations. Rates are formally allowed by the magistrates of the liberty; and the account of the expenditure is perused and allowed, having been first verified on oath before the same magistrates. There appeared a strange confusion in these accounts. Entries of rent due to *one of the proprietors*, carried on from year to year. Bills unpaid, in a long string of items of various description, amounting to 500l. or 600l. On turning back to an earlier part of the ledger, the confusion was in some degree explained by a page which had not been cancelled, when the Borough of Seaford was transferred to Schedule A. I subjoin some extracts previous and subsequent to the disfranchisement:—

	Amount of Poor Rate.			Statement of Cash Received.			Statement of Cash Due.		
	£.	s.	d.	£.	s.	d.	£.	s.	d.
Dec. 31, 1828	528	3	10	0	0	0	0	0	0
Apr. 13, 1829	522	19	10	3	14	0	0	15	0
Oct. 1, 1829	526	12	6	3	14	8	2	9	8
Jan. 21, 1830	524	19	2	4	2	8	2	9	8

A marvellous improvement in accuracy of accounts was produced by the mere contemplation of the Reform Bill:—

	Amount of Poor Rate.			Cash Received.			Cash Due.		
	£.	s.	d.	£.	s.	d.	£.	s.	d.
May 22, 1831	544	19	10	500	12	2	44	7	8
Oct. 14, 1831	811	2	3	723	17	6	87	4	9
Feb. 17, 1832	675	5	7	557	17	2	117	8	5

It was notorious that in the borough of Helston, in Cornwall, the whole poor rates of the town were paid by the patron; and when the patronage passed from one family to another, the burden of the rates followed the transfer: something like that system seems to have prevailed in Seaford.

Near this town, in the parish of Bishopstone, there is a farm of about the same extent and value as that mentioned above. There being no borough town to oppress it, the rates are 160*l.* instead of 577*l.*

GENERAL REPORT ON THE DISTURBED DISTRICT OF EAST SUSSEX.

BEER-SHOPS.

The beer-shops are considered as most mischievous. They allow of secret meetings beyond any places previously existing, being generally in obscure situations, kept by the lowest class of persons: they are receiving houses for stolen goods, and frequently brothels *; they are resorted to by the most abandoned characters—poachers, smugglers, and night depredators, who pass their time in playing at cards for the expenses of the night, in raffling for game and poultry, and concocting plans for future mischief: they are never without a scout, and are not interrupted by the observation of any person of respectability; no information can be obtained from the masters, who are in the power of their guests, spirits being usually sold without license; and not one in ten sell home-brewed beer. Similar representations are made in East Kent. A magistrate expressed his opinion that no single measure ever caused so much mischief in so short a time, in demoralizing the labourers. The evidence of the high-constable of Ashford is very strong, and his means of judging extensive,—having been called upon to attend at the numerous fires which have taken place in that district. He has been present in the condemned cells, at the last parting of the convicts from their parents and relations; and it appears that all the acts of incendiarism were perpetrated by frequenters of beer-shops. Dyke, who was executed, was taken in a beer-shop; and

* A gentleman of property in East Sussex informed me, that a small tenant of his converted his cottage into a beer-shop: he was asked how it succeeded, he answered, " If my beer-shop will not answer I don't know whose can, for I keep them a girl and a fiddle."

the two Packhams, who suffered at Maidstone, acknowledged, before their execution, that they went from a beer-shop to commit the offence.

RURAL POLICE.

A more efficient police is a matter of the greatest importance. All classes, proprietors and occupiers, magistrates, overseers,—all require it. Concession to paupers can hardly be avoided under the present insufficient police; and the magistrates consider the calling in the military very objectionable, unless in the last extremity. As to yeomanry, there is so much distress among farmers, and consequently so much discontent, that they are unwilling to enrol themselves: those who, in the good times of farming, had horses fit for yeomanry service, now make use of a cart-horse, or go on foot.

The few who are more opulent hang back; as, from living in isolated situations, their property is completely at the mercy of their own labourers.

Such, indeed, is the general insecurity of farming property, since the unhappy time of the riots, that a considerable occupier has thought it necessary to retain, in constant pay, two of the most confidential of his labourers, to watch over and report to him any symptoms of dissatisfaction among the rest, likely to lead to mischief.

The constables and headboroughs are elected at the annual meeting of the court-leet of the hundred; the chief constable is usually some small farmer or tradesman, who receives no pay, except the small fee for a summons.

The common constables are usually village artizans, competent perhaps to the forms of civil process, and putting down a village broil, but totally unacquainted with the business of police, and in case of great mobs, quite inefficient: they are changed every year, and are seldom willing to serve a second time.

SMUGGLING,

Since the establishment of the preventive service, is much diminished. This diminution has had the effect of increasing the poor-rate, or, as was expressed by an overseer, who is supposed to have had formerly a very accurate acquaintance with the business, " the putting down smuggling is the ruin of the coast." The labourers of Bexhill, and of the villages proceeding eastward towards Kent, used to have plenty of work in the summer, and had no difficulty in finding employment in smuggling during the winter.

The smugglers are divided into two classes, the carriers or bearers, who receive from five shillings per night and upwards, according to the number of tubs they secure, and the batmen.

The batmen, so called from the provincial term of bat, for a bludgeon, which they use, consider themselves as of a superior class : they go out in disguise, frequently with their faces blackened, and now with fire-arms; they confine their services to the protection of the others, and are paid 20*s.* or more per night; and many, perhaps most of them, are at the same time in the receipt of parish relief.

Large capitals have been invested in this business, particularly at Bexhill· Many of the small farmers, if they do not participate, certainly connive at these practices; those who do not directly profit by smuggling, consider that it is advantageous, as finding employ for many who otherwise would be thrown on their parishes.

The smugglers are now much more ferocious since the use of fire-arms is more constant.

The offer of 1000*l.* reward by the Secretary of State, for the detection of some men engaged in a desperate affray, caused much sensation, but was ultimately ineffectual. Many from fear left the country for France and America, but have returned since the failure of the prosecution, for want of satisfactory evidence; though, probably, not less than 500 persons in the district were fully acquainted with the transaction.

Beyond all doubt the practice of smuggling has been a main cause of the riots and fires in Sussex and East Kent: labourers have acquired the habit of acting in large gangs by night, and of systematic resistance to authority. High living is become essential to them, and they cannot reconcile themselves to the moderate pay of lawful industry.

RIOTS.

The riots in the north-east parts of the Rape of Hastings commenced simultaneously on the 5th and 6th of November, 1830. The farmers observed, that their labourers all at once left their work: they were taken away by night by a systematic arrangement; no leader could be identified, but bills were run up at the public-houses in the evening, and in the morning a stranger came and paid.

The mobs generally had written forms containing their demands, they varied a little in the amount of wages, but all agreed in the amount of " allowance" of 1*s.* 6*d.* for every child above two; that there should be no assistant-overseer; that they should be paid full wages, wet or dry; that they would pay their own rents *. There were nine cases of incendiarism that winter at

* This last point is remarkable : perhaps it may be thus explained,—that the labourers were aware that high rents, paid out of the poor-rates, formed part of the system of parish jobbing, of little advantage to them.

Battle. The mob which assembled there, on the day of the magistrates' meeting, amounted to nearly 700 : all the principal magistrates of the division, nineteen in number, assembled; the arrival of a troop of horse established order.

Though the guilt of one of the incendiaries, J. Bufford, who was executed, was clear and admitted by himself, yet the feeling of the country was so much in his favour, that he was considered as a martyr,—he was exhibited in his coffin, and a subscription made for his family.

A permanent Bench of Magistrates was established at Battle, at which Mr. Courthorpe presided, at their particular request, and directed by day and night the measures which were requisite for public tranquillity.

This harassing duty continued during a month; but from that period, a certain degree of intimidation has prevailed in this district. The assistant-overseers having been then ill-treated by the mobs, are reluctant to make complaints for neglect of work, lest they should become marked men and their lives rendered uncomfortable or even unsafe. Farmers permit their labourers to receive relief, founded on a calculation of a rate of wages lower than that actually paid: they are unwilling to put themselves in collision with the labourers, and will not give an account of earnings, or if they do, beg that their names may not be mentioned. A similar feeling prevails in East Kent: at Westwell, the farmers are afraid to express, at vestry-meetings, their opinions against a pauper who applies for relief, for fear their premises should be set fire to. Two of the fires immediately followed such a resistance; one of them happened to a most respectable farmer, a kind and liberal master, and a promoter of cottage allotments.

The allowance system is represented to be so established, that without some legislative enactment, neither overseers, vestries, nor magistrates, can make any effectual change; and that if local regulations were attempted, a repetition of the outrages of 1830 may be expected. Day wages seem to be fixed at 2s. to 2s. 3d.; which are not thought too high, were it not for the rates, but the farmers state that the present relief, coupled with that rate of wages, is exhausting their capital. The relief is in great measure compulsory; but it is also considered unnecessary,—for on an accurate examination of the population, the quantity of acres and the numbers requisite for the cultivation of the land in its present state, it is calculated that the money expended for labour, within the Rape of Hastings, is sufficient for the maintenance of nearly the whole of the able-bodied agricultural labourers and families without assistance from the rates.

Emigration has already been carried on to a considerable extent—still, in certain parishes, there is some excess.

The redundancy of labourers in this district is probably but small, but under the present state of the poor-laws, it cannot be ascertained.

The removal of that small surplus, might confine the funds of labour and rates to their specific purposes; but the inclination to emigrate has been materially checked among the idle and profligate, by the great improvement in their condition since the riots. A still more unfortunate consequence is, an unwillingness among the labourers to take land. In the most disturbed parts of this district, attempts have been made to introduce cottage allotments, but they have been ineffectual. The labourers show a decided reluctance to hire them; they think it might diminish their claim to relief, and treat with scorn those who attempt to persuade them to better their condition by economy and industry.

The accuracy of this general statement may be illustrated by the following detailed account of particular places:—

RYE.

RYE, an " ancient town" within the liberty of the Cinque Ports, is in two divisions. The "town" in the jurisdiction of the local magistrates, the " foreign" in that of the county. The accounts are kept in separate books. Population 3715, rates 21s. in the pound on a two-third value. There is a select vestry: four overseers. Those now in office are a tailor, shoemaker, butcher, and coal-dealer, with an assistant-overseer.

Formerly, a manufacture was carried on at the workhouse, which has been discontinued on account of the great loss. A considerable increase in the rates has been caused by the riots of Nov. 1830. At that period, about 1000 persons collected near the workhouse; they demanded an increase of wages, according to a printed scale which included about twenty items, embracing the different occupations in the town,—porterage, carriage of coal in barges, &c. Some of the most respectable masters in the town consider that wages were previously too low, and part of that increase remains.

The labourers, not contented with this concession, have since then demanded relief, also, to a much greater extent than previously: they have become more licentious in their moral conduct, and urge the demand on the parish for relief as a right, saying, " If you do not relieve us we shall help ourselves." In Nov. 1831, a celebration of the anniversary of the rising of the preceding year was announced by placards. The mayor and principal proprietors applied to the Secretary of State, and a company of the Rifle Corps from Dover marched into the town, and their appearance was sufficient to maintain order. A restless spirit still prevails, quite different from the former state.

The police consists of four constables chosen at the leet, and the gaoler, who acts as constable with a salary. Whether the inhabitants would be willing to come forward as special constables, depends on the political feeling of the moment.

A general habit of improvidence exists; a proof of which may be taken from the seamen employed in conveying chalk from Eastbourne. Some of these working mariners, not sharers in the craft, earn from 40*s.* to 50*s.* per week during the season, which lasts from May to October. When winter comes, all the money being spent, and the wives and children really destitute, the overseers are obliged to relieve them, and if they refuse, the magistrates cannot avoid some degree of interference.

Relief is not given to the families of smugglers when the husband has been convicted and remains in prison. It is supposed that they are supported by their confederates.

Emigration.—Many vessels sail from this port to New York with emigrants; and some American vessels have put in for the same purpose: four families have been sent out by the parish, and are doing well; the expense was paid at once out of the rates, and the cost of one large family was saved in two years.

In general, favourable letters have been received from the emigrants, who usually go 600 miles up the country. A nephew of the overseer, who went about six years ago as a labourer, provided by his friends with a small capital, not exceeding 100*l.*, has married there, and become a proprietor: he writes word that he expects to be able to provide well for his children, from the land which he has acquired.

BREDE, SUSSEX.

Expended on Poor.

£.	£.	£.	£.
In 1816. . 1003	1820. . 1323	1824. . 2009	1828. . 1506
1817. . 1241	1821. . 1745	1825. . 1753	1829. . 1795
1818. . 1494	1822. . 2021	1826. . 1834	1830. . 1765
1819. . 1447	1823. . 2325	1827. . 1470	1831. . 1970
			1832. . 2606

POPULATION.

In 1801	In 1811	In 1821	In 1831
801	787	902	1046

Note.—The increase of poor-rate, from 1816 to 1832, exceeds 150 per cent.

Acres.	Population.	Rental.	Value.	Rates in the £.	Expenditure to March, 1832.
4675	1046	2035*l.*	¾	21*s.*	2606*l.*

besides a 2*s.* rate in debt,

Wages, 2*s.* 3*d.* per day, summer and winter.
Allowance 1*s.* per week for third child; all beyond 1*s.* 6*d.*, till 12
years of age.

The parish of Brede was the first place in Sussex where the
riots broke out in Nov. 1830; several causes are assigned: the
appointment of the assistant-overseer was very obnoxious to the
paupers.   It is thought that he did not exceed his duty; but
the constant habit of resisting exorbitant claims, almost of necessity caused some degree of harshness.   Under his superintendence an attempt was made in the summer of 1829, to discontinue
regular allowances for children; to revert to the old system of
occasional relief under the direction of the vestry, according to the
real wants of the applicant; another cause arose from the law of
settlement: under the pressure of want of employment, some
parishes began to discharge non-parishioners; other parishes, in
self-defence, followed their example; in consequence of which, the
mutual tie of kind feeling and self-interest which attached good
labourers to good masters was severed; a man who had made
himself useful to a farmer by his industry, and received in return
encouragement, was forced to seek a new employer; his spirit
was broken, he became dependent, wages were calculated according to subsistence, not the value of the labour, and the complaint
was, " Now I am forced back to my parish, you know every shilling I earn, and give only what is necessary to keep skin and bone
together."
Many smugglers are inhabitants of this and the adjoining
parishes, who, from the audacity of their character, formed able
leaders of the discontented, and the employment of the preventive
service had rendered them more ferocious.
Another cause of dissatisfaction arose among the farmers, on
account of the continuance of the war-duty on hops : finding they
could not obtain a reduction, they directed their hostility entirely
against tithe.   The storm broke over the head of one, upon whom
of all others it might least have been expected that such a calamity would have fallen.
The advowson of Brede was part of the patrimonial estate of
Dr. Horne, Bishop of Norwich, and had been held for a long
period of years by some member of the family, and latterly by
Mr. Hele, the son-in-law of the Bishop; he had always been on
the best possible terms with his parishioners.   Though fully
aware of the value of his tithes, he had compounded on very moderate terms; and from the year 1803 to 1826, no alteration had

been made, though during that period most extraordinary profits had been made from the culture of hops, which in this present year will, in all probability, bring more than 20,000*l.* into the parish. In the year 1826, the farmers, under the enormous pressure of the poor-tax, gave notice to the rector that they should set out tithe in kind, and rate him in the poor-book unless he agreed to an abatement of 25 per cent. The rector refused to abate, and there being an informality, instead of submitting to this unreasonable reduction, required an increase, which the farmers agreed to pay.

Previously to the audit, Nov. 1830, a tumultuous meeting assembled near the Parsonage, where the curate, Mr. Hele's son, was living, during his father's temporary absence, clamorous for an abatement of tithe; the rector immediately returned to Brede, and sent for two of the principal farmers, and required the composition should be paid; the farmers positively refused, till they should have the sanction of the labourers, alleging, they feared some injury would be done them. On the audit-day, the rector met the farmers at the inn; it was surrounded by a body of many hundred labourers, with their wives and children. The farmers required an abatement from 715*l.* to 400*l.* The rector said nothing should compel him to give way under circumstances of intimidation. The farmers replied, that the mob without was very impatient; that the rector of Ewhurst had been obliged to flee from his house by night, and that the mob had threatened to hang over his door the farmer who managed the tithes for him. They then left the room to consult the mob, but returned, saying they would not alter their resolution. Mr. Hele persisted that he would not yield to their demands, but they might pay what they pleased to his banker, and left the parish the next day. They paid the 400*l.*, and, after the special commission, came forward and paid the remainder. The rector then returned to his parish, and the labourers, finding the promise of 2*s.* 6*d.* wages had not been kept, were ready to resent on the farmers the injury they had done to Mr. Hele. He did all in his power to repress that spirit, and in order that the farmers might be more able to reinstate themselves in the good opinion of the people, made a voluntary reduction of his tithes to the former amount.

A labourer of Brede said at the time of the riots, " We know that the farmers cannot pay the increased wages, but they have agreed to it; and we shall now join all together to get rid of tithes and taxes, to enable them to do so."

The following is the set of Resolutions drawn up by the labourers —

Nov. 5, 1830.—" At a meeting held this day at the Red Lion, of the farmers, to meet the poor labourers who delegated David

Noakes, sen., Thomas Henley, Joseph Bryant, and Th. Noakes, to meet the gentlemen this day, to discuss the present distress of the poor—

" Resolution I.—The gentlemen agree to give to every able-bodied labourer with wife and two children, 2*s*. 3*d*. per day, from this day to the 1st of March next, and from the 1st of March to the 1st of Oct. 2*s*. 6*d*. per day, and to have 1*s*. 6*d*. per week with three children, and so on according to their family.

" Resolution II.—The poor are determined to take the present overseer, Mr. Abell, out of the parish, to any adjoining parish, and to use him with civility.

(Signed) G. S. HILL, Minister.
Wm. Colman, Francis Bourne, J. Bourne, J. Ades, David Smith, sen., David Smith, jun., H. Smith, J. Bourne, jun.
David Noakes, T. Noakes*, T. Henley†, Jos. Briant.

The assistant-overseer was dragged in a cart by women to the borders of the village ; after an absence of some time he was rein-stated in his situation at the workhouse.

The rates continue at an enormous amount; the overseer says much of the relief is altogether unnecessary, but he is convinced that if an abatement was attempted, his life would not be safe ; he looks to the farmers for support, which they dare not give, considering their lives and property would be in danger, although they find that it is impossible to maintain the present wages, together with the present relief and surplus labourers, without the exhaustion of capital.

The population of this parish seems superabundant ; 35 men are on parish employ in winter, at an expense of 380*l*.

HISTORY OF THE BREDE RIOTS,

Which took place by the turning out of the Overseer on the 5th November, 1830. From a Labourer. Communicated by a Magistrate.

SEVERAL days (about four or five) before the 5th, there were three men working upon Steep-Hill road, who in conversation, stated to each other the ill-treatment which they had frequently received from Abel the overseer. Not that he had done them injustice so much by lowness of wages, as from his abusive manner. One of them said, " Let us see whether we cannot get rid of this." One said, " Let us appeal to a magistrate, and see if we can get redress." To this proposal they disagreed, as appeals had so often been made without effect. They never could find redress. Another proposed, " Let us turn Abel out of the parish."

* Since, wounded in smuggling.
† Has two cows, and receives parish relief.

They then started from their work with this idea, to visit other labouring classes, who appeared all willing to join them in this last proposal. All the labourers of the parish then agreed to meet on Thursday evening, the 4th of November, at a labourer's house. They met, and they were troubled to agree what to do. Some proposed, that those who could write should sit down and write to the parish to see if they could get rid of Abel; others said, that they would much rather take him out of the parish— that a great many of the farmers had behaved so bad to them, that they did not expect they would dismiss Abel. There was not a man who wished to do mischief—they were unanimous in a determination not to do it.

That night no determination was come to. They parted, differing about what to do. Some would turn out Abel, and some not, being afraid of laying themselves open to the law.

The determined party met early in the morning, and went round the parish, when every one joined them in their purpose.

On the preceding night, the question of wages was discussed. It is true that the labourers complained of their wages, and being together they brought forward the question; but ————— says he is quite sure, that if they had not met for the purpose of turning out the overseer, they never would have met as they did for a rise of wages. They had no idea of it; for several said they would not mind being poor, if they could but be used with civility. Some proposed 2*s.* 6*d.* a day from 1*s.* 9*d.* their usual wages, and some 2*s.* 3*d.*; but some said the farmers could not afford 2*s.* 6*d.*, considering their taxes and tithes, and the poor-rates, of which they knew the farmers were constantly complaining; but they all agreed that they should demand 2*s.* 3*d.* a day, and 1*s.* 6*d.* a head for each child, parish allowance, after the second. He thinks they did not on that night discuss whether the allowance to paupers in general was too small.

To pursue what occurred on the morning of the 5th November. —The whole assemblage stopped at the Hundred Pound to consult what they should then do. This was about 10 o'clock.

A great many proposed that some should go to the farmers, to request they would step to speak to them. The farmers then came to the assembly—F. and J. Bourne, Colman, John Ades, David Smith, jun. and sen., Henry Smith, and others. The farmers wished to go to the public-house, and to meet four or five of the labourers, to be selected from the mass, as a deputation, and then they would come upon terms, if they could agree. Four men were selected to meet them—David and Thomas Noakes, Joseph Briant, and Thomas Henley, the four hands afterwards imprisoned. The farmers and four deputies met accordingly.

The farmers voluntarily signed their hands to a paper, that this man Abel should be carried away; and consented likewise, in writing, to give 2*s*. 3*d*. a day to all labourers from the 5th November to the 25th March; and thence to Michaelmas, 2*s*. 6*d*. a day: also 1*s*. 6d. for every child, parish allowance, above the third. Upon this being announced, they proceeded to the work-house to take away Abel. The farmers in the meanwhile sent word to Abel, that he had better give himself up peaceably, as he had threatened to shoot the first man that meddled with him. On arrival at the poor-house, Abel did not deliver himself up for some minutes. ———— says that Abel swore falsely in stating afterwards that a part of the men followed him into his room with bludgeons. No one entered the doors.

They put him into a little cart, which Abel had had made to carry stone and gravel. Abel was consulted as to where he would be conveyed to, out of the parish; and he selected Vine Hall, a place on the London Road. He was accompanied by about 300 men.

NORTHIAM.

Expended on Poor.

£.	£.	£.	£.
In 1816. . 1758	1820. . 2201	1824. . 1828	1828. . 1315
1817. . 2235	1821. . 2563	1825. . 1930	1829. . 1424
1818. . 2609	1822. . 2979	1826. . 1644	1830. . 1585
1819. . 2302	1823. . 2187	1827. . 1592	1831. . 1598
			1832. . 2180

Rental, 1815, 3149*l*.

POPULATION.

In 1801	In 1811	In 1821	In 1831
997	1114	1358	1448

Acres.	Rates in the £.	Value.	Expenditure 1832.
3450	15*s*.	$\frac{3}{4}$	2180*l*.

Wages per day, 2*s*. 3*d*.

Allowance 1*s*. per week for third child.—1*s*. 6*d*. for all above three.

———

Number of unemployed labourers in winter 25 to 30. These men at one time, were required to bring up bags of beach on their shoulders for mending the roads, and were shut up in the work-house yard; the object of which was to prevent imposition on the parish, by their receiving parish pay as unemployed, when they were, in fact, getting work from farmers. This degrading mode having attracted public notice, has been discontinued, and the present plan is to require them to attend a roll-call at nine in the morning, and three in the afternoon, at the workhouse, and no work whatever is required of them. The regular scale of relief was once abolished in this parish for four or five years, till the riots of November, 1830; the mob then dictated their own terms as to allowance, and since then it is found impossible to adopt a system different from that of the adjoining parishes.

Tithes in kind are a principal cause of the bad feeling which exists in this parish. The farmers avow that they do not wish for an amendment in the poor-laws while tithe remains as at present, being aware of their power in making use of the rate as an engine against it. The circumstances of this parish regarding tithe are so peculiar, as to merit a distinct notice. The Rev. W. Lord, by a clause in his will of 1813, devised to his sister, "all his right and interest in the advowson, patronage of, and right of presentation to, the rectory and parish church of Northiam, in the county of Sussex, hoping, trusting, and requiring that she or any one claiming from her, will present no one to that rectory and parish church of Northiam, who shall not, previously thereto, engage under a bond to the amount of 5000*l.*, to be paid, &c., in default that he will continue to take in kind, and improve to the utmost of his power, by all lawful means, the income of the aforesaid rectory of Northiam."

The present rector declined every offer on the part of the parish till 1829. He then made overtures to composition, and a negotiation was in progress, but it was stopped by his receiving counsel's opinion, that he could not break through the restraint imposed on him by the bond. The employment of labourers has been thereby much checked.

The refractory spirit of the labourers in this parish showed itself as far back as 1828. The stacks of the rector were fired by an incendiary; the vestry-room was forcibly entered a few days after, and the labourers said they would help themselves; the vestrymen retired. The rector, on arriving there, found one of the labourers in the chair. Three of the ringleaders were apprehended, tried at the winter-assizes before Judge Bayley, and sentenced to three months' imprisonment. At the time of the riots in 1830, a vestry meeting was held, at which it was suggested, that a deputation of labourers should be at hand; constant work at the increased scale, or relief was one of their demands. The vestry proceeded to the consideration of the applications for relief: one of the cases was that of a collier, who had been in work at high wages all the summer, but had wasted his earnings. Two of the delegates of the labourers were called in; one of them admitted that it was a case of great injustice; but he pointed to the agreement and said, "They will expect it." It is the opinion of

an occupier of land in Northiam, who has thought deeply on the
subject, that the remote cause of the riots is the mixture of wages
and poor-rate; that for 35 years past, the labourer has not been
dependent on his employer, because parish relief having made up
the deficiencies in his earnings, the idle labourer obtains as good a
living as the industrious, and the farmer, being crippled in his
means by the necessity of paying the idle, is unable to remunerate
the deserving.

Eighteen acres have been offered to the parish to be let in
small allotments, but the labourers prefer parish pay to land. It
is the conviction of all persons that, without an efficient police, it is
impossible to effect an improvement, all are crying out for it.
The language used is—" It is a complete revolution, there is no
government, no police." The farmers would not be averse to
organize a domestic force, but for their irritation on account of
tithes.

In the adjoining parish of

EWHURST.

Expended on Poor.

£.	£.	£.	£.
In 1816..1880	1820..2049	1824..2021	1828..1343
1817..2474	1821..3101	1825..1715	1829..1362
1818..2853	1822..2909	1826..1529	1830..1594
1819..3053	1823..2684	1827..1356	1831..1719
			1832..1630

POPULATION.

In 1801	In 1811	In 1821	In 1831
847	1032	1225	1200

Rates in the £.	Value.	Expenditure 1832.
11s.	⅔	1630l.

Wages, 2s. 3d.   Allowance, 1s. 6d. for third child.

Relief* was once paid by tickets on shops to such an extent,
that one shopkeeper has received 550l. from the overseer in one
year, and the labourers complained that they were obliged to
take inferior articles at high prices. Another grievance of the
labourers in part of this district was the billet system. Farmers
turned off their men or refused to employ them at fair wages,
thereby causing a surplus fraudulently; they then took the men
from the parish at reduced wages paid out of the poor-rates.

* Evidence before the Committee on Labourers' Wages, 1824.

The reduction of rates in the parish of Ewhurst has been effected partly by adopting money payment, but principally by emigration. Since the year 1818, 100 persons have emigrated, so that there are now no supernumerary labourers. In a parish which has incurred the expense of emigration to such an extent, as to leave no more labourers than are requisite for the cultivation of the soil, in which 400 acres of hops afford employment to women and children winter and summer, and where the rate of weekly wages is 13*s.* 6*d.*, the allowance for children must be considered as compulsory,—and to that must it be ascribed that rates are still 27*s.* per head on the population, and 11*s.* in the pound on a two-thirds value.

The rector, from benevolent motives, has offered small allotments to the labourers, at a low rent: he has been able to let three acres only, and his offer of nine acres more has been rejected.

STANFORD RIVERS, ESSEX.

Population.	Acres.	Rental.	Value.	Rates in the £.	Expenditure, Year ending March, 1832.	
905	4320	4124*l.*	⅔	average 2*s.* 6*d.*	Incorporated Workhouse	126*l.*
					Out-door Poor . .	66
					Bills, Salaries, Church Rate	94
					Constables and Law .	40
					County Rates . .	94
					Total,	420*l.*

Expenditure on Poor only, excluding Salaries, 193*l.*
Weekly Wages, 10*s.* to 12*s.*

The parish of Stanford Rivers is purely agricultural, containing a tract of land of good quality. It is well situated, within 20 miles of the London market, tenanted by persons of capital, and paying fair wages, and not overpeopled; yet, with all these advantages, it was at one time pauperised to a great extent. In the year 1821 the expenditure amounted to 1191*l.*, composed of the following items:—

Weekly Pay . . .	389*l.*	
Pauper Allowances, extra .	186	
Workhouse . .	312	} 1191*l.*
Bills . .	62	
Incidental Expenses .	242	

In the year 1824 a Select Vestry was established, which effected some reduction; and in the year 1825, a gentleman of the name of Andrews, the occupier of a considerable farm, determined, with the concurrence of the rest of the parishioners, and the support of the very intelligent and experienced magistrate, Mr. Oldham, to make a bold effort to put down pauperism. The weekly pay was at once struck off; and in the year ending March, 1826, the account stood thus:—

Pauper Allowances .	127*l*.	
Workhouse Expenditure .	256	
Medical . . .	42	560*l*.
Incidental .	73	
County Rates . . .	62	

At the commencement of the new system, very numerous applications were made to the Select Vestry, but they were strictly examined : where relief was necessary, in cases of illness or real distress, it was liberally granted ; but refused, unless considered requisite; and the labourers, by degrees, learnt to depend on their own resources. The rates gradually diminished, and the money expended on the poor alone, which in 1825 amounted to 834*l*., was in 1828 only 196*l*. The Vestry determined that all capable of work should be employed, and that no relief should be given but in return for labour.

The labourers improved in their habits and comforts. During the four years that this system was in progress, there was not a single commitment for theft, or any other offence. Mr. Andrews once put this question to a supporter of his plan :—" What do the poor give in return for that which they receive from the poor-rates?" After a pause, he thus answered his own question:— " They give their honesty, their veracity, their industry, and everything that tends to make a man a good member of society."

In the year 1830, after the death of Mr. Andrews, who fell a sacrifice to his great exertions, the expenditure of the parish was rising; and Mr. Capel Cure, a principal proprietor, introduced the plan of an incorporated workhouse, as is related by Mr. Becher, in his evidence before the House of Lords. Ten parishes united to erect " the Ongar Hundred Workhouse," under Gilbert's Act, by the medium of 3½ years' poor-rate. The expense amounted to 3181*l*.

The sale of the old workhouse at Stanford Rivers, defrayed their medium, with 100*l*. over. The expense for diet, which was before 3*s*. 9*d*. per head, is now below 2*s*. No " allowance " is given on account of large families; but the children of those parents who are unable ·to maintain them, are· taken into the house, where they attend in the school, are taught to read, to sew, and knit stockings, which are given out for distribution in the united parishes.

There is no assistant-overseer in this parish, but the accounts are accurately kept by a schoolmaster, at Ongar, who acts as vestry clerk.

The salary to the surgeon is 25*l.*

Twenty-seven allotments of 20 rods each have been let this year to labourers, at 6*s.* per allotment, free of rate and tithe; it is proposed they shall hold the land by lease, from the 1st of December. The crops are great, and the land is considered a great benefit by the labourers, who are enabled to raise potatoes, instead of buying them at great disadvantage at the retail price.

The opinion of the rector of the parish is, that the morals and general conduct of his flock are improved since the new plan has been adopted. Under his auspices, with the assistance of the deputy-visitor of the workhouse, several charitable institutions have been formed; which, by making additions to the deposits of the poor, tend to encourage in them habits of providence. Mr. Capel Cure, to whom the district is indebted for the introduction of the improved workhouse, continues his services as visitor. While many parishes in the neighbourhood remain in a pauperised state, this parish is entirely cured, to the mutual advantage of the payers and receivers of rates. It is to be observed, however, that the circumstances are favourable; there is no surplus population,—a considerable portion of the land being pasture, the pressure on the capital of the occupiers has not been so great as in arable districts, and that fair wages are paid.

Ongar Hundred Workhouse.

The printed rules and regulations will sufficiently detail the general management. The governor is a retired supervisor of excise; his former occupation has accustomed him to accuracy in accounts, and his services on the Kent and Sussex coast have inured him to the firmness required in his present situation: and the most refractory have given way to the discipline of the house. The building is in general judiciously planned : the governor's apartments in the centre, between the male and female wards, and overlooking the two yards. The number of inmates at present is 62, principally aged, deserted children, and a few children of parents who are not able to maintain them. The able-bodied who are sometimes sent in, are soon induced by the order, the cleanliness, the abstinence from fermented liquors, and the general restraint, to quit, as soon as possible, and seek work for themselves. Nearly 200 persons are sent into the house in the course of the year. The able-bodied are employed in raising and drawing gravel, and in the repair of the roads. The cheapness

at which they can be maintained is a material object; for where
the charge is heavy, some obstinate paupers frequently use that
as a means of wearying out their parish and obtaining their own
way. The attempt has been made here by some families, but
they have at last given way after a fruitless attempt to recover
their " allowance." As children can be maintained here for
1s. 6d. per week, the parishes avoid the evil of the large allowances usually made for bastards, which operate as a premium
on immorality.

SAFFRON WALDEN, ESSEX.

Population.	Acres.	Rental.	Value.	Rate in the £.	Expenditure 1832.	
4762	7296	13,790l.	⅘	4s. 10d.	Poor .	2900l.
					Surveyor (paid out	
					of poor-rate) ..	900
						3800l.

SAFFRON WALDEN is a considerable market-town, in which a great
trade in malting is carried on; and from the extent of land, it is
also important as an agricultural parish. Weekly wages 10s.;
and, contrary to the usual practice of the district, there is no regular scale of " allowance " on account of families. There is an
open vestry, well attended by proprietors and occupiers; two
overseers, an assistant-overseer, and vestry clerk. Strict examination is made of all applications, and the business of the parish
seems to be conducted with great regularity and economy. The
general improvidence of the artisans who waste their summer
earnings, throws many on the parish in the winter, and this
number has been much augmented by the necessity imposed on
farmers to reduce the number of their labourers, in consequence
of the diminution of their capital, owing to a succession of bad
crops, and the general depression of agriculture. The able-bodied
are set to work by the surveyor of the roads, and paid out of the
poor-rates. Hills have been lowered and roads much improved,
but these works have been carried on not from choice, but to employ the people. In the commencement of 1830, spade-husbandry was introduced, and 52 acres of land were dug and the labour paid at a certain price per rod by the occupiers. At the same
time, at the suggestion of Lord Braybrooke, with the assistance of
Messrs. Gibson, bankers in the town, who had long been advocates for the plan, allotments of land to the labourers were introduced, in order to enable them to make additional earnings by
their own exertions. To the account published by Lord Bray-

brooke, I add a few details—first, as to the effect on the rates. The repair of the roads, which exceed 25 miles in length within the parish, requires an expenditure of about 400*l*.; but in the year 1829 the sum actually expended on the roads was 1500*l*. At the commencement of 1830, there were 136 men on parish employ, at a weekly expense of 40*l*. At the same period of the year 1831, the greatest number was 88, and the weekly expense 25*l*. In the year ending March, 1832, the greatest number out of employ was 86, and the total sum paid to them was 560*l*. less than in 1829. It is probable that other causes have contributed to this reduction; but the most competent judges ascribe much of this improvement to the allotments. The effect on the habits and comforts of the labourer has been most beneficial. In November of the year 1830, in which the system commenced, when fires and riots were prevalent in many of the adjoining parishes, this altogether escaped the infection. Not only did the labourers refrain from joining the mobs, but they went out under the orders of the magistrates to assist in putting down the riots.

It happened at this period that (by an ill-timed joke, as afterwards appeared) the notice, " 'This house to be burnt," was written with chalk on several houses, and among others, on that of a principal promoter of the allotments. Nearly 50 labourers came forward to offer to watch his premises. There are now 138 allotments, of from 20 to 40 rods each; and it may be considered that each of their occupiers is a special constable ready to protect public order in moments of difficulty, because he has now an interest in maintaining it. It is pleasant to take this more favourable view; but as the tenants are liable to lose their occupations by misconduct, those whom good motives might not influence, are bound by a tangible recognisance to their good behaviour. The produce has infinitely exceeded that of farming lands. The profit of the labour on each allotment, after charging rent and seed, may very reasonably be calculated at 3*l*. 138 × 3 = 414*l*. Thus there is a constant creation of capital, which otherwise would not have existed. The attachment of the labourers to their small occupations is increasing. Many spend their hours of leisure, and sometimes a whole day, there. They have now something they may call their own.

Since the abolition of small farms, it has been observed, that there is nothing between 10*s*. a week and a large occupation : and a familiar metaphor has been used, that all the intermediate staves in the ladder have been removed.

ASHHURST MAJENDIE.

ANSWERS TO THE QUERIES OF THE POOR-LAW COMMISSIONERS
FROM TICEHURST, SUSSEX.

Queries.	Answers.
1. Are cottages frequently exempted from rates? and is their rent often paid by the parish?	The rents of cottages have been paid to a great extent, in this part of the country, from the parish funds; but in this parish and many others, this practice is now discontinued. Cottages are frequently exempt from the poors' rates from the impossibility of enforcing the payment from the poor occupier: I believe the more general practice is not to make the attempt against their own parishioners. It appears to me to be desirable that both the occupier and the landlord should be rated where the rent is small, the poor would then feel some interest in checking the amount of the rate, and the parish would be secure from the landlord.
2. Is the industry of the labourers in your neighbourhood supposed to be increasing or diminishing; that is, are your labourers supposed to be better or worse workmen than they formerly were?	The industry of the steady labourer, who is in constant employment under the same master, I believe not to be diminished; and I believe that such labourers have no ground of complaint at the present wages of this neighbourhood; but the supply of labourers in many parishes exceeding the demand for them, and the reduced capital of the farmers not enabling them to pay for the work which a due cultivation of their farms would require, many of the labouring class, and more particularly the single men, are left in a state of idleness, or obtain very irregular and uncertain employment. The payment of such labourers being too frequently measured by what is considered necessary for *subsistence,* rather than by the *merit* of the workman,—the idle and dissolute receiving as much by aid of the poor-rate, as the most indus-

trious for his labour; and the various shifts and contrivances for giving employment and support to what is considered as surplus labour, at the least expense to the farmer,—all tend to ruin the industry of the country, and to produce much discontent and irritation amongst a large class of the agricultural population.

3. Have you any and what employment for women and children?

The women have employment in hop-pole shaving, hop tying, weeding, and haying; but the principal profit to the women and children arises from the hop-picking, which, in favourable seasons, gives a considerable sum to large families.

4. What in the whole might an *average* labourer, obtaining an *average* amount of employment both in day-work and piece-work, expect to earn in the year, including harvest work and the value of all his other advantages and means of living, except parish relief? You will observe that this question refers to an *average* labourer obtaining an *average* amount of employment, not to the best labourer in constant employment.

In many instances, since the late riots, the labourers have been receiving 2*s.* 3*d.* per day as day-wages; but I should calculate the general day-wages in this neighbourhood at 2*s.* per day, or 12*s.* per week. I think a good labourer, in constant employment, with the average advantages of piece-work, would earn 35*l.* per annum, or 13*s.* 6*d.* per week; and the best and most industrious would exceed this sum, and would probably reach 40*l.*, or something more than 15*s.* per week. It is impossible to form even a conjecture as to those who are not in regular employment, but are dismissed from day to day, when the farmer from distress is unable to pay them, or has no occasion for their work.

5. What in the whole might his wife and four children, aged 14, 11, 8, and 5 years respectively, (the eldest a boy,) expect to earn in the year? obtaining, as in the former case, an average amount of employment.

The wife, and the eldest boy of 14 years old, if in regular service as carter's mate, &c., would contribute very materially towards the support of the family; but the boy's being able to procure such a situation, or any regular employment, is very uncertain. I am in-

Queries.	Answers.
	clined to estimate the average earning of the wife and children as adding one-tenth to the husband's receipts; but this is not founded in any data that can be depended on. In good hop seasons such a family would add no trifling sum by their earnings in hop-picking. When the boy is of the age of 17 and upwards, he might very materially contribute to the general fund for the support of the family. The poor, in order to make a further claim on the parish, treat such a lad as independent of them; and even if living in the same house, as a mere lodger with the father and mother. If true, this places the young men in a situation likely to lead to every kind of irregularity, at an age when they ought to be under parental control; and if false, it is a fraud upon the parish.
6. Could the family subsist on these earnings? And if so, on what food?	I think such a family, if in constant employment, might subsist on their earnings, with prudence and economy, especially with the assistance of a garden to the cottage; but much will always depend on the good management of the wife. Their food is pork, bread, and cheese, butter, potatoes, and tea. I conceive the poor have no reason to complain of the amount of the day or weekly wages; but the hardship consists in their not being able to obtain regular employment. The distress of the farmers having led to a practice (which does not prevail so much in this parish as in many others) of dismissing their labourers from day to day, and thus throwing them for support on the poor-rate, whenever they have not pressing occasion for their labour;

and whenever such relief is to be
measured by the necessity of the
family, neither overseer, vestry, nor
magistrate, can do this with satisfaction to themselves; for one
poor family will live in comparative ease and comfort under the
same circumstances under which
another appears in great distress.
All seems to depend on such minute savings and management in
so many articles, each trifling in
itself, that a magistrate has no
measure low enough for such an
estimate; his duties, therefore, between the overseer and the pauper,
are most painful. A practice prevails in this part of the country,
which, though very plausible, I
fear is productive of evil consequences to the poor, to the rate-
payers, and also to those who appear to receive advantage from it,
—I allude to the custom of putting
out children into the farmers' service, with clothing, and frequently
with a premium to the farmer who
takes them; it deprives the poor
man of getting his children out
but through the medium of their
becoming parish paupers, as he
has no means of offering the advantages that are given by the
parish, and the children are much
worse servants, and less under the
control of their masters, than if
the clothes were provided by the
latter, as they consider themselves
under no obligation, and are careless whether they keep such places
or not. If, by this means, more
children were put out than would
otherwise get into service, it
might be considered beneficial,
but none are taken but those
which the farmers require, and to
whom they must have given clothes

and food for their services, if they had not been provided at the parish expense. The regular demand for domestic service is thus superseded by the parish supply. The farmers in this parish some time since determined to put an end to this practice; which has seldom since gone beyond giving 10s. with girls from the poor-house for clothes, and then not till after they have been tried in the place, and approved by the masters; but there is great difficulty in putting an end to this in any one parish, unless neighbouring parishes do the same, as the farmers in such case would take their female servants from other parishes on these advantageous terms, and their own pauper children would crowd their own workhouse.

7. Could it lay by anything? and how much?

As to a poor family laying by, it is quite out of the question; but if the *single man could procure regular work*, and could be induced to lay by as he ought to do, I think an industrious man might in a few years secure an independence at the present wages of the country; but if an industrious man was known to have laid by any part of his wages, and thus to have accumulated any considerable sum, there are some parishes in which he would be refused work till his savings were gone, and the knowledge that this would be the case acts as a preventive against saving.

8. Is there any and what difference between the wages paid by the employer to the married and unmarried when employed by individuals?

The most profitable and regular employment is given to the married men; and the single man, except at the busy seasons, finds great difficulty in procuring work in a great part of this country. I believe the wages *in this parish* are not different to the single men when employed by individuals; but as they are the persons generally, in most places, dismissed when any of the workmen can be dispensed with, they are in the receipt of a much less weekly or yearly sum than the married men. The most active, therefore, of the agricultural population have much idle time, acquire vicious habits, which are much promoted by the beershops, and are in a constant state of discontent, it cannot be said without reason where they are industrious and anxious to work, but not able to procure it.

9. Have you any and how many able-bodied labourers, in the employment of individuals, receiving allowance or regular relief from your parish on their own account or on that of their families?

The only mode in which able-bodied labourers, in the employment of individuals in this parish, receive parish relief, is by the payment in consequence of the size of a family; or if only partially employed, parish work, in raising stones, &c., is given, when considered necessary for themselves or family.

10. Is that relief or allowance generally given in consequence of the advice or order of the magistrates? or under the opinion that the magistrates would make an order for it if application were made to them?

The magistrates in this division have, as far as it is practicable, determined never to order relief upon any regular scale, but that each individual case should depend upon its own merits, and they very rarely interfere in ordering more than has been determined by the vestry; and when such an occasion has occurred it has generally been done by private intimation that the case deserved to be reconsidered by the vestry, and not by any positive order upon the subject: by this means the magistrates and vestries have drawn well together, and there have been comparatively but few applications to the magistrates.

Queries.	Answers.
11. Is any and what attention paid to the character of the applicant, or to the causes of his distress?	As parish allowance is reduced to the lowest amount which is conceived necessary for subsistence, however desirable it may be, it becomes almost impossible in practice to make any important difference, grounded on the character of the applicant, or the causes of his distress; but with this view some parishes prefer giving relief according to the number of the children, rather than by estimating the actual receipts of the family, considering that the former mode encourages the industrious, whilst the latter (even where it is practicable) operates as a premium to idleness and vice; since, by aid of the parish funds, the weekly receipts of the profligate idler (as the necessary subsistence of his family) are made to equal the amount of what is earned by the hard labour of the industrious. It is very difficult too to ascertain with any accuracy the real earning of the family, as some farmers, from various motives, will join with their men in deceiving the vestry as to their amount.
12. Is relief or allowance given according to any, and what scale?	Upon the late riots this parish, besides increasing wages, acquiesced in the demand of giving allowance for families, to commence with the third child; but thinking this unreasonable, the vestry afterwards determined to make some alteration; but before they carried it into effect, requested the farmers to speak to their respective labourers on the subject, —some of whom expressed their surprise that it should ever have been acceded to or continued so long; and it was then determined, without further difficulty, that when the father was on regular work, he

Queries.	Answers.

should support three children without parish relief: since that time, four gallons of corn per month have been generally allowed for the fourth child; seven gallons for five children, and so in proportion. We have few families above five entitled to claim relief, the older children being able to do something for themselves, or being above twelve years old, when we cease to give the parents relief on their account; if relief is given at all on account of the size of the family, something like a scale is almost unavoidable in practice, though in theory most objectionable.

13. Can you state the particulars of any attempt which has been made in your neighbourhood to discontinue the system (after it has once prevailed) of giving to able-bodied labourers in the employ of individuals parish allowance on their own account, or on that of their families?

In this parish we had, some few years ago, viz. from 1819 to 1823, a large apparent surplus of labourers, and at Michaelmas 1819, hired a parish farm, which was found to be attended with many evil consequences, and was relinquished at Michaelmas 1822, finding the mischief of collecting together so many of the worst characters in the parish. In Nov. 1821, a system of billeting was adopted, at which the surplus men were to be drawn for by the occupiers, at the rate of one man to 15*l.* rental, and two boys from 12 to 16 reckoned as one man; such men were to be paid 7*d.* per day by their employers, and the rest of their income made up in proportion to their families from the poor-rates; this practice was continued till June, 1822, and being found very objectionable, a different plan was adopted; viz. the surplus labourers were put up and sold to the highest bidder, to be taken by those occupiers only who had in their employ at the same

E

time, one man to every 10*l.* 12*s.*
rental, which was continued till
April, 1823 ; during these respective periods the surplus labour appeared to be large, and after a
trial of the last-mentioned experiment it was found, like all such
schemes, to be mischievous in its
result ; and by superseding the
regular demand for labour, to increase the apparent surplus, and
has been given up for some years.
A committee was therefore appointed in Oct. 1823, to find some
·public work for such unemployed
labourers; and by persevering in
the determination that such men
should never be employed in private labour of the farmer on his
lands, with any assistance from the
poors'-rate, we have never since
had a large surplus, though small
numbers, varying at different seasons of the year, are on parish work;
as far as I can learn, during the
last year about twelve men have
been so employed during the winter months, and three or four in
the summer, averaging about six
or seven during the year. But
whilst the distress of the farmer
continues, from want of capital and
credit, and the habit (which is the
unavoidable consequence) of turning off the labourer every day
when his labour is not absolutely
requisite, there must always be an
apparent surplus, or number of
persons who are paid out of the
rates for want of regular employment. Whilst there is such a fund
as the poor-rate to resort to, I fear
it is too much to expect that all
farmers will abstain from this mode
of relieving themselves at the expense of others; but this is much
less practised in this parish than in
the neighbourhood, from a know-

Queries.	Answers.

ledge that it will not lead to procuring labourers at reduced prices from the rate. All labour-rates are objectionable on this principle, and if examined will be found to be nothing more than a plausible mode of legalizing the crying evil of paying the labour out of the rates.

14. What do you think would be the effects, both immediate and ultimate, of an enactment forbidding such allowance, and thus throwing wholly on parish employment all those whose earnings could not fully support themselves and their families?

I conceive this to be quite impracticable; the farmers and the labourers would unite in resisting any such scheme, and the whole of society in this part of the country would be deranged: its effects no man can calculate.

15. Would it be advisable that the parish, instead of giving allowance to the father, should take charge of, employ, and feed his children during the day? and if such a practice has prevailed, has it increased or diminished the number of able-bodied applicants for relief?

In country parishes, not very extensive, and where the population is not very large, and where the workhouse is very well and judiciously conducted, and it is superintended by a zealous advocate and promoter of the scheme, such a plan might be adopted with success, as I believe it has been in some places; but it is impossible to secure such a management of workhouses throughout the kingdom, that they would not be made instruments of oppression in some places, and, I fear, lead to a great demoralization of their numerous inhabitants. I believe, occasionally, such an offer of taking a child into the workhouse has been made in this parish, in cases where imposition has been suspected, and the parties have desisted from making further application; but as a general law, I think it would lead to mischievous consequences, and in some cases the workhouse would be so conducted as to become an object of desire, and would defeat the object

E 2

Queries.	Answers.
	by running into the opposite extreme.
16. What do you think would be the effect of an enactment enabling parishes to tax themselves in order to facilitate emigration?	I think it desirable that facilities should be given to raising funds for emigration; having no doubt, in the present state of the agriculture of the country, that there is a surplus of labour beyond the demand. I had imagined till very lately, that if agriculture was in a healthy state, this surplus was small, though from the ignorance and mismanagement of the parochial authorities, it is in many places apparently large; but, I fear, from recent inquiries into the amount of the agricultural population in this district, I am mistaken, and that the surplus of labour is beyond what I imagined; but at all events, as a safety-valve, emigration, in my opinion, would operate beneficially, and would soon check itself. For this object I should recommend that the expense incurred should be paid in a short period, viz., two or three years at the utmost, that parishes might not be encouraged to throw too much of their burdens on their successors: the landlords, on such a subject, should have a vote in the vestry (though in general occasions I would not give them such vote), and they should pay half the expense. I believe this has been adopted in the parish of Salehurst with success, where the whole expense was paid in this manner within the year.
17. What do you think would be the effect, immediate and ultimate, of making the decision of the vestry, or select vestry, in matters of relief final?	I cannot venture to give an opinion on this question. I am well aware that the charitable and humane feelings of magistrates have formerly led to a great increase of the poor's-rate, but of late years this has been much checked in this part of the country; it is the

Queries.	Answers.
	most painful part of the duty the magistrate has to perform, and I have never been able to discover any mode of discharging it with satisfaction to myself. In those places where the magistrates draw well with the parochial authorities, the overseers would wish for the appeal as they receive assistance from the sanction of the magistrate ; but where the magistrates are very generally interfering with and controlling the proceedings of the vestry, the overseer loses all authority in the parish and nothing can go on well.
18. If an appeal from the vestry or select vestry shall continue, what do you think would be the effect, immediate and ultimate, of restoring the law as it stood before the Stat. 36 Geo. III. chap. 23. was passed, so that, in any parish having a workhouse or poorhouse, the magistrates should not have the power of ordering relief to be given to persons who should refuse to enter the workhouse or poorhouse ?	If relief is offered in ;the workhouse, it is very unusual for the magistrates in this district to order relief in any other shape ; *occasionally* a recommendation to the parish officer has been given where the circumstances seemed to require it ; but I conceive the proposal of any general law dooming every applicant for parish relief to be confined to a workhouse would rouse a most formidable resistance, and that in these times of popular excitement it could not be carried into effect without endangering the peace of the country. Many parishes in this neighbourhood are very extensive, and the number of labourers out of employ at some seasons of the year, whether from mismanagement or not, is large: if these persons, who are the idle, vicious, discontented, and the most violent of the agricultural population, are collected in numbers, instead of being dispersed, as would be most desirable, few parish officers would be found that would dare to do their duty with such a formidable body in their workhouse.

Queries.	Answers.

19. Can you suggest any, and what alteration in the settlement laws, for the purpose either of extending the market for labour, or interfering less with contracts, or diminishing fraud or litigation?

It is very difficult to propose any alterations in the law of settlement that will not furnish fresh sources of litigation ; and the whole subject is so involved in difficulties, that I had intended wholly to omit returning any answer to this head of inquiry, having no confidence in any foresight of my own upon any plan that I could suggest, and knowing too well that cunning and artifice will be at work in every parish to relieve themselves at the expense of their neighbours, and will never fail to present infinite difficulties in carrying the best principles into practice. The inclination, however, of my opinion is, that residence, if it can be free from restraint by the interference of parochial authorities, is the best foundation of settlement. But in proportion as any law on this subject gives room for parochial interference, it impedes the circulation of labour, I would suggest that if residence is adopted as a mode of settlement, it should be residence not necessarily consecutive, but during the greater part of a given period, so as to prevent, *if possible*, any contrivance by which parties or parishes may receive the benefit without the corresponding burden. Before the law of settlement by hiring and service, or apprenticeship, is abolished—unless residence or some such substitute is adopted in their place—it should be well considered whether it will not lead to much injustice towards parishes who are to bear the burdens, cruelty towards the objects of removal in illness and old age, and, unless the law of settlement by parentage is also altered, to further evil consequences. Questions on the settlement by hiring and service might

Queries.	Answers.

be much simplified, by confining it to residence in such character, but it would be tedious and useless to enter upon these details, unless any such plan is in contemplation.

20. Do you think it would be advisable to afford greater facilities than now exist, either for the union or for the subdivision of parishes or townships, for any purpose connected with the management of parochial affairs ?

Soon after the close of the war, when the agricultural labourers were increased by the disbanding of the army, and the demand for their labour was diminished from various causes, agricultural parishes very generally came to the resolution of employing none but their own parishioners, which ruined the industry of the country, and produced more individual misery than can be conceived by those who were not eye-witnesses: the immediate consequence of this determination was the removal of numbers of the most industrious families from homes where they had lived in comfort, and without parish relief, all their lives, to a workhouse in the parish to which they belonged; and without materially affecting the ultimate numbers in the respective parishes, the wretched objects of removal, instead of happy and contented labourers, became the miserable inmates of crowded workhouses, without the hope of ever returning to their former independence. Since this period recourse has been had to various plans, shifts, and devices, all bad in principle, and seldom affording even temporary relief in practice. It must be obvious that the evil of a superabundant population, even where the excess upon the whole is not large, is greatly aggravated by confining undue proportions within small local divisions; but I am not aware of any practicable scheme, by which the general evils of the settlement law can be reme-

Queries.	Answers.'
	died by the union, much less by the subdivision of parishes.
21. Can you give the commissioners any information respecting the causes and consequences of the agricultural riots and burnings of 1830 and 1831?	Having no local knowledge of the eastern part of Kent, where, I believe, the agricultural disturbances commenced in the summer of 1830, my views may be mistaken ; but the fund for labour in the hop districts depends materially, in the present distressed state of agriculture, upon the advances from the factor to the grower, on the credit of the expected crop. There being a decided failure in the gardens in that part of the country in the summer of 1830, a greater number of labourers were out of employ, and the thrashing machines became the first object of attack. Whether the burnings which had likewise commenced at this period originated with the labourers, is more than I can pretend to explain, but I am satisfied they were very soon adopted by them as a means of revenge against those whom they considered their oppressors. The lenient punishment of the Kent sessions, as well as the increase of wages which was recommended and adopted in Kent, instead of conciliating (as was expected), tended only to encourage combinations in the adjoining parts of the country. I conceive the latter to have been the more immediate exciting cause of the risings in the eastern part of Sussex bordering on Kent, where the disturbances first assumed a serious aspect. The same cause for diminution of labour, viz., a failure of the hop crop, did not exist in that neighbourhood, but there were various causes of discontent which had created a feeling

of much dissatisfaction amongst the labourers for some considerable time, and the then recent events at Paris had given rise to a notion amongst the lower orders, that the means of redressing their grievances were in their own hands, whilst the beer shops afforded facilities for union and combination which never before existed amongst the agricultural population. The several causes of discontent to which I allude were, the reduced allowances from the poor-rates, principally effected by the assistant overseers, which rendered them the first objects of attack by the labourers; the degraded state to which the single men were too generally reduced, and the numerous shifts and contrivances which had been resorted to in various parishes to relieve the farmers from the burden of what they considered surplus labour. These had long been producing an irritation which the circumstances of the moment brought into action. At the same time, various motives prevented the exertions of those who ought to have assisted in suppressing them: some of the little farmers (though I believe they did not first occasion the rising of the labourers) gave decided encouragement to them, with the hope of compelling the clergyman to reduce his tithes, and, though not so prominently brought forward, the landlord his rent; the leaders in these meetings by their placards, and by other means, endeavouring to impress their followers with the belief that the farmers were unable to pay fair wages, in consequence of the extortion of the clergyman. Many of the above class of farmers were in a state of insolvency, and quite reckless of the consequences, whilst the more respectable farmers, from the alarm for their property, occasioned by the fires, were deterred from appearing to resist the general torrent; and I am sorry to say a very general feeling of dissatisfaction against Government prevailed in this part of the country amongst the farmers, grounded on the supposed inattention to, or neglect of their petitions, which I impute to what I consider to be a mischievous practice of parochial petitioning, too generally adopted for other purposes than the benefit of the petitioners. This feeling was extensively and decidedly expressed in answer to the recommendation of the magistrates to appoint special constables, which, after much difficulty and persuasion, was at last adopted. In such a state of the country, the first risings being successful in attaining their object, and with such an exciting cause as the increase of wages and additional allowances from the poor-rates, it is not surprising that these risings should spread to a considerable extent. The petitions to which I allude were principally on the subject of the hop duty, which Government must be aware has never been paid since 1822, without remonstrance and petition.

There is one other subject connected with the poor-laws, which does not appear from the preceding questions to have attracted the attention which I think it deserves— I allude to the clergyman, or other owner of tithes, when he enters into a pecuniary composition with the respective occupiers of land, being liable to be personally rated

to the poor as an occupier of the
tithes. The certain consequence,
wherever this is adopted, is to disturb the whole labour of the parish,
as it becomes the obvious interest
of the farmer to throw as much of
his labour upon the rates as he can,
and there always will be the appearance of surplus labour in such
a parish, whether it really exists or
not. I imagine that this is not a
general practice; but recourse has
been too frequently had to it as a
means of annoying the clergyman
in the eastern part of Sussex and
adjoining parts of Kent, and invariably with the worst of consequences to the labouring population. The commissioners are
aware that this state of the law
proceeds from tithes being an in-
corporeal hereditament, and consequently not passing by parol;
for to make a conveyance or lease
of tithes effectual, it must be under seal, but the stamp-laws render
it impossible to enter into such
compacts with each separate parishioner; the lessee therefore is
not legally bound either by his
composition or agreement. I
would suggest such an alteration
in the law as to place tithes with
respect to rating to the poor and
highways upon the same footing as
land; that in all cases where the
tithe owner receives a rent or pecuniary consideration in lieu of
taking his tithes in kind, the occupier of the land should be considered also as the occupier of the
tithes, and liable to be rated as
such, whether his agreement is by
parol or by writing under seal or
not; by which means the owner
of the tithes would bear his proportion of the burden of supporting the poor as the landlord of

Queries.	Answers.

land does at present by the reduction of his rent or pecuniary receipt; but as the law now stands, the tithe-owner (though in truth a landlord or lessor) must be rated to the poor as the occupier, if it is insisted on by any parishioner, and he thus becomes liable to a large proportion of the whole rate, having no occasion (as far as his tithes are concerned) for the employment of any portion of the labour of the parish ; the evil consequences of which no man at all acquainted with the subject can doubt.   Before I leave this subject I cannot avoid noticing the circumstance of the clergy having, in some instances, been the persons who have effected beneficial reform in their parishes; but if it is to be inferred from thence that it is desirable, by rating them for their tithes, to compel them to take a part in these parochial transactions, I have no hesitation in saying it would produce the most mischievous results.

22. What is the name and county of the parish, township, or district to which your answers refer?

The parish of Ticehurst in the county of Sussex.

G. COURTHOPE,
a Magistrate resident in this parish.

My Lords and Gentlemen,

I have the honour to transmit to you, for the information of Viscount Melbourne, the following statement of the practice pursued in several of the parishes which I have visited, with regard to the management of their poor; and, at the same time, subjoin such remarks as I deem it right to add for his Lordship's perusal.

As Surrey and West Sussex consist of parishes purely agricultural, the treatment of persons applying to the parish officers for relief, or for labour, is nearly the same, varying only as respects the able-bodied labourers in the amount of abuse, as in no case have I found the parish officers able to apply the labour thrown upon them to a profitable purpose. Nearly every parish has a workhouse for itself, or the use of an incorporated one. These for the most part are farmed, the cost of maintaining the inmates varying from 2*s.* 4*d.* in agricultural districts to 5*s.* in town parishes.

SURREY.

SHERE.

This parish contains a population of 1190, and 4000 acres, of which half is waste land. There is a workhouse containing twenty-one inmates, chiefly old persons and children. It is farmed at 2*s.* 4½*d.* per head, according to the price of flour. The number of able-bodied men out of employment at one time, during last winter, was 35, and the average exceeded 20. These are put upon the roads, or to dig gravel by the load, for which there is no sale. Parish wages are,

For a single man	5*s.*
Married man . .	7*s.*
With one child . .	8*s.*
With two children .	9*s.*

One shilling and sixpence is given for every child above three.

The money expended on labour by the parish last year, 417*l.* 6*s.* 6¼*d.*

The vestry is an open one. There is no paid overseer. The whole expenditure of the parish last year was 1963*l.* The rates are 17*s.* in the pound, considered to be assessed on land at its full value.

* In 1821 and the three following years the annual expenditure from the poor-rates averaged 1050*l.* The population of 1831 exceeds that of 1821 by 113.

It is impossible to resist calling his Lordship's attention
to the deplorable condition of this and the adjoining parish of
Albury, owing to the disaffected and demoralized state of the
labouring classes, and the continual fear in which the respectable
inhabitants live of fires, or other destruction of property. It will
be in his Lordship's recollection, that this part of the country was
notorious in the winter of 1830-1 for the lawless outrages committed, both on person and property. The same spirit and inclination still exists, and the word " fires," or allusion to the occur-
rences of 1830-1, are in the mouths of all classes, either for the
purpose of producing intimidation or indicative of alarm. I
remained some days in the parish of Shere, and from what I there
saw and heard, shall not be surprised at any outrages which may
be committed. While staying in the house of Captain Hay, who
occupies a considerable farm in the parish, poison was given to
some of Captain Hay's farm stock, in the farm-yard adjoining his
house, of which five fat hogs died. No traces could be discovered,
or any clue obtained, by which the perpetrators could be found
out. The following night Captain Hay was roused, about twelve
o'clock, by the barking of his dogs, and on going out with his
loaded gun, perceived a man standing as if attempting one of the
windows, who made off immediately, and was fired at by Captain
Hay. About six months before this time the house of Captain
Hay had been attacked, all the windows and frames were broken
in, fruit-trees barked or cut over, and the hot-bed frames destroyed; an immense bludgeon was left sticking in the gravel-
walk, with threatening words written on the gravel in a good
legible hand. It is supposed that the active part which Captain
Hay took at the request of the magistrates of the Guildford
bench, in acting as a special constable, and taking command of
Shere and the adjoining parishes of Albury and Chilworth, during
the disturbances of the previous winter, has been the cause of these
attacks.

There is an organized body of men in this parish, known by the
name of " the Shere Gang," and who are the terror of the whole
neighbourhood. The members of it have always money without
any ostensible means of earning or obtaining it, as they neither
work nor apply to the parish for relief. The farmers and others
are afraid to employ them, and equally afraid to refuse them
work. When any depredation or outrage is committed, some
one or more of these is apprehended, but generally escape commitment, as no one of them was ever known *to split*, nor was any
crime ever punished upon information derived from them. One
of the most notorious was hung for burning Albury Mill, in the
winter of 1830-1, and seven or eight have been transported at

various times. Those belonging to the gang are known, and are objects of universal terror.

There is no resident magistrate in the parish, and, on a recent occasion, it was necessary to send seven miles to obtain a warrant to commit a man. Some vigorous measure of police is necessary for the security of property in this part of Surrey, as well as in the almost adjoining parishes of Woking, Purford, Egham, and Chobham, in each of which fires have occurred within the last few weeks.

SUSSEX.

KIRDFORD.

THIS parish has a population of 1623 persons, and 16,000 acres, of which 9000 are under cultivation, 3000 under wood, and 4000 waste, though some of it is good land.

The parish has a workhouse, farmed at 3*s.* 2*d.* a head per week. The number of inmates averages 44, but there are more in winter. Some of all classes are put into it.

A medical man, who resides five miles off, gets 50*l.* a year. No rent is paid by the parish. Aged and impotent persons are either taken into the house, or allowed from 2*s.* to 3*s.* a week out of it. Widows and orphans, or deserted children, the same.

If an able-bodied single man applies to vestry for relief, he is asked what he can shift for, and if he will take 2*s.* 6*d.* a week it is given to him, and no further inquiry is made after him. This generally continues for three months during the winter season; and 33 single men were so relieved last year; but at one period during the winter 43 single men were upon the parish. Work upon the roads is reserved for the married men. The scale by which these latter have been relieved, has been, since November, 1830, *at which time the scale was raised*—

For a man and wife, 1*s.* 6*d.* a day.
A man and wife, with one child, 1*s.* 8*d.* a day.
A man and wife, with two children, 2*s.* a day; and 1*s.* 3*d.* for the third child.
And the same for every child above that number.

This scale has been reduced 1*s.* a week on each class, and continues at that rate now. The reduction was made on account of the fall in the price of provisions, and because the farmers lowered the scale of their wages.

In the year 1820, the number of unemployed *married* men did not exceed 30; in 1828, it reached 60 men; in 1830, the number was 80; and in the winter of 1831, the number amounted to 85;

and there seems every probability of an increase to this number.
Every possible mode is professed to have been tried to find employment for these persons, and to reduce the expenditure of the
parish. The roundsman, or ticket system, was adopted ten years
ago, but as the farmers were jealous of the manner in which the
men were sent to them, it was abandoned.

A labour rate was tried last year and the year before; under
it it was agreed, that each farmer should employ a man, at the
usual rate of wages (then 12*s.*) for every 25*l.* to which he was
assessed. This did not employ the whole available labour, and
was soon abandoned. The number of able-bodied agricultural
labourers in the parish, as near as I could ascertain, is 190,
exclusive of about 15 mechanics, most of whom apply to the
parish for work during the winter months.

It follows from the above statement that, during last winter
(1831-2), there were 118 able-bodied men, married and single,
upon the parish: this leaves 72 labourers to do the work upon
9000 acres of cultivated land, and 3000 acres of woodland.

The general opinion, as far as I was able to collect it, seemed
to be, that there is not more than sufficient labour in the whole
parish for the cultivation of the land, but that the want of capital
among the farmers prevents the employment of it on the land.
On this subject a resident proprietor, in answer to the circulated
queries, states " that the amount of agricultural capital was
decreasing; that the poor-rate has increased of late years, and
such increase, together with three or four unfavourable harvests,
has reduced many farmers to a state of insolvency."

It seems difficult to reconcile the alleged want of capital with
the amount paid by the farmers to the poor-rate,—as the sum
levied by the poor-rate in 1823 was 2129*l.*, while that levied in
1832 was 4675*l.* The population of 1831 exceeds that of 1821
by 51 individuals only.

The vestry is an open one, well attended by the farmers. The
parish is divided into two districts, and one overseer acts in
each. The books are kept by the vestry-clerk, who has a salary
for so doing of 15*l.* a year. There is no assistant-overseer.

The subjoined statement of the expenditure of this parish, for
the last four years, was furnished to me by Mr. Hasler, a magistrate resident in the parish, and amounts to above 50*s.* per head
on the population.

ANNUAL EXPENDITURE OF KIRDFORD PARISH, FROM 1829 TO 1832.

Years.	Reliefs for Infirm, Sick, and Children.*			For Labour.			Paupers in the Poor-house.			Bills, including Law Expenses, Salaries, &c.			Total Expended.†			Amounts levied by Rate.†		
	£.	s.	d.	£.	s.	d.	£.	s.	d.	£.	s.	d.	£.	s.	d.	£.	s.	d.
1829	1974	14	8	676	6	1	360	10	4	· 05	3	10½	3216	14	11½	3917	17	5
1830	1983	16	6	890	7	4	363	18	6	332	6	3½	3570	8	7½	4296	9	4½
1831	1960	0	0½	999	10	3	366	14	4	386	8	3½	3712	12	10¾	4301	18	7
1832	2079	6	0	1209	6	1	371	9	2	‡579	9	8	4239	10	11	4675	11	8¼

The rating is upon a scale of three-fourths of a valuation taken in 1825; but now, in many instances, it exceeds the actual rent paid for the land.

* Included under this head is about 1000*l.* annually paid to labourers *in regular employment*, on account of their families. The allowance made for children to men on the parish is included under the head "Labour."

† The difference in the amount expended and the amount levied is accounted for by the balance in hand, and the uncollected rate upon cottages.

‡ Included in the bills of 1832 is 100*l.* allowed to committee for emigration for this parish.

PULBOROUGH.

THE population amounts to 1979 individuals. The numbers of acres are—4216 arable; 900 meadow; 158 woodland; 150 waste land—in all 5424 acres. There is a workhouse, which is farmed at 3*s.* a head per week; flour at 1*s.* 3*d.* a gallon; and 25 inmates being secured to the contractor. The inmates are either aged, infirm, or children, with occasionally an able-bodied man, during the winter months.

The medical man receives fifty guineas a year. One shilling a week is paid as rent for every person who has a third child; and the price of a gallon of flour is allowed for every child in family above that number. Aged and infirm persons, unable to work, if not in the workhouse, are allowed from 1*s.* 6*d.* to 2*s.* 6*d.* a week, and additional relief in cases of necessity. A similar amount of allowance is extended to widows, orphan and deserted children.

The parish possesses no means of employing labour profitably; but all able-bodied applicants for labour or relief, are put upon the roads ª, or to dig gravel in pits. For above nine months of last winter, 1831-2 there were 130 able-bodied men at parish work. During the winter months the number reached 176. The whole number of labourers, inclusive of bricklayers, carpenters,

ª The surface of the roads in many parts of Sussex is so good, that I have heard it said, " If a man finds a stone upon it, he must make a hole into which to put it."

shoemakers, &c., is stated to be 308. In the month of September parish wages were as follows :—

A single man was allowed to work four days in the week at 1*s.* a day.
A married man worked the whole week at 8*s.*
With one child, at 9*s.*
With two children, at 10*s.*

Upon my return to this parish, in the end of the month of October last, these wages had been reduced to the following scale :—

A man with a wife and two children received 1*s.* 6*d.*
A man with a wife and one child, 1*s.* 4*d.* a day.
A man and wife, 1*s.* 2*d.* a day.
Single men above 21 years received 1*s.* a day.
Ditto from 18 to 21, 1*s.* a day, for five days in the week.
Ditto from 15 to 18, 10*d.* a day, for five days:
Ditto from 12 to 15, 9*d.* a day.

Those who only work a limited number of days, are under no control, and no inquiry is made into their occupations, pursuits, or earnings during the other days in the week. The shifting system is never adopted as a permanent arrangement; although a shilling or two is given to enable a man to go and look for work out of the parish.

Cottage rent varies from 4*l.* to 6*l.*, with a garden of from 20 to 25 rods.

A select vestry existed, *in name,* up till last March, but has been discontinued *in fact* for some years. Few attend beside the parish officers. The overseers are usually farmers, but this year a tradesman is in office. An assistant-overseer was appointed ten years ago, and still continues. The present assistant-overseer receives 25*l.* He acts as vestry clerk, and also as superintendent of the men on the roads.

The rates last year reached 14*s.* in the pound, on a valuation made in 1829, and then put at two-thirds, but which is now considered rack-rent. The expenditure of last year was as follows, viz. :—

EXPENDITURE OF THE PARISH OF PULBOROUGH, SUSSEX,
from March 25, 1831, to April 5, 1832—54 weeks.

	£	s.	d.
Poor-house	265	8	3
Old, infirm, widows, and fatherless children	559	4	6
Occasional relief in illness and distress, and for clothing boys and girls going first to service	500	8	2
Medical advice	59	19	0
Repairs and additions to the poor-house	13	2	6
	1398	2	5
Relief to able-bodied men—			
In house-rent, 1s. a week for every third child	257	0	0
1 gallon of flour for every child above three	378	0	0
Poor-rates allowed to cottagers	275	5	9
Able-bodied men on the roads paid from the poor rates	1807	12	11¼*
	2717	18	8½

	£	s.	d.
Law expenses	15	4	2
Clerks' fees at the Bench	5	10	0
Acting overseer's salary	52	0	0
His and the constable's expenses	22	10	9
Beadle's salary	31	4	0
County and bridge rates	67	19	6
Churchwardens' bills instead of a rate	18	9	1
	212	17	6
Three families emigrating to Canada	120	0	0
	1398	2	5
	2717	18	8½
	4448	18	7½

or near 45s. per head on the population.
Wages in Sussex have been 12s., but a reduction to 10s. was
very generally talked of, and has taken place in some of the adjoining parishes. Many farmers make a difference of nearly one
half to the married and single men : turning them off when the
weather is wet, and only employing them for half days. When
the nature of the work admits of it, task-work is general, but rarely
above 2s. can be earned at this : constant work cannot be said to
average above eight months in a year.

* To this sum must be added 324l. expended on the roads by the way-
warden, making the total expended 2131l. 12s. 11¼d.

THE PARISH ACCOUNTS OF PULBOROUGH FOR THE LAST SIX YEARS UP TO THE 5th APRIL, 1832.

Date.	Men on the Roads.	Weekly Pay.	Monthly Account.	Shillings in the Pound.	Collected by Rates.	Received on Bastardy Account, &c.	Amount expended.	Increase and Decrease.	
	£. s. d.	£. s. d.	£. s. d.	s.	£. s. d.	£. s. d.	£. s. d.	£. s. d.	
1826–27	652 3 4	401 19 2	352 1 5½	10	2421 1 9	95 0 11	2430 4 3		
1828	750 1 0½	406 6 4	349 8 0	12	2909 0 0	56 2 10	2689 13 3	259 9 0	Increase.
1829	574 6 5	504 14 9	336 14 10½	10	2433 3 0	60 17 6	2618 19 8½	70 13 6½	Decrease.
1830	817 0 10	550 1 7	340 15 9½	10	2981 8 9	45 13 0	3162 5 1½	543 5 5	Increase.
1831	1004 19 8½	583 13 7	415 17 4	12	3583 13 6	52 9 2½	3288 5 11½	126 0 10	Do.
1832	1807 12 11½	610 16 8	505 4 4½	14	4186 4 3	71 7 7½	4448 18 7½	1160 12 8	Do.
	5606 4 3½	3057 12 1	2300 1 10		18514 11 3	381 11 1	18638 6 11		

The Way-wardens have expended about 324*l.* yearly, in addition to the sums in the column under the head " Men on the Roads."
The population of 1831 exceeds that of 1821 by 78 individuals.

The condition of this parish, possessing perhaps greater advantages of situation and soil than any other in the weald of Sussex, though, in common with most of them, destitute of the wholesome influence of a resident proprietor, is truly lamentable. The happiness and prosperity of the parish have been sacrificed, and, I fear, past hopes of recovery, by a bitter animosity which has sprung up between the parishioners and the rector, respecting the amount of composition to be paid for tithes, which are now nearly all taken in kind. The loss of independent feeling, of industrious habits, and respect and attachment for their superiors, which necessarily follow the vicious and demoralizing practice of setting large numbers of men to work together at unprofitable work and inadequate wages, to which the parish has been forced, have been the ruinous and melancholy consequences to the labouring class. In this state of disagreement, the parishioners have, for the last two years, (for the purpose, it would seem, of bringing the rector into their own terms,) been in the habit of throwing a large proportion of labourers on the roads, whose wages are paid out of the rates, and so, by means of the poor-laws, they have thrown an additional burthen on the rector as a rate-payer. In addition to this, they have lately attempted to come to an agreement under Sir Charles Burrell's Act, that each person assessed to the poor-rates should employ an able-bodied labourer for every 30*l.* of his assessment, or pay at the rate of 10*s.* per week for each man so to be employed; the result of which agreement would be to compel the rector to employ or pay for a number of labourers *, for whom in fact he has no employment—and thus the breach has been still more widened.

Whether the exercise of a little more concession on the one hand, and a little more temper and reason on the other, might not restore the tone of this parish, is well worthy the serious consideration of those who have brought it to its present most unhealthy state.

WISBOROUGH GREEN.

THIS parish has a population of 1782 persons, and contains near 8000 acres, of which two-thirds are arable, and the rest woodland or waste.

The parish has a workhouse, farmed at 2*s.* 9*d.* per head per week, but varying with the price of flour. Last year able-bodied single men were put into it, but owing to the dilapidated state of

* The whole living being rated at 1050*l.*, the number of labourers thrown upon the rector would be thirty-five, being 910*l.* a year for labour alone, and independent of a poor-rate, which certainly is a most effectual mode of reducing the church to apostolic poverty.

the house, and the want of means to enforce discipline, this course
will not be again pursued.

The medical man receives 40 guineas a year.   No rent is paid
out of the rates.   Aged and impotent persons, out of the workhouse, are allowed from 2*s.* to 2*s.* 6*d.* a week.   Widows are allowed
from 1*s.* to 2*s.* 6*d.*, according to their families and opportunities to
earn anything.

If an able-bodied single man applies to the parish, he is put to
work on the roads at 6*s.* a week.

A man with a wife is paid 7*s.* at the same work.
A man with a wife and one child, 8*s.*
A man with a wife and two children, 9*s.* ; and 1*s.* 6*d.* is allowed in
money for every additional child.

This 1*s.* 6*d.* is allowed to every labourer for his third child,
whether working for the parish or for an individual.   A tradesman, or journeyman in employment, is expected to keep three
children.

The common practice of giving a regular allowance of a few
shillings a week, and requiring no work in return, is not adopted.

The roundsman, or ticket system, did not give satisfaction,
either to the labourer or farmer, when tried about ten years ago.

The average number out of employment for the last five winters has been 80.   In the winter of 1830-1 the number exceeded
100 for a few mouths, but this was owing to the parish wages
having been raised through intimidation, which brought many
home to their parish.   In the winter of 1831-2 the number employed by the parish was 84.

There are two overseers, generally farmers.   A guardian receives
25*l.* a year, and the vestry-clerk has a salary of 10*l.*

The vestry is now an open one.   Up to the month of November, 1830, this parish had a select vestry.   This was given up, as
those who at that time composed it ceased to attend, owing to the
alarm caused by the disturbances.   The members of it were
unwilling to incur the odium which was thrown upon the vestry,
and by degrees the meetings ceased to be attended.

The parish accounts are made up half-yearly, but not printed.
The accounts of this parish, as furnished to me, are as follows,
and amount to rather more than 35*s.* per head on the population.
It will be seen that they have increased one-third in the last four
years, though the population, from 1821 to 1831, has increased
very slightly, only from 1649 to 1782.

Wisborough Green, Sussex.
STATEMENT,
Showing the Amount paid from the Poor-Rates under different Heads, as specified below, from the 25th of March, 1827, to the 25th of March, 1832.

Year ending 25th of March.	Weekly Pay.			Maintenance of Paupers in the Poorhouse.			Casual Relief by Guardian.			Relief by Order of Vestry.			Expenses of Boys and Girls in Service.			Law Expenses, Journeys, &c. in cases of Bastardy and Removals.			Employment of Poor on the Highways.			Bills including every Expense not otherwise specified.			Total.			Observations.
	£	s.	d.	£	s.	d.	£	s.	d.	£	s.	d.	£	s.	d.	£	s.	d.	£	s.	d.	£	s.	d.	£	s.	d.	
1828	657	14	6	353	5	2	48	3	0	87	17	3	90	0	6	43	7	3½	341	5	1½	491	1	10	2142	14	8	Under the head of Bills is included the sum of 191l. 5s. 11d. amount of tax remitted on small tithe and cottages occupied by paupers.
1829	711	8	3	346	13	0½	91	0	6	150	12	6	79	8	10	63	14	4½	257	6	0	505	19	7	2208	3	2	Under the head of Bills is included the sum of 200l. 19s. amount of tax remitted on small tithe, and cottages; also the sum of 18l. 9s. 3d. expended on bedding, &c. for the poor-house, not general every year.
1830	829	14	6	376	17	11½	84	4	0	205	18	6	85	17	6¼	27	19	7½	431	18	11	569	19	1	2612	10	2	Under the head of Bills is included the sum of 235l. 11s. 9d. amount of tax remitted on small tithe, and cottages occupied by paupers.
1831	898	17	6	278	8	10	104	16	1½	150	12	3	88	19	8¼	27	11	11½	980	1	2	726	7	0	3155	14	6¼	Under the head of Bills is included 19l. 6s. a balance due to Guardian on late year's account; 287l. 17s. 8d. tax remitted on small tithe and cottages; 97l. 1s. expended on bedding for the poor-house; 75l. 2s. 9d. for enlarging poor-house, and 43l. 2s. 7d. expenses of measuring land in consequence of an appeal against the poor-rates.
1832	951	5	6	293	7	0	92	18	0	246	8	0	57	11	9½	43	7	10	966	4	2	520	3	5	3171	5	10	Under the head of Bills is included 239l. 19s. 9d. expense incurred in consequence of an appeal against the poor-rates, and paid for valuing the parish, &c. There were other bills contracted to the amount of 129l. remaining unpaid, in consequence of the non-payment of the poor-rates.

WALBERTON.

THIS parish contains a population of 616 individuals and 1600 acres, of which three-fourth belongs to one person, Mr. Pryme; it has a share in a work-house incorporated with the two adjoining parishes of Yapton and Felpham. Each parish contracts for seventeen inmates, and pays 9*d.* a head per week for every one deficient of that number. The contract price is 3*s.* 1*d.* per head per week when wheat is 10*l.* a load; and when wheat advances 1*l.* per load the price rises a penny per head.

A medical man receives 16*l.* a year, and attends all the poor. No rent is paid out of the poor-rates. There are four tenements belonging to the parish, into which poor families, unable to provide accommodation for themselves, are put.

Aged and infirm persons are allowed to live with their friends, and receive from the parish something less per week than they would cost in the house. Arrangements are made to support orphans and deserted children among their friends, if they have any, rather than to put them into the poor-house. There is a friendly society in the parish, to which many from the adjoining parishes are subscribers. It is well managed and thrives.

For the last five years the occupiers of land have agreed, at the suggestion of Mr. Pryme, (a resident proprietor and magistrate, to whose residence and influence the comparatively good state of this parish is to be mainly attributed,) to employ all the labourers in the parish, in the proportion of two men and a boy for every 50*l.* assessment. By adopting this suggestion, the parish supposes that they have reduced the rates; they certainly appear to have increased the comforts and morals of the people, and, of course, have had less recourse to the objectionable plan of sending the men to the roads in gangs. The average number of men upon the roads, since the adoption of the above plan, has not exceeded four, although it had previously been twelve, and was increasing. Those who do work upon the roads get as follows:—

A single man, 7*s.*
A man and wife, 8*s.*
A man, wife, and two children, 10*s.*

At the same time it is considered, that the farmer employs *a third* more labour than is for his advantage or he would otherwise do, so that the real reduction of rate is much less than would appear. It may be doubted, indeed, whether the real expense has not increased since it has been adopted. The roundsman or ticket system is unknown in this parish, and wages are never made up out of the rates, except that an allowance of a gallon of flour is made for every child above two. It is considered that many receive this allowance who could do without it; but as they have been accustomed to it, and consider it *their right,* it is supposed that there would be great difficulty in stopping it. It is, however, at present under consideration.

Since the disturbances in the end of the year 1830, wages have been 12*s.* The farmers have very few men resident in their families, and there is scarcely an able-bodied single man in the parish, as they marry at the age of seventeen and eighteen. Those employed in the parish are all parishioners, which is another reason for supposing that the agreement to divide the labourers among the rate-payers has been less beneficial than the parishioners suppose. In fact, the very trifling decrease since 1817, when the rates were 494*l.*, though the population has been absolutely stationary since 1811, shows that no material benefit has been obtained. The occupiers of land have confined themselves entirely to the employment of these, though they are sensible that they do less work than out-parishioners.

Cottage rent is usually 4*l.*, with a small garden. The cottages in this parish are very superior, and generally contain four rooms.

There are two overseers, who merely collect the rates; a guardian is elected annually, who expends; he has no salary. The parish accounts are made up yearly, and audited by the vestry, which is an open one, and well attended by the clergyman, gentlemen, and farmers.

The expenditure for the last six years has been,

1826	£511
1827	660
1828	636
1829	515
1830	575
1831	468

The rates have varied from 6*s.* to 8*s.* in the pound. The valuation is considered to be very near three-fourths of a rack rent on land, but much less on house property.

Twenty-seven persons were emigrated, in the last two years, to York, in Upper Canada, at an expense in all of 280*l.* The owners of land paid one-third, and the remaining two-thirds are to be paid from the rates within four years.

SHIPLEY.

This parish contains a population of 1181, and 6700 acres, of which 6000 are arable, meadow, or pasture, and 700 rough or woodland. The workhouse has an average of 45 inmates, who are farmed,—

If under 16 years of age, at 2*s.* 6*d.* per head per week.
If above 16 and under 25, at 3*s.*
All above 25, at 2*s.* 6*d.*
All females at 2*s.* 6*d.*

A medical man receives 45 guineas a year. One shilling a week is now paid as rent where the family amounts to four in number; hitherto 30*s.* a year has been paid as rent for a man with three children. Aged and infirm persons, not in the workhouse, are allowed 2*s.* or 2*s.* 6*d.* a week. Widows, orphans, and deserted children, allowed 2*s.* a week.

The alternative of 2*s.* 6*d.* a week without any work being required, or the workhouse is offered to able-bodied single men—the former is usually preferred. A man and wife, without any children, may go into the workhouse, or receive in money the amount which it would cost the parish to maintain them there.

A man with a wife and one child is set to work at 1*s.* 4*d.* a day.
Ditto,   ditto   two children,   at 1*s.* 8*d.*
A gallon of flour is allowed for every child in family above two.
Single men are now (31st January, 1833) employed on the parish farm, and allowed to earn 5*s.* a week.
Married men receive 6*s.*
With one child 8*s.*
With two children 10*s.*
With three children 10*s.* for labour.
A gallon of flour is allowed for each child above two in a family ; and 6*d.* a week for rent if the family exceeds three.

The greatest number on the parish at one time last winter (1831-2) was 133, and the average of the six winter months was 108.

The parish has lately taken, at a rent of 80*l.*, a farm of 320 acres, which had been thrown out of cultivation owing to the poorness of the land and the excess of the rates. Four other farms have since been thrown up into the hands of their landlords, who are unable to find tenants for them. Those labourers only who have two children are regularly employed on the farm.

A labour-rate, under Sir Charles Burrell's act, has been adopted, by the terms of which *every* rate-payer is to pay or take out in labour a 4*s.* 6*d.* rate in six weeks. It was soon after found, although the farmers all employed men according to this scale, that the number of unemployed men was very little diminished.

There is a select vestry, and an assistant-overseer at a salary of 50*l.* a year, who makes all payments and superintends the parish labour. Sir Charles Burrell is the only resident proprietor. No clergyman resides in the parish.

The rates of the year ending Ladyday, 1832, were 27*s.* in the pound, on a valuation made about the year 1820, and then put on two-thirds, but now considered to be very nearly on the rack-rent. Great difficulty is experienced in collecting the rates; and the assistant-overseer is frequently without money when he requires it.

The expenditure has been, for the respective years ending Lady-day,

	1830.			1831.			1832.		
	£.	*s.*	*d.*	£.	*s.*	*d.*	£.	*s.*	*d.*
Monthly pay . .	884	0	3	768	4	6	1069	8	0
Work bills . . .	814	17	2½	845	13	3½	834	7	4
Clothing and keeping children	172	16	2	115	12	7	110	18	3
Workhouse account .	38½	17	5½	235	8	6	275	11	9
Casual	31½	0	5¾	604	11	11	779	12	11
Sundry expenses .	317	18	10	357	8	1½	485	3	6½
Rent paid for paupers .	300	5	11	244	15	3½	254	14	2½
Total	3,182	16	3	3,171	14	2½	3,809	16	0

amounting to 62*s.* per head on the population.

The sum expended from the poor-rate in 1822 was 2,242*l.*; from which period it gradually increased down to 1829, in which year it had reached 2,889*l.* In 1832 the expenditure was 3,809*l.*

The population of 1831 exceeds that of 1821 by 21 persons only.

HORSHAM.

THIS parish contains a population of 5105 individuals, and 9300 acres, arable, meadow, and built upon. There is a poor-house, which is not farmed, but has a governor at a salary of 30*l.* Inclusive of all expense, and the value of the labour of the inmates, the cost per head at this time is 2*s.* 8½*d.* per week, and the number of inmates is forty-nine.

A medical man is paid 70*l.* a year. It has been the practice for many years to assist in paying rent for all the lower classes who apply for it, and although the vestry is sensible of the mischievous tendency of the practice, they feel unable to refuse it. The rule is in no case to pay above 1*s.* a week. A receipt in full is, however, taken from the landlord. On an average the parish pays above 200*l.* a year in rent. Aged and infirm persons receive out of the poor-house from 2*s.* 6*d.* to 3*s.* a week. Widows receive about the same.

If an able-bodied single man applies for relief to the vestry, his circumstances are inquired into as well as the assistant overseer can effect it. The same course is pursued with the married men and those with families. There is no scale by which parochial relief is administered. A scale was sanctioned by the magistrates and other gentlemen at the time of the disturbances in 1830, by which relief was given to all able-bodied men, at the rate of 12*s.* a week, and 1*s.* 6*d.* a week for the third child, but it was found impossible to carry this plan into effect. It is difficult to say whether the complaints of the payers, when this scale was adopted, or those of the receivers, when it was abandoned, were the loudest *.

The greatest number at parish work during last winter was sixty at one time. The average of the winter months was forty-five. These were all set to spade husbandry on sixteen acres, which the parish had taken for the purpose, or put upon the roads under the superintendence of the way-warden, an unpaid officer.

No application for relief from an able-bodied man is now granted, without inquiry into his necessities and opportunities of obtaining employment for himself. To show that he has used due diligence in endeavouring to obtain work for himself, a ticket is given by the assistant overseer to each pauper, stating his name and age, whether he is married or single, his trade and number of children, and a request to the rate-payer to whom he makes application for work, to sign the ticket, and mention the day of the month on which the pauper applied.

There are four overseers, two for the town and two for the country, with one assistant at 80*l.* a year. The vestry is a select one and well attended, the clergyman being present and taking the chair.

The rates are called 14*s.* in the pound, upon an assessment called and supposed to be two-thirds on land, but not above one-fifth upon houses. The expenditure for the last four years has been

	Weekly Relief.	Casual.	Labour.	Bills, &c.	Total.
1829	£830 10 0	£792 13 7	. .	£1539 1 5½	£3162 5 0½
1830	821 19 6	772 2 1½	. .	1552 15 2¼	3146 16 9¾
1831	799 12 0	1115 1 9½	£110 8 0¼	1548 1 2½	3572 15 8½
1832	1029 14 6	945 4 4½	141 14 4	1182 4 11½	3298 18 2

During the disturbances of the winter of 1830, very serious riots took place here, the effects of which are felt up to the present time, not only in the increase of the rates, but in the disaffected and malicious conduct of the lower classes. The more respectable inhabitants live in continual dread of the destruction of their property.

I have the honour to be,
My Lords and Gentlemen,
Your obedient, humble Servant,
C. H. MACLEAN.

Lincoln's Inn, December, 1832.

* The vestry had assembled in November 1830 for the purpose of electing an assistant overseer. The labouring classes collected to the number of many hundreds from this and the adjoining parishes, obstructed the proceedings of the vestry, and with threats and intimidating language proposed a scale of 2*s.* 6*d.* a day for wages, and 2*s.* a week for every child in family above two. The vestry adjourned till next day, when the scale mentioned in the text was agreed to, but, as there stated, never acted upon.

Extracts from the Evidence taken by Mr. Wrottesley and Mr. Cameron, in Buckinghamshire, with a few Remarks arising out of them.

We have selected those portions of the evidence collected by us, which follow, with a view to illustrate the effect produced upon the habits of the labouring population, by the way in which parish relief and wages are distributed among them. The general principle which regulates the practice in respect of relief is, that all are to receive it who are in want of it, or rather (for no very rigorous scrutiny is instituted into the circumstances of each case) who appear to be in want of it. Whether that want is produced by imprudent marriages, or idleness, or thoughtless extravagance, or even by squandering resources with the deliberate intention of coming upon the parish, appears to be quite indifferent. Want, as want, constitutes a complete title to relief. Wages, considered as the result of a bargain between the capitalist and the labourer, for the advantage of both parties, can hardly be said to exist. The farmer, like the parish, commonly pays every man according to the wants of himself and his family, and then gets what work he can out of him. Under this system the lot of every man is the same. No one can raise himself by good conduct above the ordinary level, no one can sink himself below it by the opposite course. The results, as far as we were able to observe them, corresponded with the expectation which is excited by contemplating the causes in operation. The veracity, the frugality, the industry, and the domestic virtues of the lower classes must be very nearly extinct, unless the following are (which we have no reason to suppose) extraordinary instances of their deficiency.

We found the practice of giving relief without work to the able-bodied, in the shape of bread-money, prevailing in every parish we visited in Bucks, except Aylesbury. It is not systematically given in any other shape. At Marlow, however, we found money given to able-bodied men, among the numerous experiments which the pressure of the evil and ignorance of its true nature and causes have driven the parish authorities to make. The assistant overseer says,

" In the year ending March, 1831, we thought if a man applied to us for work, it was quite as well to give him a trifle, (perhaps 2*s.* 6*d.* to a single man, and more to a married man,) and let him seek work where he could find it."

The assistant overseer approved of this plan, and thought he proved the justness of his opinion by showing us that it had produced a saving during the short period in which it was tried. Fortunately, there were others in the parish who, having less interest than the assistant overseer in a plan which so materially lightened his duties, looked a little farther into the effect it was likely to have on the rates, and the parish now always finds work, or what is called work, for those who apply.

The number of labourers employed by the parish at Great Marlow, during the year ending March, 1832, was 104. They are employed in digging gravel in a field rented by the parish for that purpose, and in repairing the parish roads. A single man receives 4*s.* a week; a married man 1*s.* more for his wife, and 1*s.* 6*d.* for each child.

In order to exhibit the whole amount of the evil produced by relieving the able-bodied at Marlow, it is necessary to observe, that for many years the business of making skewers has been carried on in the town. The skewers are generally made of what is called prick wood, which grows in the hedges. The people keep donkeys, and go all over the country searching for this wood, so that when the neighbouring villagers see a man with a donkey, they say, " There's a Marlow man."

The whole business of skewer-making, or skewerting, as it is called, is involved in profound mystery. Both the capitalists and the labourers conceal with the utmost care from the parish officers what they respectively give and receive, in order that the allowance the labourers get from the parish may not be decreased in consequence of the earnings of themselves and their families as skewerters. A labourer employed by the parish at Marlow gives his work to it from six A. M. to six P. M. in the summer, and from daylight to dark in the winter; at other hours he can occupy himself in making skewers, and his children, as well as the children of widows receiving relief from the parish, can occupy themselves at all times in cutting or making skewers. Although this is known in various ways, it is extremely difficult to produce such evidence of it before the magistrates or the select vestry as will enable them to regulate the relief granted accordingly.

Mr. Field stated that he had made inquiries of one of the persons who employ the skewerters, who assured him that he did not dare tell what they earned, for that, if he did, they would not work for him. Mr. Field repeated part of the conversation which passed, as follows :

" I said, perhaps they earn 20*s.*, 30*s.*, or 40*s.* a week ? " He answered. " Perhaps they do." I said, " Perhaps 50*s.*?" He answered, " I can't say."

Mr. Field's own belief is, that a family in which there are five or six children, can earn as much as 40*s.* a week in those weeks in which they work up and sell their materials.

Mr. Gibbons, the churchwarden, states, that Dean Street is the principal residence of the skewerters; that the people in that street are observed to live very extravagantly with reference to their situation in life, and are excellent customers to the public-houses for beer.

Dr. Scobell, a very active magistrate, says, " When we impose a fine upon a man known to be a skewerter, (which we very often have occasion to do,) we almost always find that he pays his fine; whereas a man of the same station, not so employed, is seldom able to pay, and goes to the tread-mill."

This business of skewerting might, we presume, be carried on as honestly as any other business, if the allowance system did not render concealment, wherever concealment is practicable, the interest of all those who live by the sweat of their brow. In the skewerting business concealment is practicable, for the materials can be collected surreptitiously and worked up in private, and the capitalists engaged in the trade are few in number and understand one another. This concealment, which, in the occupation in question, is sought only for the purpose of defrauding the rate-payers, has all the same bad effects upon the character of the workmen as concealment employed to cover a direct breach of the laws, and the character of the skewerter has accordingly been represented to us as resembling that of the poacher and smuggler. We think it clear, therefore, that nothing prevents the whole population of those districts, in which the full malignity of the allowance system is developed, from reaching the same point of demoralization, but the circumstance that the fact of a labourer being employed, and the amount of wages he receives are, in general, matter of notoriety.

There are also three persons who employ the women of Marlow in satin stitch: one of them resides in London, the other two on the spot; and the assistant-overseer states, that he finds the same kind of difficulty in ascertaining the earnings of the women thus employed as in the case of the skewerters.

Whoever has an income, which is not large enough to make his condition better than that of a parish pauper, derives, of course, no benefit from such an income, because he is thereby excluded from parish relief. His business is, therefore, to sell or mortgage his income, dispose of the sum which he thus raises according to his pleasure, and throw himself on the parish.

Two cases came to our knowledge in which this sort of proceeding is exemplified.

The first was that of a widow, who applied to the select vestry at Marlow for relief. The assistant-overseer stated to the vestry that she had an income of 2s. a week, arising from a bequest. She admitted this, and the vestry refused relief. She then went before the magistrates, and made oath that she had mortgaged her income of 2*s.* a week for two years to come, in order to make up the sum necessary for apprenticing her son to a cordwainer, (the remainder of the sum was to come from an apprenticing charity,) and that consequently she had then no income at all. The magistrates ordered her 1*s.* 6*d.* a week for one month.

We do not adduce this case for the purpose of casting the slightest reflection on the magistrates. The woman swore, in addition to what is stated above, that she also applied on account of another child she had at home, which may have weighed with them; and even if that circumstance had not existed, we will not undertake to say that they could have legally refused to relieve the woman, because she had placed herself in a situation to require it. We adduce this case for the purpose of showing the effect which is produced on the minds of the people by the doctrine, that destitution, however produced, constitutes a claim to be supported by the community.

It is very likely that this woman was swearing to nothing that was not strictly true, but the temptation to fraud, collusion, and perjury, which such a situation must hold out, is too obvious to need further remark.

The other case was as follows :—

Thomas Easton was the surviving trustee of a Dissenters' chapel, and of some land at Princes Risborough. The land had been left by will for the benefit of a Dissenting minister and congregation, and the rents and profits had been for some time applied to the use of a Presbyterian minister and congregation. Upon that sect becoming extinct in the parish, Easton applied the rents and profits to his own use, and afterwards contracted to sell the land to his father-in-law, but no conveyance was executed. This mode of enjoying the trust property did very well until the parish officers discovered it, upon which they refused relief to all the parties, whereupon Easton and his father-in-law sold the property to a third person, disposed of the purchase-money according to their own fancies, and again claimed and were admitted to the privileges of pauperism. The father-in-law has a family, and Easton himself, who told us the whole story with great alacrity, and not without mirth, has nine children, and is now employed by the parish at 9*s.* a week.

Another case was mentioned to us by Sir John Dashwood King, which may be properly introduced here.

" There is a soldier," said Sir John, " named Durrant, a parishioner of Wendover, who has a pension of 3*d.* a week; the farmers will not employ him for more days in the week than will suffice to make up his earnings, including his pension, to 7*s.* I have given him employment, and he is a very good man. I know him well."

It is plain that this man, and every man so placed, has the strongest motives for concealing, or selling, his income. A pension from government being an income which can neither be concealed nor sold, is of no value, because the right to parish relief is abated *pro tanto*, and in this neighbourhood there appears to be no difference between wages and relief, except that one is paid by the farmers, the other by the parish.

The effects produced upon the industry of the labourers, and on the opinions of the parish officers as to what ought to be the industry of a labourer, are strikingly illustrated at West Wycombe. Mr. Dashwood has there offered to let the able-bodied paupers dig his ground at 1*l.* an acre (the cost of ploughing), but the parish has invariably refused his offers.

Mr. Dashwood informed us, that he always offers the labourers work by the grate; that they frequently refuse, and apply to the parish officers, who would provide parish employment, if he did not take care to apprise them of the circumstances. If, being thus apprised, they refuse to do so, the labourer probably goes to a magistrate, who, upon hearing the case, perhaps directs him to return to Mr. Dashwood, and take the work offered him. Then if it should happen that Mr. Dashwood has, in the mean time, hired another person, the magistrate feels himself compelled to order the parish officers to find the man employment, and so he gains his point. " It is true," said Mr. Dashwood, " the parish officers might have the men sent to prison for refusing work, but the expense generally deters them."

This dread of expense seems to arise from the circumstance that the parish officers are annually appointed, in consequence of which, it is only by immediate savings that they can gain any credit. Expense incurred with a view to remote savings would redound to the credit of future officers.

Mr. Dashwood stated also, that having occasion to clean out a piece of water, he told the parish officers there was that work to be done, but they did not undertake it. He then contracted with a man from Woburn, who undertook to do the work at so much a load, the contractor paying the labourers at 2*s.* a day, or 10*s.* a week and beer. He brought labourers from Woburn. At last a few of the West Wycombe people came to assist in the work, but one man, who was sent by the parish officers, said he was not used to water work, and would not do it. The officers did summon him, and he was sent to prison.

Mr. Dashwood said, this work would have employed the surplus labourers for two months, at least, during the winter.

G

Mr. Heath, indeed, stated in justification of the West Wycombe people, that they are unaccustomed to such work, whereas the labourers from Woburn were water-cress men, accustomed to be constantly up to their knees in water, and that he believed Mr. Dashwood did not offer sufficient wages for such work.

It would, of course, be right, in giving an account of this transaction, to state what Mr. Heath said, whatever the effect of it might be: but it seems to us, that his remark only makes the case a still stronger illustration of the mischievous effects which flow from relief to the able-bodied.

Not only do the able-bodied labourers of West Wycombe think they have a right to support at all events, and to take and refuse what work they please, without forfeiting that right, but this opinion of theirs seems quite reasonable to a man far above them in station.

The notion of wages as a contract beneficial to both parties, seems to be nearly obliterated from the minds of the people of West Wycombe.

Mr. Henry Curtis, the vestry-clerk and assistant-overseer, states, that the rate of wages paid by the parish is,—

To a single man under 20	3*s.* a week.
Ditto above 20	4*s.*
Married man without children	5*s.*
Ditto with one child	6*s.*
Ditto with two	8*s.*
Ditto with three and upwards	9*s.*

besides which every labourer, whether employed by the parish or by an individual, receives, under the name of bread money, 1*s.* 6*d.* for each child that he has above the number of three. There is one family with six children on the parish, receiving 9*s.* as parish wages, and 4*s.* 6*d.* as bread money.

We asked what wages the farmers give, the answer was, " The same as the parish."

We pointed out that this could hardly be, as the farmers would then be giving different wages to married and single men.

· Mr. Curtis then said, the farmers gave the same rate as the parish to married men, and that if a farmer refused to pay this rate, the labourer would apply to a magistrate.

' But the magistrate," we remarked, " could not make an order upon a farmer."

Mr. Curtis, after some hesitation, answered, " No; but the man would immediately come upon the parish, and the farmers never refuse this rate."

Mr. Curtis has evidently no idea that wages ought to be a matter of bargain; he supposes that the farmer ought to give 9*s.*

because that is what the magistrates would order the overseer to give.

We asked Mr. Joseph Lacey, churchwarden of West Wycombe, if piece-work was common: he answered " There is very little, it does not answer."

" Why not?"

" We have got too many people, and want to employ them."

" You mean that men would do too much work if employed by the piece."

" That is what I mean."

Mr. Curtis having stated that a man, his wife and six children had been sent to the parish by an order of removal, added, " We have admitted him into the workhouse till *we* can find a house for him."

" You mean, till *he* can find a house."

" *We* must find him a house. I do not think any landlord would let him a house, if the parish was not security. The parish is security in a great many instances; in some cases we stop part of the allowance of a family in order to pay the rent; in some cases we pay the whole rent out of the poor-rate."

Mr. Thomas Fowler, the overseer of Aston Clinton, stated that the young men of that parish " dress very smart on a Sunday, and come to the overseer next day. When they earn money at harvest time, they spend it in something fine, not caring about durability, and will come to the overseer immediately after harvest. If we refuse them, they run to the magistrates, who always side with the poor since the riots."

Mr. Edward Pheby, the overseer of Fingest, having described to us the allowance system as prevailing in his parish, we inquired if he did not think it made the people less industrious than they otherwise would be.

" Perhaps it does," he replied, " but we cannot help ourselves; if we refuse this allowance, the magistrates order it, and then there is the additional expense of the summons, &c."

" There are not, in fact, many applications made to the magistrates, for we know what they will order, and do it of our own accord to save expense."

Mr. Thomas Thom, overseer of Brierton, says, " We pay the rents of many cottagers. Some will come and say, when they have got large families, that they want to come into the workhouse, and then we pay their rents in order to keep them away, because they must have a place found them."

In looking over the parish books we found the following entry : " April 2, 1831, Mr. Stiles for William Evans at Thame, 2*l.*"

We asked the meaning of this, and the overseer explained that

a 2

" Evans used to go tramping about the country. He had been on the parish some time before, but went away into Norfolk, where he married, and then came back under an order of removal. The parish officers put him on the roads, but he soon got tired of that, and offered the overseer, if he would give him some money, not to come back so long as he was in office."

" Have you seen any thing of him since?"

" No, but he will very likely come down now after the summer is over."

We turned over the leaves and found " October 13, 1832, William Evans, 1*l.*"

" What is this?"

" I did not know he had come again."

We showed him the entry.

" This is Mr. Bond's account. There are two overseers for Brierton, and one for the hamlet of Broughton. Bond is the overseer for Broughton. Each of the three pays for the whole parish during four months in the year. I did not know he had given Evans any thing."

Mr. Thom, however, saw no objection to the payment, for he only remarked, when it was brought to his notice, " They gave Evans 1*l.* rather than be plagued with him, for he won't do any work. It is better giving him 1*l.*, than having him all the winter."

Mr. Robert Brath, the churchwarden of Stone, stated as follows:

" There is a butcher who occupies, I think, 20 acres of land, who has five or six cows and a horse. A son of this butcher, an able-bodied man, is constantly on the parish."

We asked why the 43 Eliz. c. 2, s. 7. was not enforced against the butcher.

The answer was, " I have been desirous of doing so, but I got no one to agree with me, and it is hard to incur so much ill will."

Mr. Thomas Pattison, overseer of Buckland, stated as follows:—

"There is a woman of this parish who has had two bastards by different men, and is now living with a third, who belongs to another parish; some time ago she was with child by him. He offered to marry her if the overseer would give him 2*l.*, buy the ring, and pay the expense of the ceremony. The overseer hesitated, and before the completion of the bargain, the woman miscarried. Then the man was no longer willing to marry. She is now with child again, and has made the same proposition to me, and says, " You had better give what I ask, or I shall be passed home to you."

This same woman is also an example of the sort of filial piety which flourishes under the influence of the poor-laws: for the overseer proceeded to inform us that she has an aged mother who is quite helpless.

" I told her," he said, " that if she married, she had better take her mother to live with her, offering her at the same time 3*s.* 6*d.* a week, which is 6*d.* more than we now allow her mother; she said she would not have her mother for that money."

Those whose minds have been moulded by the operation of the poor-laws appear not to feel the slightest scruple in asking to be paid for the performance of those domestic duties, which the most brutal savages are in general willing to render gratuitously to their own kindred. Why should I tend my sick and aged parents when the parish is bound to do it? or, if I do perform the service, why should I excuse the parish which is bound to pay for it?

At Princes Risborough we turned over the minute-book of the Select Vestry, and found the following entries:—

" Samuel Simmons's wife applied to be allowed something for looking after her mother who is confined to her bed : the mother now receives 3*s.* 6*d.* weekly. To be allowed an additional 6*d.* for a few weeks."

" David Walker's wife applied to be allowed something for looking after her father and mother, (old Stevens and his wife,) now ill, who receive 6*s.* weekly. To be allowed 1*s.* weekly."

" Mary Lacey applies for something for waiting on her mother, now ill. Left to the governor."

" Elizabeth Prime applies to have something allowed for her sister looking after her father now ill. Left to the governor."

We shall conclude these selections with an extract from the evidence of Mr. Thomas Raymond Barker, a gentleman who has taken great pains in administering the parochial affairs of Hambledon. He says,

" In the year 1824 or 1825, there were two labourers who were reported to me as extremely industrious men, maintaining large families. Neither of them had ever applied for parish relief. I thought it advisable that they should receive some mark of public approbation; and we gave them 1*l.* a piece from the parish. Very shortly after they both became applicants for relief, and have continued so ever since."

Mr. Barker stated that he was not aware that any other cause existed for this change in the conduct of these two men, than the above-mentioned gratuity.

CHOLESBURY, BUCKS.

POPULATION.

1801.	1811.	1821.	1831.
122	114	113	127

Sums Expended for the Relief of the Poor.

	£.	s.	d.		£.	s.	d.
1776 . . .	10	11	0	1823 . . .	184	19	0
1783, 4, 5 . .	19	13	0	1824 . . .	131	10	0
1803 . . .	36	19	5	1825 . . .	152	9	0
1816 . . .	99	4	0	1826 . . .	151	1	0
1817 . . .	116	12	0	1827 . . .	180	16	0
1818 . . .	138	17	0	1828 . . .	123	18	0
1819 . . .	155	15	0	1829 . . .	133	16	0
1820 . . .	141	9	0	1830 . . .	169	0	0
1821 . . .	186	13	0	1831 . . .	150	5	0
1822 . . .	154	3	0				

The Commissioners were informed, in December last, that the parish of Cholesbury had obtained a rate in aid. Thinking it probable that its history might afford an instructive example, they applied to the Rev. H. P. Jeston, the rector, and requested from him an account of the present state of the parish, and of the causes to which it might be attributed. It will be seen from Mr. Jeston's letters, that he was able to comply only with the latter part of the Commissioners' request.

To the Secretary to the Poor-Law Commissioners.

Cholesbury, 4th January, 1833.

Sir,

    My connexion with the parish commenced only in November, 1830, previously to which I had no personal knowledge of it, nor any acquaintance with its neighbourhood. I can find no other documents, connected with the parish, than the accounts of the different overseers from 1820 to the present time. These accounts, down to 1829, are most confused; partly from the illiterate character of the parish officers, and in other part from the very advanced age and infirmities of my predecessor having prevented him from interfering with the parish concerns.

The amount, as specified in the parish books, apparently disbursed from 1820 to 1829, appears to be greater than is shown by the parliamentary returns, of which you send me extracts; though possibly this may arise from items being brought into the accounts of each year, belonging to the previous year. It is probable the sums stated in the parliamentary returns are correct, for they were given in by persons who must have best understood the accounts.

I am informed, by the very oldest of my parishioners, that sixty years ago there was but one person who received parish relief; but it should seem that the parish, for many years past, has been an overburdened one; though within the last year the burdens have been much increased by the land going out of cultivation, and the whole population of the parish being thrown upon the rates. In fact, for some years, I understand the land was let only by means of the proprietors consenting to become guarantee to the tenant against more than a certain amount of parochial burdens, all above that amount to be considered in lieu of rent. At the present moment some of the proprietors, in answer to communications from me upon parish affairs, have confessed an intention to abandon altogether their property in the parish, rather than give themselves further trouble about it, from their actually having lost money by it, the rates having more than swallowed up the rents.

About October last, the parish officers not being able to collect any more funds, threw up their books, and from that time their duties have fallen upon myself; for the poor, left without any means of maintenance, assembled in a body at my door, whilst I was in bed, and applied to me for advice and food.

My income being under 140*l.* a year rendered my means of relief small ; but my duty was to keep them from starving, and I accordingly commenced supporting them by daily allowances of bread, potatoes, and soup. In the mean time I made several, as many as eight or ten, journeys to the magistrates at petty and special sessions, in company with the parish officers, and after a delay of three weeks, succeeded in obtaining a " *rate in aid*," for 50*l.*, on Drayton, an adjoining parish. These journeys, eight, ten, and fourteen miles each, the parish officers were compelled to go on foot, and I must have done the same but for the loan of a friend's horse.

Before the 50*l.* was obtained, the great distress of the parish and my exertions in its behalf becoming known, donations to the amount of 64*l.* were sent me unsolicited, from the neighbouring families, for the use of the poor, and to indemnify myself from the expenses I had been at; among the latter was one of 20*l.* from the Countess of Bridgewater.

The present state of the parish is this :—The *land* almost wholly abandoned (sixteen acres only, including cottage-gardens, being now in cultivation) ; the *poor* thrown only upon the rates, and set to work upon the roads and gravel pits, and paid for this unprofitable labour at the expense of another parish! I have given up a small portion of my glebe (the rest is abandoned on account of the rates assessed on it) to the parish officers, rent

free, for the use of the poor, on condition that spade-husbandry
only be made use of, and the work done by married men with
large families; but the employment this can afford must be of short
continuance.   The 50*l.* will be expended in less than two weeks;
and I have apprized the magistrates of the hundred that I shall
be compelled to apply, on Monday the 14th instant, at the petty
sessions, for another " *rate in aid.*"

I need not say this precarious mode of maintenance for the
poor is most lamentable in every respect.   It is most injurious
both to their comforts and to their morals : for it reduces, of necessity, their weekly allowance to the lowest possible pittance;
and it throws them, whilst under excitement from real suffering,
in a body on the useless labour (or rather idleness) on the roads,
with no one but myself to superintend them.   This is a source
of great anxieiy to me, and a state of demoralization to them,
from which, for their sakes, I earnestly hope some steps may be
taken to relieve them.   At present I confess I see no prospect
of permanently bettering their condition; and it is to be feared
this parish must continue dependent for support on the parishes
in the hundred, by means of rates in aid; for there appears no
probability of the land being reoccupied, and the longer it remains uncultivated the greater will be the difficulty and expense
of re-cultivation, and the less the produce; whilst the wants of
the parish will be increasing.   The able-bodied poor and the
boys are, I have just observed, deteriorating physically and
morally by reason of the want of useful and productive employment, and of their receiving parish allowance, *without any chance*
of bettering themselves by any *exertion or good conduct.*

Perhaps, situated as Cholesbury now is, if the common (containing forty-four acres of good land) were enclosed, under some
such act and for such purposes as was contemplated last session,
and if a workhouse were built, the evil under which it now suffers
might be alleviated.   But so long as it continues a parish of
its present *small extent with its present number of poor*, the property must be an incumbrance to the proprietor; for he can expect no rent, the rates assessed upon the land far exceeding its
value, amounting, as they last year have done, to more than
32*s.* in the pound at rack-rent.

My experience in parochial affairs is very limited, not having
had any thing to do with their administration previously to coming to Cholesbury, in November 1830; so that my suggestions
must be received with much allowance, and I hope to be excused
for offering so little assistance.

I have the honour to remain, &c.

(Signed)   HENRY P. JESTON.

Mr. Jeston added the following statement of the situation of all the inhabitants of the parish, and of the expense at which those who have a claim on Cholesbury are maintained. By which it will appear that, though the population has but slightly increased since 1801 (having been then 122 and now only ·139), and though of those 139 only 101 have a claim on Cholesbury, yet the poor-rates have in that time risen from less than 37*l.* a year to 367*l.* It is obvious, indeed, that the instant the poor-rate exceeds the net surplus produce,—that is to say, exceeds that surplus which, if there were no poor-rate, would be paid in rent,—the existing cultivation becomes not only unprofitable, but a source of absolute loss. And that, as every diminution of cultivation has a double effect in increasing the rate on the remaining cultivation,—the number of unemployed labourers being increased at the same instant that the fund for payment of rates is diminished,—the abandonment of property, when it has once begun, is likely to proceed in a constantly accelerated ratio. Accordingly, it appears from Mr. Jeston's statement, that scarcely a year elapsed between the first land going out of cultivation and the abandonment of all except sixteen acres.

POPULATION OF CHOLESBURY.

Parishioners not receiving Relief . .	35
Parishioners receiving Relief . . .	66
Non-Parishioners (Paupers) . . .	38
	139

Parishioners not receiving Relief.

NAME.	CALLING.
Jeston, the Rev. Henry, wife and two children .	Incumbent.
Dwight, Colly '	Servant.
Bachelor, Thomas, wife and child . . ·	{ Parish Clerk and Bricklayer.
Osborn, Mary	Publican.
„ Ezekiel	
Maunders, John, wife and five children .	Publican.
Bachelor, William	Cobler.
Wright, Robert	Butcher.
„ Ann	
Carpenter, Ruth	Bastard.
„ Mary , ...	Ditto.
„ Mary	Spinster.
Sills, George, wife, and four children . .	Butcher.
Deverill, Richard	Farmer.
„ Ann	Spinster.
Mayo, William, wife and child . . .	Farmer.
„ Thomas . . . . . ·	{ Labourer to Wm. Mayo.

35 in Number.

PARISHIONERS RECEIVING RELIEF.

NAME.	AGE.	CALLING.	RELIEF AFFORDED.					
			Per week.			Per year.		
			£.	s.	d.	£.	s.	d.
Bachelor, Charles	79	Late Parish Clerk	0	3	0	7	16	0
Thorn, Thomas .	28	Labourer						
„ Mary .	26	. . . .						
„ William .	8	. . . .	0	9	6	24	14	0
„ Elizabeth	6	. . . .						
„ Adey . .	3	. . . .						
„ Jessy .	1	. . . . . .						
Gardner, John .	18	Labourers, forsaken	0	4	0			
„ Patience	12	by their father—	0	1	0	18	4	0
„ Mary Ann	9	their mother dead	0	2	0			
Thorn, William .	50	Labourer						
„ Mary .	49	. . . .	0	8	0			
„ Eunice .	10	. . . .						
„ Lydia .	8	. . . .				52	0	0
„ William .	18	. . . .	0	4	0			
„ John . .	16	. . . .	0	4	0			
„ James .	12	. . . .	0	2	0			
„ Job . .	10	. . . .	0	2	0			
„ Joseph .	21	Labourer	0	4	0	10	8	0
Cox, Richard .	55	Labourer						
„ Ellen . .	16	. . . .	0	9	0			
„ Phebe . .	12	. . . .				40	6	0
„ David . .	10	. . . .						
„ Richard .	25	A cripple	0	2	6			
„ John . .	18	A labourer	0	4	0			
Norris, John .	28	Labourer						
„ Elizabeth	19	. . . .	0	7	0	18	4	0
„ George .	1	. . . .						
Carpenter, Ann .	70	Widow	0	3	0	7	16	0
Bachelor, Ann .	62	. . . .	0	3	0	7	16	0
Newton, David .	46	Labourer						
„ Phillis .	45	. . . .						
„ Phebe .	15	. . . .	0	9	0	23	8	0
„ Charlotte	13	. . . .						
„ James .	8	. . . .						
Sills, Mary . .	76	Widow	0	3	0	7	16	0
			£2	4	6	216	8	0

PARISHIONERS RECEIVING RELIEF.—Continued.

NAME.	AGE.	CALLING.	Per week £.	s.	d.	Per year. £.	s.	d.
		Brought over	2	4	6	216	8	0
Bachelor, Joanna	50	Widow	0	3	0			
„ Joseph	21	Labourer						
„ William	16	. . . . . .	0	4	0	23	8	0
„ Mary .	12	. . . . . .	0	2	0			
„ George	9	. . . . . .						
Gates, Rhoda .	12	Orphan	0	2	0	5	4	0
Corbett, Jane .	14	Ditto	0	1	6	3	18	0
Gurney, Edmund	38	Deaf and Dumb	0	4	0	10	8	0
Forster, William	81	Cobler	0	3	0	7	16	0
Norris, Mary .	68	Widow	0	3	0	7	16	0
Cox, Joseph . .	36	Labourer	0	4	0	10	8	0
Gates, Edward .	29	Labourer	0	4	0			
„ Mary . .	27	. . . . . .				20	16	0
„ Shadrach .	11	. . . . . .	0	2	0			
„ Jonathan .	15	. . . . . .						
Puddifoot, Sarah .	2	Orphan	0	2	0	5	4	0
Spittle, William .	58	Labourer .						
„ Ann . .	56	. . . . . .	0	8	0	20	16	0
„ Mary .	8	. . . . . .						
„ John .	4	. . . . . .						
Cox, James . .	30	Labourer	0	4	0	10	8	0
„ Ann . .	28	. . . . . .						
Griffin, Thomas .	33	Labourer						
„ Sarah .	25	. . . . . .						
„ William .	7	. . . . . .	0	9	6	24	14	0
„ George .	5	. . . . . .						
„ John .	3	. . . . . .						
„ Robert .	1	. . . . . .						
			£5	1	6	367	4	0
Gates, William .	62	occasionally . .	0	7	0			
„ Esther .	54							

66 in number
35 not relieved

Total . 101

INHABITANTS, NOT PARISHIONERS, RECEIVING RELIEF FROM THEIR OWN PARISHES.

NAME.	AGE.	CALLING.
Young, Sarah	79	Widow.
Wright, Edmund	32	Labourer.
,, Mary	23	
,, Joseph	5	
,, Sarah	4	
,, Charlotte	1	
Franklin, Fanny	57	Spinster.
,, Hannah	54	Ditto.
Young, Thomas	39	Labourer.
,, Ann	46	
Philby, Henry	27	Labourer.
,, Elizabeth	26	
,, Ann	5	
,, Elizabeth	2	
Joiner, Joseph	47	Labourer.
,, Sophia	46	
,, Sophia	4	
,, Ann	2	
Guttridge, Joshua	51	Labourer.
,, Charlotte	45	
,, William	22	Labourer.
,, Ann	20	
,, Elizabeth	18	
,, Hannah	16	
,, Joseph	14	
,, Margaret	12	
,, Phebe	10	
,, Caddy	7	
,, Sarah	5	
Badnick, Charles	22	
,, Mary	18	
,, Ann	1	
Prickett, Ann	30	Spinster.
Carter, Ann	17	
Gates, John	31	Labourer.
,, Ann	30	
,, Adey	3	
,, Maley	1	

38 in number.

After the preceding pages had been in print, the Commissioners received the following letter from Mr. Jeston :—

To the Secretary to the Poor-Law Commissioners.

Cholesbury Parsonage, Great Berkhampstead, Feb. 2, 1833.

Sir,

I am sorry to state the condition of my poor is again becoming very distressing. The rate in aid for 50*l.* is exhausted ; and the able-bodied poor have again resorted to me for relief, the parish officers being afraid to employ them, on account of possessing no means of remunerating them for their labour. The donations which I received from the neighbouring families are expended, with the exception of 20*l.* presented to me by the Countess of Bridgewater. I rejoice that this sum enables me, which otherwise I could not have done, to set the married men with families to spade-husbandry on a piece of my glebe; the labour on the piece given by me to the overseers for the use of the parish being for the present necessarily discontinued on account of their having no funds to pay for digging it. This land, about two or three acres, I have given to the poor themselves, as garden-ground.

The present unfortunate condition of the parish officers is an evil which, I fear, must recur as often as a fresh rate in aid is required ; for the magistrates to whom, about a fortnight ago, I applied for further assistance,—the rate in aid which they had granted being *nearly gone,*—then informed me they had no power to interfere, nor to grant an order for another rate, till the former was *quite expended.* Whenever, therefore, the one rate in aid is exhausted, and before another can be obtained, an interval of at least three weeks must expire, and, during that period, the poor can be afforded no relief. In the present instance they can obtain none for three weeks to come but what is advanced by myself; and this, should the evil continue longer, it will be out of my power to render. This circumstance will continue to be a source of much uneasiness to me, inasmuch as it is of very bad tendency to the poor themselves. For the poor-laws have produced so much dependence and improvidence among them, that if for a few weeks only they are deprived of parish aid, they incur debts, and become behindhand in their rent; and, to avoid discharging it, voluntarily quit a comfortable cottage for one much less so : and thus a spirit of recklessness and dishonesty is promoted, detrimental to the moral character of the very best of them. I have always remarked, that from the moment a pauper quits a comfortable dwelling for a poorer and less comfortable one, his character invariably alters for the worse; and he soon becomes idle and dishonest; he betakes himself to the pot-house, and from thence to poaching, which at once incapacitates the body for labour through the day. I can perceive these effects already in more than one of my poor.

There is another circumstance which augments the evil under which the parish of Cholesbury now labours, which is, that although nearly the whole of the land is now abandoned, the parish officers are called upon to furnish the full assessment of *county* rates as hitherto. It is true, these have not yet been enforced, but the officers have repeatedly expressed to me their fears of having their goods distrained on this account; and, for their sakes, I attended at the late Quarter Sessions at Aylesbury, and prayed the bench to exempt, for the present, the parish from paying county rates. The magistrates took the matter under their consideration, but I was at last informed it was out of their power to grant the thing I prayed for.

Having obtained the consent of the trustees of the principal farm in the parish, now abandoned, to let it at a nominal rent till Michaelmas next, and having found that if I could obtain a *rate in aid* for 120*l.*, I could induce persons to come forward and take the land at 5*s.* an acre,—by reason of that sum enabling me to guarantee the occupier for that period from a greater burden of rates than 10*s. in the pound at ruck-rent,*—I, at my last interview with the magistrates (for whose most ready and obliging compliance with my wishes, as far as lies in their power, I am most thankful), solicited them to grant a rate in aid to the above amount, to carry the parish officers on till Michaelmas next. They did not, however, feel justified in making an order for so great a sum, nor prospectively for so long a period. Had I obtained the sum stated, the parish officers themselves had, by my advice, agreed to become the occupiers, who, by employing all the surplus labourers on the land, would have greatly lightened to other parishes the burden of supporting the poor of Cholesbury. The probable amount required by *rates in aid,* for the same period, I now estimate at about 180*l.* Thus, if the farm in question had been occupied, an expense of 60*l.* might have been spared, and the poor have been employed *usefully and with satisfaction to themselves.*

Having failed in this attempt, I confess I now see no prospects whatever of the parish being relieved from its present degraded and impoverished state. The situation of myself and the parish officers is a most painful one; for besides the continual calls upon their time, which to them is no small loss,—they being little better than paupers, and obliged to labour hard for their bread,—I experience that we are exciting unpleasant feelings against ourselves from the other parishes in the hundred, who dread being called upon, by rates in aid, to assist in the support of the poor of another parish. And, in fact, this mode of supporting the poor of an insolvent parish, is a great grievance to the one rated, as the one selected for that purpose is generally that in which, through good management of the poor, the rates are so reduced as to attract the notice of neighbouring parishes.

The parish of Cholesbury does not exceed in extent the size of a moderate farm, and the whole is to be bought for about 2000*l*. I wish government would purchase the whole, and try the experiment of allotting it exclusively to the able-bodied paupers. I would gladly dedicate my time to the project; and I have reasons to think, that at the expiration of two years (the parish in the interval receiving the assistance of rates in aid), the whole of the poor would be able and *willing* to support themselves, the aged and impotent of course excepted.

I have the honour to remain,
Sir,
Your very obedient servant,
HENRY P. JESTON.

P. S. If the burden of supporting the poor of an insolvent parish could be thrown on the county, or the hundred, it would be little or not at all felt.

My Lords and Gentlemen,

In compliance with Lord Melbourne's wishes, as conveyed to me by you, I have selected six of the parishes in the district which I visited, viz.—

Cranbourne		
Poole		
More Crichel	. .	Dorset.
Hasilbury Bryan		
Dunstew	.	Oxfordshire.
Calne	. . .	Wiltshire.

I have endeavoured in this selection to illustrate the points mentioned in his Lordship's Letter.

I am, my Lords and Gentlemen,
Your obedient Servant,
D. O. P. Okeden, Assist. Commissioner.

More Crichel, Dec. 25, 1832.

CRANBOURNE, DORSET.

Population, 2158.

Number of acres in the parish—

	Acres	Roods	Poles
Common, or heath land .	4604	.. 1	.. 5
Woodlands . .	1347	.. 1	.. 28
Arable land . .	5006	.. 1	.. 37
Pasture land . .	2093	.. 3	.. 13
Total acres	13,052	0	3

Rate about four shillings in the pound rack-rent—payment to paupers of different descriptions both in and out of the poor-house.

1830 . .	£1693 18	8¾
1831 . .	1370 9	7
1832 . .	1541 9	4½

Cranbourne parish contains five tithings, viz., Alderholt, Boveridge, Blagdon, Fairwood, or Verwood, and Monkton-up-Winbourne. Over each of these there is a tithing-man, and a constable of the parish resides at Cranbourne. The magistrates hold a petty sessions at Cranbourne once a fortnight. In the tything of Farewood there is a large pottery of the coarsest earthenware, which affords employment to about 100 men and about ten boys, who turn wheels.

The agricultural labourers amount to 800
The pottery ditto . 100

The average wages of the agricultural labourers are 8*s*. per week—at the pottery they are perhaps 9*s*. per week.

The women have employment only in the fields.

The woods afford very profitable piece-work labour, in fencing, hurdling, and fagotting, at each of which employments an able-bodied man may earn from 12*s*. to 14*s*. per week.

The rents of the cottages in Cranbourne parish are high, and run from 3*l*. to 5*l*. per annum, and the gardens are small except at those cottages which border on the heath-land. Here, too, the labourer has another great advantage—he is allowed to cut turf for himself gratis, so that his fuel costs him nothing but the labour, and his vicinity to the heath does not require carriage home.

Ten acres of land have lately been given up to the poor by Lord Salisbury, the lord of the manor. This is divided into 24 parts, and let at the rate of 1*l*. 3*s*. per acre.

A speculation of building small houses for the poor has lately been undertaken in the tithing of Farewood, and a large population of 300 or 400, raised round the pottery. While the works continue, the pressure will not fall on the parish ; if they fail, the pressure will be very great. Every house is taken as soon as it is finished, and at a very high rent.

All the cottages are rated, but many returned "rates uncollected :" this the parish makes up by a small increase of rates.

A few house rents are paid by the parish for labourers with large families ; but no number of children are a plea for the relief of an able-bodied man in employ. A child or two are occasionally taken into the poor-house, if their support at home presses hard on the parents, and if they request the children to be taken.

The strictest investigation takes place into character.

A sum left by the will of a parishioner to be annually given in clothing to the poor is used as the reward of industry and good character.

No distinction is made, by individuals, in the wages of single and married men.

If a man belongs to a friendly society, and is thrown out of work, by illness or accident, the parish gives him the full benefit of his society's allowance, and look to the wife and children.

There is a poor-house, containing this year, 1832, 28 inmates, and a few orphans and bastards. The 28 inmates are made up of

> 12 old infirm women
> 16 old infirm men
> —
> 28

There are about 8 children in the house, all very young.

H

There is no contract, and the expenses of each individual, for lodging, bedding, clothes, food, medical advice, and all expenses of the house, amount to about 3*s*. 10*d*. per week.

No work is done in the house.

There are now, December 15, 1832, only eight persons out of employ, who have applied to the guardian for work.

The parish of Cranbourne is governed by the Gilbert act, and has four overseers, six visiters, a treasurer, and a guardian of the poor. The latter is a paid officer, and is in fact the working overseer. His salary is 70*l*. per annum.

The loss by bastardy last year was as under:—

> Amount of bastardy-orders made £114
> Collected by the guardian . 23
>
> Loss . . £71

The committal of women who have had two or three bastards avails little, either as punishment to them, or as terror to others.

There is no female tread-mill at Dorchester, and the hard labour of the women consists in washing the jail linen, and keeping the female wards clean; in fact, of their usual occupations. I once went to one of the female wards at Dorchester, where I saw 15 women with 18 bastards. The room was clean, had a good fire in it, and one and all declared they had rather be there in winter than at home. As for shame, it is out of the question.

Emigration is unknown.

In my report on Dorsetshire I cited a remarkable act of swindling, by the late guardian of the poor of Cranbourne, to show the necessity of parish accounts being audited by regular accountants, and not by the loose and irregular auditors of a vestry.

GENERAL OBSERVATIONS.

I HAVE selected the parish of Cranbourne, in Dorsetshire, as affording a remarkable instance of the great improvement in the character and comfort of the poor, by an emancipation from the most systematic and constant interference of a resident magistrate that perhaps was ever displayed. The Rev. H. D——, the late vicar of Cranbourne, was a county magistrate, he attended very little to any business except that of poor-management. This formed the whole employment of his life. He affected the mischievous honour of "the poor man's friend." His house was a daily petty sessions. He made scales, and small codes, and issued orders and recommendations of the most preposterous and illegal description.

The overseers gave up the contest; the justices were beaten by him, and the parish was a scene of discontent and demoralization.

About four years ago this vicar died. Some new magistrates had begun to act in the Cranbourne division; they heartily joined the others in establishing a new system in so large a parish as Cranbourne. A meeting of farmers, rate-payers, &c., was called at the petty sessions, and it was declared that from that time no scale or head-money should be allowed : that every case should rest on its own merits, and that able-bodied men in employ should not be relieved on account of their families. There was a little discontent at the pottery, but in the end, as the magistrates were firm, the opposition ceased. The magistrates have met with complete success. They refer every case back to the vestry, and hardly ever hear of it a second time.

They hear few cases at their own houses, and in every way interfere as little as possible. Three years and a half have created a change most pleasing and satisfactory. The old poor, regularly paid, are satisfied; those whose applications are refused by the vestry acquiesce in the decision; and I can assert, as one of the magistrates of the division, that the complaints which used, in the late vicar's ' time, to amount to at least 20 in a week, do not amount now to that number in a year.

If the rates, though they are lessened, and lessening, do not show the diminution which might be expected, it is owing to the swindling acts of the late guardian, and which are wholly unconnected with the relief of the poor.

He has made over his property to the parish, and the whole is in a train of settlement, by which I hope the parish will soon be repaid its losses.

The excess of 1832 above 1831 is owing to bills left unpaid by the late guardian.

The actual poor expenses of 1832 are less than 1831.

Ludicrous as it may appear, and almost incredible, I must mention that the late vicar's power was so highly estimated, by the paupers, that the printed scales and rules, which he issued and signed, were called by them " Mr. D.'s Acts of Parliament," and a pauper actually once threatened me with the consequences of disobeying them.

Cranbourne, as a parish, lies under great disadvantages. Its population is 2158, and scattered over a wide extent.

There is a large parish church at Cranbourne, a chapel-of-ease at Farewood, and the same at Boveridge.

These are to be all served every Sunday. The poor, so numerous, are to be visited at their homes, and their *temporal*, as well as spiritual, wants inquired into.

The whole income of the vicar is 125*l.* per annum. A curate, of course, is out of the question, and no individual is equal to the adequate, or to anything like the adequate, discharge of the duties of a vicar of Cranbourne.

The great tithes which are in the hands, principally, of Lord Salisbury, and another person, amount to 2500*l.* per annum.

I have universally found that of all the blessings of a parish, few, indeed none, are equal to the pastoral care of the clergyman, and his advice and guidance in the temporal concerns of the poor, whom circumstances render so helpless.

Cranbourne suffers much by beer-houses, which are numerous, and which are more dangerous in proportion as they are established in heaths, and places at some distance from the villages.

I am personally so well acquainted with Cranbourne, that I have not quoted the names of many intelligent persons from whom I have received much information. The present vicar, the Rev. F. Pare, deplores his inability to perform half the duties which his responsible situation entails on him.

HASILBURY BRYAN, DORSET.

Population—611.
Number of acres in the parish.

Pasture-land .	2020
Arable do.	250
Woodland do. .	27
Common do.	150
Gardens .	7
Total acres	2454

Expended on the poor, as per book for one year to Lady-day 1832, 413*l.*

There are 77 agricultural labourers. In summer none are out of employ, in winter not above five or six are unemployed. These are put on the roads, or, if family men, relieved by the scale as settled at the petty sessions at Sturminster Newton. In short, the scale system, and the making up of wages is complete. There is no workhouse, but there are eight cottages belonging to the parish, in which there are 14 families lodged.

Hasilbury Bryan is seated in a rich grass vale, and the farms are principally pasture farms, whence cheese, butter, and cattle are sent to Smithfield market. The wages may be thus stated:—

	£.	*s.*	*d.*
Man, 26 winter weeks at 7*s.* . .	9	2	0
16 summer do. at 9*s.* . .	7	4	0
10 weeks hay and corn harvest, at 9*s.*⎫ per week, and beer, the beer valued⎬ at 2*s.* 6*d.* . . ⎭	5	15	0
Fuel given or carried . .˙	1	0	0
Man . .	23	1	0

	£.	*s.*	*d.*
Wife, button-making per week .	0	2	6
Boy, do. . . .	0	2	0
2 children buttoning and bird-⎱ keeping . . ⎰	0	2	6
	0	7	0
	0	52	0

		£.	*s.*	*d.*
	364	0 18	4	0
Total per annum		41	5	0

Thus the family would receive above 13*s.* 6*d.* per week.
Soon after the riots of 1830 a new and more liberal scale was
made by the magistrates of the division; and in February, 1831,
an order was given to the overseers of Hasilbury Bryan, requiring
them to relieve 10 families, all able-bodied, and in employ by the
new scale. The overseers contended, and the clergyman protested
against this order in vain. In this district, indeed, the overseers
know so well the inutility of resistance, that to avoid trouble,
expense, and reproof, they generally accede to the demands, and
settle all claims, not by character or merit, but by the rules of
addition and subtraction. I have already named, in my report on
Dorsetshire, the district of Sturminster Newton, as the worst
regulated as to poor concerns, with the highest proportionate rates,
in the county. It is certain that in no district is there so much
magisterial interference.

BASTARDY.

The allowance is from 1*s.* 6*d.* to 2*s.* per week. No regular
bastard account is kept in the parish. There are now five bastards, who cost the parish nearly 15*l.* per annum.

GENERAL OBSERVATIONS.

I have selected the parish of Hasilbury Bryan, from its affording the singular case of a rector of great intelligence, and of the
most correct views on the working of the poor-laws, being thwarted

by the overseer and Magistrates. When I name the Rev. Henry
Walter, I need hardly enlarge on his knowledge of the poor-laws.
His examination before the House of Commons on the Labourers'
Wages Committee, will prove my assertions.

Mr. Walter determined in 1823 to put an end to the illegal
system of roundsmen or stem-men, and he appealed to the Dorsetshire July Quarter Sessions against the rate made for that purpose. His appeal was successful; and no appeal from the decision
of the magistrates against the rate to a superior court ever took
place. But mark the consequences,—Mr. Walter's legal expenses
exceeded 90*l*. The expenses of the parish and overseer were paid
by a rate made on purpose. Mr. Walter, indeed, succeeded; but
the practice continues, and the relief of the able-bodied men in
employ, according to their families and the scale, is universally
bestowed. I fear Mr. Walter's appeal in 1823 did not conciliate
the magistrates; and certain it is, that in some remarkable cases,
the bench of the division have done all in their power to counter-
act Mr. Walter's efforts. Still his zeal for the true interests of the
poor in his parish is unabated; and he proves how the evils of a
bad system may be mitigated by a constant watchfulness and
well-applied kindness, though he is not permitted to use his judicious efforts for the introduction of a good management.

MORE CRICHEL, DORSET.

Population—304.

Poor expenditure to Lady-day, 1832, for one year, 124*l*. 7*s*. 8*d*.,
being 10*l*. less than the former year.

Number of acres about 1860 ; viz.—

Woodlands		150
Arable	.	880
Pasture	.	630
Downland	.	200
	Total . .	1860

There are about 25 men and 10 boys able for field and barn-
work, which are quite sufficient for the labour of the parish, with
the women to weed, &c.

There are none on the poor-book but the old and infirm, and
widows, with four or five very small children. There is no scale
nor make-up system. Every cottage has a large garden, and potato land is let to the labourers by the farmer at the usual rate.
There are never any men out of employ: indeed, for the road-
work, or draining, or any extra job, application for labour is
made to the neighbouring parishes, which abound in superfluous

labour. The mode in which the cottages are let in this parish conduces, in my opinion, more to preserve the spirit of independence and attachment to the soil than any I know. It is the letting of cottages on their lives to the poor. No one who has not witnessed it can imagine the struggles that are made, the privations that are undergone, to purchase these copyholds of inheritance. For a good cottage and about a quarter of an acre of garden the price is about 40*l.*; of this they generally have half the sum laid by, and raise the other half by mortgage, paying it off in about five years by instalments. The rates are scarcely 1*s.* in the pound.

BASTARDY.

There has been but one in the parish for seven years, and for that the money is received regularly from the father.

No emigration by the parish has been ever heard of; two boys were sent last year by subscription, at the rate of 7*l.* each, which left them 1*l.* each in their pocket on reaching Montreal.

GENERAL OBSERVATIONS.

I have selected this parish, because it exhibits a proof of what may be done by good management and constant watchfulness. There has been but one instance in five years of any appeal to the magistrates, from the decisions of the vestry.

The property being only in two hands, a regular system has been practised for above 30 years, and no increase of cottages allowed above the requisite habitation required for the sufficiency of labourers of the parish. I wish to mention here a curious instance of the dealings of the poor at their hucksters : the enormous profits of the shopkeepers, and the badness of their articles, induced one of the landowners here to furnish a shop with goods (tea, rice, sugar, treacle, &c.) of excellent quality, which were supplied to the poor at prime cost. A better tea than they used to get for 6*s.* 10*d.* per lb., was supplied at 5*s.* 2*d.* per lb., and everything else in proportion. The two shopkeepers who formerly made a livelihood by their trade were pensioned off. Ready money (that is, one week's credit) was required. In one year the old shopkeepers threw up their pensions, and returned to their trades, and *all* their customers followed them. The fact is, long credit is given; and one of the shopkeepers confessed to me that if one out of three paid, he made a very comfortable profit. So that the fashionable coachmaker in Long-acre and the petty huckster of a petty village proceed on the same principle of dealing.

In this village, some of the copyholds, about five or six, have from six to ten acres of land. These families have universally done well.

POOLE, DORSET.

Poole is a town and county, having its own quarter sessions and gaol. It is entirely governed by its own magistracy, without any interference of the magistrates of the county.

Population, 6459.

Annual sum expended on the poor for the year ending Lady-day, . . . 1830	£3265	8	6
Ditto . . 1831	3149	13	0
Ditto . . . 1832	3440	17	6

There is but one parish in Poole, St. James's. Poole is governed, as to the management of its poor, by the Gilbert Act.

The assistant-overseer has 30*l.* per annum. The guardian acting, Mr. Hooper, who is the entire manager of all that relates to the poor, has 130*l.*

The acting guardian and visiters settle the relief to be allowed to each pauper. There is scarcely ever an appeal to the magistrates.

THE WORK-HOUSE.

The numbers, ages, and sexes of the inmates of the work-house are at present, December, 1832,

Old and infirm men, some above 90	37
Ditto women, three above 92 .	42
Under 13 years old—boys	21
Ditto girls . .	29
Total inmates .	129

There are generally about five or six more, somewhat younger than the old men and women, who do the work of the establishment.

The women are mostly widows. The men have been sailors and mechanics. The old men occasionally pick a little oakum, and some of the less infirm sweep and clean the streets. These employments may save the parish about 40*l.* per annum.

The men and women are separated, except in the case (there are only two cases) of an old married couple.

The board, lodging, clothes, fuel, and all expenses of the house, and medical advice, for each individual, amounts to a sum not exceeding 3*s.* 10*d.* per week.

The children are well instructed, go to the Sunday-schools, and to church or meeting-house. The boys are apprenticed to the sea line. There is a very accurate and constant visitation of the out-poor at their houses, and every means are used to ascertain their characters, and the validity of their claims on parish aid. The men, of the out-poor, are principally old sailors and some mechanics. The women, widows of those classes with families. When they have fathers or children able to support them, the parish does not relieve the poor, but apply for, and procure, from the magistrates, an order on the relations.

If able-bodied men apply for relief they are sent to the parish farm. Such applications are rare, and the applicants soon find work again.

The out-door women are employed to make up cotton shirts, for the Newfoundland sailors. The sailors in the Newfoundland and coasting trade get about 2*l*. 10*s*. per month.

A good mechanic earns about 50*l*. per annum. About one-tenth of the resident poor are non-parishioners. The total number of poor relieved out of the work-house are generally 700. The residences of the poor are rated, but the rates never demanded. There is a loss of about one-third in every rate on this item, as the landlords are not made to pay the rates. There are twenty-five bastards supported by the parish at 1*s*. 6*d*. per week. The fathers are generally strange sailors, who get away. I think this is a small number of bastards in proportion to the population, and may be accounted for by the abundance of prostitutes at Poole.

REMOVALS AND APPEALS.

The expenses of removals are as under:—

	£.	*s.*	*d.*
For 1829	32	5	6
1830	27	11	3
1831	21	8	9
Total of three years	81	5	6

Expenses of appeals:—

	£.	*s.*	*d.*
For 1829	14	10	6
1830	21	13	0
1831	19	9	3
Total of three years	55	12	9

The accounts are all kept by the acting guardian, and submitted to, and passed, monthly, by the other guardians; and every quarter they are audited and signed by the visiters.

The accounts are published annually, and sent to all the rate-payers.

CHARITABLE INSTITUTIONS.

The charitable foundations of Poole are as under:—

1st. Twelve alms-houses, vested in the corporation by Christopher Jolliffe, Esq. They are occupied by twelve poor old men, who only receive, besides their lodging, some coals at Christmas.

2dly. Six alms-houses are left to the corporation as trustees. In these reside twelve old women, who receive, besides their lodging, 6d. a week each. These are Rogers's alms-houses.

3dly. 300l. left by W. Bennett to the corporation, as trustees, the interest thereof to be distributed by them annually to the poor.

A few smaller sums have been left to the corporation, as trustees, at various times; the interest to be applied to coals, or bread, or schooling.

GENERAL OBSERVATIONS.

I have selected the town of Poole as an instance of the best management of the poor I have met with.

The interference of the magistrates is unknown. The present acting guardian took on himself the management in 1815. In four years he reduced the expenditure 2,600l.; and though the population has nearly doubled since that period the rates have never exceeded what they were after that reduction.

CALNE, WILTSHIRE.

Population—Parish and Borough	4795
Bowood Liberty .	81
Total	**4876**

The hamlet of Bowood consists only of the mansion of the Marquis of Lansdowne, and a few cottages and one farm-house. So that in considering the population of Calne, as applicable to the poor-rates, it will be fair only to consider the population of the borough and parish, viz., 4795.

Of these the males are .	2296
females	2499
Total	**4795**

The number of inhabited houses is	962
do. uninhabited	33
Total houses	**995**

There are   393 families employed in agriculture.
There are   368   do.   in trade.
Other families 351

Total   1112

The parish contains about 8,000 acres of land.

The money expended on the poor last year, that is, for one year to Lady-day, 1832, 4961*l.* 17*s.* 9*d.*

The items of this annual expenditure, which I took from the parish pay-book are as under:—

150 old men and women past work, at 72*l.* per month	£936	0	0
27 widows with young children	370	10	0
30 old men and women in work-house	208	0	0
6 children in the poor-house	45	10	0
41 bastard children, to whose mothers is paid yearly	71	12	0
84 able-bodied labourers with families, whose wages are added to by the magistrates' scale	455	0	0
Extra relief to poor persons in sickness, out of work, and loss of time	591	2	7
Payments to Calne poor in other parishes, and funerals	320	7	4
Payments to surplus labourers employed on the parish farm or roads (for one year)	1081	15	10
Tradesmen's bills, about	350	0	0
Officers' salaries, medical attendance, law bills, &c.	300	0	0
Rent of parish farm	132	0	0

1 year's total to Lady-day, 1832   £4961 17 9

On the above account, after expressing my surprise that any bench of magistrates could be found to sanction it, I would make the following remarks:—

Of the fifth item for bastards, there is so little ever received on the orders that it is not worth speaking of,—the whole is nearly clear loss.

On the ninth article or payment of able-bodied surplus labourers, I found the whole labour was allowed to be utterly unproductive.

The parish farm is a great loss every year, and is used merely as an excuse for labour, to keep the men employed on it out of mischief and thieving.

The poor-house contains 60 old men and women, about thirty of each, who receive 2*s.* 6*d.* per week, and keep themselves. The management has lately been improved, which has occasioned some decrease of rates.

The few children there are kept at about 2*s.* 9*d.* each per week. The rents of the cottages are from 3*l.* to 4*l.* per annum, with very little garden ground.

Wages, in general, are low—not above 8*s.* per week; but the labourers employed on the property of the Marquis of Lansdowne, both at Calne and in the neighbourhood, have 10*s.* per week, and potato land.

The operation of the scale system is complete.

Calne labours under the disavantage of having had a manufacture, which lately has fallen into decay—a manufacture of coarse cloths and serges; so that many men have been thrown out of employ, as manufacturers, who are unused to, and nearly incapable of, the least sort of field labour. I met many of the paupers who came either for increase of pay, or for other relief. I never, even in Oxfordshire, heard demands made with more brutal insolence. "We will have our right by the scale, or Mr. Overseer shall take the consequence," was often repeated.

The assistant-overseer, and the other parish officers, allowed that *no attention whatever* was ever paid to character; but that the most notorious drunkards, swearers, and thieves, with wives and families, were all duly relieved by the arithmetic of the magistrates' scale. I asked them if they never took these men before the bench for punishment. Their answer was, that they had so often been reprimanded, and triumphed over, (to use their own expression,) that they had given it up in despair, and relieved all alike, bad and good, meritorious and profligate.

GENERAL OBSERVATIONS.

I have selected the town and parish of Calne not as a single but as a strong example of a bad system of working the poor-laws, uncounteracted, except in one instance, the improved management of the poor-house, even by common care and prudence in the parish officers. The same prevails in the adjoining parishes.

The rigid adherence to the scale, and the total disregard of character, have produced every evil of which they are capable. The overseers never appeal to the magistrates, knowing that they would be reprimanded, and the insolent pauper supported by the scale. Thus, with the appearance of no appeal to the magistrates, the magisterial interference is unbounded, complete, and, by tacit consent, always in exercise, and ever producing evils of the greatest magnitude and worst description.

The whole pauper-management is one great vice,—throughout the whole of the district which includes Calne; which must be entirely attributed to the scale system, and the making up of wages from "the book."

DUN'S TEW, OXFORDSHIRE.

The property of this parish belongs, almost entirely, to one individual, Mr. Bolton, whose attention to the concerns of the poor cannot be surpassed. He is well supported by the rector, the Rev. W. Gordon, a most intelligent, active man. From Mr. Gordon, with whom I had many conversations, I received the detailed account of his own parish, as well as much information respecting the poor-laws in Oxfordshire, as given in my report on that county. Mr. Gordon is a magistrate for Oxfordshire.

Population—450.
Number of acres in the parish, about 1716.

Of these there are about 24 acres of road and waste, very little pasture, the whole chiefly arable land.

The amount of the sum expended on the poor for one year, to Lady-day, 1832, is 682*l.* 13*s.* 6½*d.*

The system of the scale is in full operation here, as it is in all Oxfordshire, and also the roundsman practice.

Of these evils, which account for the rates being so high (6*s.* on the rack rent), Mr. Gordon is fully aware. He cannot, unsupported as he is by the other magistrates of the district, alter the system, but he does everything in his power to mitigate its evils.

His affability and good arrangements have, at least, produced an orderly and satisfied race of paupers. The cottages are by far the best I ever saw. They belong to the lord of the manor, and are let low, varying from 1*l.* 10*s.* to 2*l.* 10*s.* They have good gardens, and the farmers all let potato land to their labourers.

The wages of an able-bodied man are 9*s.* per week, 12*s.* in hay harvest, and 15*s.* in corn harvest, so that altogether his earnings alone amount to above 25*l.* per annum. The wives earn about 6*d.* a day, weeding, &c., and in hay-time 8*d.* a day and beer.

The roundsmen, who are the less able of the workmen, gain 7*s.* a week.

Boys on the round have about 3*s.* a week after 12 years old.

The number of persons receiving parish allowance, when I was in Oxfordshire, in September, 1832, was as under:—

Aged, sick, and infirm . . .	32
Children	81
Men, boys, and girls, on the round, whose wages are paid in part	27
Total relieved	140

Besides this there were entries of medical advice, rents paid, make-ups for loss time, &c., to about 30 more, making on the parish books, 170.

In the winter months of December, January, and February, I have no doubt the numbers are increased to above 230, or more than half the population of the parish.

In Dun's Tew, as in all the Oxfordshire parishes, the early marriages of mere boys is frequent, for the avowed purpose of increasing *their income* by allowance for increase of children. There is no select vestry, no assistant-overseer, no workhouse. There are 64 agricultural labourers. Mr. Gordon is fully aware of the great evils that have been produced by the scale and head-money system. He sees what it has done, what it is doing, and he foresees all these evils tenfold multiplied, in ten years, if the system is allowed to continue. He assures me, and I was assured of it at every bench in Oxfordshire, that the magistrates of that county are also so fully aware of this, that they are ready to concur in, and to support, any measure proposed by Government for arresting the increasing curse.   .

GENERAL OBSERVATIONS.

I have only one observation to make on Dun's Tew, which is the remarkably good effects which may be produced on a bad system by the constant care of an intelligent clergyman, who devotes himself to the temporal as well as spiritual wants of his parishioners. If I have arrived at one opinion more decided than any other on the poor, it is, that the loss of such a clergyman is not to be made up to a parish by any means whatever. The poor live a life of expedients,—to use their own phrase, " they live from hand to mouth." They are like children, they want constant help and advice. The greatest blessing to them is a clergyman, constantly living with them, who is not only their teacher in religion, but their friend and guide in their worldly affairs.

REMARKS.

I have thus selected, according to the wishes of Lord Melbourne, six places, from amongst those which fell under my observation, in the district entrusted to me; and I have so selected them as to illustrate the points enumerated in his Lordship's letter to the Central Board of.Poor-Law Commissioners. I have selected

CRANBOURNE, DORSET,

As an instance of a large and populous parish, which, after suffering for many years, by constant magisterial interference, has, by a complete change of system, risen to comfort and content, and in which the most satisfactory improvement in morals, appearance, and character of the poor, has succeeded to depression and degradation.

HASILBURY BRYAN, DORSET,

As an instance of what may be effected, even under a bad system, and magisterial interference, by an active and intelligent minister, who, perhaps, has few equals in his correct and extensive knowledge of everything connected with the operation of the poor-laws.

MORE CRICHEL, DORSET,

As an instance of a small parish, as well managed with regard to its poor concerns as the poor-laws will allow, and where magisterial interference is unknown.

POOLE, DORSET,

As an instance of a large, trading, populous, borough town, where perfect confidence being placed by the magistrates in the decisions of the vestry, and in the management of the assistant-guardian of the poor, no interference takes place, and where all that relates to the government of the poor seems to me to be of unrivalled excellence.

CALNE, WILTSHIRE,

As an instance of every unmitigated evil that can arise from a most corrupt and vicious working of the poor-laws.

DUN'S TEW, OXFORDSHIRE,

As an instance of the evils of a most vicious system mitigated, and rendered, at least, harmless, by the care of an active and intelligent minister.

In the whole district that fell under my care, I do not hesitate to pronounce a decided opinion, that the poor of boroughs, where little or no magisterial interference takes place, are superior in moral character and appearance to the majority of country parishes. I have instanced Poole, I could support it by the cases of Bridport, Devizes, and Marlborough.

D. O. P. Okeden,
Assistant-Commissioner.

Dec. 27, 1832.

My Lords and Gentlemen,

In compliance with your requisition, I submit to you the results of my inquiries in the city of Oxford.

I have the honour to be,
My Lords and Gentlemen,
Your obedient Servant,
H. Bishop.

CITY OF OXFORD.

The population of the eleven united parishes, according to the Parliamentary Returns of 1831, amounts to 16,425.

Annual value of real property, according to the Property Tax Returns of 1815, £37,853.

The city of Oxford and its suburbs comprise 14 parishes. By a private act, 11 Geo. III. c. xiv., 1771, eleven of these parishes are incorporated, and possess a workhouse. The parishes which are not united are three in number—St. John's, a very small parish, lying in the very heart of the city (population, 122) St. Giles's, and St. Clement's.

Here, then, lie close at hand some materials for estimating the advantages or disadvantages of uniting several parishes under one administration. But it ought to be remarked that the mere amount of rate, whether estimated per head or by its per centage, will furnish but a deceitful test. St. John's is so small a parish, has so few paupers, even in proportion to its size, and from its situation is so incapable of greatly extending its population, that it may fairly be put aside. St. Giles' and St. Clement's are very considerable parishes, and are so situated as to contain much more than their due proportion of paupers, while a smaller amount of rateable property is contained within their limits. St. Thomas' doubtless contains a very large pauper population, but it possesses likewise some of the most valuable property in the whole city of Oxford, as well as a large tract of highly-rented land.

The local act for the city of Oxford is very long, and generally admitted to have many faults, and probably this is the case really in more instances, than those usually insisted on. Under this, act, thirty-four guardians are annually elected, and the office *may* be compulsory: those who have served it may be compelled to serve again, after an interval of five years. A guardian frequently is re-elected; but all go out of office in July. This appears to be one of the blunders of the act, for every year there is too large a proportion of the guardians seceding from office; and even the substitution of one who has previously served the office in the place of the retiring guardian, does not remedy the evil of so large a number coming into the new board, and the result actually is, a great degree of unsteadiness in the management of the house and of the poor generally. The paupers themselves are aware of the effect of this change of administration, and consequently July is the period of the year when the greatest number of improper applications and fraudulent attempts are made on the board. This I learnt from one who had served the office of governor and guardian together for more than three years, with great zeal and equal advantage to the public.

Overseers of the poor are appointed for each parish, but the whole of their duty consists in collecting the rate which they have been enjoined to make by the precept of the guardians. The guardians perform those duties which are ordinarily discharged by the overseer. To them all applications for relief ought in the first instance to be addressed, unless made to the governor, or at once to the court, which assembles every Thursday in the afternoon or evening.

The overseers when they have collected a rate pay it into the hands of the treasurers, and the governor has the power of drawing upon them without check. This absence of all control over the governor has already, in one instance, produced its fruits. A very few years ago, the governor absconded with many hundred pounds of the public money, and has never been heard of since.

One great cause of the Oxford Act working so badly arises from the low qualification for the office of guardian; in many instances very improper persons are elected, and though, in themselves, they may be respectable and intelligent men, and fit to conduct the business of a *single* parish, yet they are quite unequal to discharge the duties which they are forced, perhaps, to take on themselves.

There appears to exist a great deal of *jobbing* in the conduct of the house.

The average number of persons in the workhouse is 234, the greatest number 258 ; yet for these large numbers no contract is entered into, and the reason assigned for not doing so, is that articles so supplied are commonly inferior to the samples. The real reason was, however, contained in a supplementary cause, *viz.* that it was right that the trade of the house should be distributed.

In the relief of paupers great partiality appears to exist. Any person who can make interest, or who is connected with a member of the court of guardians (and this last is a circumstance of no uncommon occurrence), obtains a very different measure of attention and assistance from one not so situated.

The absence of all responsibility, of all inspection, and the non-

I

publication of the names of paupers, gives great facilities to the indulgence of these inclinations; and, without doubt, many are permitted to enjoy regular pensions, who would be ashamed of receiving parish aid, if it were publicly declared that they were on the list of paupers. Many persons also receive it, of whose circumstances such evidence could be tendered as would render it impossible to continue them on the list.

These abuses were heavily complained of by some, who, from having held seats in the court, had opportunities of seeing and knowing the secret springs which influenced the members; many also admitted the justice of the charge, and not one denied it.

Another evil of the Oxford Act is the size of the court. Thirty-four is too large a number to be invested with executive power. The number of those who actually meet varies so much as to give the character of a new assembly almost to each meeting; and, consequently, even during the year, the body is deprived of all steadiness of conduct.

In every respect, and in every department, the system works ill. Impositions by claimants are very frequent; and nine-tenths of the paupers are reduced to, and kept in that state, by their own vices or improvidence.

The remarks hitherto made apply to the workhouse, and yet much remains to be said on that head. In the city of Oxford, the house of industry of the united parishes, as it is most improperly called, is that to which all arrangements for the management of the poor are made subservient.

But in this house of industry there are no means of employment for the paupers. There once was some weaving, but this has been abandoned for some years. The Commissioners for Lighting, Cleansing, and Paving, have made a contract with the guardians of the house for cleansing the streets. This finds occasional employment for a few old men. They also contract for digging and breaking stones to repair " the mile-ways," as they are called. And this is the whole of what is done by those in the house, beyond the little which is required for the immediate service of the establishment.

A few out-paupers are also employed (chiefly young men and boys) in breaking stones at so much per load.

The following anecdote will show the state of subordination of the paupers :—

It was judged proper to employ the inmates of the house in *wheeling* the dirt of the streets out of the city in barrows, instead of carting it away. The men resisted this arrangement, and instead of carrying the contents of their barrows to the appointed spot, they one and all emptied them in the centre of the town, where the four main roads meet and cross, at Carfax. The mayor and one of the city magistrates, intimidated by this act of insubordination, sent for the governor, and entreated him to give up the plan: fortunately, he possessed greater firmness, and refused to give way, and he succeeded in reducing the paupers to order; his year, however, expired, and the plan, I believe, was abandoned by his successor.

Great improvement in the internal management of the house seems to have taken place under the present master, who appears to have done all in his power, but he is sadly hampered by the interference of one or two meddling and mischievous guardians.

The house is clean, and as regular in its arrangements as its defective construction allows. There is, however, a lamentable want of means of classification, even the sexes cannot be kept separate. The house stands in the middle of a garden, or piece of ground between three and four acres in extent: this lies in one allotment, without the slightest internal fence or division, and surrounded by a high wall. Visitors are admitted by a porter living in a small lodge at the gate. The house opens into this piece of ground; consequently all, men, women, and children, may meet in this space, even after dark. It is hardly necessary to add, that there is, to speak in the most cautious terms, strong suspicion that the bastardy list has been swelled even within the walls.

The diet-table of the house has been constructed on too liberal a scale; the inhabitants of the workhouse are better fed than they could expect to be at their own homes.

The house is not an object of terror, but rather of desire, to the young and able-bodied pauper. There is no seclusion or confinement. Permission, it is true, must be asked to leave the walls, but it is never refused, and the pauper, when once out, need not return till bed-time.

There is, in fact, no government in the house. One guardian frequently undoes what another has done. There is, at the present moment, a guardian, who, probably from a morbid craving for popularity, goes about to the gangs of men that are occasionally set to work (for the house has 16 acres of pasture land to keep cows and horses on, in addition to the garden ground) and will order the men to go to the house and get bread and cheese and beer, in addition to their pay. This took place lately, in the case of eight men engaged in cleaning a ditch, and so far were they from deserving encouragement, that the whole eight did not do the work of two men.

It may be added to these observations, on the authority of a competent judge, well and practically acquainted with the Oxford workhouse, and several of the London ones, that had the houses in town been so managed, and the poor kept as they are in Oxford, their numbers would have doubled.   In London, so far from allowing the sexes to mix, it is common to separate man and wife. At the date of this report (August 17, 1832) there were in the house 247 inmates, one-sixth of whom, at least, were able-bodied men, and women with illegitimate children, and all the labour from the garden, scavenger's work, stone-breaking for the mileways, &c., would perhaps occupy 15 men—the guardians had, on Saturday last, (this is dated August 17,) to set 53 to work.

This time last year, the weekly pay for work was 6*l.*, now it is 22*l.*   The amount of out-door relief by the present board, which commenced July 12, has varied from 90*l.* to 120*l.*

No accounts deserving that name are kept; there is one ledger, in which appears the entries for labour, house, and out-door work.

A difficulty is found in getting out the females from the house; respectable people are unwilling to receive them into their families as servants.   Necessaries are never given to bad characters, but they, like others, are relieved in money; the alleged object, therefore, of guarding their families from want is defeated, and so much more money is put in their hands to waste in intemperance and profligacy.

Nearly 130 illegitimate children are paid for by the house; the bastardy debt due to the united parishes, is now 1054*l.*, which the late governor as well as the master of the house concurred in representing to me would be dearly purchased at 100*l.*

The following are some few of the applications which the writer of this report witnessed on a Thursday night.

One woman, receiving 6*s.* per week, asked for 2*s.* more, because she had to support two boys, her sons, of the respective ages of 16 and 17.   This application was made when harvest-work was at its height.

Another person, who deals in cottons, tapes, &c., and travels the country, came to ask for (rather to demand) her annual clothing.

A third, an habitual drunkard, ruined by the facility of obtaining parish aid, and who but for that might have done well, but now allows his wife and family to continue in a state little above starving, came to ask for work, and obtained 7*s, without work.*

A fourth, receiving 12*s.* per week, obtained 2*s.* this night : he wishes to have " a fixed income " (his own words), that he may know what he has to depend on.

A woman in the house stepped forward, and complained that she had been obliged to *go* without *tea* and *sugar,* in order to have her shoes repaired, and wished for money to pay the shoe-mender.

Many other cases might be enumerated, but sufficient perhaps have been stated to show the nature of the applications, and the description of applicants; and there cannot be a doubt that *every* case which came before the Court of Guardians this night (which with the other applications occupied considerably more than two hours) not only might, but ought to have been dismissed at once, without further consideration.

By a balance-sheet, from July 11, 1831, to July 9, 1832, it appears that the total expenditure on account of the poor of the united parishes of the city of Oxford, exceeds 10,000*l.* It has increased with fearful rapidity, and is still increasing. It is impossible to say where it will stop, unless some fundamental change takes place in the management of the poor.

ST. GILES'S, OXFORD.

POPULATION 2000; acres 800; equal portions of pasture and arable.

There is no select vestry in the parish, the name creates a prejudice against it, which cannot be overcome.

This parish is divided into two districts, one within, one without the jurisdiction of the city of Oxford. This division of jurisdiction has been the cause of considerable difficulty and dispute, as to the mode in which rates should be levied and enforced.

There is a poor-house situated in the county part of the parish; but this house, though newly built, at some considerable expense, is merely a pauper barrack. There is no master or mistress now, and the occupants are congregated together as in a collection of cottages. It is, as might be expected, a very grievous nuisance to the neighbourhood: women of the town with their bullies have been residing there, and robberies have been effected by its inmates. It is at the present time in rather better order. Still, however, as a place of regulation or discipline, it is worse than useless. The parish, however, contrives to extract this good from it. If there is a pauper likely to be troublesome, and to summon the overseer before a magistrate, the parish authorities remove him to this house if possible, and, by so doing, bring him under the authority of the county magistrates, who are much more pains-taking in their inquiries than some, at least, of the city magistrates.

The petty sessions of the county magistrates possess likewise this advantage over the city court, that the overseer has greater personal security and freedom from insult in the former than in the latter. The city magistrates themselves are perhaps civil, but lukewarm and indifferent to the overseers, and the precincts of the court are beset by a number of blackguards, who assail the overseers with scoffs and jeers and insults, sometimes almost with personal violence. This the overseers have to encounter in their official character,—as *such* they are marked out for insult,—and this conduct seems to meet with no check or animadversion even from the magistrates.

The following case deserves to be fully detailed.

The pauper in question, by trade a leather-dresser, has, for some years past, preferred parish and casual relief to the honest gains of his employment. The overseer stated eighteen years as the period of his present mode of life. The pauper seems to think it is not quite so long; he talks of thirteen : however, he does not violently impeach the overseer's statement, which may therefore be assumed to be tolerably correct.

He belongs to an incorporated or combined trade ; the directors of this combination issue tickets to the members. These tickets are renewed from time to time. The holder of one goes about from place to place, but must not take the same road more than once in six months. With these intervals he is again and again assisted, and, as in the present case, for a very long space of time together.

This ticket is available in every part of the United Kingdom where a club or lodge of the trade is established. The individual in question might have had work at 1*l.* per week, but he refused to take it, or indeed 30*s.* per week ; nothing under 2*l.* will satisfy him, and when pressed for reasons to account for his refusing such offers —when asked whether it would not be better to get 1*l.* per week than to trust to casual sources of support, he replied, that he should not like to be " turned black," (quere—returned black ?) which would be the case if he worked under price.

Thus then, as far as an individual instance will avail, and it seems to be a fair sample of the general system, we see the effects of parish aid upon the combinations for raising and keeping up wages, whose ramifications extend over the whole of these kingdoms. This man gets a ticket; he is, by his own admission, a most worthless fellow, to use his own mild and gentle language, he has been " a very *foolish* man, his fault has been drinking." Though at times of his life, and that too for long periods, he has been earning from 2*l.* to 3*l.* per week, he has neglected to make the slightest provision for his future necessities; his health has been greatly impaired by his vicious habits; his character, probably his value as a workman, has been lowered by his own deliberate acts, yet he is not to take employment but at the highest wages; and in order to support him in this unreasonable demand, he gets a ticket from the trade, for which he pays 1*s.* 6*d.* per month, constantly: this furnishes him with his own support as a vagabond; for when he is at home his relief from the trade ceases, and the intervals of travelling are filled up by parish aid: his wife and family, let it be observed, are constantly on the parish, for *he* only travels his rounds. No source of support is objected to by his fellows, nothing incapacitates him from receiving the benefit of his ticket, but honest industry in his own trade: let it be known that he has once been guilty of this— of making the best terms he could—of agreeing for what his services are worth, and supporting himself and his family honestly and in comfort—and he is struck off the list, and denied all future benefit from this fund; the payments to which are in a manner compulsory, and raised from all in the trade. It is probable that this fund, if honestly, and fairly, and properly expended, might nearly destroy all necessity for the members of this trade having recourse to parish aid: so far, however, from the funds being applied to such honourable and beneficial purposes, they are made to contribute to the support of combinations. Even the magistracy of the country becomes subservient to the objects of these combinations, for this pauper is under the patronage of a city magistrate, whose name is known, and can be disclosed, with evidence of his conduct; who brow-beats and insults any overseer that refuses to comply with these demands. In reliance on this protection, the man's wife lately told the overseer that she had once made one, who filled his office, " tremble before his betters, and would do so with him."

This man's history is not yet concluded; and the sequel is important, as it exemplifies the inveterate habits of pauperism, and the skill and perseverance with which they are followed up by those who have once been introduced to them.

This same individual has a child ill, which had been sent into the infirmary of the city and county; of course, during the time the child is in the house, he is off the father's hands, and the parish refused to make any allowance to the parents towards his support: this man went to the infirmary, and removed the child, in order to enable him to claim his allowance from the overseer for this week. The pauper himself complains of illness, but will neither accept the advice of the infirmary as an out-patient, nor of the parish medical man, but has gone, or is going, the round of the medical men of the city, begging from any of them a certificate of his inability to work.

A pleasure fair was held, according to custom, a week or two before the present time, in this parish. The pauper in question was seen drinking and idling during the fair. He was warned that he would be refused relief, on the ground of his having wasted both his money in drinking, and his time. " I don't care," was his reckless reply; " I won't work during holiday-time." He had his method of compelling parochial assistance. On the following Thursday, he went to the infirmary, and begged a blister, which he was wearing when the writer of this report saw him, and then presented himself for relief. A complaint had been made against him, and with very great difficulty the city magistrate was induced to record him as a vagabond; still, notwithstanding, the man obtained on this occasion 3*s.*

It is hardly necessary to add, after this long history, that here character is not at all attended to, when relief is to be given, nor under the interference of the magistrates is the vestry allowed to regard it. The individual above spoken of says the magistrates " would not hurt him." There is, in fact, no instance of any of these idle, insolent paupers having been punished for the last twelve years.

It appears, on investigation, that, in seven cases out of ten, the paupers are idle or drunken, abusive or thieving. " I don't care for your work, I can get as much from the parish," is their constant language.

In the list prepared for payment this week, containing 50 separate cases, one is ill, two are idiots; of the rest not one does any work, and it is useless to divide the cases into casual or permanent, for the casual, when once on the list, always continue there.

An instance of the improvidence of relief appeared in the case of a boy, deaf and dumb certainly, but the son of a tradesman, a butcher, perfectly able to support his child, who, nevertheless, is kept by the parish.

Another person receives 2*s.* a week for *getting work.* This is during the harvest.

An inhabitant of this parish, once an overseer, applied on behalf of a woman, who, he alleged, was ill, but begged that it might not be known that she had parish aid; it would so distress her, not to receive it, but to have it *known* that she received it. Her dress gave no evidence of her want of such assistance; it was much above the rank of those who might be expected to look for parish help, of many, indeed, who have to contribute to her assistance. On her it was proposed to settle 4*s.* or 5*s.* per week.

A widow, who has some friends among the efficient parties at the vestry, receives 1*s.* 6*d.* a week, though she is in possession of a very considerable sum of money at the saving bank.

A boy has 4*s.* a week, because he has so bad a character that few or none will employ him. The parish let him out at 2*s.* per week, when they can get anything for him to do, and pay 2*s.* more for him.

A woman says she was not bred up to work, and won't work; she does not even choose to knit, and during the last month she received 6*s.*, 4*s.*, 4*s.*, and 3*s.* in the four weeks, week by week.

These various persons are supported in their applications by the city magistrates; and the parish authorities and vestry, knowing how useless it is to look to them for countenance, prefer paying these people their annuities to contesting them and failing *.

A considerable quantity of casual relief takes place in clothing. Shoes are made by parishioners, who charge 14*s.* a pair, for articles which would be sold to private individuals for 12*s.*

No balance sheet is published, neither are the paupers' names printed. No visitation of them at their houses takes place. They have been all ordered to attend a vestry for examination, and the absentees were struck off, but were, however, restored to the pay-list the next week.

There is no parish work of any kind. The paupers, at one time, were set to stone-breaking; but it was found that they destroyed their tools, and that their earnings were insufficient to pay for the repairs.

The assistant-overseer is generally a decayed tradesman, with a salary of 50*l.* per annum. He was to have lived in the poor-house, and taken the superintendence of the paupers; but the present one, finding the place, or the inhabitants, disagreeable, left the house and came to Oxford, and no notice has been taken.

The annual amount of money actually expended on the poor is 1317*l.*

The overseer comes into office every year, and this is a great evil, as the new officer is always assailed with a number of false complaints.

The present overseer appears to be a most intelligent and respectable man, anxious to put everything on its proper footing, and capable of improving the parish very materially, if he was not fettered by opposition and the badness of the magistracy, as well as by the faults of the existing law, or practice, which has grown into something resembling law.

The rates are fast increasing in amount, while the difficulty of collecting them is growing in an equal ratio. About ten rates in the year used to be sufficient, now one is required every three weeks.

* These various cases can be identified by the names of the parties, if necessary, and many others of a like kind might be multiplied; these are only given as samples of what actually takes place in this parish.

The fees of the magistrates' clerk, already too high, are rising rapidly. The examination of a pauper, and order of removal, used to be 7s. 6d., or 8s. 6d., now, however, it is 13s. 6d.

The charge for the overseer's warrant of appointment is doubled, but no resistance, or even remonstrance, is hazarded, as it is necessary to stand well with the court; and any one resisting would run the risk of incurring their displeasure, at least their suspicion.

The following instance of the justice with which fees are exacted is worth observation:—A man was convicted of assaulting an overseer most violently; his punishment was three weeks' imprisonment, and to find security for his good behaviour for twelve months, and the parish had to pay the fees for his giving the security.

St. Giles's has the character of being a " good parish:" landlords, therefore, can let their houses at a very high rent. The speculation of building houses, and those of the most wretched description, is encouraged; very few rates are collected from them, and thus it happens that acres of land, which used to bear their share of rate, now, in their more valuable state, and increased rent, contribute nothing, though they greatly augment the parish burthens.

There are at the present time eleven bastards on the weekly list—the parish receives for two only.

It is well known, that for from 3l. to 4l., and a treat, many men consent to be sworn to as the fathers of illegitimate children, knowing that the parish cannot enforce payment against them; and that, generally speaking, it will not be attempted. The mother is, of course, a party to this arrangement, and has her advantage, either promised only, or actually performed; at least she is not worse off, for the parish pays for the putative father, whether it recovers the money or not, and the mother has her share of the price of her perjury from the real father.

One girl, for whose child the parish receives the money, swore her infant to a boy aged only fifteen, a servant in a gentleman's family: the poor lad remarked, " This was very hard, this was too bad; the child ought to have been sworn to my young master;" and there was little reason for suspecting his veracity.

Another woman has brought three illegitimate children on the parish, and, for her last, she was committed to prison for three weeks. She told the vestry that she would, if put to gaol again, swear the child to the overseer; she is now pregnant a fourth time. This same individual says openly to the vestry, " If you don't give me some relief (enough, in fact, to support her in idleness), I will bring you some more bastards to keep,"

The difficulties under which this parish is labouring seem to be caused by the combined badness of the law and of the administrators of it, that is, the magistrates in great measure; for there is no superfluous labour, provided the labourers would only conduct themselves in such a manner as to make them worth employing. But those who want labour done, prefer employing out-parish men, or will rather leave undone that which, if well and sufficiently done, would yield them a profit, or be, at least, a source of pleasure and satisfaction. Those labourers who have families say, we can get 10s. or 12s. per week from the parish, why should "we slave ourselves for this sum?"

ST. CLEMENT'S, OXFORD,

Population 1886. Value, (1815,) 1352*l*.

AFTER the detailed report of St. Giles's, it is hardly necessary to say much of this parish, which presents the same features of mismanagement. Increase in the amount of rates,* decrease of the means of paying them, destruction to the industry and character of the labourers, and the steady growth of every species of vice and profligacy, while the interference of the magistrates, though not, in this parish, carried to such an extent as in some others, and by some benches, yet still exists to a very mischievous extent, and in a very bad manner,—by recommendations chiefly; these are enough to promote the spirit of discontent in the paupers, to discountenance the overseer, and to screen the magistrate, even from the trifling responsibility which attaches to the making of an order, the check which the law imposes, by requiring that every order shall be signed by two magistrates, and, of consequence, that every case requiring an order shall be heard by two magistrates being removed.

The only peculiarity is to be found in the extent of the speculation for building small tenements, and in some of the local circumstances which have attended that speculation.

St. Clement's, like the rest of Oxford, was originally situated on a thick bed of gravel resting on clay. As long as the buildings were confined to the gravel, the inhabitants enjoyed a healthy soil and means of good drainage; as soon, however, as they were pushed off on the clay, a very considerable change took place both in the houses, the inhabitants and their health. Nearly half

---

* There has been an assistant overseer; but he is on the point of retiring, being unable to raise the rates. His nominal salary, 20*l*. per annum, has remained unpaid, from the poverty of the parish; and from the like cause, the poor last week (Aug. 20, 1832) were not paid at all.

the deaths of Oxford, from cholera, took place in St. Clement's; on inquiry, it appeared that the majority of those cases were in the newest houses, near the river, upon the clay banks.   It is impossible to estimate, with any thing like accuracy, the number of new houses, but there are whole streets and rows built in the cheapest manner.   There may be exceptions to this statement, but, in general, the speculation has paid so well, that the cupidity of those who have more money than conscience has been strongly stimulated.   Cottages, costing on an average from 100*l.* to 120*l.* let for 9*l.* per annum, some, which have been built for 140*l.*, have let for 10*l.* per annum, and upwards.   These cottages have yards, perhaps, but the bit of ground attached to them is too small to merit the name of a garden.

These exorbitant rents are, in fact, levied to a considerable degree upon those who pay rates.   For, in the first place, by the abstraction of so much property from rateable wealth, the remainder has to bear a heavier burden; and, secondly, the rents are carried to as great a height as possible, upon the supposition that tenements so circumstanced will not be rated; the owner, therefore, is pocketing both rate and rent.   Thirdly, the value of his property is increased precisely in the proportion that his neighbour's is deteriorated, by the weight of rates from which his own is discharged; neither is this all—as it is always regarded by the tenant as a desirable thing to escape the payment of rates, the field for competition is narrowed, and a very inferior description of house is built for the poor man.   In order to make out a case for the non-payment of rates, it is sometimes necessary, perhaps, to have inconveniences and defects—and thus it happens, that a building speculation depending on freedom from rates for its recommendation, always produces a description of houses of the worst and most unhealthy kind.   Those who would build for the poor with more liberal views and greater attention to their health and their comfort are discouraged, and a monopoly is given those whose sole end is gain, by whatever means it may be compassed.

August 20, 1832.

My Lords and Gentlemen,

In compliance with Lord Melbourne's wishes, I submit the following extracts from the results of my inquiries in the county Cambridge. The following are a part of my observations on the subject of

THE MAGISTERIAL CONTROL.

When pressed on the subject of their management, overseers invariably excuse themselves by alleging the want of co-operation and protection from the magistracy in their endeavours to check the demand on the parish funds. Even the paid officers, both in town and country, justify themselves on these grounds for sparing the time, trouble, and expense of contesting with the pauper the question of relief before the individual magistrates, or the bench in petty sessions. Of the many whom I have seen, one and all are in this story. But the Commissioners will probably consider that I have found a higher and a better authority on this subject in Dr. Webb, master of Clare Hall, the present vice-chancellor of the University. He has acted as county magistrate for more than sixteen years; and being resident a great part of the year at his vicarage in Littlington, he has personally superintended the relief of the poor in that parish, as well as in Great Gransden, in Huntingdonshire, where the college have been obliged to occupy a farm of 700 acres, in consequence of their not being able to obtain a tenant for the same at any price. He is strongly of opinion that a great part of the burthen of actual relief to the poor arises from the injudicious interference of magistrates, and the readiness with which they overrule the discretion of the overseer. He has attempted in both the parishes above-mentioned to introduce a more strict and circumspect system of relief —with great success in Littlington, as appears by the descending scale of poor-rates in that parish since 1816; the population at the same time having nearly doubled itself since 1801*. In Gransden, he had found less success, being seldom personally present there, and acting principally through his bailiff. Also he had had less time by some years for effecting any steady improvement in that parish. He showed me, however, by a reference to the books, that he had made the practice of allowing relief to married men, when employed by individuals, in respect of their families, entirely disappear from

* In 1816 the rates of this parish were 242*l.*
    1828 they were   .   . 116*l.*
Since 1801 the population has increased from 350 to 622.

the late accounts. The principal impediment to the introduction of a better system, he found in the power of the pauper, when refused relief by the overseer, to apply to the bench in petty sessions ; which nothing but the advantage of an intimate knowledge of his own parishioners, and of uniting in himself the functions, not the office, of overseer and magistrate, enabled him, by perseverance, to overcome. The following case is a sample of their unwillingness to take the circumstances or character of the applicant into due consideration. He refused relief (Nov. 27th, 1829) to Samuel Spencer, knowing him to have received a legacy of 400l. within two or three years before the application. The man applied to the bench in petty sessions, where Dr. Webb produced to them an extract from the will (proved 1826), and the assurance of the executor that he had paid the pauper money since proving the will, to the amount above-mentioned. Notwithstanding this, they made an order of relief; and the man (able-bodied) has been from time to time on the rates ever since.

I have conversed with several magistrates on the subject of the magisterial control; and some I have found disposed to take the same view of it as Dr. Webb; though certainly none so confidently and unequivocally. Amongst these I should mention Mr. Metcalfe of Foulmire, a most active and intelligent magistrate, to whom this county is indebted for the introduction of the improved system of parish account keeping, given in the Appendix to Mr. Pym's Evidence before the House of Lords, in 1831 *. The greater part, however, are rather disposed to recriminate and cast upon the parish officers the charge of an insufficient and inattentive discharge of their duties. They complain that whereas the magistrates feel every disposition to inquire into the circumstances of every application for relief, it is quite impossible to get overseers to attend the bench, and follow up their own refusals for relief with the proper zeal and regard for their parishes; that very often surliness of behaviour, and even cruelty towards the poor, is combined with great extravagance and recklessness in their expenditure.

There is probably a great deal of truth in these statements on both sides of the question : certainly, between the two, affairs go on very ill in this county; but whatever portion of the blame of mismanagement attaches to either, is probably due rather to the nature of the respective functions, than to the personal misconduct of those who discharge them. Under the continually increasing pressure of the rates, the viciousness of the system

---

* Observe the divisions of items in page 137 of this Report.

is making itself daily more felt and acknowledged in all quarters; and although every one has his favourite schemes of partial im provement, these are announced rather with expressions of despe. than hope, as regards any material and permanent success; *rns so far as my inquiries have at present extended, I have rewery to think that opinion points rather to total change of system than to partial and palliative amendments.

That a sense of the necessity of some vital change in the ad- ministration of the poor-laws is becoming universal among the magistrates themselves, there cannot be a stronger demonstration than the following fact. At the time of the disturbances two years since, a general meeting of the bench of the whole county was convened at Cambridge for the purpose of deliberating on gene- ral measures. The meeting was very numerous, consisting, as my informant believes, of 28 gentlemen. A part of the business transacted was the passing of a vote or resolution to this effect, " that the poor-laws are badly administered in this county." The vote passed with only one dissentient voice.

The following is a copy of a printed scale of relief issued by the town magistrates of Cambridge. It exceeds the scale used in the rural parishes by half the quartern loaf (value $4\frac{1}{4}d$. at this time) in each of the allowances. The country scales are also printed; and, with the exception above-mentioned, the terms used in those I have seen, are precisely identical with the following:—

Copy of a printed Scale of Relief.—Town of Cambridge.

The churchwardens and overseers of the poor are requested to regu. late the incomes of such persons as may apply to them for relief or em- ployment, according to the price of fine bread ; namely—

A single woman . . . . the price of $3\frac{1}{2}$ quartern loaves per week.
A single man. . . . . ditto. . $4\frac{1}{2}$ ditto.
A man and his wife . . . . ditto.. 8   ditto.
Ditto ditto and 1 child. . . . . . ditto. . $9\frac{1}{2}$ ditto.
Ditto ditto and 2 children. . . . ditto . . 11   ditto.
Ditto ditto and 3 children. . . . ditto. . 13   ditto.

Man, wife, 4 children and upwards at the price of $2\frac{1}{2}$ quartern loaves per head per week.

It will be necessary to add to the above income, in all cases of sick- ness or other kind of distress, and particularly of such persons or fami- lies who deserve encouragement by their good behaviour, whom parish officers should mark both by commendation and reward.

By order of the Magistrates assembled at the Town-hall, Cam- bridge, Nov. 27th, 1829.

A. Chevell,
Clerk to the Magistrates.

The intrinsic mischief of such an invention is much aggravated
' the bad effect which its publication and the nature of the ex-
ns used, must produce on the minds of the paupers, to
' it is exhibited on every occasion of dispute between them
ie overseer.   It certainly does seem to me calculated to
 ͠   the notion of an absolute right to relief, independent of
any circumstances beyond the mere application for it ; and to
judge from the demeanour I have witnessed in petty sessions,
that suggestion does not appear lost upon the pauper.   The eyes
of the county magistrates have been for some time open to the
impolicy of this proceeding; and I have not seen any scale of
theirs dated later than 1821.   The present town scale, it is seen,
bears date 1829.   Which of the two set the example I do not
know, but the gentlemen of the county seem to have repented
first.

MODES OF RELIEF.

With regard to the modes of relief used in this county, I have
found very little variation to prevail in the different parishes
which have been the objects of my investigation ; none certainly
which present any important feature for remark.   The practice
of payments out of the poor-rates, in direct aid of the wages of
men employed by individuals, I have not met at all at present.
That, however, of making allowance for the families of persons in
full employ, is by no means uncommon : that of roundsmen, I
believe, exists nowhere at all within the county.   It was once
very general in that part of the county which adjoins Bedfordshire; but the only instance, I believe, now remaining in that
neighbourhood is Tadlow, a small parish, little burthened with
rates; but here the roundsman is paid full wages by the individual who employs him.   The conflicting interests and jealousies
of the different classes of rate-payers, rather than a sense of its
illegality, have caused the disappearance of this objectionable
practice.
    The grand items of disbursement in the heavily burthened pa-
rishes are found to be these :—
    1. The permanent weekly pay, as it is called, to the aged, the
impotent, and widows.   I have found that widows universally, in
town and country, get their three shillings a week without reference
to the amount of their earnings.   The admission of this as an
unquestioned title to relief is one of many premiums on marriage.
    2. *Paupers working for parish.*—There is often difficulty in
getting at the true amount of this, from the surveyor's rate either
merging in that of the overseer's, on being applied to the employ-

ment of paupers at parish wages, and consequently no work done; a clear perversion of this fund, out of which fair wages ought to be paid for real work done, under strict superintendence. For this reason there is no dependence on any of the rate-returns made yearly to Government; this kind of relief being often very considerable in its amount, and usually omitted in the returns. This item is almost always clear loss, except so far as some improvement of the roads is effected *.

3. *Occasional and casual poor.*—The amount of this item is always very great in proportion to the rest, but it has little to do with the casual poor in the legal sense of that term. It is principally applicable to cases of temporary infirmity, real or pretended sickness in parishioners, and to the maintenance of the families of men in individual employ, and full pay;—" making up the incomes" is the expression used in the scale.

There is no species of relief, however, recommended by the circumstances to which Item 1 is applicable, which does not become, when systematically administered, highly objectionable in a moral point of view; as removing every active motive for economy and good habits, and greatly enhancing the ordinary temptations to vice which attend a time of prosperity. But the operation of Items 2 and 3, combined with the working of the magistrates' scale, seems fraught with transcendant mischief, whether morally or politically considered. One very pernicious effect is that arising from the interested preference shown by the employer to men with families, whereby the young men are thrown upon parish work—so ruinous to all habits of industry; and every motive suggested for an early and improvident marriage. When the farmer employs the young single man, it is seldom or never by the great, as it is termed, but at daily wages, little above those of parish employment, which as easier work, and often no work at all, he prefers. A still worse preference, though equally natural, is that which distinguishes between the destitute person, and the person possessed of the present means of support, postponing, of course, the claims of the latter; whereby the disposition to save earnings is not only discouraged but actively thwarted, and the gifts of fortune become a sure inducement to idleness and ruin. More than one case was mentioned to me of persons who, having been detected in the possession of property, the result of former economy, were refused, not relief, but even employment, until they had rendered themselves worthy of their hire, by wasting in idleness their previous accumulations.

* On this point see the following case of Gamlingay.

K

LITTLINGTON PARISH.   TITHES.

the parish of Littlington I found, by examination of
oks of the later years, that the advantages of a strict
ion had not been able to check a rapid increase of the
: population, it should be observed, had increased, by
cess alone, from 505 in the year 1821, to 622 in

for the three years preceding 1830 stand thus:—

POOR-RATE.

1827	.	£138
1828		116
1829	. ,	124

the expenditure rose to 213*l.* deducting the county
331, it was 227*l.* During several years preceding 1830
id little or no surplus labour; at the present time they
ile-bodied men doing parish work. My informant, Mr.
the overseer, a considerable occupier, told me that
i mode of management was, no doubt, very beneficial
h, but that they had every prospect of the rates con-
:reasing. That the land within the parish was amply
i employ all the labour, if fairly cultivated; but that
rious causes, much of the land was in a very low state,
s were yearly becoming worse. Amongst those causes
irized the low state of profits, the consequent decrease
and spirit, and the particularly hard pressure of the
 this parish. It is a light chalky soil, naturally poor,
: of a very high degree of cultivation by the aid of arti-
ire. That the taking of tithes in kind was a great
id impediment to the cultivation of land of this charac-
)oke from the effects produced by it on his own prac-
hat of his neighbours. Some time before the inclo-
/ebb let the tithe to Mr. Dickerson, an occupier within
and bound him by an agreement to allow every occu-
ve his own tithes at a fair valuation, if he wished it.
s after, on a disagreement between Dickerson and the
s, Dr. Webb insisted on the fulfilment of this contract;
'atford, an eminent surveyor at Cambridge, was em-
make a valuation. The difference of Mr. Watford's
on different small occupations of land, lying inter-
gether in an uninclosed state, Mr. Kimpton describes
roduced a strong impression upon his own mind and
: other occupiers, as to the inexpediency of outlay upon
s description, when subject to a fluctuating amount of

tithe. The difference of these estimates was owing altogether to the difference of cultivation, the natural quality of the land being the same, and requiring constant supplies of artificial manure to make it productive and keep it so. The land in the occupation of Mr. Dickerson himself, the tithe-occupier, at this time, was remarkable for its high state of cultivation; a crop of turnips on one acre of it, Mr. Watford assured me himself he considered worth nearly the fee-simple of an acre adjoining, in some other person's occupation. Had the former been exposed to valuation for tithe at this time, not only might the profits of so expensive an outlay have been absorbed for this turn, but the punishment would have endured during the whole term of the composition. Whether, therefore, the crops be subject to tithe in kind, or to composition for certain periods, the occupier of lands of this description must feel himself greatly fettered in its cultivation. In some cases the indisposition to cultivate seems to have arisen in part from irritation of mind on the subject; a Mr. ——, occupying 300 acres, abandoned the cultivation of his land almost altogether, being a person of capital, and independent of farming profits.

GAMLINGAY.

PROBABLY the county furnishes few worse examples of oppressive rates, aggravated by extreme mismanagement, than the parish of Gamlingay, in the hundred of Longstow. It contains something more than 4080 acres, of which

    1880 are uninclosed arable land,
    1500 inclosed ditto and pasture,
     700 waste.
    ————
    4080

The present population is 1319. The advantages afforded by the waste land in a supply of fuel, and the permission to build cottages on it*, have attracted the poor from the neighbouring parishes; and a vast quantity of settlements have been made by the farmers letting their land during a part of the year to be dug for potatoes at high rents. As many as thirty families have been introduced in this way. The eldest of my informants (all occupiers) remembers the poor-rate amounting to only 50*l.*—that was sixty years ago; the expenditure of the year ending March, 1832, was 1427*l.* The annual value as assessed in 1815 was 2945*l.*; an estimate of the present actual rental, furnished me from the best authority, states it at little more than 2000*l.* The rates,

---

* Lords of the Manor, Merton College, Oxford.

therefore, have already approached to very nearly 15*s.* in the pound, and the constant decrease of capital and cultivation threatens a further augmentation. The increase of the last over the preceding year was 100*l.* The disbursements of the last year stand thus :—

Aged, impotent and widows	£318	0	0
Paupers working for parish .	615	0	0
Materials, tools, &c. .·	54	0	0
Occasional casual poor relieved for sickness, &c. . }	316	0	0
Medical attendance . .	54	0	0
Law expenses, removals, &c. .	17	0	0
Bastardies . .	10	0	0

The wages paid to men employed by individuals are about 6*s.* a-week to single men, to married men with children from 9*s.* to 10*s.*, further allowance from the rates according to the number of the family. The parish is regulated by the bread scale in use in this part of the country, otherwise called the Magistrates' Scale. The result is as follows :—

A single man .	£0	3	0
Man and wife	0	5	0
Ditto with one child .	0	6	0
Ditto with two children . .	0	7	0
Ditto with three children . .	0	8	0
Ditto with four children . .	0	9	0

There are at this present time between seventy and eighty men and boys (not counting old men) employed in parish work : they began with eight or ten immediately after the harvest, and the number has been rapidly increasing up to this time. The average throughout the whole year is understated at forty; and so it should appear, from the actual disbursement applicable solely to this item last year, viz. 615*l.* The sole employment is that of collecting stones from the surface of the land, for which they are paid at the rate of 2*d.* per bushel, until they have earned the sum allowed by the bread scale, they then do as they please for that week.

This account of the stone-gathering seemed rather a puzzling one. In the first place it must soon fail as a source of employment. 2dly, If it did not, the actual value of the stones would be 1½*d.* per bushel to sell in this country, and by keeping the men at work in this way the parish would lose nothing. 3dly, I was told it was rather an injury than a benefit to the land. 4thly, I found on the receipt side of the balance sheet the item, " Produce of work done by paupers," 11*l.* 10*s.*, to be set against 615*l.*. the expense of their employment. It seemed to me, therefore, on the whole that this employment could be little else than a nominal one; but I was not fully satisfied on the point, until leaving the village, after finishing my inquiries, I encountered a group of boys and men, eight or ten in number, from the age of sixteen to twenty-five, about a stone heap, busily employed, some with their hands, some with large sticks by way of bats, in returning the collected stones to the impoverished acres.

My interview with the overseers (the appointment I had made with them having become known) was voluntarily attended by about six of the other principal occupiers. The external appearance of these men betokened a want of agricultural capital; and they spoke of their parochial burthens in a despairing and almost reckless tone. They could not help themselves. They had in vain attempted several times to share the whole labour of the parish amongst themselves, according to the extent of each man's occupation; a strong practical objection was found to this in the quick recurrence of Saturday night, whereas the rate collector called upon them only fourteen times in the year. It had been attempted to employ the surplus labour in the drainage of the uninclosed lands; but so partial an appropriation was strongly protested against by the rate-payers in respect of land inclosed. They showed me the fragment of a proposition to set the paupers to spade-labour on the parish account; it failed for want of unanimity in the vestry. An inclosure which would give them great temporary relief, and better them permanently to a certain degree, was opposed by Merton College, Oxford, in which body lay a great part of the proprietorship, as well as the tithes : a kind of property which few owners are willing to commute for an allotment of land; yet that is a condition upon which both cultivator and rent-owner usually insist. Under these circumstances they seemed to have abandoned all thought of mitigating their burthens by a strict and proper administration of parochial affairs. Such, in fact, was the abandonment of public principle in the parish officers, that, while employing paupers on the parish account at the expense of 615*l.* a year without any return, they are at this very time called upon to defend an indictment at Quarter Sessions for the infamous state of their roads. On this point I am bound to say, that, if the evidence be properly arranged, they must suffer a verdict.

DECREASE OF FARMING CAPITAL.

It is the opinion of Mr. James King, of Tadlow, an active and enterprising farmer, who knows the parish of Gamlingay perfectly well, that this enormous superabundance of labour arises, in great measure, from want of capital in the farmers to employ the quantity of labour which the land deserves. He should allow three or four men to each hundred acres; whereas, he believes, about one man is the proportion actually employed in that parish. Mr. King himself farms 1100 acres (and has done so for many years) under Downing College; he pays for his labour about 18*l.* a-week; he considers that, in bad times, it is necessary to the interest of the farmer to grow the more corn, if he can find the money to do it with.

Mr. King is much confirmed in this account by the universal complaint in this part of the country, that substantial tenants cannot be found at the lowest assignable rents. I subjoin a few facts on this subject, which have fallen under my personal observation. The parish of Hatley St. George in this neighbourhood consists of 1000 acres; there are only fifteen labourers in the parish, whereof seven able-bodied men are now employed with parish pay upon the roads. Mr. Ingle, the overseer, my informant, occupies himself 306 acres, and has in vain attempted to bring the other three occupiers to an agreement to share the labourers according to the number of acres. The great objection here, as in Gamlingay, was to the Saturday-night payments. Very respectable occupiers of land find it necessary in these times to take a great part of the manual labour upon themselves, assisted by their sons.

Mr. Quintin, of Hatley St. George, proprietor of a great part of that parish, and a gentleman of considerable landed property in the county, tells me, that he has a farm situate in Little Gransden for which he cannot get a tenant. It has been thrown upon his hands for two years past; he is willing to let it on a short lease for 5*s.* an acre; that it is land from which he has himself obtained, during the war, from twenty to thirty bushels of wheat per acre.

Downing college has a property of about 5000 acres in this country, lying principally in the parishes of Tadlow, East Hatley, Croydon, and Gamlingay. It is found impossible, notwithstanding the lowering of the rents to an extreme point, to obtain men of substance for tenants. Several farms of considerable extent have changed hands within the last five years, from insolvency of the tenant in some cases; in others from the terror of that prospect. The amount of arrears at this present time is such as only a collegiate body, situated as Downing college is, could bear. The estates are large, applicable, for the present, in part to the college stipends, in part to a building fund; the latter, of course, suffers. I draw from authentic sources in this case, being myself a fellow of the college.

The answer given by Mr. Withers of Wimpole, land-agent to Lord Hardwick, to query 28, No. 2, of the Commissioners' queries, deserves attention on this subject. He says, " Diminishing rapidly (speaking of farming capital). A great dealer in artificial manures (such as oil-cake, dust, bone-dust, malt-dust, &c.) told me lately, that the farmers in Cambridgeshire purchased of him no more than 2000*l.* worth of such manure last year, (1831,) whereas the usual annual amount has been 4000*l.*; consequently the soil must deteriorate."

The deficiency of agricultural capital, arising from whatever causes, is no doubt one great cause of the present extended pauperism; it is also certain that in a very great degree that deficiency of capital is itself reacted upon and aggravated by the evil it assists in producing; and where this latter effect has resulted to any great extent, it is difficult to conceive how, under the most favourable circumstances, capital can be well reclaimed into the channel it has deserted,—those impediments remaining unabated which drove it from its course. A vital change in the poor-law system must precede, in such cases, the return to a sound state of agricultural speculation.

INCLOSURES.

The Commissioners must be familiar with the two principal obstacles which oppose themselves to the obtaining acts of inclosure, in those parishes which would receive very great benefit from the adoption of such a measure, viz. the great addition which the expense of obtaining the act makes to the other considerable expenses of the inclosure, and the difficulty of arranging satisfactorily to all parties with respect to the tithes. I shall therefore only say upon this subject, that in the several parishes so situated in which I have made the inquiry, uniformly these two obstacles have been put forth as impeding the arrangement. I can mention Shelford, Melbourn, Gransden, Gamlingay as places so situated, in which I have locally received this information; and I believe it to be equally true of a vast number of parishes within the county of Cambridge *.

On this head, the parish of Gamlingay already described as

* Dr. Webb, himself a great promoter of inclosures, effected on behalf of the college a rescue of the tithes in the case of Littlington above-mentioned. Again, at Duxford, a parish in this county, inclosed some years since, the struggle about the tithes is said to have been very severe. They were owned in part by Clare Hall, and partly by another college in Cambridge; the other proprietors were obliged at last to yield the point; but such was the spite against the tithe-owners, that instead of assigning them, as they wished, separate divisions of the parish, they have compelled them to take each their moiety from every individual field.

containing, out of 4080 acres, 1880 acres uninclosed arable land,
and 700 acres of waste, deserves further remark. I have no
doubt, and, in so saying, I am giving effect to better opinions than
my own on this subject, that the present miserable condition of
this village is owing, in great measure, to the want of a sufficiently
interested or a sufficiently wise proprietorship of the land. It is
shared, with a slight exception, between the colleges of Clare-hall
and Downing, Cambridge, and Merton college, Oxford. The
first of these has a small proportion,—the last by much the greatest
part of the ownership, besides the manor and the tithes. With
respect to the proportion now enjoyed by Downing college, the
ownership remained in abeyance for many years during a chancery
suit, in which the heir-at-law contested his right. At this period
I am told that great part of the mischief accrued. The objections entertained by Merton College to an inclosure of the parish,
as stated by them very lately in answer to a general proposition
to that effect, are grounded on these two reasons :—

1. " The general expenses of the inclosure, and the improba-
" bility of a return for the outlay.

2. " An unwillingness to abridge the little benefits which the
"poor parishioners derive from the waste land in its present "state."

As to the first objection, better judges, probably, than the fellows of Merton college, assure me that it is far from being justified
by the circumstances or the character of the land: as to the
second, they are probably at too great a distance from the spot to
know, that at some seasons of the year there are 100 labourers out
of employ, and that the average throughout the year is more than
40; a mischief arising in great measure from " the *little* benefits
" which the poor parishioners derive from the waste land in its
" present state ;"* and a mischief which the inclosure would for a
certain time almost altogether remove, and diminish permanently
to a very great degree.

SITUATION OF THE RURAL PARISH-OFFICERS.

The tone assumed by the paupers towards those who dispense
relief in the oppressed agricultural districts is generally very insolent, and often assumes even a more fearful character. At Great
Gransden, the overseer's wife told me that two days before my
visit there, two paupers came to her husband, demanding an increase of allowance. He refused them, showing at the same time
that they had the full allowance sanctioned by the magistrates'
scale. They swore, and threatened he should repent it ; and such

* This is true twice over ; the little benefits brought them there, (as is seen
before,) and they are too little to do them any good, compared with the effect
of an inclosure.

was the violence of their temper and demeanour, that when they left the house she ran after them, and called them back, fearing they would do some mischief, and prevailed upon her husband to make some further allowance.

Mr. Faircloth came about two years since into the occupation of a farm in the parish of Croydon, where the rates amount (including surveyor's rate) to about five shillings in the pound. He immediately took on himself the parochial management, and partly by adopting a stricter system of relief, and partly by the additional employment, which, being a man of capital, he introduced into the parish, he reduced the rates from 435*l.* in the year ending March, 1831, to 342*l.* in the year ending March, 1832, being a saving of nearly 100*l.* His improved management, however, of the relief, made him very unpopular amongst the labourers of the parish, into which he was introducing employment in the place of pauperism ; and a few weeks after last harvest, they gathered in a riotous body about a threshing-machine which he had upon his premises, and broke it all in pieces. The Rev. Mr. Dawes was on the spot a short time after ; and before the party had dispersed, he tells me he heard the following expressions :—" It's almost as good as a fire !" " He's not going to lord it over us any longer !" and similar demonstrations of personal resentment to Faircloth for his conduct as overseer.

At Guilden Morden,* in the same neighbourhood, a burning took place three weeks ago of Mr. Butterfield's stacks, to the amount of 1500*l.* damage. Mr. Butterfield was overseer ; and the magistrates have committed for trial, on strong circumstantial evidence, a man to whom Butterfield had constantly denied relief, because he refused to do work for it. The evidence against him partly consists of previous threatening language and his behaviour during the fire, at which he exulted, saying, " Butterfield ought to be in it."

A fire occurred about six weeks since at Swaffham, on the other side of Cambridge, in the direction of Newmarket. Messrs. Ellice, Gibbons, and Chambers, the principal occupiers appointed to meet together for the purpose of coming to a joint resolution to reduce the wages to 9*s.* instead of 10*s.*, at which point they had been artificially maintained since the harvest. The object of this meeting having transpired, a threatening letter was sent them ; and on the morning of the day on which they were to have met, Mr. Gibbons' ricks were set fire to and consumed.

* There was a fire at this place in November, 1831, on a Mr. Westropp's premises. There was no clue to the motive, further than the circumstance that he paid low wages.

I have found, and it is not to be wondered at, that the apprehension of this dreadful and easily perpetrated mischief has very
generally affected the minds of the rural parish officers of this
county, making the power of the paupers over the funds provided for their relief almost absolute, as regards any discretion
on the part of the overseer.

LINTON.

GAMLINGAY, oppressed and ill-managed as it is, is not the
worst place in the county. At Linton the rates press more
heavily on the rental, and the administration is, if possible, worse.
The two cases, however, present very distinct, and even opposite,
features. Instead of an impoverished race of farmers, as at Gamlingay, screwing down a miserable, ill-lodged, and ill-fed population to the very letter of the bread-scale, and with difficulty producing their rates at fourteen instalments in the year, we find at
Linton a substantial set of farmers, giving a fair degree of cultivation to the land, producing their four shillings in the pound
(like rent) four times a year, for the purpose of maintaining, to
the extent of just one shilling above the incomes laid down in the
bread-scale, the best fed and most comfortable and thriving
population of paupers in the county of Cambridge. I had only
been half prepared for this the day before at Fulbourn, where
they keep their parish-pay at 6d. above the bread-scale in all its
departments. The recommendation of the magistrate is pleaded,
but there is no new scale. Some considerate landlords must be
suffering for this.

The present population of Linton is 1678. The assessment in
1815 was 3,120l. The whole number of acres is 3,600, of which
600 are inclosed and the rest open field. The following is a copy
of their balance-sheet for the year ending March, 1832.

RECEIPT SIDE.	£.	s.	d.	DISBURSEMENT.	£.	s.	d.
Rates during the year, viz.,				1. Relief to aged, impotent,			
4 rates at 4s. in the pound	2108	7	4	and Widows . . .	793	2	11½
For work done by paupers	0	0	0	2. Paupers working for parish	527	6	4
By re-payment of loan . .	1	8	0	3. Medical attendance, fune-			
Recovered for bastards . .	8	1	7	rals, rent, &c. . . .	107	6	10
For rent	3	2	6	4. Occasional & casual poor	688	17	9
				5. Tools, materials, clothing,			
	2121	0	0	fuel, food, &c. . . .	108	18	2½
				6. Law expenses, orders, &c.	65	2	1
				7. Bastardy expenses . .	63	6	0
				8. County rate	41	5	8
				Constable's expenses, &c.	12	1	0
				Militia	1	18	0
					2428	13	11
				Deduct	2121	0	0
				Balance due to overseer .	307	13	11

With respect to Item 1, I can only say, that its amount is monstrous, and utterly unaccountable, in a population of 1678 persons, except from what has been already remarked on the profuseness of the relief.

I am possessed of some explanation of Item 2. There is no return from it on the receipt side, the only employment alluded to having been bestowed on the roads, which for some years have been in a state of excellent repair, and therefore little work wanted. About three years since, at the suggestion of Mr. Fisher, the very amiable and intelligent rector of the parish, spade cultivation has been tried on some of the private farms. About 100 acres a-year have been since dug in this manner. The farmer pays 1*d.* a rod; this, although 13*s.* an acre instead of 10*s.*, the cost of ploughing, is no loss to him, except that his horses are idle: the parish pay the pauper 2*d.* per rod for the work, if a single man; if a married one, 2½*d.* or 3*d.* according to his necessity. The officer told me that 70*l.* a-year was thus got by the parish from the farmer in aid of the rate; but although it furnished severe employment, and thus drove away many applicants, it did not produce in any other way a saving to the parish; for that the single labourer would earn more than his 1*s.* a-day by this work, and they always gave him a greater allowance than when doing nothing on the road; and even thus it was often necessary to stop him, lest he should earn too much. Then why not put it to him at 1½*d.* per rod? The answer to this question, by a person who paid 391*l.* for rates last year, was given with great naïveté—" Well, Sir, there is something in that to be sure!" The 70*l.* above-mentioned is not made a part of Item 1.

A further fact is, that of sixty men now unemployed, a smaller portion only are agricultural labourers; the remainder are artizans, labouring mechanics, &c., Linton being the emporium of the local trade of this part of the country. These men earn throughout a great part of the year from 18*s.* to 1*l.* 1*s.* a week, and in winter regularly fall upon the rates. They detest the spade labour; and it is obvious, that were relief given to them only through that, and at low wages, they would save their earnings for the winter season. The excuse made, however, for not pressing them in this way is, that they are a desperate set, and would not bear it, and would not mind what they did. They have, indeed, given some tokens of deserving this character. In 1830 two men were hanged for burning the stacks of Mr. Chalk. It was in evidence on the trial, among other things, that they had uttered threats against Mr. Chalk, for some offence given them by him in vestry. The outrage committed, about three weeks since, in the streets of Linton, upon the persons of Lord Godolphin and

Mr. Adeane, acting there as magistrates, is probably known to the commissioners. Mr. Adeane's life has been only within these few days considered out of danger.

The same remark applies to Item 4 which I have made on Item 1, with this addition, that the farming wages for all persons here are 9*s.*; and that a great part of this item goes indirectly in aid of these, that is to support their families, or " make up their incomes," as the magistrates express it.

I have the honour to be,
My Lords and Gentlemen,
Your obedient servant,
ALFRED POWER.

MY LORDS AND GENTLEMEN,   *Dec.* 12, 1832.

IN compliance with your request, communicated to me by your Secretary on the 4th instant, to be furnished with a detailed account of the administration and practical operation of the Poor-Laws in some of the parishes I have visited, for the information of Lord Melbourne, I have now the honour to send you a particular account of four parishes in which the poor-rate is administered entirely by the parochial authorities, and of an incorporation of forty-six parishes, where it is controlled by a Board of Directors and Guardians.

The administration of the Poor-Laws by corporate bodies prevails to a considerable extent in the county of Suffolk, and seems to me to be attended with advantages which deserve attention.

I have the honour to be,
My Lords and Gentlemen,
Your faithful and obedient servant,
HENRY STUART.

*To the Commissioners for Inquiring into
the Administration and Practical
Operation of the Poor-Laws.*

SUFFOLK.

FRISTON PARISH, IN PLOMESGATE HUNDRED.

Acres, 1500.   Population, 1831, 466.
Expenditure on Poor, 1829, 607*l.*, and since increasing.

THE rate-payers of this parish devolve the whole administration of the poor-laws on an assistant overseer. The vestry is so ill attended, that when a meeting is called to make a rate, it frequently happens that no more are present than the churchwarden and assistant overseer. The annual meeting for electing parish officers and auditing accounts is better attended ; but the vestry take no active interest in the affairs of the parish.

There is no resident clergyman or gentleman, and divine service is only performed once a fortnight by a curate who lives some miles off. The only school in the parish is a Sunday school belonging to a dissenting chapel.

The assistant overseer was appointed merely to save trouble ; and as he is not backed by the authority of a vestry, he admits that his services are of little avail towards the good management of the poor. He is a blacksmith, and seems to be a man of good sense ; but the qualities which chiefly recommended him for the office are, great personal strength and undaunted resolution. He collects the rate, and disburses it without either assistance or control.

Relief to those who are out of work or who are unable to work is administered according to a scale, which is understood to be sanctioned by the magistrates ; and the amount in money varies with the price of flour. The scale in use, when I was in the parish, allowed to

	s.	*d.*
A single man, per week . .	4	0
Man and wife . .	5	6
And for each child under 14 . .	1	0

When above that age they have 3*s.* a week on their own account till they come to be considered men. Whenever a lad comes to earn wages or to receive parish relief on his own account, although he may continue to lodge with his parents, he does not throw his money into a common purse and board with them, but buys his own loaf and piece of bacon, which he devours alone. The most disgraceful quarrels arise from mutual accusations of theft ; and as the child knows he has been nurtured at the cost of the parish, he has no filial attachment to his parents. To men who have work an allowance of 1*s.* per week is made for each child over three ; but where the man is understood to be earning good wages, it is attempted to avoid this payment.

The rate of wages in the parish is 1*s.* 8*d.* when employed by the day, and a stout and willing labourer may earn 2*s.* 4*d.* at piece-work. The women and children are sometimes employed by the farmer, but more frequently they are hired by men, who contract for hoeing wheat and such work at a price per acre, which is considerably under what a labourer could undertake it for. These contractors give constant attention to their gangs, and some have accumulated money.

In administering relief an attempt is made to ascertain the amount of the applicants' earnings, but no attention whatever is paid to character. Although the assistant overseer is a man of courage, yet he admits that relief is frequently given under the fear, that if it was refused it might expose his person or property to secret injury. No labour whatever is required in return for relief.   *

There is a poor-house, with about two acres of land attached to it, which is given to a man with a large family for the purpose of keeping him off the parish. He is bound to receive any one that may be sent to it, and is paid 3s. a week for the maintenance of each. The only inmate is an old man who is a cripple.

The rent of cottages is occasionally paid by the parish, and the rates are not collected on cottages occupied by labourers.

There are a few labourers who still own the cottages in which they live; formerly, there was a great number who had grants of land on the common, but they have gradually parted with them for the purpose of completing their title to the parish fund, and have sunk down to pauperism. Before the importance of keeping off settlements was known, a great many were made by hiring and service by farmers, who employed labourers from adjoining parishes.

The pressure of the poor-rate is ascribed to an excess of population, and to the want of sufficient capital, preventing the farmer employing so many men in cultivation as is required, aggravated by negligence in attending to parish affairs. I was informed by the principal farmer, that he had frequently attempted to rouse his neighbours to a sense of the necessity of taking a part in the business of the parish, but with so little success, that he had given it up in despair.

The population have the character of being the greatest poachers in the neighbourhood ; and being near the preserves of several noblemen, they have every opportunity of carrying on their depredations ; which they pursue without any fear of being exposed to want, as they are always sure of maintenance from the parish or in jail.

STRADBROKE PARISH, HOXNE HUNDRED.

Acres, 3000.   Population, 1831, 1527.
Expenditure on Poor, 1829, 2026*l.* 16*s.* and since then increasing.

THERE are only two farms in this parish so large as 160 acres. A great proportion of the land is in the hands of small occupiers of from 50 down to 10 acres, many of whom are owners of th farms which they cultivate.

The vestry does not take any efficient part in the management of the poor, neither do they appoint any committee for that purpose.

The clergyman of the parish is resident, but there is no landed gentleman within the hundred who lives on his estate. There is an endowed school in the parish for the education of seventeen boys. The master also receives scholars who pay fees, but very few come to him. The rector has frequently endeavoured to unite the parishioners in some plan for the employment of those out of work, either by distributing them among the occupiers, or by hiring land on which to set them to work; but, although when assembled in vestry no opposition was made to the proposal, and the advantages which might be expected to result from it were fully admitted, yet, after using his best exertions, he has never been able to carry any plan into execution.

The administration of the poor-rate rests entirely with the parish officers, who have the assistance of a clerk in keeping the accounts.

The relief given to the aged, the infirm, and otherwise helpless, who are considered constant pensioners, is paid at the village shops. This mode of payment is preferred by the paupers, as it gives them credit for any little necessaries which they may require before the pay-day comes round. The parish officers declare that they are are always ready to protect them from any imposition which may be attempted; and I could not learn that the system was considered objectionable.

The relief to those out of employment, or who are suffering from sickness or any other casualty, is distributed every Saturday morning by the overseers and churchwardens. It is regulated by a scale which allows the value of a stone of flour each to husband and wife, half a stone for each child, and 6d. a head for other necessaries to the parents, and 3d. a head to the children. The practice of taking flour as the standard for ascertaining the sum required for maintenance, completes the degradation to which compulsory relief has brought the lower orders, as the price of all the other necessaries of life does not invaririably follow the price of that article. At this time it happens that the reduction in the amount of allowance, which followed the fall in the price of flour, has abridged the comforts of those who depend on parish relief. The pauper, therefore, does not, and cannot thank God for an abundant harvest, although he may be ordered to do so.

It is the practice to deduct any earnings, which can be ascertained, from the allowance. Such deductions do not appear to be regulated by the sum earned, but by the number of days on which work has been obtained. A case was mentioned to me, of nine men who had been able to earn 15*s.* each by task work in three days, who came to the parish for the other three days of the week during which they had no employment. The overseer being aware of the profitable work in which they had been engaged, offered 1*s.* a day for the lost days instead of 1*s.* 6*d.*, which would have been their allowance according to the scale. This the men rejected, and left the work which they then had, and went to a magistrate to complain. The magistrate did not make an absolute order, but sent an open note by the complainants, appealing to the humanity of the overseer, and recommending a favourable consideration of the case. The men being acquainted with the contents of the note, backed the recommendation of the magistrate with such threats of violence, as induced the overseer to pay the demand through bodily fear.

Besides relief in money, it is common to give shoes and other articles of clothing to those who require them.

There is a poor-house belonging to the parish: the number of inmates averages about thirty; no work is carried on in it, and it is merely a receptacle for the aged, the orphan, and bastard children, and for others who are without a home.

Although the parishioners do not take any general interest in the management of the poor fund, they are constantly complaining of the amount of the rates. The parish officers, for the purpose of exonerating themselves from all suspicion of malversation, have for the last two years published quarterly a detailed account of their disbursements ; with the names of those who have received relief within that period, distinguishing the cause for which it is administered. From the account for the quarter 17th March to 17th June, 1832, it appears that there was disbursed within that period,

	£.	s.	d.
On account of sickness and other misfortunes, requiring temporary assistance	65	12	2
For the permanent list of the aged, and otherwise impotent	118	3	1½
For unemployed labour	328	18	4
	512	13	7½

The total number of names on the list among whom the above sum was distributed, is	212
The number of children	327
Of the 212 there appear to be 104 married men. Their wives	104
Number of persons receiving relief	643

This does not include those in the poor-house, or the expense of maintaining them.

The extent of pauperism in this parish is attributed to a super-abundant population; the inconvenience of which would not be so much felt, were it not that deficient capital on the part of the farmer, together with the low price of agricultural produce, prevents the employment of so many labourers as the proper cultivation of the soil requires. For the purpose of getting rid of a portion of the unemployed labourers, forty-six persons were induced to emigrate, in 18:30, at the expense of the parish. Of these forty-six persons, fourteen were married, eight single, and twenty-four children. This emigration has not, however, been sufficient to afford any perceptible relief; for so crowded was the population, that the cottages which were vacated by the emigrants were immediately tenanted by married persons who had lived doubled up in houses with other families. The accounts received from the emigrants express satisfaction at the change they have made; and the parish is endeavouring to raise means to send out others who are desirous to remove. Only one of the first party has come back. He is a man of a dissolute and abandoned character, who immediately returned to his station on the pauper roll. Besides the inconvenience produced by the superabundant population, there are other causes which contribute to increase the number of paupers, and to add to the amount of the expenditure. The circumstances of the small occupiers are described to be such as to place them on the very verge of pauperism: besides, they all have relations who are absolutely in that state. Those who are in this condition do not hire labourers at the ordinary rate of wages, but obtain such labour as they require, on low terms, from those who are receiving parish relief. This they conceive to be not only to their own advantage, but doing an act of kindness to their friends, as well as keeping up a system to the benefits of which they may soon be obliged to have recourse themselves. It is well known to the parish authorities, that underhand employment is given to a great extent; and for the purpose of checking it, they oblige all who are out of work to show themselves daily at a fixed hour to the overseer. This, however, has no effect; as leave of absence is very easily obtained to enable them to pass muster, and to receive the reward of their knavery from the parish. The poor-rate is considered by the lower orders as a fund in which they have an absolute property, and they do not scruple at artifice, fraud, or violence, to establish their right to it. This feeling contributes more than any other cause to the progressive increase of the poor-rate, and to the general demoralization which prevails in the lower ranks of society. It exists to a great extent in the parish of Stradbroke, to which the enormous and increasing expenditure on the poor bears witness.

WICKHAM MARKET, PARISH, WILFORD HUNDRED.

Population, 1831, 1202.
Expenditure on Poor, 1829, 543*l.* 7*s.* and since then increasing.

THE great road from London to Yarmouth passes through this parish—and although it is not a market town, yet, being centrically situated, it is a place of considerable resort—besides, a number of the inhabitants have their settlements, and give their labour, in the adjoining parishes.

There is a select vestry, and an assistant overseer, under the 59 Geo. 3. The vestry meets once a fortnight for the purpose of receiving applications for relief, and transacting other business connected with the administration of the poor fund. Regular minutes of their proceedings are kept, and entries are made of such circumstances as come to their knowledge as may be useful in regulating the allowances of those who are already in receipt of relief, or of those who may thereafter come to require it. These memoranda are found to be extremely serviceable. The assistant overseer pays the poor according to the orders of the select vestry, and any relief he may have administered on his own responsibility during the interval between the meetings of the vestry, is carefully inquired into at the next meeting. The certainty of this investigation keeps him constantly alive to his duties.

The clergyman is resident, and takes an active and judicious part in the business of the parish. It has unfortunately happened, that one of the inhabitants, who is a tradesman of property in the village, has taken umbrage at some of the proceedings or persons of those who compose the vestry, which he displays by creating disturbances at their meetings, which have become so unpleasant, that the clergyman and many of the most respectable members have withdrawn themselves from that regular attendance which they were in the habit of giving. If this continues, the worst consequences must result from it.

There are no able-bodied labourers who receive parish relief except in cases of sickness, and some small occasional assistance which is given during winter to such as are getting advanced in life. There is a good understanding among the occupiers, who keep the labourers themselves, their wives, and children in constant employment. A sort of agreement exists among them, that each shall employ a certain number of men, according to the extent of their occupations: this agreement is not very scrupulously adhered to; but although some do not employ so many as they have engaged to do, yet such of their neighbours as are in a condition to employ more than the number allotted to them, contrive among them to find work for such labourers as would otherwise fall on the parish for support.

This parish was formerly included in the incorporation of the hundreds of Loes and Wilford, which was dissolved about six years ago, and being then deprived of a workhouse, they have not found it expedient to build one for their own use. There are several cottages belonging to the parish, which are given rent free to old and infirm people; and for those who cannot be accommodated in this way, lodgings are provided, or board and washing is found for them.

No complaints reached my ear in this parish of superabundant labour or deficient capital. The vigilant management which has been established is to some extent accounted for by the active part taken by one of the inhabitants, who, having been very forward in bringing about the disincorporation of the hundred, has exerted himself to prove, that the workhouse system has no effect in lightening the burthen of the poor rate, or in bettering the condition of the lower orders. This man possesses energy and judgment, and by his influence with his neighbours, the affairs of the parish are conducted advantageously to the rate-payers and beneficially for the poor.

Within the last two years the expenditure on the poor has increased. This is accounted for by the typhus fever having carried off a great number of people, which not only occasioned a great immediate expense, but has left many widows and orphan children chargeable to the parish, who will continue a burthen for some years to come. Before this load is removed another similar casual affliction may occur and prevent its being diminished, or it may even add to its weight. Even when the ruinous practice of giving relief to the able-bodied from the parish funds is avoided, by the rate-payers keeping them in employment, the most extensive evils arise from the certainty of support which the poor-laws afford, when sickness or old age come on. The dependence which all have on that provision does away with the necessity of providing by their own industry and management for a season of calamity, and the parish is exposed to demands which can neither be foreseen nor prevented.

LITTLE LIVERMERE, BLACKBOURNE HUNDRED.

Population, 1831, 185.
Expenditure on Poor, 1829, 209*l.* 10*s.*

THIS parish is the property of one gentleman, and is farmed by one tenant, who concentrates in himself all the powers of vestry, churchwarden, and overseer.

The system of bread allowance prevails in all the surrounding parishes, which, at the present price of flour, gives to a man, his wife, and four children, 10s. a week, and 1s. 6d. a head for every child beyond that number. When the wages of a man do not come up to the statement, as it is called in this district, it is made up by the parish.

When Mr. Rodwell, who is the present occupier of this parish, came into possession about five years ago, he sent for the labourers for the purpose of coming to terms with them; but they declared it was immaterial to them what wages he allowed, as they would be made up by the statement. He, however, gave them to understand, that he would not deal with them in that way, and offered them such wages as he considered just, and promised to keep them, their wives, and children in constant employment. This caused great dissatisfaction for some time, and there were constant threats held out against him, and appeals made to the magistrates, from whom many verbal messages were received, but to which no regard was paid, as work was always to be had. For the purpose of keeping the women and children in employment, as much work as possible is done by manual labour, and they are kept as constantly engaged as the men. When wheat is to be dibbled, or such work is to be done as requires a number of hands, it is let at so much an acre to one man, on condition of his employing as many children belonging to the parish as may be sent to him. In more severe labour, which can be done by men, the use of horses and carts is avoided as much as possible. The soil being light, claying is required, and the clay is removed by wheel-barrows. This is hard work, but being let by the yard, good wages can be earned at it; and men who have complained of the severity of the employment, on being offered lighter work at day's wages, have refused it.

From this system of constant employment a man with several children earns large weekly wages. Mr. Rodwell allowed me to extract from his book of accounts the sum earned in one week (in the month of May when employment is not easily obtained), by a man and his three boys, which amounted to 1l. 2s. 6d. In answer to the queries of the Commissioners, Mr. Rodwell has stated that an average workman will earn in the year about 35l. at task-work, and 30l. at day-work, and that his wife and four children, of the ages specified in the queries, can earn 2s. 4d. a-week, summer and winter, weather permitting. He further states that the family can subsist on these earnings, and describes the food. In reply to the question whether it can lay by anything, he says, " A careful man, with an industrious wife, *could*, and if they were not confident of parish relief, *would*, make provision against sickness and old age." Mr. Rodwell has a thorough knowledge of the whole economy of rural life, and his opinion can be relied upon. He describes, that although only five years have elapsed since all allowance to able-bodied men has been discontinued, he can perceive an improvement in the general character and condition of his labourers. Where bread allowance exists to the greatest extent, the income of the labourer is larger, by the amount of the parish allowance, than the wages earned by Mr. Rodwell's labourers—their comforts are fewer and their character is miserably degraded. The only case in which I was able to ascertain the total income of a labourer, in the receipt of bread allowance, was in the parish of Whatfield, by the kindness of the Rev. Frederick Calvert, the rector, whose attention has been attracted to the evils of the system by the extent to which it exists around him, and I beg to state it here. A labourer in that parish with a family of five children, received in

Wages from 1st June, 1830, to 1st June, 1831 . £33 6 10
From the parish, from Easter, 1830, to Easter, 1831 . 24 4 0
_____
£57 10 10

The wages noted here are merely those received from one master, for whom he usually worked. It is considered more than probable that he had opportunities of earning money, when professedly unemployed, of which he availed himself, and also that his wife and family derived the usual advantages from gleaning. The man is considered to be an excellent workman, but he is withal a worthless and profligate fellow; he, however, does not greatly differ from the general character of the labourers in the parish, where the abuse of bread allowance prevails to an enormous extent. When Mr. Calvert first came to reside in Whatfield, he was desirous to try to make at least one family respectable and independent, and engaged as a bailiff a man with a large family, of whose character he had received a favourable report, to whom he gave, comparatively speaking, very high wages, with the understanding that he was no longer to consider himself a pauper. Still it was found that he was not quite satisfied without obtaining the permission of his master to go to the parish for assistance in the payment of his rent—which permission was refused. Mr. Calvert was grievously disappointed when he found that the yearly receipts of the pauper must have exceeded that of his bailiff by about 15*l.*, which, as he justly remarked, was a premium on profligacy and idleness, which made his theory of rewarding good conduct and industry perfectly ridiculous.

Although Mr. Rodwell's character is well known to those about him, yet the habit of relying on the parish for the supply of every want is so firmly fixed, that he is constantly exposed to the most extravagant applications, which it requires the most persevering firmness to resist. A young man belonging to his parish and in his employment married, and for some months lived with his wife's relations, but some disagreement having taken place, he and his wife were immediately turned out of doors. They both came to Mr. Rodwell, as the overseer, at a late hour in the evening, and required to have a house provided for them. On being informed that an overseer was only obliged to find work, the man took a different view of the law, and expressed his determination not to quit the house till lodgings were found for him. Both he and his wife were instantly removed by force. Next day the ejected party complained to the magistrates, and brought an open note from them recommending that a home should be found for him, which, when presented, was thrown into the fire. As the man slept in an adjoining parish, he threatened to absent himself from work for the purpose of making himself chargeable. He was immediately offered work, but refused it, and after a week's absence applied again to the magistrates, who, having probably heard of the reception the open note had met with, gave him a sealed expostulatory letter to the overseer, which produced no more effect than the open note. Finding that the overseer was inexorable, the man at last returned to his work, and found lodgings for himself. All this happened within the month preceding my visit to the parish, and I had the opportunity of seeing such of the documentary evidence relating to the transaction as then remained in existence.

Although this mode of dealing is not likely to attract settlements, yet it is thought necessary to use the utmost vigilance to keep them off. Mr. Rodwell hires his domestic servants only for fifty-one weeks, for the purpose of preventing a settlement by a year's service. This has sometimes occasioned him inconvenience; for, where the servant has suited him, and he has expected his return, the man has taken some whim during his days of emancipation, and engaged himself to another master. The landlord's seat being within the parish, settlements are frequently acquired by persons living in his service. As, however, nothing is given out of the parish to a person who is able to work, those who require relief are obliged to earn it by their labour within the parish. The butlers and grooms are in this way generally got rid of within a week, as relief is invariably administered to them in the shape of task-work.

It might be expected that where no parish allowance is made to married men on account of children, that a check would be given to early marriages—but that is not the case, for the certainty of provision in sickness and old age renders it quite unnecessary to enter into any prudential consideration before entering into the state of matrimony. The united ages of a couple, who were married in this parish within the last few months, were thirty-four years.

Even in this parish, where so vigilant a management prevails under such advantageous circumstances, there is a considerable expenditure on the poor, although the population is so small; and it cannot be otherwise till, by a perseverance for a course of years, the out-settlements are reduced in number, and relief is confined to those who live within the parish.

INCORPORATED HUNDRED OF BLYTHING.

The forty-six parishes of which this hundred consists are incorporated for the management of the poor. The incorporation does not take any charge of the relief given to able-bodied men out of employment, nor of the expenses incurred in the maintenance of bastard children, beyond receiving such as may be sent into the house of industry.

The government of the incorporation is vested in twenty-four directors and twenty-four guardians. The directors are landed proprietors and magistrates, and are elected for life ; the guardians are elected periodically, and the qualification for the office is being assessed at not less than 60*l.*

A committee, consisting of two directors and two guardians, who serve in rotation, meets every Monday at the House of Industry, for the purpose of ordering relief, and a quarterly general meeting assembles to control the whole management.

The establishment of the House of Industry consists of a governor, a matron, and a visiting guardian whose duty it is to superintend the farm, and to take a general charge of the provisions and other necessaries which are purchased for the house. There are besides a chaplain, a schoolmistress, a clerk, and a house-surgeon.

All paupers admitted into the house, are dressed in the clothes of the incorporation, and their own are laid by and are returned to them when they are discharged.

Unmarried males and females, whether grown up or children, are kept separate; but married persons are permitted to sleep together, a separate apartment being allotted to each couple. No spirituous liquors are allowed; but smoking is permitted in the yard. The disobedient and refractory are punished, by order of the Committee, by solitary confinement or a diminution of diet; and, in aggravated cases, they are handed over to the magistrates, to be dealt with according to law. A room is set apart for receiving visitors; but the inmates are only allowed to go to it by the special permission of the governor, except in cases of sickness, when the visitors are permitted, under proper regulations, to go into the wards to see their friends. No one is allowed to go out of the house without leave. To the aged people, who conduct themselves well, more liberty is allowed.

There are fifty acres of land, which are cultivated by the inmates, and the produce is applied to the use of the house. The employment within doors is spinning hemp, knitting, weaving, shoemaking, and other occupations, by which every one who is capable of work is kept in constant activity. The produce of this labour is consumed in the house; and some articles, such as sacks and coarse linen, are sold. The profits of the manufacture, which are not charged with the labour employed in it, amount to 100*l*. or to 150*l*. a-year. There is a school for the children, in which they are instructed in reading, and the girls are taught to knit and sow.

The diet of the inmates is regulated according to their age. To all persons who are above fifty-five years of age, and children under thirteen, meat is allowed twice a week, and to the old a daily quantity of beer. Those who are under fifty-five have meat only once a week, and no beer.

The number of inmates, when I visited the house, was—

> 106 men,   of whom 69 were over 55 years.
> 101 women, of whom 55 were over 55 years.
> 136 boys, } of whom 60 were under 4 years.
> 88 girls, }
>
> ———
> 431

The weekly expense per head, for the year ending Lady-day, 1832, was—

> For maintenance and clothing   .   .   2*s*. 11*d*.
> Expense of establishment   .   .   .   1   1½
>   ————
> Total expense per head for the week   4*s*.   0½*d*.

The expense per head for the year, during the same period, was—

> Maintenance and clothing   . .   .   £7   14   10
> Expense of establishment   .   .   2   19   3¼
>   ————
> Total expense per head for the year   £10   14   1¼

Each parish is charged with the expense of maintenance and clothing, according to the average number of poor they have had in the house during the year. The expense of the house, which comprehends all salaries, law, and miscellaneous charges, is paid by each parish, according to the whole amount disbursed for it by the incorporation during the year.

All children, who are sent from their respective parishes to be bound as apprentices by the incorporation, are taken into the house on the 1st of October, and are bound out the Easter following,—according to the laws of the incorporation, by which every occupier is obliged to receive one apprentice for every 50*l.* of his assessment, or to pay a fine of 10*l.* for every one he refuses to take. Those assessed under 50*l.*, down to 10*l.*, are also obliged to take one in their turn. The order in which the apprentices are imposed on the occupiers, is regulated according to a table, of which the following is a copy :—

	No.	Order of Apprenticing.					
Every person occupying £300 per annum, who should have	6	1st	3d	6th	10th	15th	21st
Ditto 250	5	2nd	5th	9th	14th	20th	
Ditto 200	4	4th	8th	13th	19th		
Ditto 150	3	7th	12th	18th			
Ditto 100	2	11th	17th				
Ditto 50 ..	1	16th					

The children are distributed, by ballot, among those who are liable to receive them, regard being had as to whether the business of the master is suitable for the child. The period of servitude is regulated so as to expire when the apprentice has reached the age of eighteen.

Compulsory binding is so obnoxious to the rate-payers, that, in order to abridge it as much as possible, those who are liable to receive an apprentice, are allowed to take any child they choose within their own parish, which exempts them from having one forced on them from the house. Notwithstanding this option is allowed, there are from sixty to eighty children sent every year to the house to be bound out. The object in sending them to the house is, that they may be trained to habits of industry before they go to their service. However desirable this may be, I am inclined to believe that great mischief is done by familiarizing the minds of the children to the restraints of the workhouse, which destroys all reluctance to being sent back to it in after life.

The great advantages of the workhouse, beyond being a place of refuge for the aged and otherwise impotent, are considered to lie in its being a place of restraint to which the parishes can send idle and refractory paupers, who are unwilling to exert themselves

to find employment, or to retain it when they have it. I am informed, that it frequently does operate in this way, and that
when able-bodied men find that they have to change their dress,
and to be subjected to a rigid discipline, they contrive to shift
for themselves. On the other hand, many who have not the
spirit to avoid such degradation, very soon become reconciled to
their condition; and as the expense of maintaining them in the
house exceeds the sum they are content to receive out of doors,
the parish is soon glad to take them home again.

All law-suits are conducted by the clerk, who has a salary,
beyond which he is only allowed for his outlays. The law expenses are defrayed from the funds of the incorporation, and are
charged to the expense of the establishment. When parishes
belonging to the incorporation dispute among themselves about
settlements, each pays its own expense; but when any parish
gets into litigation with one not belonging to the hundred, the
suit is carried on at the expense of the incorporation, provided
the appeal is approved by the board. The adjoining parishes
complain loudly of the litigious spirit of the incorporated parishes,
who, as their expenses are defrayed from a common fund, resist
every attempt at settlements being made upon them, or enter into
expensive law-suits for the purpose of getting rid of them.

Medical relief is furnished by the incorporation; and each
parish is charged with a proportion of the expense according to
the number of paupers belonging to it. An annual census is
taken of those receiving parish relief, of whatever kind, within
the hundred.

The out-door relief, administered to the aged, the infirm, and
those labouring under sickness, or any other calamity which incapacitates them from supporting themselves, is all passed through
the incorporation, and is regulated by the weekly committee.
The overseer of each parish attends the committee with a book,
in which are entered the names of all those for whom relief is
requested; against which are set the occupation of the applicant,
the cause of complaint, and the number of his children, with the
sum which the vestry and overseer consider it right to allow,
together with the number of weeks for which it should be continued. The amount of relief sought is either granted, modified,
or totally rejected by the committee.

It is the earnest recommendation of the directors and guardians
that a select vestry, or a committee of vestry, should meet for the
purpose of minutely investigating the circumstances of the applicants before their names are forwarded to the committee, and
also that each parish should appoint an assistant overseer. I
have observed, that where there are assistant overseers, the busi-

ness of the vestry is generally more vigilantly attended to by the parishioners.

It may appear that it is unnecessary to carry the amount of relief applied for to be approved by a distant body, who must frequently be ignorant of the peculiar circumstances of the case; but in fact it is found to be very useful, for the directors and guardians, being all men who are acquainted with the affairs of their own parishes, or who are experienced in the management of the poor, from the attention they have given to the business of the incorporation, are well qualified to examine the overseer as to the necessity of each case, and to judge of the amount of relief which it requires. I have seen this controul very beneficially exercised, not only in curtailing allowances which had been carelessly made, but in admonishing the parish officers to be more attentive to their duties. When the amount of relief is settled, it is paid to the overseer. These applications are made not only for the poor who have settlements in the parish, but for those belonging to the other parishes of the incorporation who may be resident within it, of whose wants the overseers can inform themselves more effectually than if the inquiry was left to the officers of the parish to which they belong. Separate accounts are kept for each parish, and the amount of relief is carried to the debit of the parishes to which the paupers belong.

The funds for the purposes of the incorporation are furnished by quarterly assessments on the parishes of which it is composed. The amount to be levied is regulated by an average of the general expenditure for the three preceding years. Warrants are issued to the treasurer, who receives from each parish the amount of its contribution. Any difference between the amount levied and that which has been disbursed for each parish is merged in the funds of the incorporation.

The original Act for this incorporation was passed 4th Geo. III., and subsequently amended. The contribution to the funds was regulated by a standard taken from an average of the expense of the poor within each parish for the seven years previous to the incorporation. The altered circumstances of many of the parishes caused this mode of levying the contribution to press very unequally. Soon after this grievance began to be felt, another and more formidable arose,—which was, applications for relief to men out of employment, which first came to be demanded in 1815, within the two last quarters of which year a sum of 1376l. 14s. 9d. was disbursed in this way. The total expenditure, under the same head, within the succeeding year, amounted to 2704l. 5s. 5d., which so alarmed the directors and guardians, that a committee was appointed to investigate the whole state of affairs. This committee presented a report in 1817, which reprobated the discontinuance of certain allowances which the labourers had formerly enjoyed,—exhorted the individual parishes to devise means of employment within themselves,—and recommended that a new Act should be applied for to remedy the evils arising from the inequality of the assessments. On this report resolutions were adopted, but it was recommended that no application should be made to Parliament for a new Act till it was seen whether any general measure would result from the labours of the Committee of the House of Commons on the Poor Laws, which was then sitting. Having waited in vain, a new Act was obtained in 1820, which settled the system of assessment as it now exists ; and in 1824 the incorporation gave up the charge of relief to the unemployed, as it was found impossible to exercise an efficient controul over it.

As the rate now raised in each parish is not confined to the support of the funds of the incorporation, but is partly diverted to the relief of the able-bodied, some parishes avail themselves of the opening this gives, to withdraw a portion of the support given to the impotent from the controul of the incorporation ; and by thus diminishing the sum paid for them by the committee, they lessen the charge on them for the general expense of the establishment, which is regulated by the amount of the disbursements for each parish. This petty fraud is one of the chief difficulties with which the corporation has to contend.

The appointment of assistant overseers seems to be essential to the efficiency of this mode of managing the poor, as the overseers of those parishes which have none, overlooking the general benefits which the incorporation confers, consider their journeys to the hundred house as an intolerable grievance, which is not attended with any corresponding advantage. Most of the parishes have assistant overseers, and the business which they have to transact with the committee enlarges their intelligence, by bringing them into frequent contact with men of superior education and understanding, and gives an *esprit de corps* to the body, by making them acquainted with each other.

It would appear, by comparing the expenditure on the poor in this hundred with that of those immediately adjoining, which are not incorporated, that the mode of management which it has adopted tends materially to lighten its amount:—

	Population, 1831.	Assessed to Property Tax in 1815.	Expenditure on Poor 1829.	
Blything Hundred	. 23,829	£.87,405	£.13,449	10s.
Hoxne	. . 16,399	80,255	20,568	10
Plomesgate	. . 11,385	42,053	10,253	14

The managers of the incorporation being composed of an equal number of land-owners and land-occupiers, the probability, and, I believe, the fact is, that they do come to a more just conclusion on the matters brought before them, than when the decision is left entirely to the prejudices and partialities of a parish vestry. All applications for relief being referred to the incorporation, any pauper who has cause of complaint appears before the committee, where he and the overseer are heard, and the case determined. The magistrates are thus, to a great extent, relieved from the interminable appeals that are made to them for relief from unincorporated parishes, and the chief questions brought before them, connected with the poor-laws, are those of settlement.

It is to be lamented that no effectual means have been discovered to bring the relief to the unemployed under the controul of a mixed body, such as the court of directors and guardians of this hundred ; but it has been felt by experience that a sufficient jurisdiction cannot be established over this branch of expenditure, as it is found that the occupiers of individual parishes do not exert themselves to find means of employment within themselves, when there is a common fund to which application can be made for this purpose. Throughout this hundred, which seems to be admirably managed in every other respect, each parish deals with its unemployed poor according to its own notions of management, and allowances without work,—nominal work on the roads,—allowances to large families,—roundsmen, and other expedients are resorted to.

This incorporation gives general satisfaction to those who are within it. There are discontented persons, but their objections are limited to individual part of the expenditure, such as the salaries of the chaplain and visiting guardian, and the journeys which the overseers are obliged to make to the house.

My Lords and Gentlemen, ·

According to the directions of your Secretary, I have selected the following parishes from among those which I had occasion to examine. ·

The facts connected with them serve to show the degree in which pauperism may depend upon the administration of the law, and the evils that follow from the exercise of that power by ill-qualified persons.

I have the honour to be,
My Lords and Gentlemen,
Your obedient servant,
Charles Pelham Villiers.

*To His Majesty's Commissioners for
Inquiring into the Practical Ope-
ration of the Poor-Laws.*
December 24th, 1832.

WARWICKSHIRE.

RUGBY.

In 1814 pauperism was fast increasing in this parish. Able-bodied paupers in the employment of individuals were relieved in money; allowances were made according to the number of their children, and the rounds-men system was practised. In this year, land was purchased and allotments were offered to the labourers at a full rent, which were accepted by many, who, in consequence, became less dependant on the parish. Orders, however, were frequently made by the magistrates upon the overseer, and the practice of giving relief in aid of wages continued. The rates in 1817 were rapidly increasing. In 1819 an incorporated workhouse was established under the provisions of Gilbert's act, with a visitor and guardian. The parish resolved that, subject to the discretion of the visitor and guardian, all relief on account of children should be given in the house, either by taking in the children, or, in case of any interference by the magistrates, by ordering the whole family to be placed there, and that all women with bastard children, applying to the parish, should be relieved only in the house, and be made to work if able

—the money ordered upon the fathers, if recovered, being applied to the support of the child.

In 1821, certain charities, bequeathed to the parish of Rugby, were appropriated for the purpose of an annual distribution of prizes to the labourers who maintained their families with the greatest credit. By these means the number of applications to the parish have been diminished, the rounds-men system entirely abolished, and the interference of the magistrates stopped.

The influence of this system upon the rates will be shown by the following returns:—

		£.	s.	d.
1816	. . . . .	431	13	0
1817	. . . . .	754	11	0
1818	. . . . .	1069	1	0
1819	. . . . .	1290	13	0
1820 (Workhouse was established)		874	2	0
1821	. . . . .	892	19	0
1822	. . . . .	810	12	0
1823	. . . . .	665	12	0
1824	. . . . .	583	10	0
1825	. . . . .	484	10	0
1826 } Outstanding law-bill paid off		546	4	0
1827 }		603	18	0
1828	. . . . .	379	10	0
1829	. . . . .	402	10	0
1832	. . . . .	843	8	11

The number of bastards in the book for five years is eleven. The dislike to enter the workhouse, and the hope of improving their condition, have altered the character of the labourers; they are now observed to be industrious, contented, and well conducted.

Annual value, 5275*l.*—Number of acres, 1526.

Population 1811 . . . 1805
1831 2501

STRATFORD-UPON-AVON.

Prior to the year 1821 the rates in this borough had been increasing. The five immediately preceding years were as follows:—

				£.	s.	d.
Year ending at Lady Day, 1816			. .	1031	0	0
,, ,, ,, 1817			. . .	1393	0	0
,, ,, ,, 1818			. .	1499	0	0
,, ,, ,, 1819			. . .	1682	0	0
,, ,, ,, 1820			.	1829	2	8

In this year a select vestry was established, and a paid over-seer appointed. The vestry elected a permanent chairman; a governor and matron were appointed to the workhouse, and, in cases of orders made by the magistrates in opposition to the judg-ment of the vestry, relief was only given in the house. The meetings of the vestry have been weekly, and the attendance of the members and chairman peculiarly regular. The result of their vigilance will be seen by the following statement:—

POOR RATES.

				£.	s.	d.
Year ending at Lady Day,	1821	.	. .	1647	3	7
,,	,,	,,	1822	. .	1420	17	9
,,	,,	,,	1823	. . .	1155	17	1
,,	,,	,,	1824	. . .	1043	8	2
,,	,,	,,	1825	. . .	1026	14	6
,,			1826	. .	1035	11	6
,,	,,	,,	1827	. . .	1000	7	10
,,	,,		1828	. .	1046	4	0
,,	,,	,,	1829	. . .	911	19	2

An increase of the rates observed in the returns for the years 1830 and 1831, was attributed by the chairman to unusual sick-ness and distress, occasioned by a typhus fever.

There has not been any charge of cruelty or oppression against the select vestry or the overseer. In this borough, a paid officer of police was appointed in the year 1820, whose services are found extremely useful. The labourers bore a good character: there were riots in the neighbourhood, but not a man from this borough was suspected.

Population, 3488.

This borough is the only place in the division not subject to the jurisdiction of the county magistrates, and the only one where it is said the rate-payers are not dissatisfied.

As illustrative of the mode in which the poor-law is admi-nistered in this division, a case was mentioned of a magistrate reproaching an overseer, the father of the witness, for his folly in not relieving a worthless fellow who had summoned him, as, from the nature of i his character, he might fire his stacks! As illustrating the opinion which prevails of the mode of dispensing relief in this division, my attention was requested to an applica-tion being then made to an overseer of one parish. The ap-plicant, a strong, able man, aged thirty, who had walked from Birmingham in the morning, stated the times to be so hard that he could not live—he wanted some assistance from the parish. On being asked as to his intentions if this was granted, he ex-pressed his desire to become a " green-grocer." On being further

questioned as to his views if it was refused, he stated the necessity
he should be under of coming entirely upon the parish, and
bringing his mother with him. The accommodation was refused,
on the ground of its having been discovered, two days only before,
that his mother, who had been receiving 7*s.* a week for the whole
year from the parish, had an elder son, who had a good house, a
coal wharf, and several men in his employ at Birmingham.

WORCESTERSHIRE.

OLD SWINFORD.

This parish is managed by a select vestry. The governor of
the workhouse receives a salary and is required to pay the poor.
The attendance of the vestry is extremely irregular. The accounts
were in great confusion, the workhouse was in a filthy state, and
little order or discipline maintained. There had been a case of
affiliation by one of the inmates on the day upon which the
house was inspected.

A debt of 700*l.* was then due from putative fathers; sixty-seven
bastards were on the books; one woman had borne seven, and
had received pay for each. The parish itself was in debt to the
amount of 500*l.*, the residue of a debt of 1100*l.*

The rates are not collected from between two and three hundred cottages, which belong to the manufacturers, who stop the
rent out of the wages of their men who occupy them.

A gentleman in this neighbourhood had lent the overseer, who
had not the means of paying the poor, between three and four
hundred pounds, to prevent his distraining upon these cottages,
as the occupiers would then have thrown themselves entirely upon
the parish. Rents are also occasionally paid, to prevent this.

It has been the practice here to relieve men with families, without inquiring into the amount of their earnings, and not to refuse
relief unless they were shown to exceed 25*s.* a week. The
people are chiefly engaged in the manufacture of nails. A large
family is considered to be a source of profit. Women object to
marry till they are pregnant. If the trade is good, there is employment for women and children; if bad, they are supported by
the parish. The trade not having of late been good, a man had
deserted his family, consisting of a wife and nine children; the
place of his resort was known, but it was considered better eco-

M

nomy not to bring him home and punish him, as the parish would, in either case, have to support the family.

The character of a large portion of these people is notorious in the neighbourhood, and it appeared that no person, either vestryman or county magistrate, would venture to take an active part in the control of the parish.

The annual expenditure for the poor in the parish, from what could be collected from the books, and from other evidence, must amount to, if not exceed, 2000*l.*

The condition of the people is said to be deteriorating.

Annual value of the property in 1815 . . £5514
Population in 1801, 3766; in 1831, 6490.

KIDDERMINSTER.

THE mode in which the affairs of this populous parish are administered will best appear by the following extracts from a report drawn up and published by a committee, appointed by a vestry, to inquire into the management of the poor, and the expenditure of the money raised for their relief, dated 6th April, 1832:—

" The committee attended at the pay-table at the poor-house several successive weeks, and the result of their observation was a discovery of various instances of imposition:—first, pensioners receiving 3*s.* 6*d.* a week, to whom the overseer had thought it right to refuse relief, subsequently received, by virtue of an order of magistrates, 2*s.* 6*d.* a week from the parish, making, with their pensions, 6*s.* a week, whilst to paupers in like circumstances as to age, health, and number of family, the total amount of weekly relief was only 3*s.* 6*d.*; secondly, instances occurred of relief intended for a family having been given to the head of it: one, two, and, in one case, three members of *that* family applied for relief themselves, at different times of the same day, and obtained it; thirdly, persons representing themselves as having no employment, when on inquiry they had full employment at that time.

" The committee next directed their attention to the books and accounts. The year fixed upon was from that ending Lady-day, 1830, to that ending Lady-day, 1831. It appeared that the whole property rated for the relief of the poor, consisted of 2826 houses, *whilst* 525 *only paid rates;* the remaining 2301, which ought to have produced a sum not less than 2383*l.*, had in fact paid nothing; that thereby one-third of the value of the property rateable is exempted, to the manifest injury of those persons upon whom a grievous burden is made to fall; and further, upon careful comparison of the assessment upon different productive properties, it appears that such properties are unequally assessed.

" The committee next examined into the management of the poor-house, and were here struck with an allowance made to paupers in the house of twenty-five per cent. upon their earnings, thereby, with their food and clothing, placing them in a better situation than the independent poor; moreover, the earnings of paupers were not regularly accounted for. That land, which had been purchased some years since by the parish, contiguous to the house, had been cultivated by the plough and the expense of team hire, instead of the spade, notwithstanding the difficulty of finding employment for paupers; that private advantage had been derived by the governess of the workhouse by keeping fowls and making carpets; that a practice, which appeared of long standing, prevailed, of paupers disposing of portions of their food, in order to spend the money at the ale-house; that the expense per head in the house was 3s. 1d., not including the produce of the land, and after deducting their earnings and various items sold; that the weekly relief to paupers in the parish was 3128l. 13s. 9d.; that upon questioning the governess as to the admission of paupers in the house, her answer was, ' that if the circumstances of the in-door paupers were examined closely, the result would be that at least forty would be turned out;' that the paupers were not kept in regular employment.

" That a practice had obtained of labourers being engaged at half or even one-third of the usual rate of wages, upon an understanding with their employers that the difference would be made up to them from the parochial funds.

" With a view to prevent some of such practices in future, the committee beg to recommend that the magistrates be respectfully requested to take into consideration the propriety of not ordering such relief to pensioners as shall place them in a better situation than paupers in equal necessity; that overseers be requested to deliver relief to the heads only of families; thirdly, that the manufacturers be earnestly requested to inform themselves as to the necessities of their workmen. But, without the slightest reflection upon any individual, the committee beg to state, that without an extensive superintendence beyond what any overseer can give, practices of injurious tendency will take place, and needless expenditure be incurred ; and should the great proportion already stated, of the property of the borough, which is at present wholly unproductive, continue so, *the committee are decidedly of opinion that many of those who have hitherto paid rates will be compelled to leave the town, or become paupers themselves.*

" For the above reasons, the committee earnestly recommend the appointment of a select vestry, under the 59th Geo. III. The committee have reason to doubt the necessity for a standing overseer.

" The committee have taken into consideration the propriety of making a new assessment, and an application to parliament to regulate the affairs of the poor, but as this would cause much delay and expense, they think it best not to advise either until the select vestry shall have been tried."

Previously to this inquiry, the parish had been managed by an assistant overseer, with a salary, subject to the jurisdiction of the borough magistrates. One of these authorities was a linen-draper, having considerable property in small houses ; the other a manufacturer of bombasin and carpet, having many workmen in his employment.

The workhouse is capable of holding 300 persons; about 135 are inmates at present, apparently subject to little restraint, and without any classification : one woman, living in the house with her husband, was observed far advanced in pregnancy, and had borne other children there.

A select vestry has since been appointed. The overseer, who is an upholsterer, stated the disbursements, since his appointment, have amounted to 100*l.* a week out-pay, exclusive of the house and other expenses, and the whole annual expenditure would nearly reach 10,000*l.*

Value in 1815 . . £13,960.

Population 1801 . . . 6110
    ,,   1811 . . . 8038
    ,,   1831 . . . 14,981

The population is chiefly employed in weaving carpets, and they have heretofore earned high wages; the increase of their numbers and their general improvidence have occasioned a great fall in wages, and much distress.

BENGEWORTH, SAINT PETER, EVESHAM.

In the year 1815 the parish adopted the provisions of the 22d Geo. III. Three guardians and a visitor were appointed, and also a governor to the workhouse. The overseers only collected the rates. No relief was given without the sanction of a guardian.

One of the guardians, elected in 1815, was continued in office for fifteen years. This gentleman united in himself the several offices of magistrate, guardian of the poor, surveyor of roads, assessor of taxes, and was besides a medical man. He resided in the parish, and was constant in his attendance at the meetings. He became acquainted with the circumstances and character of the poor. His various offices enabled him to detect as well as to punish frauds whenever they occurred, and thereby prevented many from being attempted. He was re-elected guardian each year, and was uninterrupted by his colleagues in the execution of his duties.

The following reduction in the rates is said to have resulted from his management :—

Amount of Rates, for the		£.	*s.*	*d.*
Year ending Lady-day, 1812 .	.	547	5	7½
„ „ 1813	.	649	19	1
1814 .	.	797	19	8
1815	.	703	6	8
„ „ 1816 .	.	508	2	2
„ „ 1817	.	456	0	0
Gradual reduction until the year 1824, when it was 1824 .	.	340	0	0
A variation in amounts until the year 1830, when it was 1830	.	304	1	7

In the year 1800 the amount of the rate was 351*l.* 6*s.* 10*d.*

Population, 1801 . . 672 | Population, 1831 . . 965.

The utmost number of inmates in the workhouse has been eighteen, the least twelve. They have been fed, clothed, washed for, physicked, and kept warm for six hundred and fourteen weeks, at 2*s.* 5¼*d.* a head per week.

GLOUCESTERSHIRE.

STOW-ON-THE-WOLD.

This parish has no land attached to it. The poor are managed by the overseers, annually elected, and the accounts are said to be inspected at an open vestry.

Able-bodied labourers apply here to the overseer for employment, who is unable to provide any. They are then sent round to the householders to employ them, at the wages they choose to give, and if insufficient, the difference is made up out of the rates. Others are paid 2*s.* 6*d.* or 3*s.* a week, no work being required of them. Others obtain work in the neighbouring parishes, and

apply to the overseer for relief, who has no means of ascertaining their earnings. Single men only are refused. People
recently married are sometimes relieved, and also upon the birth
of their first child. An instance was mentioned of a man who
had lately lost all his children, saying publicly, that it was a sad
thing for him, as he had lost his parish pay, and that, had all
his children lived, he should have been well to do.

The establishment of a workhouse, desired by some of the inhabitants, is successfully opposed by some of the tradespeople,
who let houses for the use of the poor.

Riots and destruction of property were carried to great lengths
in this neighbourhood. Some of the magistrates raised their scale
of relief upon this occasion, and went round themselves to the
farmers, to insist upon their giving higher wages, and making
larger allowances to men with families.

The influence of the magistrates' interference on the conduct
of the paupers is much complained of. The following returns
show the prospects of the parish :—

Amount of Rates for the	£.	s.	d.
Year ending Lady-day, 1826 . .	366	13	0
,, ,, 1827 .	417	19	0
,, ,, 1828 . .	418	14	0
,, ,, 1829 .	472	9	0

The only return received from the parish officer was for the
year ending Lady-day, 1832, which was 500*l*.

Annual value of the property in 1815, 687*l*.
Population, 1240.

DEVONSHIRE.

HARTLAND.

Population . . . 2193, chiefly agricultural.
Annual value of property in 1815, 9091*l*.

THIS parish is managed by twenty-four persons, who style themselves the " Elders :" they are self-elected. They take the office of
overseer in turn, and appoint some of their own body to keep the
accounts, which are allowed annually by the magistrates They
meet once in the beginning of the month, and dine at the parish
expense, asking friends to dine with them. Some time after
dinner, the paupers who cannot get work are brought in one by
one, are put up to auction, and the elders bid according to the

value they fix upon them, the difference with what is necessary for their subsistence being made up from the rates.

The soil is poor in this parish, and some land is gone out of cultivation. The chief employment for the surplus population is on the roads; the magistrates order the paupers to be paid at the same rate as other labourers : they do not seek for work out of the parish.

The rates here are levied by the "elders," and the inequality of the assessment is much complained of. One property, worth 20,000*l.*, is said to be exempted altogether, which is ascribed to the influence of the proprietor with the "elders ;" while their own properties are also unfairly rated. Those who complain are afraid of appealing against the rate, on account of the expense, and of making enemies in the parish. Some of the small farmers have lately emigrated, and settled in Upper Canada.

NORTH MOLTON.

THIS is the largest parish in the northern division of Devon, comprising an extent of 19,000 acres, principally pasture land. The population in 1831, 1937, chiefly agricultural.

It is managed by the overseers annually chosen, and by one with a small salary.

The ticket system, allowances for children, and relief of different kinds to men in the employment of individuals, have long obtained here.

In the commencement of this winter the farmers sent back all the men who had been billeted upon them by the overseer, stating that they could not afford to employ them, and the overseer, upon two occasions lately, has been unable to pay the poor, in consequence of the rates not being collected.

An agreement has, however, been entered into between the parish and the farmers, at a vestry holden for that purpose, for the latter to pay the billet men 7*d.* a-head, and to take one for every 8*l.* of rent; the rest of their wages to be made up out of the rates ; and that this should be continued throughout the winter. The farmers used to pay a larger proportion of the wages.

Much of the land in this parish is notoriously neglected, and the farmers state that their rates are so heavy that they have not the means to cultivate it properly.

The assessment is made on two-thirds of the actual value, 3997*l.*

	£.	*s.*	*d.*
Rates ending Lady-day, 1828 . .	865	17	0
„ „ 1829 . .	868	14	0

The average payment for every month during the last year has been 100*l.*, making for a whole year, 1200*l.*
The population in this parish is greatly redundant. The following items appear in the monthly charge for October:—

	£.	*s.*	*d.*
To Robert Gould's wife in child-bed . .	0	5	0
Emanuel's, do. . . .	0	5	0
Catherine Nutt, extra trouble in child-bed .	0	8	6
Mary Bawdon, for delivering Ann Nutt .	0	2	6
Do. W. Bawdon's wife	0	2	6
Ann Lewis, in child-bed	0	16	0
Mary Bawdon, for delivery of Ann Lewis .	0	2	6
Ann Lewis and child	0	4	6
Ann Loosemore's necessities . . .	0	3	0
Returned Billets	0	12	10
Six heads, at 9*s.* each	2	14	0
Monthly pay to John Allen and wife, aged 50 and 49, (two children).	1	10	0
Monthly pay to Robert Blackford and wife, aged *eighty and seventy* (infirm) .	0	10	0

Eighty persons, between the ages of 20 and 50, receive regular monthly pay, chiefly for children.

Small farmers here are much disposed to emigrate. The brother of the overseer, a farmer, had lately settled in America, and was prospering. The farms in this parish are generally small; an answer in this case to the notion that large farms have occasioned pauperism.

There were considerable riots in 1830 in this division of the county.

My Lords and Gentlemen,

In some parts of the district assigned me, the radical vice of the poor-law system has not hitherto shown itself in practical operation. In others, its existence is but indistinctly traceable. In all, its growth and development as yet bear no comparison with the height which it has reached in the southern counties. By radical vice, I wish to be understood to mean the maintenance of the able-bodied out of local, often inadequate, funds, whether or not administered on a regular allowance-system*. Comparative exemption from this evil in the northern counties has been imputed by some as a merit to their inhabitants. They ascribe it to good management. I ascribe it to good fortune. In the northern division of Northumberland, comparative thinness of population, attributable in some degree to the *hinding system* of hiring labourers—in the district of the Tyne and Wear, employment given by collieries, &c.—in South Durham, indeed throughout the county, recent public works have deferred the evil day of pauper maintenance. Let any one of these causes cease to act in its present extent (and the last of them at least is of a manifestly precarious nature). What ensues?—The process of the southern counties—a process hitherto escaped in many places by mere accident—a process actually commenced in the southern part of this favoured region.

I proceed to offer a few instances illustrative of these remarks.

I have the honour to be,

My Lords and Gentlemen,

Your most obedient servant,

Temple, January 28th, 1833.   JOHN WILSON.

DURHAM.

DARLINGTON.

Darlington is the first place in which I have happened to find subsisting the provisions of the 22d Geo. III. c. 83, and in which the affairs of the township are administered by a visitor and

---

* The township of Winlaton, near Newcastle, affords a striking instance of the intolerable burthens often thrown on narrow localities by casualties impossible to provide against. The failure of the iron-works of Crowley, Millington, and Co. in 1815, raised the rates in that township at once to 16s. in the pound on the rack-rent, while the adjacent townships remained at 2s. or 3s. It also, in a manner, compelled the adoption of the allowance-system, which Winlaton township has never since been able to throw off.

guardians, according to that act. It is the first place also in which I have found the allowance-system avowedly and regularly established.

Allowances to able-bodied labourers in this township are graduated according to the numbers ih their families; and whenever the wages of any class of labourers (for example of the linen-weavers, who have latterly been the most distressed) fall below the amount appointed by this scale, the difference is made up, as a matter of course, by the parish. The scale awards 2s. a head a week to heads of families, and 1s. 6d. for each of the children under twelve years of age. This is the minimum of allowance paid by the parish in all cases. A further sum is occasionally granted to *deserving objects;* and presents of sums of money are often made by the parish for special purposes. But I am now speaking only of the regular allowance. Suppose a single man to earn 2s. a week, he could put forward no claim to relief*. Suppose another, earning the same wages, but possessing besides a wife and six children. Then 2s. a head for himself and his wife, and 1s. 6d. a head for each of his children, give a total amount of 13s. weekly. In this second case *the family-man* has a recognized claim on the parish for an allowance of eleven shillings weekly, making up his earnings of two shillings by the above-mentioned graduated scale.

This, it may be said, is an extreme case. I answer, it was only selected by way of illustration. A case, however, of ordinary occurrence, is that of a labourer earning 5s. or 6s. a week in the employ of an individual or of the parish. He must content himself with these wages—*if he is a single man.* But if he has shown foresight sufficient to provide against a rainy day, by getting a wife and six small children, his income rises from *five* or *six* to *thirteen* shillings weekly, *seven* or *eight* of which are paid by the parish.

"As a principle," the parish set their faces against paying rents. But although they do not profess to pay their pauper's rents, Mr. Laidler (a guardian) told me that they often give them money to pay their rents with. (This is doubtless better than taking houses for them, and thereby giving encouragement to the most sinister speculations.) Entries often appear in the pay-books of sums of 1l. and upwards, given for purposes of the kind above-mentioned, by order of the parish committee.

* I merely mean to state that 2s. is the utmost weekly pension, or allowance, *gratuitously* given to a single able-bodied labourer. An applicant of this description, if he said that he could not live on his wages, would probably be taken into the poor-house, or set to work by the parish at, perhaps, 5s. a week. But he would not receive *for doing nothing* more than 2s. a week, while the sums which a married labourer receives for doing nothing increase with the birth of every additional child.

On the shortest interruption of work, were it only for a couple of days, the weavers, who (from the competition of linen woven at Irish wages) are the class most constantly burthensome to the parish, immediately make application to have their average, as it is termed, made up.

Some remarkable instances of this occurred on Wednesday, January 9th, at the meeting of the parish committee who, in this township, discharge much the same functions as a select vestry.

One applicant owned he had earned 21*s.* during the last fortnight; but because he had not applied within the last month to the parish, and his average during that period had not been made up, (he had four children,) he now applied to have the deficit made up, which was done accordingly.

Another man was earning 9*s.* a week. He had six children; 4*s.* were handed over the table to him immediately.

A third had seven children, with himself and his wife making nine in family. He stated that his average earnings were 9*s.* a week. Last week he had been out of work for a day or two, and consequently had only earned 5*s.* The parish had found two days' work for him, which made up his earnings to 7*s.*; 7*s.* 6*d.* additional were handed to him over the table.

I need not report a dozen similar cases which were despatched like the foregoing, in my presence. Yet do people in this district talk as glibly as any of the abuses of the poor-laws *in the south!*

The improvident and reckless spirit practically generated under this allowance-system, cannot be better exposed than in the following passage, extracted from a pamphlet addressed to the working classes, which, though anonymously printed, is ascribed to eminent practical authority in this town :—

" In further considering the subject, I am inclined to believe, that youth is far more uniformly the happiest period of life amongst you, than amongst those of greater worldly riches. The well-behaved apprentice has a light heart and many sources of enjoyment ; and if he be not so unwise as to marry immediately he is out of his time, these sources of enjoyment are greatly increased by more freedom and more money. He can probably earn as much for himself as his shopmate must *make serve* for a family of half-a-dozen persons. This cannot be denied ; and yet how rarely do we find the youth of twenty-three with ten pounds in his pocket! "

" Somehow he always contrives means to spend what he gets. It might often create one's pity to see how the hard-earned money of a young man's prime is wasted with a few drunken companions, who will hang upon him as long as he has anything, and then desert him; or his imprudence gets him into various and nameless scrapes; or he spends his money in foolish extravagances or fashionable clothing, not so serviceable by far as that of a more common description; as if, by outvying his masters in the quality and cut of his coat, he is in any degree raised above his real standing. However, the last means of expenditure is infinitely better than the others, and is some little evidence of respectability, as the arrant rake commonly rakes on till he has hardly a coat of any kind to his back."

I was informed by the same gentleman to whose pen is attributed the pamphlet, from which the foregoing passage is an extract, that eight shillings a-week would amply cover the single working man's weekly expenditure in the necessary articles of lodging, washing, and board. Nevertheless, wages of eighteen or twenty shillings and upwards disappear with uniform celerity, and leave the workman liable, on the first " turn of trade," to be thrown partly or wholly on the parish.

BARNARD CASTLE.

Barnard Castle, a town which has always been reckoned rather heavily burthened, is the second case of a fixed and avowed system of allowance. The standard of allowance, fixed and enforced during the last year by order of the magistrates, is as follows :— 2s. 6d. each for the father and mother of a family, 1s. for each of the children under twelve years of age; an aged or infirm person, incapable of earning anything, sometimes receives as much as 3s. The parish is at liberty to exact such an equivalent as it can get by putting able-bodied paupers to work; and a stone-quarry in the neighbourhood furnishes work for a certain number. But, such as it is, even this compensation is out of the question in cases where the workman is in full employ at inadequate wages. By inadequate wages, I mean wages which do not come up to the magistrate's standard. I put the case to an ex-assistant overseer, to whom I had been recommended as the most intelligent man in his station. Suppose a man has ten children, and receives 9s. a week wages, that is to say, 6s. short of the standard set up by the magistrates, would the parish be considered obliged to make up the deficiency? He replied, *it would*. I asked, whether that clause of the 43 Eliz. empowering the assessment of relations for the support of paupers was acted upon frequently. He said, that since 1827, when he first became town-clerk, till May-day last, when he quitted office, he only could remember one or two instances in which orders had been made upon relations; the leaning of the magistrates was against it. The select vestry were necessarily better judges of the character of applicants than the magistrates could be. When the vestry knew the real state of a man's affairs, they were always disposed to be " good to him." When a difference occurred between the overseers and the magistrates, the former had five miles to go to justify or explain themselves. When any remonstrance was made by them on account of the applicant's bad character, the reply of the magistrate commonly was, that the children must not suffer for it.

Sometimes a sort of contract is made between the overseers and the pauper, that the latter, in consideration of a certain advance from the parish, shall not trouble it again within a term agreed between the parties. The usual duration of this term is a quarter or twenty weeks, and as much as 3*l.* or 4*l.* is sometimes advanced in this manner. These advances are laid out perhaps in articles of pottery, in order to commence a petty trade. Sometimes the contract is broken, and in any case the pauper does not forget to come at the expiration of his term, to negotiate a new one, or obtain an allowance on some other footing.

The fruits of this system of allowance to able-bodied labourers are exhibited in a practice adopted in this place by the master-manufacturers in the carpet-weaving line, which forms a principal occupation of its inhabitants. The masters take a number of boys into their employment on the footing of apprentices, not, however, bound by any indenture. These they employ just as long as they like, with wages fourpence in the shilling lower than those of regular journeymen. While business continues pretty brisk, they keep the journeymen in work along with these boys, but whenever they get what is termed a *bad order* from their London correspondents, the journeymen are turned off immediately. They are thus thrown on the parish at every moment of stagnation. Weavers are frequently known to *get their web out* (finish their web in the loom) on Friday or Saturday, and come for relief to the parish on Monday night. " In Barnard Castle," my witness said, " this system is becoming horrible." He added that " the parish was made use of like a depôt for soldiers;" meaning, that workmen were billeted on the parish whenever they were not required on active service.

Some of the masters, who do not give into this mode of employing boys, from time to time put their men *upon stint*, that is to say, allow them to perform a certain quantity of work and no more. The carpet-weavers of this town are between three and four hundred in number, and of this number occasionally fifty or sixty are out of work. Some of these exert themselves to look out for work elsewhere, but their more usual habit is to come upon the parish. On an average, half of the whole number may be reckoned as being kept *upon stint*.

This method of putting workmen upon stint, it is said, is adopted in order, at a time of slack work, to avoid turning hands entirely out of employ, lowering the rate of wages, or glutting the market with over-production. These appear sufficient reasons; yet it does not seem the less an abuse, that the hands thus *half* dismissed from active service should have half their wages made up by parish allowance, and should thus be in some sort quartered on the public, till it shall suit their commanding officers to call out their whole effective force.

Property in Barnard Castle has been losing its value for some years, a circumstance ascribable in no small degree to the accumulated burthens of poors' rate, highway rate, church rate, tithe, &c. Land which has been taken into cultivation of late years, is likely to go out of cultivation again at present. The following is an instance of the fall in the value of property. A portion of land was left to the parish some time back, called Sanderson's Charity, for the maintenance of two poor men. It has generally been let by the parish officers for a term of three or four years. Four years ago it let for 22*l.*; last spring, no more than seventeen guineas could be got for it.

REMARKS.

After describing a state of things like that which exists in these townships, the question very naturally suggests itself—Who is to blame? For *somebody to blame* we always hope to find when we trace abuses. The answer seems at first sight quite inevitable —the magistrates and master-manufacturers. In Barnard Castle, these two classes of persons seem to divide the honour of figuring as the proximate cause of the ills of the allowance system. In Darlington, the master-manufacturers have it all to themselves, without intervention of magistrates; the provisions of the 22 Geo. III. having enabled the parish authorities to regulate their workhouse system, &c., at their own discretion.

So strong was my impression of some sinister interest lurking at the bottom of this system of allowance, that while on the spot I spoke of it in no very measured terms, as a system which could benefit only the master-manufacturers. The first suggestion which rather shook my preconceived opinion, was made to me by Mr. Mewburn of Darlington, who pointed out that in a town divided by religious sects, partialities would be shown, or at least would be sure to be suspected, in the distribution of parish relief to each denomination of applicants, were it not for the establishment of an invariable standard, notorious and applicable to all. So much in excuse of the fixed and graduated scale of allowance.

In the second place, I beg to direct attention to the opinion stated in one of the returns made to the central board by Mr. Walters (of Darlington), whose sentiments deserve every attention, as those of an intelligent and most respectable tradesman, many years employed in parish offices, and now in no shape interested in any sort of abuse.

In replying to Queries 21 and 22, in the second set of queries for rural districts, which run as follows:—

21. " Can you state the particulars of any attempt which has been made in your neighbourhood to discontinue the system (after it has once prevailed) of giving to able-bodied labourers, in the employ of individuals, parish allowance on their own account, or on that of their families ?"

22. " What do you think would be the effects, immediate and ultimate, of an enactment forbidding such allowance, and thus throwing wholly on parish employment all those whose earnings could not fully support themselves and their families ?"

Mr. Walters affirms, that " An enactment forbidding such allowance, under present circumstances, would operate to the injury of the parish ; and were relief withheld when the trade is, as at present, depressed, *many women and children would be deserted, by the husband leaving them to go in search of work.*"

Here is an instance of apprehended abandonment of children (apprehended be it remembered by excellent practical authority), encouraged, it may fairly be assumed (in the words of my instructions), " *by the father's reliance on their being maintained in his absence by the parish.*"*

Mr. Walters's short statement seems to me to make it abundantly obvious, that so long as the radical vice of the system, *parochial* maintenance of families, shall *legally* continue to exist, its natural offspring, the allowance system, *illegal* though it may be, will in some cases present the milder alternative, in a choice of evils. Take the case of any manufacturing town, like Darling-

---

* A gross instance of children being deserted by the father, in well-grounded reliance of their support by the parish in his absence, met my eye in the vestry minutes of Gateshead :—

" Joseph Mitchell has left his family to seek work. His wife and five children are on the parish. Ordered five shillings a-week."

This man, as the vestry clerk informed me, was an able workman, but so indifferent in his character that he never could long retain employment. His desertions of his family, it seems, recur periodically. His wife is supposed to have an understanding with him on that subject, and always to part amicably on such occasions.

ton. Let a manufacture, linen or woollen, have flourished long
enough to collect around it a whole population of operatives, who
with their families contrive to acquire settlements. A disastrous
" turn of trade" takes place, disabling the employer from affording
any longer to his workmen the rate of wages requisite to decent
subsistence. What is to be done? Common sense, in a sound
state of society, would dictate—If the concern is a losing one,
close it—if you have too many hands, turn some of them off. But
it is not lawful, under the present system, to follow the advice of
common sense. What is to be done then? The recipients of
short wages present themselves as applicants for parish relief.
General principle recommends that they *throw themselves wholly
on parish employment.* But it is not *possible*, under the present
system, to comply with the demands of general principle. The
idea of abandoning even a losing manufacture, which employs its
hundreds or thousands of hands, would strike the rate-payers with
horror. The whole support of the workmen, or if the workmen
absconded, of their families, thrown on a populous and already
burthened township, would be absolute ruin. It seems better to
the rate-payers that the manufacture should go on, though at
some loss to the parish, and probably with little profit to any one
concerned in it, and that, by means of the allowance system, applicants for relief should continue at least to contribute to their
own support by their usual labours, than that, through the abolition of that system (be it illegal or no, I do not stop at present to
inquire), the whole weight of their maintenance should be thrown
upon the parish, compensated only by such proceeds as are commonly netted from parish labour!

NORTON.

The following is an extract made from the returns of John Cartwright, Esq., from the extensive agricultural parish of Norton
near Stockton :—

" For some few years past this parish and the surrounding
neighbourhood have been peculiarly circumstanced,—large public
works have been proceeding, and the best of the labourers have
been employed on them. As the work is usually by contract, the
spirit and industry of such men have improved. Otherwise alteration, for the worse, I think, would have been perceived."

Mr. Cartwright made the following *vivâ voce* remarks on the
same subject:—

" During the last few years, public works (railways, &c.), have
employed all our best labourers, and the inferior hands, who at
other times would have difficulty in finding employment, and

would be reduced to go round the parish as house-row labourers, are now the only labourers left for common agricultural work."

Three years ago a considerable number of labourers were thrown on the parish, and sent round with the overseers' tickets as house-row labourers. Mr. Cartwright said that he paid those who were sent to him the current wages, and did all he could to discourage the practice of making up wages by parish allowances. He added, that in presiding at petty sessions, he always refused to pass parish accounts which bore on their face such items of expenditure. But on afterwards inquiring of an old inhabitant of the parish, for many years a member of the select vestry, I found that at the period referred to, the vestry, in agreeing on the value to be placed on each individual's labour, and on the proportion of hands to be allotted to each occupier, had also established a regular scale of allowances to be paid by the parish in proportion to the numbers in a family.

Mr. Cartwright made a remark which seems to corroborate the view which regards the allowance-system as a symptom, rather than source, of the evil. It was this,—that the practice of making up short wages from the poor's-rate, which he checks as illegal whenever it comes before him in a direct manner, may easily be carried on indirectly, without any positive breach of law. For example, if a pauper is ostensibly thrown on parish employment, there is nothing to prevent the overseer from setting him to work under a third party, the said party paying the man's wages *to the overseer,* and the overseer making up whatever amount above those wages may be necessary for the labourer's subsistence.

As an example of the difficulties and hardships attending removals, Mr. Cartwright stated the following case:—" A family of four or five children becomes chargeable to the parish by the father falling sick. Having taken the sick man's examination, I make out an order of removal, and suspend it till he is able for the journey. Now, if his parish happens to be Stranton, a place at nine miles distance, and I remove him thither, he would find there, at this very moment, the farmers paying 8*d.* and 9*d.* a day for the work of an able-bodied labourer, and making up whatever further sum might be required for his subsistence from the parish rates. A labourer removed under such circumstances will probably return again to Norton, as I (said Mr. Cartwright) have no means of putting an end to his contract with his landlord here. He sickens again, and becomes thus again chargeable. The law says, ' *Send him to the House of Correction ;*' but in the meantime what is to become of his family ?"

" There is a case," continued Mr. Cartwright, " in this parish, of a woman, the mother of two bastard children—children

N

namely begotten during the lifetime of her husband, but under
circumstances occasioning the sessions to decide, on an appeal,
that they should be bastardised. The husband died. The woman
was again found with child. Her two already existing children
were within the age of nurture. The mother and children could
not be sent to the House of Correction together; nor could the
mother be separated forcibly from the children. This woman
persisted in keeping herself concealed in a neighbouring village,
intending to come, at the last extremity, clandestinely, and lie in
at her old lodgings in this parish. I got her sent to her parish
at last. The overseer there gave her a guinea to induce her to
go away again, and look for shelter elsewhere, that the birth of
the child might not bring a burthen on the parish. The woman
induced a wandering vagrant here to say he would marry her.
Banns were published, and lodgings taken. The fellow was believed to have two or three wives living already. The marriage
was prevented, or the child would have been born here in spite
of all that could have been done to prevent it."

LONG NEWTON.

In Long Newton, a small agricultural township, containing between three and four hundred inhabitants, the house-row mode
of employing labour is practised, and the wages are habitually
made up from the rates. I regret my inability to give any particulars regarding this parish at present, as on the day on which
I visited it, the acting overseer, in whose custody were the parish
accounts, was unfortunately out of the way. Notwithstanding its
small population, and the charitable efforts of the rector, Mr.
Faber, this parish gives more trouble to the justice-bench at Stockton, with pauper applications, &c., than many of much greater
extent. I asked Mr. Faber how it happened that the recently
opened sources of employment on the railways, &c., did not draw
off the surplus labour. He ascribed it to the want of spirit and
enterprise in the people, who would rather hang on the parish at
home than seek for subsistence elsewhere.

HURWORTH.

This township suffers from its vicinity to Darlington, and from
part of its population being of the same depressed description—
weavers. Here also peeped out more of the spirit of the south
than I have happened to meet with in other parts of this district.
Threats of an incendiary kind have been held out against obnoxious individuals; and Mr. Raine, an acting magistrate, in-

formed me that in one instance in which he had summoned two youths for a slight trespass, some of his young trees were cut down and strewn before his windows, by way of earnest of what he had to expect in proceeding further. Mr. Raine very properly visited the offence for which the lads were summoned with the severest penalty of which the case would admit. A similar spirit was displayed on the dismissal of the assistant overseer : the farmers, who chiefly compose the select vestry, grudging, with an ill-judged economy, the payment of the salary of that officer. His dismissal was so pleasing to the rabble of the township, that they broke into the church and rang a merry peal on the joyful occasion.

The parish accounts are kept in such a slovenly and confused manner, that nothing was to be learned from a cursory view, which was all I could give them. I could not even ascertain distinctly from the overseer what was the number of houses rented parochially for paupers, which, Mr. Raine informed me, was one of the great abuses in the management of the parish, which is destitute of a workhouse. Certain persons have speculated in purchasing houses to let to the parish, or paupers who have their rents paid by the parish, a practice which not only raises the rents of lodgings on the working class, but inevitably opens the door to jobs of the grossest description. Mr. Raine has promised to supply the commissioners with the results of his local experience on these and other subjects *.

Extracts from the Vestry Minutes.

L—— ordered to be employed whenever work can be got for him, and at other times that he receive 6*d.* a day, and that he be decently and sufficiently clothed.

H. J. has a wife and family; lives at Yarm; had 3*s.* a week former winters; allow the same when he cannot get work as a fisher ; pay his rent *as usual.*

Dixon, one of the overseers, mentioned to me the case of a young man, seventeen or eighteen years of age, who is wholly dependent on the parish. When farm-work can be found for him, he has his food for sole wages. Two young men have been sent for a calendar month to the House of Correction for refusing to go to work upon the roads : 6*d.* a day is the wage allowed for that description of work; 1*s.* a day is generally given to old men. The house-row mode of labour is habitually practised ; and a

---

* Since the above statements were written, the promised returns have been made from Hurworth, and generally go to confirm the facts which I have mentioned—in particular the speculations in houses by tradesmen and others.

gentleman with whom I conversed has sometimes had men employed on his grounds receiving 1s. a day from him, and perhaps
another from the parish.   At the time, he said, he considered
himself relieving the parish by this proceeding, but should not
repeat it, now being convinced of its illegality.

To the greater part of the matter of the foregoing pages, I have
been favoured with the following instructive, and in some degree
encouraging contrast, in the shape of a letter from Mr. Little of
Stanhope, a populous and extensive parish in the lead-mining
district of Durham.   In the returns already received by the
commission from that gentleman, occur the following remarkable
expressions :—

" It may seem harsh to say that I fear great harm is done to
the labourer by the public contributions from the rich.   The free
school, the lying-in hospital, the soup-kitchen, the distribution of
grain, &c., in times of scarcity, and many other similar institutions, all tend to make the labourer look to others, and feel no
anxiety to save for such emergencies.   These public charities
create the necessity they relieve, but they *do not relieve* all the necessity they *create.*"

He adds, with a true dignity of character which almost guaran-
tees soundness of judgment :—" I have for twenty-five years had
the management of several hundreds of labourers, and during that
period have attentively observed their habits, *for which observation
I had the peculiar advantage of having been one myself till I was
twenty years of age.*"

It is chiefly to Mr. Little, who is an agent of the Lead Company, that are owing the exemplary parochial reforms introduced,
within the last ten years, in the parish of Stanhope.   The following letter was written in reply to my request for further details on
several points which had come under discussion in conversation
between myself and the writer :—

                                          Stanhope, 28th Jan. 1833.

My Dear Sir,
          Yours of the 25th came to hand yesterday, and I hasten
to meet your wishes in the best manner I am able.

The resolutions of the Select Vestry, having reference to the
relief of able-bodied labourers, are as follows :—

" 6th *April*, 1830.—No relief shall be given in aid of wages ;
but whenever a person shall have constant employment, he shall
maintain himself and his family upon his wages, whatever they
may be.   When however sickness, old age, or other infirmity
shall render him unable to perform *full work*, a small assistance

may be given as casual relief; and also where his wages are proved to be *very low*, and some extraordinary sickness prevails in his family.

" No relief shall be given to pay any rent or debt, nor (except in case of sickness) so long as the person asking it shall have any property, cattle, or furniture, beyond what is absolutely necessary in a poor man's house.

" The letting of the workhouse shall be so managed, as to ensure that *full* and *constant* work be provided for all its inmates, and that they be compelled to work."

You will perceive, that upon the management of the workhouse must depend our power of acting on the other resolutions.

It is let at 1*s*. 10*d*. per person per week, with a salary to the master of 10*s*. per week, and he has *all* the earnings of the paupers. With this stimulant, he takes care to have at all times plenty of work—quarrying, draining, breaking stones for roads, &c. &c., and any pauper refusing to work as much as he is able is sent to the tread-mill as idle and disorderly.

An indolent labourer (and they are always the first in want) comes with his family, on the vestry refusing him relief, and instead of finding himself relieved from labour, is compelled to work harder than before, and he soon applies to the vestry for a few shillings to go and seek work; and on obtaining it, by the parish aiding in the removal of his family, they get rid of him altogether; and the lesson is not lost upon others, who would have come in like manner had he seemed comfortable.

I will mention a case which has occurred since you were here. A young man, named Lowes, (who never liked hard work, as I well know, having once employed him,) with his wife and two children, had gone to work at the collieries, and after a short trial was removed from hence to Middleton (Teesdale) on the plea of ill-health. He was kept by that township for several weeks doing nothing, though no one could perceive that he ailed anything, when they discovered that he belonged to this parish, and removed him accordingly to us. The fellow instantly went back to his former employment at the collieries, and we have heard no more of his illness. Query, who were his best friends—those who would have kept him a pauper for life, or those who compelled him to exert his powers and support himself and family?

The opinion I so strongly expressed to you upon the propriety of throwing the able-bodied labourer upon his own resources has been formed by observation of a great number of similar cases.

From the accounts shown to you it would be apparent, that we do not neglect the means of supporting our present paupers cheaply. But this is with us a secondary object,—the prime one being to prevent others from becoming so. Pauperism we consider nearly as infectious as small-pox, and without constant vigilance it would soon overspread the whole parish.

I state fearlessly that even our north-country labourers do not, as a whole, perform more than *three-fifths* of the work they might, without detriment to their health. And the great object should be to encourage them to exert their *full powers.* This cannot be done directly by the legislature, but it should boldly sweep away everything having an opposite tendency. All payments for doing nothing—all interference with the application of wages—everything calculated to make them depend upon any person but their immediate employer; and on the other hand by facilities for inclosing commons, making rail-roads, and other public works, endeavour to increase the sources of beneficial employment.

I assume it as certain that no man will work *hard* without the *hope* of thereby bettering his circumstances, and also that without such *hope* there is no hold upon the labouring classes. I may in proof refer to the apparently anomalous circumstance, that the Irish labourer, without poor laws, and the labourer of the south of England, under a lax administration of them, seem to be nearly in the same moral condition, which I ascribe to the want of the *all-moving stimulus of hope.* They are so situated that neither can look to improve their condition by any exertion or good conduct of their own, and becoming reckless and degraded in feeling, they give a loose to their appetites and passions without thinking of consequences. Hence indolence, habits of dissipation, improvident marriage, turbulence and crime—everything in short which leads to misery and pauperism.

The greatest boon the Commissioners can bestow upon this and the adjoining lead-mining parishes, is to recommend that a residence of *five* or *seven* years (the person not being a pauper) should supersede all the present modes of obtaining settlements.

At present, in these parishes, the labourers remaining are mostly employed on rather better wages, and the poors' rate is not increasing ; but I fear that the demand for men at the collieries in the eastern part of this county has ceased, and that many of our labourers will be returned upon us in the spring. What is then to be done, I cannot understand. In the mines they cannot be employed, and the land is unable to maintain them in idleness.

I see thousands of acres around me totally barren, which might be converted into excellent pasture, and the land now in culture is capable of being made twice as productive. But the difficulty is to get the superfluous labour applied to such improvements.

With the spirit of industry and independence which so generally
pervades our workmen, I will not, however, despair. It is a
much harder task to create such spirit where it has unhappily
been extinguished.

I am, my dear Sir, truly yours,

JOSEPH LITTLE.

MY LORDS AND GENTLEMEN,

In compliance with your request, that a selection should
be made of a few parishes most strikingly exhibiting circumstances connected with the administration of the poor-laws,
within the districts which we have jointly examined, we beg to
notice the following:—Leicestershire, Hinckley and Loughbo-
rough ; Derbyshire, St. Werburgh, in the town of Derby, and
Shardlow.

In making this selection it is intended to illustrate, by the parishes taken from the Leicestershire report, the effect of the worst
administration of the poor-laws in full operation.

By that of St. Werburgh, in Derby, a parish is intended to be
shown " that has been bad and is improved," or the counterac-
tions produced by better principles and management.

By the comparative statement of a few points of the parish of
Chesterfield with the same points in that of St. Werburgh, it is
proposed to mark the different results where only ordinary care is
opposed to the ever-springing evil.

Having no striking instance to adduce of an *improved* parish
relapsing in any marked degree, we would only beg to observe
that the occasional fluctuations in many have appeared to us to
be in exact proportion to the relaxation of the antagonist muscle,
or as the principle of non-admission of any right of dependence
whatever on other than individual exertion, is adhered to or de-
parted from.

The parish of Shardlow is given, as instancing the power of
supporting a better principle through the means of an effective
workhouse system.

We are, my Lords and Gentlemen,

Your very obedient, very humble servants,

HENRY PILKINGTON,
REDMOND PILKINGTON.

Kensington, Jan. 10, 1833.

LEICESTERSHIRE AND DERBYSHIRE.

HINCKLEY, LEICESTERSHIRE.

Population.

1801.	1811.	1821.	1831.
5070.	6058.	5835.	6468.

Manufacturing and agricultural.

Size . . . 3500 acres | Population . . . 6491.

		£.	s.	d.
Poor's rates 1829	. . .	3009	4	0
„ 1830-31 .	.	4107	4	5
„ 1831-82 .	. .	4127	0	0

From the accounts exhibited by the overseers, it appears, that the rates amount to nearly 15*s.* a head, on the whole population ; that they increased 1000*l.* on a comparison of the year 1829 with that ending 25th March, 1830; and that they continue to increase annually.

The following cases, taken without selection, will point out the weight of the poor-rate in this parish :—

Mr. Preston, on 155 acres, paid	.	.	£.165	5	0
Mr. Bonner	60	„	.	.	.	60	0	0
Mr. Sanson	70	„	.	.	.	108	15	0
Mr. Cheekland	36	„	.	.	.	42	7	6
Mark Blakeman	100	„	.	.	.	60	0	0

This evidence was obtained from the small proprietors and farmers, who sought us, desirous of pointing out the present state of the parish, and expressed it to be their opinion that the poor's rates were likely to continue to increase. In addition to the poor's rates, there are county, highway, and composition rates,— the three last making together a serious addition. Likewise tithes, which the proprietors and farmers said " hinder us making the best use we can of the small capital which remains to us."

There are from twelve to fifteen tenpenny rates made in the year for the poor—seldom less than thirteen—and about two for the church and county rates. The land is generally valued at about one-half the rack rent, in some instances at two-thirds, and in some near the town at about one-third. The houses generally at one-third.

In 1829 there were 1160 occupied houses in Hinckley, and

90 empty ones ; since that time the number has increased. Of these only 406 paid rates ; and consequently there were 763 which did not pay, they, however, in consequence of the local act, are now charged; these houses belong to both landowners and tradesmen, but the greater part to tradesmen.

The proprietors and non-proprietors in this parish are changing places, the proprietors doing little more than holding their land for the benefit of others, as the poor's rates, in many instances, consume three-fourths of the rent of the lands. On the general distress of the agricultural part of the country very many farmers, among whom were all those above-mentioned, stated that there could be but one opinion. Their capital had been long declining, and total ruin must ensue, not only to farmers but to landlords themselves, unless government should take their case into consideration, and that speedily, and make an alteration in the poor laws.

The wages of the manufacturing people were necessarily so low that from the most laborious exertions they could hardly procure a subsistence ; between 6*s.* and 7*s.* being the extreme weekly earnings of an industrious man; and he must work 14 hours a day to get that sum : Mr. May, a master manufacturer, stated that he had known the time when a stockinger could earn 1*l.* per week ; they had only one sort of manufacture—the " plain frame."

Mr. May gave us the following scale of the possible earnings of a manufacturer and his family—

	s.	*d.*
Man, if industrious and steady, working from 14 to 16 hours a day	6	6
Woman sometimes as much as a man ; but then she must be a very good hand ; and either have no children or household affairs to attend to, or entirely neglect them.		
Children, 8 years of age, per week	6*d.* to	9*d.*
„ 11 „	1	0
„ 14 „	2	6

The above wages are calculated as clear earnings, independent of the outgoings—as rent of frame, winding, &c.

We found that the following might be something near a statistical account of the population of the parish of Hinckley :—

Population	6491	Males	3109
		Females	3359

MALES.

Labourers employed in agriculture .	97
Agricultural labourers not employed .	21
Occupiers of land employing labourers . .	32
Males employed in manufacture . .	692
„ „ retail trade . . .	367
Labourers in trade	120
Other males differently employed . .	116
Wholesale merchants and capitalists, and profes-	
sional persons	57
Male children of all ages and manufacturers out	
of employ	1607
	3109

Of this population there were 420 able-bodied persons receiving relief, 360 were regular and 60 casual. A short time since 1000 persons were receiving relief.

The payment of rents for the paupers amounts to 10*l.* a-week—520*l.* a-year.

The relief for bastards has amounted of late to 150*l.* a-year. The amount recovered from the putative fathers does little more than meet the expense attendant upon the recovery. The common allowance is 1*s.* 6*d.* a-week.

The relief given in the workhouse is confined to the aged, infirm, and children: the inmates at present amount to 85.

Aged and infirm men	. .	35
„ „ women	.	20
Boys ⎱ of ages from	.	19
Girls ⎰ infancy to eleven years	.	11

The expense of maintaining in the house is 2*s.* 6*d.* per head for food alone. There is but little work given to the inmates of the poor-house. The manufacture of hosiery had been tried, but had been almost entirely abandoned owing to the loss which had accrued to the parish. The overseers themselves were manufacturers of hosiery, and may have disliked the competition with their private interests, which arose from the goods made in the workhouse entering the same market with their own.

Hinckley suffers severely by the settlement laws, in consequence of the number of boys who, when trade is brisk, come in from the neighbouring villages to be hired as apprentices. Many of the adjacent villages are thus getting rid of their own surplus population, and are not paying more, some not so much, as 2*s.* 6*d.* in the pound.

The parish accounts are very irregularly kept, and it was very difficult to obtain them. The overseers keep the accounts in private books, and frequently omit to tranfer them to the parish books.

There is an assistant-overseer. A select vestry of 21 members, also churchwardens and overseers. Two overseers are elected annually. They do not act at the same time, but for separate portions of the year ; and as the office is never held more than one year by the same individual, the overseers generally leave office even before they become acquainted with the business. The overseer collects the rates, and the assistant-overseer distributes the allowance to the out-poor, and visits them at their houses to ascertain their wants.

Of the magistrates great complaint was made ; by injudicious conduct towards idle imposing paupers, they have greatly increased both the amount of pauperism, and the feeling in the paupers of their right to aid from the parish funds. The magistrates very seldom know the paupers, and yet on application for relief, they are in the habit of sending them with a recommendatory letter to the vestry. Experience has shewn that it is very dangerous to resist these recommendatory letters. Mr. Atkins, a hosier and overseer, refused to comply with the recommendatory letter of a magistrate, the mob assembled and threatened to pull down his house if the order was not obeyed.

In case of any tumultuous rising, the town would be entirely at the mercy of the mob ; there is no resident magistrate, there are only two constables, and they are not at all qualified to be of any service ; the five headboroughs would not act during any danger ; the only reliance in case of any real tumult, therefore, would be on such military as might happen to be quartered in the neighbourhood.

When we asked some of the rate payers, whether they had any knowledge of the causes of the incendiary fires which had taken place in the neighbourhood, they made very little reply : indeed, they seemed to shun the question. One of them said, " It would not be over safe to have all we have talked about to-day mentioned in open air." We observed at several other places a similar disinclination to speak on this subject.

It was generally stated by all with whom we conversed, that " they could expect no relief but from an alteration, not only in the laws relating to the poor, but in the mode and spirit in which those laws are to be administered ; and that if one or more magistrates with a salary were appointed by Government, with a good and effectual police under them, who should have the entire superintendence of the poor laws, such a measure would be of the greatest benefit, and do more to repress the daily increasing spirit of pauperism, than all their own combined efforts put together, situated as they were between two fires,—the magistrates on one side and the poor on the other."

LOUGHBOROUGH.

MR. MOTT, one of the overseers of this parish, told us that he considered pauperism to be increasing. He said, poor infirm people often get relief who have children of their own able to take care of them. Relief is continually given to able-bodied men without their being set to work; and the knowledge which the paupers have that the magistrates will order them relief, makes hundreds apply who otherwise would make a shift to provide for themselves. Mr. Cartwright, another overseer, said, a workman has very little incentive to work, because, by going to the magistrates, he can do much better for himself, as they will order him from the parish much more than he can make by his earnings. The magistrates, Mr. Cartwright observed, continually grant relief after it has been judged right by the overseers to refuse it. He further remarked, " The only shield which the overseers have against the magistrates, is threatening to take the pauper into the house." The magistrates are not particular about character, as in the instance stated to us of William Orford, who having been flogged in the market-place for theft, upon applying for relief, stating that he was only earning 4s. 2d. per week, had been refused by the overseers ; this man upon applying to the magistrates received an order to the overseers to make up the difference to him between 4s. 2d. and 6s. 6d. Mr. Cartwright also stated, that they have now an obstinate reprobate on the parish of the name of Charles Chester, who a short time back was in possession of three cows and 60l. in money, which had been left to him. He soon spent all, and has now come upon the parish for relief, and sets them all at defiance : he has even, as he himself declares, " to spite the parish," by increasing their burthens, married a woman from another parish.

Mr. Mott said, " In case of a bad character applying, we do as well as we can with him : we generally threaten to take him into the parish-house, or the man and the magistrates together would beat the parish." " Was it not for fear of the magistrates," he added, " we should much oftener refuse relief than we do : some rascals quite beat us. A fellow of the name of Lockwood married a very worthy woman of this parish. He has five children by her, whom with his wife he refuses to maintain. We have sent him to Leicester gaol for the last three months, but he still refuses ;" solely from the reliance he has that by the aid of magisterial interference he shall beat the overseers.

The magistrates' scale of allowance is,

	s.	d.
For a man	3	0
—— woman	2	2
—— children under eight . .	1	4
—— children eight and under fifteen .	1	9½
—— children fifteen and above . .	2	0

Bastardy cases, Mr. Cresswell stated, were very numerous—they had sixty-two on the list at present. Magistrates order 1s. 6d. They have several aggravated cases. Three sisters of the name of Dalby, all with child by one man, and he a married man, were passed from another parish, in which they resided, to this, which was their settlement: all had 1s. 6d. allowed to them by the magistrates. Two of the sisters again with child by the same man: these two have been sent to the house of correction. Mary White has had eight bastards by six different men: now married, and receives 1s. 6d. for her last child: for former children has received for two at a time. Total expense of bastards for the last year, as follows:—

	£.	s.	d.
1st quarter	56	6	2
2d quarter	54	3	0
3d quarter	62	9	4
4th quarter	53	8	10
	226	7	4
Recovered from fathers .	152	0	0
	74	7	4

To this loss should be added the expenses of recovering from runaway fathers, which is always considerable.

ST. WERBURGH, DERBY.

A judicious alteration in the management of this parish, seems alone to have counteracted the evil tendency, or natural operation of the existing laws and usages. Its history is this. From the year 1821 to 1826, the average assessment was 3500l. per annum; from 1826 to 1831 the average has been 1800l.

The population in 1821 was 5317; in 1831 it had increased to 6341 ; thus exhibiting decreasing rates with an increasing population.

In was in 1826 that Mr. Mozley was appointed overseer. He found it under the management, or rather mismanagement of a general vestry, the chief evils of which were in operation, namely, the defencelessness of overseers on appeals to the borough magistrates.   The indifference or inattention of all to the concerns of the parish, the whole management being committed to the overseers for the time· being ; the influence or representation of any, or every, respectable tradesman causing numbers to be placed on the poor-book, each providing in this way, without apparent expense to himself, for some favourite or dependent.   Under these circumstances, the above gentleman was induced to exert himself in order to procure its being placed under Mr. Sturges Bourne's Select Vestry Act ; which after much difficulty he effected, being opposed alike by the borough magistrates and the poor themselves ---the former jealous of the control being thus taken in some measure out of their hands, and the latter disliking the interfering of a select vestry with their appeals to the magistrates.

He found a long list of pensioners in various parts of the kingdom, to whom, through the overseers of the different parishes in which they resided, very considerable sums were annually paid, and many of whom, as may be supposed, were very improper characters to receive it.   He wrote immediately to all the overseers to inform them, that after a certain time no further payments would be allowed on their account, but that if any paupers in those several places could not subsist without parish relief, they must come and seek it in the workhouse of their own parish— " nine-tenths of these he never heard of again."   He appointed a new governor and matron of the workhouse, also an intelligent assistant overseer, choosing a stranger to the town, with consequently neither friends to serve, nor acquaintance to favour. This person, Mr. Moody, was also soon after appointed overseer of the roads, having thereby not only a better opportunity of giving employment, but being a judge of the quantity of work to be expected from ordinary labour, the plea of inability to perform such quantity, as, paid by the piece, would procure to the labourer the magistrate's allowance, was not available : if such quantity were not done he paid them accordingly, and if appeal were made to the magistrates, he ordered the complainant into the workhouse.

On examining the workhouse, and seeing its incomplete condition, and inconvenient arrangement for the proper accomplishment of the purposes required ; and knowing at the same time the advantage to which it had been instrumental, we could not but be struck with the superior importance of the principle which guides the management than the perfection of the means.   The relief of the impotent, and the repression of pauperism was the double object to be attained ; the different effect therefore of the same circumstances on the *proper* and the *improper* inmates of a workhouse were deemed most important to be kept in view.

The order, regularity, cleanliness, and confinement (for none were allowed to go out without an order) which are indifferent to the one, are insupportably irksome to the other; such regulations therefore were minutely framed, and rigidly exacted; and it was found accordingly that what in fact contributed to the well-being and comfort of the former, the latter were quickly induced to fly from; and such it was remarked seldom returned; and although stating, before they entered, their inability to find work, were soon after quitting the workhouse observed to be employed—in the latter case it was presumed they sought for employment, in the former not.

The parish allowance of diet was alone permitted; and no presents of tea, sugar, or tobacco suffered to be made.

Relief out of the house was considered objectionable in principle, and resisted as much as possible, and only given on strict investigation. On relief being ordered by the magistrates, the whole family were in preference sometimes taken into the workhouse, the moral effect being deemed of more importance than the increased expenditure. A, getting relief at his home, B inevitably demands it; but A, going into the workhouse, deters B from the application : it is the difference of using either end of the magnet. An instance was adduced by Mr. Mozley of an order, on appeal, for 3s. 6d. per week being made by the magistrates—the family were ordered into the house, and on their refusal no allowance was made: the magistrates surprised at such conduct, inquired if such sum were considered too large. Mr. Mozley's answer was, "he found no fault with the sum, but the principle." The silk-throwster, in whose employ the family had been, and who was displeased at the conduct pursued, confessed soon after, that the family were doing very well without parish pay; indeed, that they were more comfortable and respectable than before: their dependence was gone—except upon themselves.

All relief to able-bodied men in the employment of others was refused : the overseer, employed them wholly or not at all, paying by the piece. The workhouse children even were not allowed to be employed at the mills, but at the same wages as the more respectable poor (those not claiming relief) would accept for their children : the effect of a contrary practice was thus instanced. A poor person, not on the parish, offered her child to work—"At what wages?" inquired the employer; " 2s. per week ;" " 2s. ! ! why I give but 1s. 6d. to that girl both older and bigger"—the older girl was a pauper. The consequence of the withdrawal of pauper children from the mills was thus stated by Mr. Mozley : " for every 5s. thus lost by the parish treble the sum was gained by sustaining the wages of the respectable poor, and preventing their requiring parish relief also."

No houses were exempted from rates—the landlords being charged in respect of houses of 6*l.* per annum and under, and who generally, therefore, compounded, paying half the assessment up to 4*l.* and two-thirds from 4*l.* to 6*l.*; on these terms the houses were paid for whether occupied or empty.

The accounts are now kept correctly in a simple and intelligible form—they are passed half-yearly at a general meeting of the parish, and printed and distributed annually, together with the names of paupers, both regular and casual, stating the relief paid to each—the names likewise were given of those within the workhouse. The mothers' names of bastard children were in like manner stated, and those of the fathers who were in arrears with the parish.

As illustrating the effects of different management, we beg to place a few points of the above parish in juxtaposition with the same points in another parish, in which reversed results might have been expected.

Township of the Borough of Chesterfield.	*St. Werburgh's Parish in the Borough of Derby.*
Population, 1831, 5700.	Population, 1831, 6349.
Total assessments in the years 1831 and 1832, 2645*l.*	Average of five years' assessment, 1800*l.*
Resolved not to act under *Sturges Bourne's* Act.	*Adopted Sturges Bourne's* Act.
Relief given to able-bodied without work.	*No relief* given to able-bodied without work.
No employment for able-bodied men.	Employment found for the able-bodied, who are paid by the piece.
A commodious workhouse.	Inconvenient workhouse.
Paupers only employed in sweeping the streets and running errands.	Paupers not allowed to go out but by special order.
Poor in the workhouse October, 1832, 30.	Poor in the workhouse, October, 1832, 42.
Out poor, October, 1832, 149.	Out poor, October, 1832, 88.
Rates not collected in the year ending Lady-day, 1832, 113*l.* 9*s.*	No houses exempted from rates. Landlords charged for houses of 6*l.* and under.

SHARDLOW.

THE following account of the parish of Shardlow we beg to offer, as illustrating the effect of workhouse management administered by houses of industry under Gilbert's Act.

It is taken principally from the examination of Mr. Dowles, the governor of the House of Industry, and also from a correspondence with which we were favoured by one of the visiters of the house.

The origin of the house in question was thus stated by the governor :—

" The relief ordered by the magistrates being according to a certain scale, the paupers used to set the parish at defiance. It was a case of this kind that first set on foot the establishment in 1812. A man of the name of Roberts, of Shardlow, with seven children, had *one pound* per week ordered by the magistrates, against the sense and representation of the parish. Finding themselves without remedy, the parishioners, assisted by a gentleman of the name of Flack, took advantage of the act 22 Geo. III. (Gilbert's Act), and associating with four other parishes, built this House of Industry, whereby, if they cannot make a bargain with the pauper, to accept such relief as they think right beneath the magistrate's allowance, they avoid the necessary compliance therewith, on the appeal of the pauper, by offering to receive him into the house, and providing work for him therein."

An instance of the effect of such offer occurred a short time ago :—A woman, Mary Savage, complained that she was ill, and totally unable to do anything for herself; she accordingly kept her daughter at home, as she said, to nurse her, and demanded 6*s.* a week of the parish, on account of the unavoidable loss of such sum, being the weekly earnings of the daughter. The parish refused ; the magistrates ordered it on her appeal ; the offer of the house was then made ; this was declined however— and the following morning the mother was washing at her door, and the daughter was gone out again to work.

Previous to the establishment of this house, the average rates of the parish of Shardlow were 570*l.*—since that period they have been reduced full one-third. In the year ending 1832 they were 344*l.* 2*s.*

The population in 1811 were *seven hundred and fifty*—in 1831, *one thousand and ninety-one.*

Forty-two parishes have since joined the association.

Spondon, the last (1830) associated, saved 292*l.* 10*v.* 6*d.*, the price of their admission, in the first year, being one-half of their previous assessment.

Sutton Bonnington joined in 1816; its rates were then 690*l.*; they have since fluctuated between that sum and 400*l.*, giving an average annual reduction of 150*l.*

The comparison of this parish with the neighbouring one of Kegworth, in Leicestershire, *not* incorporated, is thus made in a letter addressed by the governor of the house to the overseers of the parish of Matlock:—" They are similar, or nearly so, in extent, population, and employment, both agricultural and manufacturing; while the rates of the former have decreased, those of the latter parish, which, prior to the date above-mentioned (1816) were less than those of Sutton, have been progressively increasing, and at this present time are nearly double the amount."

Though intended as a house of industry, the old, and those unable to work, are admitted upon sufferance, the rooms not being otherwise engaged; and such indeed, at the time of our visit, formed one-half of the occupants. The number of inmates at that time were ninety—accommodation can be afforded for one hundred and fifty.

The employments provided are manufacturing hemp, grinding corn, framework stockings, making list shoes, whip-cord, winding cotton, list carpeting, running lace, seaming and sewing, working in the house and kitchen. Work twelve hours, including meals.

By the governor's returns it appears that the able-bodied, last year, earned their subsistence, within a fraction.

The sexes are kept apart—except that husbands and wives are allowed to sleep together when rooms are at liberty. None are allowed to go out without express permission of the governor.

The food is good and abundant; expense 2*s.* 6*d.* per head per week.

We close this account with an extract from a letter with which we were favoured from one of the visitors :—

" I will take the liberty of observing, that from the experience I have had since I was appointed visitor, the good effects of our system is shewn in the general moral improvement in the habits of the poor connected with us. They know that if wasteful and improvident of their means they will in the end be driven into the house : they dislike it as being separated from their connexions, as a place of restraint, and where after all they must work as much as if they did so of their own accord at their own homes."

STAFFORDSHIRE.

My Lords and Gentlemen,

In compliance with your request I transmit a very short account of two parishes in my district, which appear to me the most remarkable.

In Wolverhampton the increase of the poor's-rate in ten years appears to have been nearly one hundred per cent.; and yet it is in my opinion difficult to find fault with the management, or to attribute the increase to any cause within the power of individuals to mitigate.

In Tamworth, too, the increase is great; but there I did not find the same care as in Wolverhampton in keeping the parish accounts; nor has it the advantage, like Wolverhampton, of the superintendence of a select vestry, and intelligent overseers.

So far then, these cases are different; but after all, I am compelled to say, that the difference between the best and the worst management is of comparatively slight moment. The evil, which is admitted on all hands to be great and growing, must be met, not by local palliatives, but some general and vigorous improvement of the whole system throughout England.

No one can quarrel with the principle of so much of the 43d of Elizabeth—" *relieving the lame, impotent, old, blind.*"

Assist this good law by a simple and general law of settlement, which will at once put an end to perjury and litigation, with its enormous expenses, and take care that the administrative part of the system be committed to a more judicious selection of overseers, chosen from a more intelligent and better-educated class, and freed from the control of the justices of peace. I would make the overseer a superior officer, and unite other duties with those which at present devolve upon him—the superintendence of the high roads in each district for instance, or the regulation of the police. And if ever it shall be deemed advisable to proceed with a bill once laid on the table of the House of Commons by the present Lord Chancellor, for " affording to the people of this realm the means of having their suits tried as speedily and as near to their own homes as may be for the avoidance of expense, vexation, and delay," I do not see why such an officer as is here recommended may not be found capable of fulfilling part at least of the duties of this local court.

I subjoin the cases to which I have already alluded, giving it as my opinion, that almost all the abuses arise from the want of a proper law of settlement, and from intrusting the administrative part of the system to the hands of the ignorant and the needy, freed too as they are from all real responsibility,—the control of the magistrates being in general, when not mischievous, wholly inefficient.

> I am, my Lords and Gentlemen,
>> Your very obedient servant,

Lincoln's Inn, Old Square,   D. C. MOYLAN.
> Jan. 11.
_____

The parish of Wolverhampton is divided for the maintenance and support of the poor into the several townships of Wolverhampton, Willenhall, Bilston, and Wednesfield. Of these, the principal is Wolverhampton, which contains 24,732 inhabitants; value of real property as assessed in 1815, was 33,000*l.* Since 1824, when the poor's-rate amounted to 3637*l.* it has gradually increased to the sum of 7573*l.*, the amount *expended* by the overseers for relief of the poor in the year ending 25th of March, 1832. In the current year it is also on the increase. The overseers estimate the probable amount up to next Lady-day at 8000*l.*, besides 100*l.* granted out of these funds to the Board of Health.

With every advantage calculated to keep in check the portentous evil, it is extending itself here. With a select vestry, regularly and efficiently attended, with a workhouse well conducted, and on the most economical terms consistent with the well-being of the inmates; with overseers, all men of high character and active habits, and amongst them one of the principal iron-masters of the town, whose habits of business, joined with a willing devotion of his time to the concerns of his public office, fit him to detect any error in the management of the poor; with two intelligent salaried assistant-overseers; with a perfect system of keeping the parish books,—the evils of pauperism and poor's-rate are increasing in Wolverhampton to an alarming extent !

Tuesday in every week is pay-day for the out-poor, and at half-past six in the morning I found the overseers at their work. It occupied them until near two o'clock. Upwards of 300 persons received relief. Tickets are given to paupers, and the amount paid at the workhouse every Tuesday to *the bearer.* Although in particular cases this may be unavoidable, it appears to me as a general custom liable to much objection. Indeed, I found afterwards on inquiry, that it enables the pauper often to anticipate his allowance, and raise money upon the ticket. In many cases it is lodged with the immediate landlord (where there is sub-letting), as security for the tenant's rent.

The overseers, in answer to my inquiry as to their giving relief by way of loan, stated that, often when they feel a disposition to do so, they are restrained by this consideration. It appears that persons to whom they had on former occasions extended relief in this shape, exposed themselves, in their endeavours to turn it to account, to the penalties awarded by the Hawker's and Pedlar's Act (50 Geo. III. c. 41.) They even assured me, that they (the overseers) had actually, in more than one instance, to pay out of the parish funds the penalty thus incurred by paupers who had been relieved by way of loan.

It may not be improper here to notice what appears to me a defect in the sec. of the 59 Geo. III. which authorizes relief by way of loan. I cannot imagine the reason for limiting the power of overseers in extending relief in this shape to such persons only as are most unworthy of it. Why exclude from this benefit the poor man, who, by unavoidable misfortune, and not his own fault, has become an object of charity? The words of the act are,— " Whenever it shall appear to the overseers, to whom application is made for relief for any poor person, that he might, but for his *extravagance, neglect,* or *wilful misconduct,* have been able to maintain himself, &c., it shall be lawful for the overseers, &c., to advance money, weekly or otherwise, to the persons so applying, by way of loan only, and to take his receipt for and engagement to pay every sum so advanced," &c.—sec. 29.

The power of relieving by way of loan is, therefore, in most parishes, a dead letter. The overseer generally has discernment enough to appreciate the security which the law directs him to require for his advances, viz.—the simple receipt of this man of " *wilful misconduct.*"

Amongst those whom I had an opportunity of consulting in Wolverhampton, there is I think a general feeling in favour of throwing the rate upon the landlords in the case of tenements under 6*l.*, and I had pointed out to me an illustration of the impolicy of the law in limiting the power of vestries to houses of 6*l.* rent. An immense number of small houses occupied by poor labourers are let at the rate of 5*l.* 19*s.* 11¾*d.*

On another point I found the same coincidence of opinion. I mean the effects of the New Beer Bill on the working classes. It is not, perhaps, in a large town like Wolverhampton that these effects are most appalling. They are, in their worst form, found no doubt in small towns and villages, where this pernicious Bill (11 Geo. IV. and 1 Will. IV. c. 64.) has caused unspeakable misery and pauperism. In Wolverhampton, too, it has multiplied the allurements which always before led those classes, least able to resist temptation, to squander their savings in such a way; and surely no arguments of financial expediency should weigh against these results!

In the adjoining township of Bilston, forming part of the parish of Wolverhampton, there is a select-vestry and assistant-overseer, who is also governor of the workhouse. The annual value of this township in 1815, was 15,634*l.*

The population in 1821, was 12,000
And in   1831   14,500

The amount of poor's-rate in 1829, was £1554
          „   in 1830   2145
          „   in 1831   2532
And in the year ending 25th last March 2914

A very considerable increase is likely to take place this year, owing, no doubt, in some measure, to the fearful pestilence with which this town has been lately visited.

TAMWORTH.

The parish of Tamworth, which, for other purposes, comprises several surrounding townships and hamlets, is confined with regard to the support of the poor to the town, exclusive even of the Castle Liberty.

It contains a population (in 1831) of 3537 persons. The population in 1821, was 3574.

Shewing a falling off in the number of inhabitants of 37 persons.

In the same period the poor's-rate has increased:
    In 1821 it was under   .   .   £1000.
    In 1829 .   .   .   .   .   1200.

It had increased in the year ending the 25th March, 1832, to 1600*l.*

And it is expected to exhibit this year a still further increase.

The gradual increase in the amount of poor's-rate during the last few years in Tamworth may, perhaps, be thus accounted for. It appears to have been formerly the practice for the great manufacturers of this neighbourhoood to take apprentices for seven years, securing them thereby a settlement in the parish. When the period of apprenticeship expired, these were replaced by more youthful hands, who in their turn made room for others, and thus multitudes of children from London and other places were brought and settled in Tamworth. These individuals are now constantly returning from Nottingham and Lancashire to Tamworth as their place of legal settlement, and it is likely for some years longer to be subject to this burden.

Besides, the numbers who are now employed in the neigh-

bouring manufactories of Bonchill, Fazeley, &c., all have their
lodgings in Tamworth.

The unfairness of conferring *settlement by residence* is here
seen. Can there be any mode so unobjectionable as by *birth*?

The surrounding hamlets are not taxed in the same proportion
as Tamworth. The labourers and artisans who give the benefit
of their daily labour to those hamlets, lodge in Tamworth; and in
sickness become chargeable there.

The only workhouse in the district is at Tamworth. The surrounding hamlets contribute to the support of one in the distant
parish of Roselston.

The master of the workhouse is also assistant-overseer and
vestry-clerk; and to the duties of these offices, he adds those of
police constable for the borough.

Up to the present year, it had been the practice to afford
relief in aid of wages, but it is now, as I was informed, discontinued; though from what I could collect of the feeling of the
overseers, it is by no means unlikely to be resumed before the
winter passes. The overseers appear to have no better reason
for its discontinuance than that no case has yet occurred for its
exercise.

Nothing, I think, strikes one more than the unfitness of the
men who (particularly in small places) fill the responsible office
of overseer. From the temporary nature of the appointment,
it would, indeed, be difficult for them to acquire a sufficient
knowledge of their duties; to say nothing of the unreasonable-
ness of expecting from men engaged in their own concerns,
such a devotion of their time, without remuneration, as would
qualify them for the discharge of those duties. It necessarily
follows, that the assistant-overseer is often left in the exclusive
management of the poor, and almost unlimited control of the
parish funds.

There being no select-vestry, the parishioners of Tamworth
appear to give themselves little trouble in examining or auditing
the accounts. In answer to my inquiries upon this point, I was
assured in general terms, that *they had always given satisfaction,—that he who runs may read,*—and though the accounts are
not published, *they are always accessible to such as may require to
see them.*

The workhouse is an excellent and commodious one, in a dry
and healthy situation, large enough to accommodate the aged
and impotent paupers of the entire parish, if the various townships were consolidated

At present there are only 27 inmates :—

> 4 Males from 48 to 70 years of age.
> 9 Females　　28 to 70　　,,
> 6 Girls　　　1 to 15　　,,
> 8 Boys　　　4 to 10　　,,

They have separate sleeping apartments. I found it impossible to learn the expense per head. There appears to be no separate entry in the books, for each pauper, to show the date of his admission or departure. Indeed the mode of keeping the accounts generally requires revision, and shows the want of some efficient superintending authority.

There were formerly several Benefit Societies and Silk Clubs at Tamworth. By bad management, and in some cases dishonesty, the funds were dissipated, and the institutions dissolved. Time must elapse, and the tales of distress related to me be forgotten, before anything like confidence in such societies can be restored. One upon Mr. Becher's excellent plan was established here lately, and liberally encouraged by the neighbouring gentry. Yet it does not prosper. Only 14 became subscribers at its foundation in February last, 6 in March, 3 in April, 5 in May, 1 in June, 1 in July, 2 in August, and none since.

But there is a stronger and more deplorable cause for this apathy in the working classes. The English peasant no longer looks on parish relief as a degradation : such a feeling is extinct, and there is no more terrible effect of the poor-law system than a general change like this in the national spirit.

It does not appear that this parish has of late years spent much in litigation arising out of the poor-laws. But the hardship is felt of being obliged, in case of an appeal, to send officers and witnesses to Stafford, or to Warwick, 29 miles off. This often induces officers to submit to an order which they believe to be illegal.

The question of reform in the composition and jurisdiction of inferior courts here, of course suggests itself; but I shall reserve for my general report the remarks I have to offer upon this subject. It is one that can never be lost sight of in framing an amendment of the poor-law system.

LONDON AND BERKSHIRE.

My Lords and Gentlemen,

In the course of my inquiries into the practical operation of the poor-laws in the Metropolis, some points occurred which induced me to avail myself of an opportunity of visiting one of the agricultural counties, for the purpose of investigating different modes of administration and their effects, in the agricultural parishes and in those of less populous towns, and of comparing them with similar operations in some of the larger parishes in London. The cases of parishes which I have selected, in obedience to your request, I believe to be instances of the common operation of the poor-laws in the districts which I have visited. I visited other parishes on the reputation that they were under peculiar management. Mr. Milman and Mr. Winkworth had sent in answers to your queries; but I went to the parishes to which the evidence chiefly refers, and took the examinations of the other witnesses without selection or previous information with relation to them: excepting that, at Windsor, a magistrate of that town, to whom I had applied in the first instance, referred me to the assistant-overseer, as the person the best qualified to give me information; but stated, that he thought I should find nothing of peculiar importance in the parochial management. The gentlemen to whom I first applied at Reading were not aware that any one parish within the district was deserving of attention more than another, if at all; and I went to the workhouses on the chance of obtaining information. I consider the testimony of the two first witnesses (Mr. Hodges and Mr. Winkworth) to be exemplificative of the usual management of the out-door poor. The testimony of the governors of the workhouses at Reading exhibits the state in which I most frequently found the in-door paupers of the smaller town parishes; though I have not met with a more striking instance of the profusion, ignorance, or wanton levity with which the parochial business is conducted, than was apparent at St. Lawrence parish. Where the allowance to the paupers in the workhouse was less, as in most of the agricultural parishes, the condition of the independent labourers, as compared with the general condition of the paupers, appeared to be much the same.

I have not attempted to arrange the selection in any geographical order; as the evidence given by several of the witnesses examined in the metropolis, related to other districts where they had also become conversant with the administration of the poor-laws; and as I have added proofs and illustrations obtained from disconnected sources. Although the selection I have

made consists chiefly of fragments, serving to show the character
of the mass of evidence collected, it is much longer than I
desired to make it, but I trust that it will not appear dispropor-
tionate to the importance of the districts visited, when it is considered that the metropolis comprehends one-eleventh part of the
population, and pays nearly one-seventh of the total amount of
rates raised for the relief of the poor in Great Britain.

I have the honour to be,

My Lords and Gentlemen,

Your very obedient and very humble Servant,

EDWIN CHADWICK.

London, Jan. 24th, 1833.

---

*Evidence of Mr. Charles Hodges, Assistant-Overseer to the
Parish of Windsor.*

" The parochial affairs of this town are managed by a committee
of twelve inhabitants, and by the parish officers. As the assistant-
overseer, I receive a salary of 100*l*. When a poor person applies
for permanent relief, I inquire into the circumstances of the case,
and report to the committee. Casualties are relieved by ' the
overseer in pay.' There are four overseers, and they each take
it in turn, for three months, to pay all the parochial demands.
Casual relief is seldom given without consulting me. Every
shilling or sixpence of casual relief spent is now entered into a
book, and the account is examined and passed weekly. I think
it requisite, as a security, that all accounts, consisting of numerous items for small sums, should be examined at short periods.
This practice has been adopted with us about two years, and has
been productive of considerable saving. This saving has been
accomplished partly by looking after the accounts, and partly by
looking closely after the objects relieved. The practice of making
short settlements, and rendering the accounts of each item to the
board, is very serviceable to the latter object, inasmuch as gentlemen at the board frequently contribute useful information on the
inspection of these items. If the accounts were for long periods,
and the items very numerous, they would not be so frequently
examined. In summer quarters the average casual relief may be
about 7*l*. weekly ; in winter it may be double that amount."

" We have no labour to give our paupers but work on the roads.
They work from six o'clock in the morning in summer until five
in the afternoon, and in the winter from seven until four. To
single men a shilling a day is given. To married men with two
children we give 1*s*. 6*d*. a day ; to men with larger families

we give 2*s.* a day. About twelve men, with large families, have
their rents paid by the parish. Generally I expect, when we
are informed of an application for relief from a large family of
eight or nine children, that two or three of those children are
grown up and capable of work. Provisions are, I think, dearer
somewhat here than in the agricultural parishes: the loaf is a
penny or a halfpenny dearer here. We do not consider that 12*s.*
a week is more than sufficient in this district to maintain a labouring man and his family. Private individuals do not give more
here than 12*s.* a week to a day-labourer. No distinction is made
by private individuals between married and single men; they give
them the same wages."

" Is the parish work here piece-work?—It is not.

" Then your paupers work less than other day-labourers, do
they not?—Yes: they work less time.

" And within that time do they do as much work?—No, sir,
they want a good deal of looking after: they are always on the
look-out for me, or for any overseer. There is a superintendent,
but he is in fact a pauper, and he is rather easy with them.

" How much less time do your parish-labourers work than industrious labourers, who maintain themselves?—About one hour
daily, summer and winter. They have also opportunities of picking up a shilling by odd jobs in the town.

" Then a pauper with a family gets from your parish the same
wages as an industrious labourer; they moreover get their rents
paid; they have opportunities of picking up additional shillings,
and they work less time, and do less work than the industrious
labourer. And they are also relieved from the burthen of looking
out for work?—Yes, that is the case. Formerly we used to give
labourers 1*s.* 6*d.* per day, but they complained to the magistrates that it was not enough to support them, and the magistrates
recommended that more should be given. The paupers always,
when they think they have not enough, run to the magistrates, and
this is a check to any strictness on the part of the overseers.

" What is there to prevent the industrious and independent
labourers who have large families throwing themselves on the
parish, and placing themselves in the more advantageous situation
of paupers?—Only the sense of degradation.

" Is this sense of degradation diminishing?—It is.

" What is the characteristic of the wives of paupers and their
families?—The wives of paupers are dirty, and nasty, and indolent; and the children generally neglected, and dirty, and vagrants, and immoral.

" How are the cottages of the independent labourers as compared to them?—The wife is a very different person: she and her

children are clean, and her cottage tidy. I have had very extensive opportunities of observing the difference in my visits; the difference is so striking to me, that in passing along a row of cottages I could tell, in nine instances out of ten, which were paupers' cottages, and which were the cottages of the independent labourers.

" And what chance do you see of dispauperizing any of the paupers?—None, with the present generation of them, unless with very severe measures indeed. When a family is once on the parish, it is very difficult to get them off. We have cases of three generations of paupers. If the overseers were to adopt severe measures to put a stop to the system, the paupers would run with piteous tales to the magistrate, who orders the relief and censures the overseer. If overseers are strict, their conduct is also censured by the local newspapers. Tradesmen in these places will not make themselves martyrs.

" What do you think of the expediency of withdrawing all appeal to the magistrates?—I think it would be advantageous to give the final decision in all applications for relief to the committee for the management of the poor-rates. The thing desirable is, to remove the responsibility from individual overseers. If the decision were with the committee they would be a satisfactory check to any undue rigour on the part of individuals, and would at the same time know more of the merits of each case, and of the testimony, than can be known by the magistrates. One individual may be indiscreetly severe, but in a board selected from such a town as this, it is impossible that a whole board should sanction it.

" Within your experience, how many overseers have been disposed to act with strictness?—In the course of about nine years I have observed about four individuals so disposed out of thirty-four officers *.

* Nearly all the permanent parochial officers to whom I have put similar questions, have given similar answers, as to the proportion of those who were disposed to act harshly towards applicants for relief. It appeared from the individual instances which they adduced, that nearly all the persons so characterised were men of inferior education, who had risen from the lower stations in society. Sometimes a tradesman, serving the office of overseer, will treat with harshness or neglect applications made to him for relief whilst he is engaged in business; but from the testimony which I have received, it may be stated as a general rule, applicable to the questions of making the decisions of elective vestries final on applications for parochial relief; that the chances amount almost to certainty, that in boards, composed of individuals such as usually serve parochial offices in the towns, there will always be a secure majority for the protection of deserving applicants. This is, indeed, admitted by every one of the few experienced witnesses who have thought magisterial interference necessary for the

" Have you refused applicants relief unless they went into the house?—Yes; and a large proportion decline going into it, and we get rid of them.

" Are there many charitable ladies in your district?—Many ladies very charitable indeed, Sir.

" Now do these paupers, whose wages and residences you have described, receive in addition to their other advantages of rent-free cottages, easier work for shorter times than independent labourers, derive advantages from the attentions of charitable ladies?

" Yes; the ladies are very charitable to them, and are cheated on all sides by them, and imposed upon by piteous stories.

" How long do you think it will be, under these influences, before all the industrious and independent poor will better them-

protection of the poor. The following is an extract from the examination of Mr. Carvill, the assistant-overseer of the parish of St. Bride's, in the city of London :—

" I think the present mode of transacting parochial business a great grievance; and that there should be one magistrate to attend to parochial business. I think there should be a magistrate to appeal to, as parish officers are sometimes disposed to be harsh towards the pauper. How many parish officers have you known as serving since you were in office?—Twelve. Of that twelve, how many were characterised by undue severity?—Two. What do you consider the general average proportion of men characterised by such a disposition found serving such offices?—I think about two in twenty; indeed, I might say, not one in twenty. Were the men to whom you allude men of education, or men who had been raised from the lowest ranks of life?—They were men comparatively uneducated: they were the most uneducated. Nineteen out of twenty of the persons chosen as parish officers in the city of London, you would then consider as disposed to deal fairly and humanely to a pauper, whatever might be their interest in getting rid of his claim?—Yes, I have no doubt whatever of that. And lean to the side of benevolence rather than of undue severity?—Yes. And would protect the fair claim of a pauper?—Yes. Are you confident of that?—Yes, I am confident of that. If then the final decision of a pauper's claim were left to a board composed of men, nineteen out of twenty of whom are disposed, as you state, to ' lean to the side of benevolence rather than of severity,' and to ' protect the fair claim of a pauper,' whatever might be their supposed pecuniary interest in getting rid of that claim, do you think there would be any danger?—I have not had any experience of the working of a large board of officers."

From the testimony I have received in other cases, I am led to believe that in most instances where an overseer who has risen from a lower station in society is " disposed to be harsh towards the pauper," it will be found that this overseer comes to a conclusion more quickly than his brethren, by judging from his own experience what frugality and industry may achieve, or from knowing better what a person of the condition of the pauper might do. This conclusion being usually enunciated without the reasons, and with uncontrolled temper, has the appearance of harshness and cruelty, though it may be substantially just. But be the explanation what it may, the whole evidence, which I have received, proves that on all boards indifferently chosen from the middle classes, the deserving applicant will have a " secure majority."

selves by getting large families and becoming paupers?—I cannot say, Sir.

" On a further examination of this witness, as to whether other paupers than those, the rents of whose cottages were paid by the parish, had not demanded similar benefits. He stated that they had ; and that the complaints from other paupers, " who did not see why they had not as much RIGHT as others to have their rents paid," had become so numerous, that the committee had determined that no new applicants should have their rents paid, and that the practice should cease as the present possessors of the privilege died off.

" The witness, in answer to further interrogatories, stated :— In Windsor we have often a great number of artizans and labourers brought into the town by the works carried on at the palace. About five years ago we had three or four hundred additional labourers. In cases of sickness, or of improvidence, we had sometimes to remove them to their parish. But, more frequently, the mechanics had clubs, and the parish was greatly relieved by their declaring on their clubs on such occasions. In consequence of a suspicion that Government wanted to get hold of their money, the labourers who had constituted clubs in this town broke them up. We had four clubs, we have now only one, and that will shortly be broken up. I never heard the regulations under the new act particularly objected to. These clubs were, when in operation, a great relief to the parish, and their dissolution will be a severe misfortune to it. We have a savings bank in this town, but I cannot state what is its progress. Mr. Adams, the carpenter, who employs about ten or twelve men, has instituted a fund among his men, who each contribute 2*d.* a week to provide for casualties. In this way a considerable fund has accumulated, and from this fund casualties have been provided for, and the parish has at various times been saved serious expenses. Mr. Ramsbottom, the brewer, has made up a fund of this sort, and when a workman is sick he is allowed from this fund the same wages as when he is in health and at work. In this instance, also, the parish has been saved from serious burdens. I think it would be of very material assistance to all parishes if the employers of workmen would patronize trade clubs of this sort, and take the trouble of them."

" In this town there are various ancient charities, and we have had instances of people settling in the parish for the purpose of obtaining a share of the produce of these charities."

*Evidence of Mr. William Winkworth, the Overseer of the Parish
of St. Mary's, Reading.*

" In this town great advantages would be derived by an union of
the parishes. There would be great gain derived from an union:
first, in obtaining more efficient officers and administrators; next,
in systematic and united management; thirdly, in more economical expenditure; and, fourthly, in finding things for labour,
and in directing the labour of the able-bodied paupers."

" The town, for example, wants draining. We have brick-
makers and carpenters, and other labourers, on the parishes, receiving relief; and the whole town might be well drained by
the labour of these paupers, at the expense of materials only,
bricks, wood, mortar, and sand. This, however, is a work
which the parishes cannot, or will not, undertake separately: it
is prevented by petty jealousies and dissensions, and the want of
able officers to direct the work of the paupers. The owners of
premises well situated and well drained, say, " Drainage is a
benefit to the owners of the property, and we do not see why we
should be called upon to contribute money for their benefit."
The owners of the houses where the drainage is most wanted say,
" We can get no rents to pay for the work, and the nuisances
which are caused by the want of it must therefore continue." No
account is taken of the necessity of finding work of any sort for
the able-bodied paupers: nothing can be done with the separate
parishes governed by open vestries, no cordial co-operation can be
got, and the benefit of considerable labour is lost. As the surveyor of the road from this town to Basingstoke, and also of the
road from hence to Shillingford, I can state, from my observation
of the several parishes (19 in number) through which these roads
pass, that very considerable labour might be found, under good
direction, in improving their private roads. This is an instance of
the sort of work which might frequently be found for paupers. In
some of the parishes the roads are kept in very good order,—but
this is mere accident; whilst in the immediately adjoining parishes
more money will be expended, and the roads will, nevertheless,
be in so bad a state, that the parish is indictable for them. The
most conspicuous examples of the skill used in one parish, rarely
produce any imitation in the next parish. The farmers, in
general, steadily adhere to their old practices, and never willingly
conform to any improvements; they employ waggons where carts
would serve much better: they throw down on the roads materials totally inapplicable, and think they can mend them with big
loose stones, which stones would really be useful, if they were
broken up."

" I have sometimes twelve and sometimes thirty men in my employment as surveyor, but I have no paupers. I will not have them. I cannot trust them. They are so lazy and demoralized, that they cannot be got to do anything without constant goading and superintendence *. They require a superintendent to every half dozen of them. Sometimes one of them is appointed as a superintendent of the others; but that is of very little use, as it requires some one constantly to superintend the superintendent. Small parishes have no officer who can be employed, nor can they pay any one who can be depended on, to see that the paupers do their work properly. Independent workmen, who have not been demoralized by being admitted on the parish, do not require the same expense of superintendence.

" If several parishes were united, they could afford to pay for some one to direct the labour of the paupers for the whole of them.

" If provisions were supplied and all parochial work were performed by contract, excessive waste would be arrested. I think that it is only by the union of parishes, under a select vestry, that proper officers can be obtained, or systematic management be instituted. I am confident that a select vestry would save more

---

* I found that the witnesses in all the parishes, town or country, agreed as to the superior value of non-parishioners as labourers. In examining one witness (Mr. J. W. Cockerell, the assistant-overseer of Putney) as to the operation of a birth settlement, and the removal of paupers from his parish to their settlements in the rural parishes, I asked him whether there were not many of the paupers who had applied for relief from his parish, and who had withdrawn their claims when they were told that they would be removed to their parishes in the country? He stated that many had refused; and in answer to further questions as to what became of these persons who refused to be removed, he stated (as all the other witnesses, who had the means of observing the subsequent conduct of the applicants, stated) that these paupers remained, and afterwards attained a much better condition than they had ever before attained while they considered that parochial resources were available to them on the failure of their own. He cited the cases of nine families who had applied for relief, but had refused it when they were told that they would be removed. Six of these families, he said, had not only been saved from pauperism, but they were now in a better situation than he had ever before known them to be in. In two instances particularly, the withdrawal of dependence on parochial relief had been the means of withdrawing the fathers from the public-houses and beer shops, and making them steady and good workmen. " Indeed," said he, " it is a common remark amongst the employers of labourers in our parish, that the non-parishioners are worth three or four shillings a week more than the parishioners. This is because they have not the poors-rates to fly to. The employers also remark that the non-parishioners are more civil and obliging than the others." In this parish the usual wages of the single labourer are about 12s. per week ; and the deterioration of the labourer by the influence of the present system of administering the poor laws, may therefore, according to the witnesses' statement, be set down as from five and twenty to more than thirty per cent. Other witnesses declare that the deterioration is much more considerable.

than one-third of the expense in this district. The obstacles to the union of the parishes here arise chiefly from the wealthy and less burdened parishes, who object to the union on the ground of an apprehended increase of their rates from the greater burdens of the parishes chiefly inhabited by the poor. But I would meet this objection, by allotting to each parish only its own share of burdens; by allowing each to raise money as they pleased, and only uniting them for the purpose of expenditure."

Some conception of the state of the out-door poor in some of the agricultural parishes may be formed from the fact stated by the Rev. Mr. Cherry, of Burghfield, who says :—"The difference between parish work and private work is exemplified by the fact, that in many instances single men in our parish have preferred six shillings a-week for working on the roads or in the gravel-pits, to seven or eight shillings a-week for working for the farmer."

Mr. Clift, the assistant-overseer, gave stronger instances; and stated that he had known instances where the men who received six shillings a-week from the parish, had refused nine shillings a-week from the farmer.

The following extracts from the evidence of one of the assistant-overseers of Lambeth parish, and from other officers of the London parishes, exemplifies the effects of the system in the metropolis :—

Mr. Luke Teather, Assistant-Overseer of St. Mary, Lambeth.

" If you could get hard work for your able-bodied out-door poor, so as to make their condition on the whole less eligible than that of the independent labourer, what proportion of those who are now chargeable to the parish do you think would remain so ?—On a rough guess, I do not think that more than one out of five would remain.

"Can you state any facts to justify that conclusion ?—Yes ;—the instances of the proportions who have left us on their having had work given them. Some time ago, for instance, we had a lot of granite broken; there were not above twenty per cent. of the men who began the work who remained to work at all ; there were not above two per cent. who remained the whole of the time during which the work lasted. Many of them, however, were not idle men ; but they found other jobs."

Mr. Oldershaw, the vestry-clerk of Islington, states :—" It sometimes costs us more—(the grinding corn by a mill)—than the wheat ground ; but then it keeps numbers away, and in that way we save. When it became known that we could not get work for the whole of our able-bodied, we had, in two or three days, one-third more of this class of applicants, and unless we had been able to provide work of some sort so as to keep the great body of the able-bodied employed, we should have been inundated with them."

With the view of reducing the parochial expenditure of the populous parish of Marylebone, the stone-yard was discontinued, as it was believed to be conducted at a loss, and the able-bodied paupers receiving out-door relief were no longer employed. Soon after this proceeding, the able-bodied applicants for parochial relief increased in such numbers, that it has recently been found necessary to recur to the use of the stone-yard to stem the influx. Nine hundred of the applicants for relief were set to work : only eighty-five have continued at work. The average wages were from 10s. to 12s. per week, but some got as much as 18s.

In the agricultural parishes I found that, although the circumstances of an out-door pauper, as to whether he were or not in employment, and his capability for labour, were in general sufficiently well known; and although the mischievous character of demands and allowances of parochial relief to out-door paupers was distinctly perceived by parish officers, yet they made the allowances under fear of personal consequences. In one parish, where the rates had been reduced nearly one-half, and the condition of the labourers improved by the partial adoption of a more strict system of administration, the progress of improvement was stopped by the farmers, who were paralysed with terror by the acts of incendiarism which prevailed in adjacent parishes.

In the metropolis I have found this cause—the fear of violence from the out-door paupers—in direct operation, as an obstacle to retrenchment, in only three or four parishes. In most town parishes the chief causes of profusion are—first, an uncontrollable facility and temptation to fraud, which appears to be unavoidable in the administration of any out-door relief in towns, when not given in the shape of wages for labour; next, the ignorance of the annual officers; and often, the operation of interests on their parts at variance with their duties. The frauds committed in consequence of the facilities which the system of granting out-door relief affords, are such as these :—parties receiving relief as being out of work, when they are in work ; parties who have received relief in consequence of being actually out of work, continuing to receive relief after they have obtained work ; parties who have received out-door relief in money on account of sickness, continuing to receive that relief after they have recovered ; women receiving relief on the ground that they have been deserted by their husbands, whilst their husbands are living with them; women receiving relief for themselves and families on the pretence that the husband is absent in search of work, while he is absent in full work; parties continuing to receive pensions for children or relations, as if they were alive, when they are dead. The following extract from the evidence of an experienced and able parish officer (Mr. Huish, assistant-overseer of St. George's, Southwark) will afford examples :—

" The most injurious portion of the poor-law system is the out-door relief. I do not serve a day without seeing some new mischiefs arise from it. In the smaller parishes persons are liable to all sorts of influences. In such a parish as ours, where we administer relief to upwards of two thousand out-door poor, it is utterly impossible to prevent considerable fraud, whatever vigilance is exercised.

" Has the utmost vigilance been tried ?—Suppose you go to a man's house as a visitor:—you ask where is Smith (the pauper)? you see his wife or his children, who say they do not know where he is, but that they believe he is gone in search of work. How are you to tell, in such a case, whether he is at work or not? It could only be by following him in the morning; and you must do that every day, because he may be in work one day, and not another. Suppose you have a shoemaker who demands relief of you, and you give it him on his declaring that he is out of work. You visit his place, and you find him in work; you say to him, as I have said to one of our own paupers, ' Why, Edwards, I thought you said you had no work?' and he will answer, ' Neither had I any; and I have only got a little job *for the day.*' He will also say directly, ' I owe for my rent ; I have not paid my chandler's shop score; I have been summoned, and I expect an execution out against me, and if you stop my relief, I must come home,' (that is, he must go into the workhouse.) The overseer is immediately frightened by this, and says, ' What a family that man has got! it will not do to stop his relief.' So that, unless you have a considerable number of men to watch every pauper every day, you are sure to be cheated. Some of the out-door paupers are children, others are women; but, taking one with another, I think it would require one man's whole time to watch every twenty paupers.

" Some time ago there was a shoemaker, who had a wife and family of four children, who demanded relief of the parish, and obtained an allowance of 5s. per week. He stated that he worked for Mr. Adderley, the shoemaker, who now lives in the High-street in the Borough. The man stated in applying for relief, that, however he worked, he could earn no more than 13s. per week. A respectable washerwoman informed me, that the way in which this family lived was such, that she was convinced the man earned enough to support them honestly, without burthening the parish, and that it was a shame for him to receive relief. In consequence of this information I objected to the allowance : but one of the overseers, taking up the book, said, ' But here is the account, signed by Mr. Adderley himself : can you doubt so respectable a man ?' Still I was not satisfied ; and I watched the man, and found him going to Mr. Pulbrook's, in Blackfriars Road. When the man quitted the shop, I went in and asked whether the man who had just left worked for them. Mr. Pulbrook stated that he did work for them, and had done so during the last twelve months : that he was one of the best shoemakers who had ever worked for him ; that he earned only about 12s. a week, and that he (Mr. Pulbrook) regretted he had not more work for him. The man had left his book, which I borrowed. When the man came to the board, I said to him, Do you know Mr. Pulbrook, of Blackfriars Road? 'Yes, I do very well.' Do you ever work for him ?—'I have done a job now and then for him.' I then asked, whether he had not earned as much as 10s. or 12s. a week from him. His reply was ' No, never.' I then produced the book between him and Mr. Pulbrook, from which it appeared that he had earned from 10s. to 12s. per week for the time stated. This took him by surprise, and he had no answer to make. The relief was refused him, and he never came again; I afterwards ascertained, that, in addition to the 13s. a week which he earned from Mr. Adderley, and the 12s. a week which he earned from Mr. Pulbrook, his wife and himself worked for Mr. Drew, the slopseller, living at Newington Causeway, and earned 7s. a week from him. On the average of the year round they did not earn less than 30s. per week. The man was afterwards spoken to about the loss of the parish allowance, when he said,— ' I did not like to lose it : it was a d—d hard case; it was like a freehold to me, for I have had it these seven years."

" No inspector would have found out such a case except by constant watching or favourable accidents. It might be supposed strange that a shoemaker could have earned no more than 12s. a week; but his answer was, that his bodily infirmities were such, that he could not sit long enough to enable him to earn more than such a sum. This morning, I said to a man of the name of Taylor, a tinman, who is receiving 4s. a week,—'Taylor, how can you come here and waste your time to get your lazy shilling, whilst, if you staid at home, you might earn your honest eighteen-pence, and set your family a good example ?' His reply was, ' I have no work ; I can't earn anything.' I answered, ' Why, every time I pass your house, except on relieving days, I always find you hammering.' ' Yes, so I may be,—penny or twopenny jobs : will you find me work ?' I replied, ' That I could not seek pans to mend for him.' He went away with his money. Had I positively challenged this man, the first question with the annual officers would have been, ' What is your family?' ' There are six of us,' it would be replied. ' What a family for a poor man to maintain !' exclaim the overseers ; ' let him have the money.' The overseers are in perpetual fear of a man with his wife and family coming into the workhouse. They usually say, in such a case as this, ' We pay 4s. per head for their keep in the workhouse; here is six times 4s.—what a difference this is ! Let us keep them out at all risks.' We have had instances of sawyers leaving their work and paying men to work for them, whilst they came and got relief. Within these few days we found out the case of a cabinet-maker named Baylis, working for a Mr. Edwards in Lambeth Walk, and at the same time receiving 6s. 6d. per week from us, under a pretence that he was out of work. In fact, such discoveries are perpetual.

" Does the practice of obtaining out-door relief extend amongst respectable classes of mechanics, whose work and means of living are tolerably good ?—I am every week astonished by seeing persons come whom I never thought would have come. The greater number of our out-door paupers are worthless people ; but still the number of decent people who ought to have made provision for themselves, and who come, is very great, and increasing. One brings another ; one member of a family brings the rest of a family. Thus I find, in two days' relief, the following names :— ' John Arundell, a sawyer, aged 55, *his son* William, aged 22, a wire-drawer ; Ann Harris, 58, her husband is in Greenwich Hospital ; her son John and his wife also come separately, so does their son, a lad aged 18, a smith.' Thus we have pauper father, pauper wife, pauper son, and pauper grandchildren frequently applying on the same relief-day. One neighbour brings another. Not long since a very young woman, a widow, named Cope, who is not more than 20 years of age, applied for relief; she had only one child. After she had obtained relief, I had some suspicion that there was something about this young woman not like many others. I spoke to her, and pressed her to tell me the real truth as to how so decent a young woman as herself came to us for relief: she replied that she was '*gored*' into it. That was her expression. I asked her what she meant by being *gored* into it. She stated, that where she was living there were only five cottages, and that the inhabitants of four out of five of these cottages were receiving relief, two from St. Saviour's and two from Newington

parish. They had told her that she was not worthy of living in
the same place unless she obtained relief too. I was completely satisfied of the truth of her statement by inquiry. Her
candour induced me to give her 5*s*., and I offered her a reception
in the house for herself and child. The consequence was we never
heard any more of her."

The most experienced witnesses declare, that the only test of
the merits of such cases is, by taking them wholly on the parish.
The parish officers of St. James's, Westminster, state, that " on
one occasion, in the month of November last, upwards of *fifty* paupers were offered admission into the workhouse, in lieu of giving
them out-door relief, and that of that number only *four* accepted
the offer;" and that since then the same system has been pursued
in a number of instances, and attended with a similar result.

Mr. John Myles, a very experienced officer, states, that the
city parishes are in general very wealthy, and do not make the
requisite inquiries. The frauds, too, are of a nature which cannot be detected in the present state of things, except by accident. One mode of working the fraud is by a combination of
this sort:—There are three old women, for instance, one residing
in Cripplegate, one in St. Sepulchre's, one in Bishopgate, or in a
different part of the town. These three women will lay their
heads together, and agree to acknowledge each other as residents,
by which they are enabled to obtain relief from several different
parishes, by giving a different residence to each parish where they
claim relief. Thus, when the officer makes inquiry at the house
of the old woman in Bishopgate, whether Mary Jones, the old
woman of Cripplegate, lives there? the old woman at Bishopgate says, ' Yes, she does; we live together; she is a worthy
creature, and in a very necessitous condition, and has suffered very severely.' The old woman of Cripplegate will go and
lodge at times with her friend at Bishopgate, in order to give a
colour to her statement and make other persons corroborate it;
and so on with the others. By accident, I once detected a man
who was an inmate of Lambeth workhouse, and at the same time
receiving a pension of 5*s*. a week from our parish, and 5*s*. a week
from St. John's, Hackney*. I constantly hear of these frauds in
the other parishes."

Mr. Miller, the assistant overseer of St. Sepulchre's parish,
London, where the rate-receivers now equal in number the rate-
payers, says, with respect to the out-door relief, " No industry,
no inspection, no human skill will prevent gross impositions under

---

* Since this evidence was given, one case has appeared before the public,
in which a man defrauded fourteen different parishes in the metropolis.

this mode of relief. From the very nature of it there must be an immense deal of fraud."

The Rev. Mr. Whately said, in advising parish officers :— " Never flinch at the expense ; you are ruining yourselves by not taking the parties wholly upon the parish, and subjecting them to strict regulations." The same gentleman contends that all out-door relief ought to be given in kind, so long as such a mode of relief is retained. The best effects followed the discontinuance of money allowance in his parish of Cookham, which is now nearly dispauperized *.

ST. LAWRENCE, READING.

In this parish

In		the No. of Houses was		inhabited by		Families		No. of Individuals
1801		574		706		3170		
1811		703		760		4627		
1821		774		862		3091		
1831		789		900		4048		

* He stated in his evidence the following case, to serve as an example of the effects of the change of system, in respect to out-door relief by money payments. A man, who went by the name of Webb, was hanged for horse-stealing. He left a widow and several small children. The widow applied to the select vestry for relief the week after his execution. It was suspected that they possessed resources which would enable them to provide for their own wants, without parochial relief; and in consequence of this suspicion, the vestry ordered them to come to the workhouse three times a week for such relief in kind as was deemed necessary. The woman begged to be allowed the money, or less money than the value of the bread,—which was refused. The result was that she never applied, and she never received any relief whatever. "In this case," said he, " as in almost all others, it would have been utterly impossible for the parish officers to have ascertained whether the pauper did or did not possess the suspected resources. Had relief such as was requested been readily granted, as it generally would, under the in-fluence of the feelings of pity, and from the impulse of a blind benevolence, or from the love of popularity, in appearing to yield to the demand for assist-ance in a case so deeply affecting the sympathies ; or from a dread of un-popularity, from the imputation of hard-heartedness " towards poor children, who could not be supposed to participate in their father's crime ;" or from the love of ease, and the want of firmness to refuse,—a WHOLE FAMILY would have been placed as paupers, or consumers of the labour of the industrious : the children of the woman would have been further demoralized, and ren-dered as miserable themselves as they would have been worthless and mis-chievous to others. The course of blind benevolence would have been real cruelty, and the extra indulgence applied for would moreover have been in-justice towards the children of the meritorious, to whom the rule was ap-plied without relaxation." All the members of the family are well known to Mr. Whately, in whose parish they reside, and they are in a satisfactory and thriving condition ; so that in this case, which will apply to all others, the pauper would have had the relief of the exact kind suitable, (i. e. *bread*, not *gin*,) had it been absolutely necessary, but, as it was unnecessary, was thrown on her own resources.

The amount of real property in 1815 was 13,051*l.*
The expenditure on the poor was—

	£.	*s.*	*d.*
In 1804 .	1444	0	0
1815 -	2464	0	0
1821	2859	0	0
1830 .	2912	0	0

The churchwardens of this parish could give me no information; but they stated that the governor of the workhouse knew every-thing about parish affairs, and that he was the only person who could give me full information.

I began my inquiries of the governor by asking him what quan-tity of food he gave to those under his charge?—"Quantity! why, a bellyful. We never stint them. I stand by the children myself, and see that they have a bellyful three times a day."

" What descriptions of food do you give them? — Good wholesome victuals as anybody would wish to taste. You shall taste it yourself. We give them all meat three times a week. The working men have a bellyful. We never weigh anything, and there is no stint, so as they do not waste anything. Then they have good table beer and good ale."

" How many paupers have you generally in your workhouse? —From forty to fifty."

" And what is the quantity of meat usually consumed weekly by that number?—Seldom less than 150 pounds of meat."

" Do you find them in tobacco or snuff?—No, Sir; but if they get a few pence, or if their friends choose to give it them, we do not debar them from anything, so long as they do not make beasts of themselves."

I requested to be shown the house. Everything appeared re-markably cleanly and in good order. He requested my particular attention to the goodness and cleanliness of the sheets and bed-ding, and the general comfort. He dilated on the quality of the bread, which he showed me. He also gave me some of the table beer and ale to taste. I must do him the justice to state that it was excellent. The table beer was such as in the metropolis is called table ale. But besides these liquors for the use of the pau-pers, he produced a third specimen, still superior, of which I tasted. This was a most potent beverage. It was two years old; and he said he generally reserved it for the overseers after the performance of a "dry day's work." The paupers themselves appeared to be very strong and healthy, and the children the most so of any that I had observed in the district. He pointed out to me one pauper, a remarkably hale-looking man, of 63, who had with his wife, been on the parish more than 40 years, and in all probability would live more than half that time longer on their charge. The governor, it appeared, had been a farmer many years ago. I asked him—

" Do you think the condition of these paupers better or worse than the condition of the agricultural labourers thirty or forty years ago?—A great deal better off than the labourers forty years ago."

" Than the agricultural labourers of any class?—Yes, sir, I know they are a great deal better off."

" And what is the present condition of the independent labourers, as compared with that of the labourers at the time you mention?—I think they are not quite so well off. To be sure, they got less wages, and clothing was dearer : they only got 7*s*. a week. But then, on the other hand, they only paid 8*d*. for the gallon loaf. I think they were better off. There are too many labourers now, and labour is more uncertain than it was then."

" I may say, then, that not only is the condition of those under your care better, as regards food, clothing, lodging and comfort, than the labourers who toil out of doors ; but that they are under no uncertainty, and have no anxiety about providing for themselves?—Yes, Sir, you may say that. You may say, too, that they are better off than one-half of the rate-payers out of the house. I know the rate-payers; I know what it is to be a rate-payer; and I know that a great many of them are worse off."

In the course of my inspection of the workhouse, I observed that the men's rooms were all locked. I inquired the cause of this —that they may not come in and lie down before bed-time.

" That is, I suppose, that they may not escape from their work ? — No, Sir, we have no work here, even for those that might work : it is that they may not come up here and lollop about, and roll about in their beds after dinner, or when they are tired of doing nothing."

" How does this sort of life agree with them on their first entrance?—Wonderfully well in general. Sometimes when they come in very low, and on the brink of starvation, the great change in the way of living is too much for them ; but when they get over the change they go on surprisingly. Their friends, when they have any, come in to see them, have sometimes been quite surprised at the change, and hardly knew them again, they were looking so well. We had an old woman brought in not long ago ; she was so very low and feeble, that you would have thought it impossible she could live long ; but now she is one of the most active women of her age, and will live, I dare say, a great many years more ; they will say themselves they never were so well off before. There are some, it is true, who cannot bear even our regularity, and prefer the dog's life of hunger and liberty; but in general they never leave us."

In answer to my interrogatives, as to the general character of the inmates, he declared that the great majority of them were undeserving characters, who had been reduced to poverty by improvidence or vice.

The male and female paupers were separated in the night, but in the day the young girls, and the mothers of bastard children, and all classes, might meet and converse together in the yard.

On examining the books containing the list of the out-paupers, I found the management equally characteristic; out-door paupers having nearly the same amount of wages allowed them without work, that could have been obtained by independent labourers by hard work : the pauper having, in addition to the money payments, frequent allowances of clothes from the parish, and payments on account of rent, and " other advantages." I made inquiry into the case of the persons by the same name first presented on opening the book, when I found them to consist of a pauper family of three generations, the whole of whom received upwards of 100*l.* per annum from the parish. The parents of the pauper stock were described as remarkably hale old people in the workhouse, who had lived on the parish upwards of 40 years. The father was the man who had been pointed out to me, as an instance of the care taken of the inmates, he having lived so long and so well on the parish. I took down their names in the order which exhibits the genealogy of the *living* pauper family :—

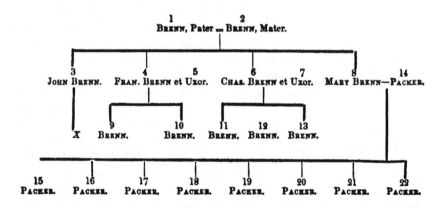

I asked the governor how this last and most widely-spreading branch arose? "That" said he, "was one of our overseers' doings. I warned him against it, but he would do it. Brenn's daughter became pregnant by a weaver, named Packer, and the overseer made him marry her; and see what the parish has got by it!—

eight more mouths to feed already, and eight more backs to find clothes for."

" How many more paupers do you consider the parish may receive from this said stock ?—Two or three score, perhaps." The progenitors lived in the workhouse at an expense of not less than 10s. per week, (the average expense of the inmates, children included, being about 5s. per week each), Charles Brenn, who was an out-parishioner, received 7s. 6d. per week, besides shoes and stockings; Francis Brenn received 6s. 6d. a week; John Brenn is a mechanic, I believe a weaver, at present resident in London, and had 3s. a week sent to him,—on what ground except as a patrimonial claim, on what evidence except his own statement that he wanted it, and must return to the parish if it were not sent to him, I was unable to ascertain. Packer, for himself and family, received 13s. a-week of the parish, and " various other advantages." I inquired with respect to the out-door paupers in general, as well as with respect to this pauper family, in particular whether they got no additional " relief" from charitable foundations and benevolent people ?—" Yes," said the governor, " we have a great many benevolent people in this town, and they help. There is always something or other given; a great deal of coal is given away, and the churchwardens give away linen."—He admitted, in answer to further inquiries, that the greatest impositions were practised on the most humane people. One of the paupers had declared to him, that he had as many as six shirts at a time given to him by different benevolent people. It was intimated that, as a matter of course, these things went to the pawn-shop for drink. He expressed an opinion that coals were the best commodity to give away—" as coals cannot be pawned !"

On inspecting the accounts of the disbursements, I found that the supplies of meat and various other commodities were purchased of different tradesmen. This was done to " give each tradesman a fair advantage," and " that they might have no ground of complaint." For the same reason it was a rule never to buy anything out of the parish. The overseers are mostly small tradesmen.

The governor " could not make it out," but the poor's-rates were increasing : they were 3s. 6d. in the pound the last half year, and a 4s. 6d. rate must be called for, for the next half year, and the parish was already 200l. in debt.—" Something," said he, " must be done."

ST. GILES'S, READING.

In my visit to this workhouse, I was accompanied by the Rev. Mr. Milman. I stated to the governor of this workhouse that the governor of St. Lawrence's workhouse had declared that the paupers in that house were better taken care of than the paupers in any other parish in the town? " But we, Sir," said the governor of St. Giles's workhouse, " give ours one · hot-meat dinner a week more than they do in St. Lawrence parish." " And what quantity do you give them at each meal ?—We have never any stint."—On such an examination as I was able to give of the accounts of commodities supplied to the workhouse, I was satisfied that this was the case. The beverage of the paupers was table-beer and ale. Four hogsheads of beer, and about 36 gallons of ale, were brewed in the workhouse from 10 bushels of malt. They had two generations of paupers on the parish. When people were once on the parish, and in the workhouse, it was remarked they never got them off except by death. When the girls who were old enough were got out to service, they frequently went back to the workhouse complaining that they were badly treated,—meaning that they had not been so well treated as in the workhouse. These girls, when they returned, were in consequence made to wear a linsey-woolsey gown, and a close cap, which prevented their hair being seen. This, it was imagined, would operate to deter them from throwing themselves so readily out of their places. Their conduct was too frequently wanton and improper. The able-bodied paupers, who were mostly out-paupers, were idle and dissolute, and the parish officers could never manage with pauper labour. The farmers of that parish got work from " foreigners," as they could not rely on pauper labour.

The house, though not so airy as the workhouse of St. Lawrence's parish, seemed to be regulated much in the same manner. The children were very hale and clean. There appeared to be the proper separation by night, but by day the society in the courtyard was indiscriminate. In the course of my examination of the place, the governor more than once volunteered a repetition of his statement, that they gave one hot dinner a week more than in St. Lawrence's parish.

The allowances of money to the out-poor did not appear to be as considerable. There was, he told me, a vast deal of charity in the parish, of which the out-door paupers partook; fuel, and food, and clothes were given away in great quantities. The pawnshops, he said, were full of the clothes given away by benevolent people.

All the labourers in that parish sent to the workhouse for caudle when their wives lay in, and 5s. each was given them on the occasion. Benevolent people also gave caudle; and a society, in which there were young as well as old ladies, provided the labourers' wives with linen; a pair of sheets were given to the woman, and a set of baby linen was provided for the child. One half of the linen was left with the woman for the use of the child, the other half was returned to the society.

After some delay I have obtained the following copy of the accounts of the expenditure for the maintenance of 62 paupers in the workhouse of the Parish of St. Giles, during three months:—

AN ACCOUNT of Provisions, Clothing, &c. used in St. Giles's Workhouse, from 1st of August to 31st of October, 1832.

Of whom Purchased.	Articles.	Price.		Amount.		
		s.	*d.*	*L.*	*s.*	*d.*
Mr. Thomas Champion.	8 sacks of flour. . .	48	0 per sack.	19	4	0
.. ..	7 do. do. . . .	40	0 ...	14	0	0
Mr. William Cottrell ..	88 lbs. *bacon** . . .	0	7¼ per lb. ..	2	15	0
Mr. Webb	114 .. beef	0	5 ...	2	7	6
..	92 .. do.	0	6 ...	2	6	0
Mr. Ferris	2 tons of coal . . .	26	0 per ton .	2	12	0
Mr. William Champion	81¼ lbs. *bacon*	0	6¼ per lb. ..	2	2	5
.. ..	2 cwt. 3 qr. 20 lb. cheese	50	0 per cwt..	7	6	6
.. ..	13¼ lbs. *lard*	0	7½ per lb. ..	0	8	3
.. ..	56 .. soap	64	0 per cwt..	1	12	0
.. ..	1 .. *mustard* . . .	1	6 per lb. ..	0	1	6
.. ..	56 .. sugar	0	6 ...	1	8	0
.. ..	4 .. *tea*	5	6 ...	1	2	0
.. ..	1 .. *ginger*	1	6 ...	0	1	6
.. ..	5 .. *starch*	0	11 ...	0	4	7
.. ..	1 bushel of salt. . .	1	9 ...	0	1	9
.. ..	2 cwt. 26¼ lbs. cheese	46	0 per cwt..	5	2	11
Mr. Wren	204 lbs. beef	0	5 per lb. ..	4	5	0
.. ..	211 .. do.	0	5 ...	4	7	11
Mr. Steward	314 .. *bacon*	0	7½ ..	9	9	9
.. ..	2 bushels of salt . .	1	9 per bush.	0	3	6
.. ..	3 lbs. *arrow root* . .	2	6 per lb. ..	0	7	6
.. ..	3 .. *sago*	1	0 ...	0	3	0
.. ..	322 .. *bacon*	0	7¼ ...	10	1	3
.. ..	136 .. do.	0	7½ ...	4	5	0
Mrs. Slaughter	1 sack of beans. . .	23	0 per sack.	1	3	0
Messrs. Philbrick . . .	Leather		. . . .	5	14	0
Mr. John Smith. . . .	1 bushel of oatmeal .	15	0 per bush.	0	15	0
.. ..	4 lbs. *tea*	5	0 per lb. ..	1	0	0
.. ..	1 .. do.	6	0 ...	0	6	0
.. ..	2 .. *coffee*	2	4 ...	0	4	8
.. ..	1 .. *pepper*	2	6 ...	0	2	6
			Carried forward .	105	4	0

* The articles marked in *italics* would, under a strict diet, for the able-bodied be deemed superfluities. If beef is consumed by able-bodied town paupers, bacon cannot be necessary.

Of whom purchased.	Articles.	Price.			Amount.		
					£.	s.	d.
		Brought up . .			105	4	0
Mr. John Smith. . . .	1 .. *allspice*. . . .	2	6	...	0	2	6
.. ..	56 .. *sugar*	0	6		1	8	0
.. ..	40¼.. *butter*	0	10¼	...	1	15	5
.. ..	6 dozen candles . .	6	3	per doz..	1	17	6
.. ..	1 lb. *blue*	2	0	per lb. . .	0	2	0
.. ..	2 cwt. 1 qr. 3 lb. cheese	59	0	per cwt..	6	19	7
.. ..	73¼ lbs. *bacon*	0	7	per lb. . .	2	2	10
.. ..	83 .. *do.*	0	7	...	2	8	5
Mr. Henry Johnson . .	142 .. beef	0	6	...	3	11	0
	63 .. *do.* . . .	0	5¼	...	1	8	10
Messrs. Willats & Bland	54 gallons of beer . .	0	6	per gall..	1	7	0
.. ..	1 barrel do. . .	18	0	per barrel	0	18	0
.. ..	2 do. do.. . .	18	0	...	1	16	0
Mr. John Champion . .	6 sacks of flour. . .	44	0	per sack.	13	4	0
.. ..	2 do. do. . .	44	0	...	4	8	0
.. ..	1 bushel of bread . .	11	4	per bush.	0	11	4
Mr. Bannister	235 lbs. beef.	0	5	per lb. . .	4	17	11
	174 .. do.	0	5	...	3	12	6
Mr. Ayres	2 tons of coal . . .	26	0	per ton..	2	12	0
Mr. W. Truss.	1 bushel of bread . .	10	8	per bush.	0	10	8
.. ..	67¼ lbs. *bacon*	0	7	per lb. . .	1	19	4
Mr. Pratt	Coffin			. . . .	0	16	0
Messrs. Letchworth . .	Clothes			. . . .	6	16	6
Mr. Durbridge	1 bushel of bread . .	10	8	per bush.	0	10	8
Mr. Robinson.	10 .. malt . .	9	6	...	4	15	0
	10 lbs. hops.	1	8	per lb. . .	0	16	8
Mr. Holly	2 tons of coal . . .	27	0	per ton..	2	14	1
					179	5	8

It may be observed, that in this one bill there are four different tradesmen, Messrs. Webb, Wren, Johnson, and Bannister, who supply " beef," and four different tradesmen, Cotterell, Champion, Steward, and Smith, who supply " bacon," for the consumption of the paupers in the workhouse. A similar practice prevails in most of the parishes. The governor of St. Lawrence's workhouse assigned the prevalent reason for this distribution of the custom for the supply of the commodities, i. e. to give such tradesmen a " fair advantage," and to prevent complaints. In some places each tradesman in the parish supplies the goods in his turn. Thus butcher A. supplies the meat this week, and B. the next week, and so on until all the butchers of the parish have had their turn. In nearly every instance I found the commodities supplied unexceptionable, or superior in quality, and the prices what are called " fair:" that is to say, they never exceeded the retail price in the market, and were often somewhat below it.

I could not readily ascertain the local market prices of the

various commodities consumed in the workhouses I visited, but I
have very little doubt that it may be stated generally of the workhouses throuhgout the country, in all the smaller parishes, that,
were the quantities of goods to be allowed to continue as at present, an enactment, providing that all goods for the workhouse
should be supplied by contract, would save from 15 to 20 per
cent. (or whatever may be the difference between the retail and
the wholesale prices of commodities) of the present expense of
maintaining the in-door paupers.

In some instances, the parish officers stated, that the supply of
goods was by contract ; but I generally found that, from the neglect of proper publication, the contract was a mere form, as the
supplies were usually taken from tradesmen resident in the
parish. In one parish, where the supply of bread for the parish
was put out to contract, I found that the contract was held jointly
by two bakers, who, being the only bakers in the parish, had
agreed to divide the supply and settle the prices between them.

The examination of this system developes a strong under-cur-
rent in favour of profuse management and open vestries. A very
intelligent officer of a large parish in Berkshire, where this system
was in operation, stated to me in his evidence,—

" If the legislature provides that the supply of goods for the
use of the poor in the workhouse shall be by contract, we shall
have a select vestry, (meaning an *elective* vestry,) and if we have
a select vestry we shall have some reduction of the profusion and
mismanagement, and a proportionate check to the increase of
pauperism. On the present system, the smaller shopkeepers,
who have always under their influence a number of the poorer
rate-payers, and those of their own class, can get up a majority
to carry anything in the open vestry, and prevent any efficient
reform."

Very great mischief appears to have been created by the am-
biguity of the term ' Select Vestry.' Where complaints have been
made to me of the profusion prevalent in parishes under the government of open vestries, and I have asked of the witnesses
whether no attempt has been made to obtain a select vestry,—the
reply has usually been, that they would by no means resort to a
form of government so much worse. I found that they understood
the term *select vestry* to mean not an *elective* vestry, but a *self-
elected* vestry, of the character of those which have been covered
with so much opprobrium in the Metropolis. When the same
witnesses have been asked, whether they thought any improvement in the administration of their funds would be effected by
confiding it to a board elected by the whole of the rate-payers,
they have usually stated that that was the very form of manage-

ment which they thought desirable to control the expenditure of the money. In nearly every instance of the government of parishes by open vestry, I found that practically the government was in the hands of a small body of parishioners; the numbers attending the vestry being usually a very small minority compared with the entire body of rate-payers; so that the management was, in these so-called open vestries, by a select body often of the worst description,—namely, of those directly or indirectly interested in profuse expenditure. In one instance, where a parish is under the control of an open vestry, or a minority of the smaller rate-payers, it was admitted that the object of the "clamour and blackguardism" which prevailed at the public meetings was to drive away the larger rate-payers.

But though a crowd or a fluctuating body—*i. e.* an open vestry —is utterly unfitted for detailed management, and though a representative committee or board may be the better instrument for economical management, these bodies are almost equally apt to degenerate into compact combinations of numbers of tradesmen, bound together by mutual local interests. Here and there a few persevering individuals thwart these interests,—which can only be withstood by constant exertion and public attention, and by exterior securities.

Mr. Richmond, one of the guardians of the poor in St. Luke's parish, Middlesex, stated, that " in compliance with our local act, some of the articles of consumption, in the parish, are advertised for in the public papers to be supplied by contract or tender. But there was no such provision for nearly two-thirds of the commodities supplied. When I came into office, it was a recognised principle, that the purchase of these commodities should be confined to the tradesmen of the parish. The effects of the patronage incident to purchases of goods, to the amount of upwards of twenty thousand per annum, from shopkeepers within the parish—patronage exercised by a board, who are themselves tradesmen or shopkeepers, or connected with shopkeepers,—may well be conceived. For several years I have contended, but unsuccessfully, for the universal application of the principle, that contracts should be taken from those who made the lowest tenders, wherever they resided, provided they gave the requisite securities for the due performance of the contract. On investigating the purchases of goods within the parish, I found that some of the charges were upwards of forty per cent. above the market prices. Whatever opposition may be made against an extensive or efficient reform, or generalization of the management of the funds for the relief of the poor, will be based on the retention of the parochial patronage and power. Although such a motive will never be ostensibly avowed, I have no doubt they will even assume that extended management will be more profuse than their own."

The following is the governor's list of the paupers by whom the provisions described iu the preceding account were consumed :—

PAUPERS in the Workhouse from 1st of August to 31st of October, 1832.

15 MEN :—			19 WOMEN :—		
Names.		**Age.**	**Names.**		**Age.**
Abbott, Thomas	. . .	69	Boult, Margaret	. . .	32
Bateman, Thomas.	. .	79	Bawtree, Sarah	. . .	23
Hawkins, Thomas.	. .	63	Clack, Amelia .	. . .	66
Lloyd, George .	. . .	69	Bowsher, Hannah .	. .	21
Lovell, William	. . .	69	Dell, Sarah .	. . . .	50
Parker, James .	. . .	73	Dyer, Hannah .	. . .	68
Pitman, Thomas	. . .	69	Goddard, ——	. . .	76
Pocock, Austin .	. . .	61	Goddard, Sarah	. . .	36
Plumridge, Joseph	. .	43	Green, Sarah .	. . .	52
Prior, James .	. . .	22	Hudson, Mary .	. . .	73
Spraggs, Joseph	. . .	34	Higgs, Jane	. . . .	23
Stevens, Samuel	. . .	71	Knight, Catherine.	. .	52
Ware, William	. . .	19	Mitchell, Mary	. . .	40
Weddel, William	. . .	63	Washbourn, Mary.	. .	58
West, Daniel .	. . .	43	Wicks, Elizabeth .	. .	52
Wellman, Francis .	. .	76	Walters, Jane .	. . .	45
			Wren, Elizabeth	. . .	28
			Perry, Frances .	. . .	58
			Perry, Sarah .	. . .	52

9 BOYS :—			18 GIRLS :—		
Names.		**Age.**	**Names.**		**Age.**
Applegath, Richard	. .	9	Aldrige, Eliza .	. . .	19
Applegath, Thomas	. .	8	Applegath, Charlotte .	.	10
Brookes, James	. . .	10	Billinger, Mary	. . .	15
Baskerville, John .	. .	9	Dell, Eliza .	. . . .	9
Harris, James .	. . .	15	Harris, Ann	. . . .	13
Parr, Robert	. . . .	20	Messenger, Ann	. . .	19
Scofield, James	. . .	15	Pile, Esther	. . . .	11
Sweetsur, John	. . .	13	Penny, Caroline	. . .	10
Ware, Charles .	. . .	11	Penny, Sophia .	. . .	8
			Penny, Eliza .	. . .	6
			Patey, Elizabeth .	. .	5
			Porter, Elizabeth .	. .	9
			Sweetsur, Elizabeth	. .	11
			Sweetsur, Mary .	. .	9
			Spraggs, Rose .	. . .	6
			Ware, Mary	. . . .	18
			Ware, Caroline	. . .	10
			Webb, Mary .	. . .	12

It appears by the governor's return, that the weekly consumption of these paupers, the majority of whom are old men, old females, and young children, is upwards of three pounds of meat, including a large proportion of bacon, one pound of which, as food, is usually considered to be equal to one pound and a quarter of meat. I have compared the diet of the paupers in this small parish with that of the paupers in one of the large metropolitan parishes (Lambeth), where the allowance of food is deemed mischievously profuse. In Lambeth workhouse the allowance of food is, to the adults, seven ounces of meat (clear of bone when cooked) three days each week. The quantity consumed by the same number of paupers as those in St. Giles's workhouse, Reading, would, according to the Lambeth diet table, be in three months .   .   .   .   .   .   1274 lbs. The quantity actually consumed by the paupers at Reading (allowing a loss of nearly one-third in cooking and for bone) is, during the same period   ·.   .   2399 lbs. showing a waste or over supply of 1125 lbs. during the thirteen weeks, which, during the year, makes a loss of 4500 lbs. unnecessarily consumed by 62 paupers.

It has appeared to me, that the force of the temptation to pauperism and crime can be duly estimated, or satisfactorily accounted for, only by means of a closer inquiry than has hitherto been instituted, into the condition and modes of living of the independent and hard-working classes, as compared with the condition and modes of living of those who, without labouring, or with less labour, are supplied with the fruits of labour. The importance of this relative view of the condition of the paupers and independent labourers is indeed indicated by every witness who has had much experience in parishes or districts affording wide fields for observation.

Mr. Wall, the vestry-clerk of St. Luke's, Middlesex,—a parish with a population of 46,000, and a work-house containing 600 paupers, and a proportionate number of out-door poor,—was asked—

" What is your opinion of the present characters of the paupers in your district?—Many of them are hereditary paupers; and it is found a most difficult thing. when a person has once become a pauper, to emancipate him from that condition. The majority of the other paupers have been reduced to a state of pauperism by improvidence or by vicious habits, rather than by unavoidable causes. Many of them might now obtain work if they were sober. Many of the mechanics now chargeable to the parish previously had wages, from which they might have made adequate provision for their later years. But even the reflecting amongst them are well aware, (and state it when remonstrated with,) that there is a sure provision for them and their families, do what they will. *That provision is a better maintenance, better food, and better lodging than the poor working people or mechanics generally have. Able-bodied persons are anxious to come into the workhouse. Persons who come into the house in consequence of sickness or accident, find the mode of living so good or so much better than they expected, that they are* ANXIOUS AND ENDEAVOUR TO REMAIN THERE. Under these circumstances, it is not surprising that these persons will not deny themselves any indulgence for the sake of making a provision for the future. The recklessness of the people in indulgence is quite frightful."

Mr. Drouet, the resident governor of Lambeth workhouse, who had also been the governor of Gosport workhouse, stated—

" I know the condition of the poorer of the independent working men. I can speak more particularly of the condition of those at Gosport, as I have been in the habit of going round collecting with the overseers there; and I can state, from what I have seen, that the poorer of the rate-payers fared worse than the paupers in the workhouse of that place. I have seen a very poor rate-payer dining on potatoes, and that for days together; and I have gone back to the workhouse, and helped to serve the paupers there with meat and with dinners comparatively sumptuous.

" Have you seen the poor rate-payers doing without such things as beer and butter?—The very poor rate-payers hardly ever think of such things, unless it be on the Sunday. I have known the rate-payer, if he is a poor agricultural man, go out in a morning with a bottle of water and a piece of bread (perhaps a pound), made of flour with the bran in it, and when he returned home he would expect a supper of potatoes, with a little skimmed milk thrown over it; this skimmed milk was perhaps given him by the neighbouring farmer. This is common in the country about Gosport, and also in Bedfordshire and Northamptonshire.

" What was the comparative fare of the pauper in the workhouse at Gosport?—I can state, with respect to Gosport, that although the fare is much more scanty than that of other parishes, there being no butter or beer allowed, yet it is much better than that of the labourer out of the house. The man in the house gets more meat, more food of every sort ; he is sure of a hot breakfast being prepared for him, without the trouble of cooking it; he is also sure of a hot dinner ; he is better clothed, and better lodged, and sleeps better, and works less time, and does less altogether. When a poor family has once been driven into the workhouse, the proof they give of its being better is, that they never can be got out of it. There are very few instances of their getting away. I have heard them express their regret, when they first come in, that they had not come in sooner. I have heard this too from people whom I had before heard pitying the poor people in the workhouse, and hoping they should never come to such a state of things themselves. Amongst several who have been striving to keep out of the workhouse, when one part of them have been driven in, their representations of its superior comfort have induced the rest to come in. This was the case at Gosport.

"Is your dietary at Lambeth much higher than at Gosport? —Considerably higher. In Lambeth they have beer, and butter, and sugar; they have also more meat, and the women have as much as the men. They have five feasts in the year: a pea-feast, a bean-feast, two mutton-feasts, and a plum-pudding-feast. In Newington, Mr. Mott was bound to give salmon once when in season, and mackarel once."

Mr. Charles Mott, who has been many years concerned in the management of several other very populous parishes, and is now the contractor for the maintenance of the poor of Lambeth workhouse, illustrates this state of things by other facts which he adduces in his examination, subsequently given in this selection.

Mr. Joseph John Hubbard, who has been accustomed to transact the parochial business of six parishes in the city of London, in speaking of the attractions of workhouses, gave the following instance of their force:—" I know one instance where a stout, able-bodied man, who had been a mechanic, having got into a workhouse, became so fond of it that he never would stir out of it, if he could help it, and kept there with his wife and children. An annuity of about 100*l.* a-year was left to him; but he was so lost to every feeling of independence, or rather so much alive to the comforts of a workhouse, that even with this annuity he would not quit the parish (St. Stephen, Coleman-street.) We continually took him before the magistrate for riotous conduct, and refusing to work, but he repeatedly told the magistrate that he never would work—that no one should make him; and, in short, that he would do as he liked, which was to remain in the work-house. The parish received so much of this man's dividend as was wanted to reimburse them, and he continued upon the parish, having his wife and children constantly in the house."

The concurrent testimony of numerous witnesses to the same effect might be stated.

I have endeavoured to ascertain from several of the magistrates who are advocates for the allowance system, or for the regulation of wages, in what way the labouring man within their districts expends for his maintenance the sum which they have declared to be the minimum expenditure, to sustain life? Some of these gentlemen admitted that they did not know; others stated that they laid it down as a general rule, that a labouring man must have bread and meat; but whether three or four loaves of bread, whether a pound or a pound and a half of meat, constituted the least quantity requisite as food for a given period, none of them could state. Several promised to make inquiries on the subject, when I asked them how they could safely set aside the decisions of the parish officers, or determine with due precision what was the minimum allowance of money for the labouring man's subsistence, unless they knew how many commodities were absolute necessaries for him, and the exact quantity and the price of each.

Whilst complaining of the effects of. the beer-shops established under Mr. Goulburn's Act, the same magistrates have frequently stated that habits of drunkenness prevailed with the whole of the labourers within their districts, and that these labourers were accustomed to carouse during one or two days in the week, gambling and indulging in the most vicious habits. Having received evidence that so large a proportion of the agricultural poor-rate is expended in aid of wages, I have been startled by the declarations that the habits of dissipation had become so prevalent. In answer to further inquiries, I have received assurances that the habit is *general;* that there are few, if any, exceptions. I have again asked whether the exceptions are formed of those who received parochial relief, and I have been assured (and satisfactory evidence has been adduced to me), that the agricultural labourers receiving poor's-rates in aid of wages are to be found at the beer-shops as frequently at least, as the independent labourers. The questions which have appeared to me naturally to follow are,—Do you consider beer or gin a necessary of life to the paupers?—if it be admitted that beer is a necessary of life to the independent labourers, the quantity required for intoxication can hardly be necessary, ought you not then to ascertain and deduct the amount of money spent in drunken revelry? As it must be presumed that a man pays for the beer he drinks at the beer-shops, (which beer is not deemed absolutely necessary for his subsistence,) is it not clear that you have not arrived at the minimum allowance? If, for example, you order wages to be made up to a man to the amount of nine shillings a week, and you find that he gets drunk one or two days in the week, and that his excess of drink costs him two shillings a week, since he actually lives on seven shillings a week, does he not prove by so living that seven is all that he really requires?

It was observed by Colonel Page, one of his Majesty's deputy lieutenants for Berks, in his communications with me, that the magistrates, from their ignorance of the habits of the labouring classes, are extremely unfit judges as to the amount of relief to be administered. " To a gentleman," said he, " a shilling appears an extremely small sum, but it often procures two, or even three days' subsistence to a labouring man; and hence the most benevolent men commonly make the most profuse and injurious allowances*."

A magistrate, who takes great interest in the welfare of the poor, and another gentleman, both of whom are trustees of the savings-bank at Reading, in answer to my inquiries as to the description of labourers who were depositors in that bank, expressed their conviction that no agricultural labourers, or at least, not more than one or two, were to be found amongst them ; as it was concluded that their wages would not enable them to lay by anything. Having ascertained that a number of the labourers in Cookham parish were depositors in the savings-bank at Maidenhead, I was not satisfied with this information, and requested the secretary of the Reading savings-bank to examine the books of the institution, and inform me whether there were no agricultural labourers connected with it. His return was, that he found amongst the depositors—

" 98 agricultural labourers, having deposits to the amount of 3753*l.* 17*s.* 2*d.* averaging to each depositor upwards of 88*l.*"

I made a similar request of the secretary of the savings-bank at Newbury, where I learned that, out of 593 depositors, the great majority of whom were of the labouring classes, there were—

138 agricultural labourers, whose total deposits amounted to	£5672
3 thatchers	209
2 shepherds	74
4 woodmen	365

It appears also from an official return, that there are at present 647 depositors in the savings-bank at Abingdon, " out of which (the secretary states) about 100 are agricultural labourers, but we have never distinguished that labourer from any other."

---

* I have found the same opinion stated in the following terms, in his work on the poor-laws :—" Unfortunately the magistrates, by whom these abuses are to be corrected, bring to the decision of questions between the overseers and the poor, feelings, which, though highly honourable to themselves, are frequently not controlled by that discrimination which previous acquaintance with the subject requires, and habits of expense, from their stations in life necessarily formed upon a scale higher than that required for the necessary and even comfortable subsistence of the day-labourer; and hence, their interference has in many cases hitherto tended rather to encourage than correct mismanagement and improvidence."

I may further illustrate this by reference to an account of the depositors in Exeter savings-bank on the 20th of November, 1829, with which I have been favoured by Mr. J. Tidd Pratt. This bank serves for the greater proportion of the county, and the number of the depositors excludes the supposition that what they do is not evidence of the capabilities of each class. The following is the account :—

		£	s.	d.
808	small farmers, the total amount of whose deposits is . . .	41,621	8	1
2072	agricultural labourers and husbandmen	70,688	3	10
478	tradesmen and small shopkeepers .	26,643	2	8
2376	artificers, mechanics, and handicraftsmen	94,668	13	8
140	labourers in the employ of tradesmen and artificers . . .	4,601	10	1
452	females engaged in trade or business	14,282	19	8
492	apprentices	3,351	1	8
202	carriers, drivers, guards, messengers, and porters	8,873	0	11
396	schoolmasters and mistresses, clerks, shopwomen and shopmen, teachers and governesses . . .	18,970	1	3
888	male servants . .	45,550	2	7
3497	female servants . .	102,882	2	7
536	seafaring persons . . .	24,447	18	1
43	soldiers	1,014	6	7
133	lower officers of the revenue and pensioners	8,942	7	11
93	officers on half-pay, clergymen, dissenting ministers, and professional men, &c.	6,459	1	5
212	females of small means, unconnected with business, or not particularly described	12,215	8	10
*8047	children of all classes . .	127,064	8	5
20,865	individuals entitled to . .	612,273	18	0
258	friendly societies . . .	41,351	11	3
115	charitable institutions and societies	14,902	17	7

Total amount £668,528 6 10

In 1828, the total number of depositors in Berkshire was 7007. There were also 70 Friendly Societies. I have not been able to obtain the subsequent accounts from any other places in the county than those I have mentioned. Mr. Pratt has examined for me the official returns made in the year 1827 from 273

. * A large proportion of the deposits in the names of children are known to be made to evade the limitation of the amount of deposits.

savings-banks in England and Wales, from accounts made up to November, 1826. The total number of depositors in these banks was 288,798. Amongst them were 9082 small farmers, and 29,020 agricultural labourers *. Notwithstanding the reduction of interest on deposits in savings-banks, I am informed that the number of deposits from the working classes has, on the whole, increased, and is at the present time increasing, from every part of the kingdom, Ireland included.

It may be supposed that the greater number of these depositors are single men. If so, the number of depositors, and the amount of the deposits, may perhaps be admitted as facts to show that if there were no bounties on marriage, by allowances to married labourers because they are married, the single labourers would be in a condition to lose by such marriages as those now usually contracted. The general answer to the inquiries I made on this subject from the persons connected with savings-banks were to this effect :—We see them, and know from their appearance that they are the persons they describe themselves to be; but whether they are married or single, we cannot tell. The greater part of them appear to be steady middle-aged men." We know that some of them are married men. For sufficiently good reasons, (which will appear in the subsequent portions of the evidence,) the agricultural labourers are at pains not to be known as depositors, and save clandestinely.

Loud and general complaints of the profligate conduct of the young men, and their intemperance at the beer-shops, do not favour the supposition that many of them put by anything from their wages. Having asked one of the officers of a savings-bank whether the agricultural labourers often received legacies, he replied, " Sometimes, but not often ; and when they are left here, they do not remain here long. A legacy, we observe, does more

* The witnesses who have been instrumental in the new and improved systems of management in the several parishes in which I have found the progress of pauperism has been checked by more strict administration, express their conviction that, if the exemptions from the consequences of improvidence were abolished or diminished—that is, if the bounties on improvidence were removed—savings-banks and such provident and admirable institutions would increase in number and importance. Amongst others, the Rev. Mr. Whately, of Cookham, expresses a strong opinion that this would be the result, and speaks confidently. from experience, of the effect of a more strict administration within his parish, where many of those able-bodied persons who have been accustomed to receive parochial aid, became frugal and depositors in savings-banks when they were thrown on their own resources. Whilst the number of the deposits from the adjacent parishes and in the neighbouring savings-banks greatly diminished, in consequence of the reduction of the interest on deposits, the number of depositors from Cookham increased. I have similar evidence from parts of the metropolis.

harm than good to a labouring man; and it may in general be said, that the care taken of money is in proportion to the labour bestowed in acquiring it. When a labouring man receives a legacy, and is induced to place it in a savings-bank, he is never content until he gets it all out, and it is spent usually in drink. " If every farthing of the money in the savings-bank from my parish," said the ·Rev. Mr. Whately, " were swept away, much good would nevertheless have been done in the formation of temperate habits."

Generally the married man is the best labourer, and obtains the highest wages and the most constant employment. In the greater number of cases of persons ascertained, from sources independent of the savings-banks, to have been depositors, they were married men. Mr. Tidd Pratt, who is in the habit of visiting the savings-banks, for which he is officially engaged, has had very extensive means of becoming acquainted with the individual depositors; and he has stated to me his conviction that the greater number of the agricultural depositors are married men. The unmarried agricultural labourers who save at all, he states, are usually members of benefit societies, which they prefer for the opportunities of conviviality which those societies afford. He states, from his own knowledge, that the number of deposits from the heads of families of agricultural labourers is actually much greater than it appears to be, since they are made by the wives of the labourers, and usually entered as from " female " depositors, without the addition of any specific description by which they might be known as belonging to the agricultural classes.

So far as I have been able to examine the answers to the query circulated by His Majesty's commissioners, whether the family of a labouring man in full work could lay by anything? it appears that a great majority of the respondents state positively that the labouring man cannot save anything. About half the respondents from Devonshire make no answer to the query. W. J. Coppard, the minister of Plympton, St. Mary's, says, " *A few* have trifling sums in the savings-bank." The other respondents either express a strong doubt whether anything could be saved by a labouring man, or declare positively that he could lay by nothing; yet we find upwards of 70,000*l.* saved, under all obstacles, by two thousand labourers, or by one out of every ten heads of agricultural labourers' families in this same county.

The larger proportion of the magistrates, clergymen, and parish officers who are respondents from Berkshire, declare that the labourer could not save; only three or four indicate a belief that he could. Colonel Page, who is one of the trustees of the

savings-banks at Newbury, says, "Hard to answer." Mr.
Walker, the magistrate of Lambeth-street, observed to me,
"Nothing is more difficult than for a gentleman to form a correct estimate of the means of living of a labouring man. Let
any scheme for his maintenance be devised by a gentleman, and
you will always find that the labouring man will live at a cheaper
rate than that estimated."

I have generally found the estimates of magistrates and others
as to the means of living or saving, and consequently of the
allowance from rates which ought to be made in aid of wages, vary
with the individuals and the customs of the place, rather than
with the prices of provisions. In the metropolis, lodging is somewhat dearer to the labouring man ; but Mr. Mott, and other well-
informed witnesses, declare that the markets are greatly in his
favour; that he may often purchase fish and other commodities
cheap ; and that, on the whole, he may live as cheaply, if not
more cheaply, here than in the rural districts.

About thirty labourers in the metropolis, when interrogated by
the governor of the Cold-Bath Fields House of Correction, stated
that they could live on 1s. a day. Labourers and others, earning
such wages as 2s. per day, are found to be depositors in the savings-banks of the metropolis. The following are the statements
of some of the respondents (clergymen and gentlemen serving
parochial offices in the metropolis) to Queries 35, 36, 37, 38—
What can a family earn, and whether they can live on these
earnings and lay by anything?

The answer from Chiswick states that a family might earn 49l.
per annum, on which they might live, but could not save. St.
Anne and Agnes, and St. Leonard, Foster-lane—family might
earn 60l. ; could not live on it. St. Botolph without, Aldersgate
—family might earn 63l. 18s., on which they might subsist, but
could save nothing. Mile End, New Town, and St. Mary's,
Somerset, City of London—family might earn 65l., on which
they might live, but could not save anything. St. Leonard, East-
cheap—family might earn 78l. ; could not save, and cannot
ascertain whether they could live upon it. St. James's, Westminster—man might earn 78l., besides material assistance from
his wife and children : might live on wholesome food, but cannot
attempt to say whether they could save. Holy Trinity the Less—
family might earn 93l. ; might live on spare diet ; could not save
anything. Mr. Baker, the coroner and vestry-clerk of St. Anne's,
Limehouse, states that a family might earn 100l., on which they
could live, but *not* save. Hammersmith—a family might earn
49l. 8s., which would give them wholesome food, and they might
and *do* save.

The extract I have given will, perhaps, suffice as a portion of the evidence tending to show the state of information on which rates of wages are determined, and adjudications are made on appeals against the allowances of parish officers. But on the part of those parish officers who come more immediately in contact with the labouring classes, and have the means of obtaining better information to determine as to the absolute necessity of the relief, I commonly found, in the districts where the allowance systems prevails, that they were daily acting in the teeth of conclusive evidence, constantly obtruded on their notice. At Newbury, for instance, on examining the books in the presence of the assembled parish officers, I found that they gave relief in aid of wages. The officers expressed a decided opinion that it was impossible for labourers of that class to subsist without such assistance as they received from the parish. The following is an extract from my notes of the examination of these officers:—

" Are those whose names appear in the books as persons receiving relief in aid of wages, all the labourers of this class or of those conditions residing within the town?"—The parish officers declared that they were only as a minority of those in the town. [Colonel Page, who did me the favour to assist me in the inquiry, observed that they did not probably form more than one-tenth of all the labourers in the parish.]

" Do the rest of the labourers receive no higher wages than those who obtain parochial relief?—We believe that their wages are the same."

" Amongst the large class of labourers who do not come for relief, is there not the usual proportion of married men, and many with large families?—Yes, we know there is."

" And yet, working at the same description of work and receiving no higher wages than the others, they maintain their families without asking aid of the parish? — Yes, they do do it, but how they do it we cannot tell. They are above coming to the parish."

" Is the fact that these independent labourers *do* live without receiving relief in aid of wages, any proof to your minds that others *may* live without rates in aid of wages? Is the occurrence of the fact before you any evidence of its possibility?"

To this interrogatory I received no answer; and I passed on to another head of inquiry.

Similar answers were given by the parish officers of Bethnal Green, to similar questions with relation to the silk-weavers. In Bethnal Green it is pronounced impossible that weavers who have families can live without relief in aid of wages. In the adjacent parish of Mile-End, New Town, which is chiefly occupied by silk-weavers, the parish officers state that they give no relief whatever to workmen when at work ; and the workmen or this parish do not appear to be more distressed than the weavers of Bethnal Green, though working for the same market, and at the same average rate of wages.

The evidence with relation to the labourers in agricultural districts which I visited appeared to establish these facts : that the labourers have now the *means* of obtaining as much of necessaries and comforts as at any former period, if not more :— *i. e.*, that their wages will go as far, if not farther than at any time known to the present generation: that, although the position of the agricultural labourers may be (as the subsequent evidence will show), relatively to others, one of great disadvantage, it is nevertheless a position, from which they may fall still lower, and that the single labourers are aware, that if the factitious inducements to improvident marriages afforded by the ordinary administration of the poor-laws were removed, it would be their interest to remain unmarried, until they had attained a situation of greater comfort and secured the means of providing for their offspring.

The Rev. H. C. Cherry, the Rector of Burghfield parish, near Reading, stated to me, in his account of the discontinuance of the allowance-system in that parish, that " the whole of the single labourers, including those who were on the parish, as well as those who were independent, hailed the notification" (that rates would no longer be allowed in aid of wages) " with great satisfaction, as they considered that it would render wages in future more proportioned to their labour, and that single men would have a better chance."   Mr. Cliff, the assistant-overseer of the same parish, stated, that "whilst the allowance system went on, it was a common thing for young people to come to me for parish relief two or three days after they were married :—nay, I have had them come to me just as they came out of church, and apply to me for a loaf of bread to eat, and for a bed to lie on that night.   But this sort of marriages is now checked, and in a few years the parish will probably be brought about.   If the former system had gone on, we should have been swallowed up in a short time.

" Is your knowledge of the individuals resident in your parish such, that you can state, without doubt, that there are persons in it, now single, who would, under the influence of the system of allowing rates in aid of wages, have married, had that system been continued?—I have no doubt whatever that several of them would have married: I know them so well that I am sure of it."

Similar effects had been produced by the allowance system in

Swallowfield; but, by the abatement of the cause, the effects have ceased. In these parishes every marriage, and its chief circumstances, was known to one or other of the parish officers. I thought this an opportunity to bring to the test the evidence which I had everywhere received as to the operation of the allowance system, and of the chief effects which its discontinuance may be expected to produce. I therefore framed a schedule under the following heads, and requested the Rev. Mr. Cherry, the minister of Burghfield, and Mr. Russell of Swallowfield, a magistrate and landed proprietor, to fill them up :—

" State the number of marriages which have been solemnized in your parish during each year, from 1810 to 1832, or for as long a period as may be practicable.

" State how many of these marriages, according to the best of your knowledge, have been improvident; *i. e.* with so little provision (even for persons of the lowest class of life) that it may be presumed the marriages would not have taken place, except on the assurance derived from the previous mal-administration of the poor-laws, that provision for the children would be obtained from the parish.

" How many children have been born of parents so married ?

" The number of these children who have in any way become chargeable to the parish.

" The number of bastards born in the parish during each of those years."

The following are the returns which have been furnished :—

	BURGHFIELD.					SWALLOWFIELD.				
Year.	Marriages.	Improvident Marriages.	Children from improv. marriages.	Children Paupers therefrom.	Bastards.	Marriages.	Improvident Marriages.	Children from improv. marriages.	Families chargeable.	Bastards.
1810	4	1	5	all	2	2	—	12	2	—
1811	6	2	7	do.	1	2	—	10	1	—
1812	7	1	5	do.	1	4	—	16	4	—
1813	9	2	4	do.	5	—	—	—	—	—
1814	4	0	—	do.	0	1	—	6	1	3
1815	7	0	—	do.	4	2	—	5	2	—
1816	2	0	—	do.	3	3	—	14	3	1
1817	4	1	4	do.	1	1	—	4	1	1
1818	8	2	2	do.	4	1	—	2	1	3
1819	3	0	—	do.	2	—	—	—	—	—
1820	10	2	10	do.	3	1	—	2	—	—
1821	6	1	4	do.	2	—	—	—	—	1
1822	3	0	—	do.	1	2	—	7	2	—
1823	6	2	6	do.	3	2	1	6	1	—
1824	7	0	—	do.	2	1	—	5	1	—
1825	4	0	—	do.	0	2	—	7	—	—
1826	4	1	3	do.	3	3	1	9	2	—
1827	6	2	unkn	own.	0	—	—	—	—	—
1828	5	1	3	do.	4	3	2	5	2	2
Select vestries. 1829	8	2	1	do.	1	1	—	1	1	—
Select vestries. 1830	0	—	—	—	0	1	—	1	—	—
Select vestries. 1831	2	—	—	—	1	—	—	—	—	—
Totals. . . .	115*	20	54		43†	32‡	4	112	24	11

It will be seen that in Burghfield, out of one hundred and fifteen marriages, twenty were improvident, and that fifty-four pauper children were the produce of these twenty improvident marriages. The allowance system has been discontinued in the parish only two years. In each parish the witnesses spoke confidently of the effects produced, and spoke not from any returns, but from their own knowledge of the circumstances of every party in the parish. For this reason, I consider these returns to be much more satisfactory than any to be obtained from parishes of greater extent; for in those the knowledge of the individual cases must be

* Average 5½ and a fraction per annum: reduction since 1829, 60 per cent.

† Average 2 per annum: reduced 75 per cent.

‡ Average 1½ and a fraction per annum: reduction 75 per cent. for last three years: reduction since select vestry 66 per cent.

indistinct in proportion to their number, and the distance of their residences.

Mr. Russell states in a letter to me, in explanation of his returns,— :

" The heading of column four, I have been obliged to alter from ' Paupers therefrom' to ' Number of families relieved.' Owing to the mode in which relief is indiscriminately given in this county, under the name of ' bread-money,' the number of *children* that have become chargeable cannot be distinctly stated. All that can be done is to state the number of *families* who have received relief collectively by having. their. earnings made up by the parish to the amount of their ' bread-money.' Out of thirty-two marriages in the twenty-three years, twenty-four or three-fourths of the whole have received relief. In the course of the whole twenty-three years, there have been only four marriages in the parish that I consider as improvident; that is to say, as having been contracted under a manifest reliance upon parochial relief. No such marriage has taken place since the establishment of our Select Vestry in the spring of 1829; but I cannot under-take to say that any such would have taken place, if the vestry had not been established,* nor any improvement made in the way of managing the affairs of the parish.

" The difference between the number of bastards set opposite the last five years in column 5, and the number given to the corresponding years, in one of my answers to the ' rural queries,' arises from this—that the present table states the number *born*, and my answer, the number *chargeable*, in each year.

" During the ten years, from 1813 to 1822, there were thirteen marriages, producing thirty-four children, and ten of those families received relief. During the last ten years there have been eleven marriages, producing forty children, and yet only seven of the families have received relief.

" During the four years preceding the establishment of our Select Vestry, viz. from 1825 to 1828, there were eight marriages, of which three were improvident; producing twenty-one children ; and four of those families received relief. During the four years that our ves-try has been in action, there have been only two marriages, neither of them improvident, producing two children ; one only of those families has received relief, and that because both the husband and the wife had children by former marriages."

---

* The other witnesses, who, from their situation in life, are probably much better acquainted with the labourers in the parish, spoke confidently as from a knowledge of the influencing circumstances of individual cases, that the decrease of cases of bastardy and a reduction of such marriages by one half, had been solely caused by the improved parochial administration. :

" There has been no bastard born in the parish since the establishment of the select vestry.

" The marriages included in the table are those of the agricultural labourers only."

The Census for the parish of Swallowfield for 1801, apparently included the population of another district which is now separated from it.

	In 1811 the number of inhabitants was						365
	1821	.	.	.	.	.	347
	1831	.	.	.	.	.	390
Burghfield	1801	.	.	.	.	.	738
	1811	.	.	.	.	.	791
	1821	.	.	.	.	.	881
	1831	.	.	.	.	.	965
Cookham	1801	.	.	.	.	.	2239
	1811	.	.	.	.	.	2411
	1821	.	.	.	.	.	2734
	1831	.	.	.	.	.	3337

In Cookham, from the number of the inhabitants and various other causes, the circumstances of a large proportion of the parties who marry could not be distinguished. But the removal of the bounty on improvident marriages afforded by the allowance system, has been attended by a marked check to the population. The Rev. Thomas Whately states in his evidence:—

" I have examined the register of baptisms, and taken three periods of nine years each; the last is that during which the new system has been adopted; the other two comprise the eighteen years immediately preceding it." The respective numbers are 593, 706, 676 : hence, in the first period, the *in*crease was 19 per cent., and in the latter period the *de*crease was 4·3 per cent., and this decrease of procreation was going on during a period in which the population was increasing at the rate of 22·2 per cent.

Very marked effects with relation to bastardy were produced in this parish by the adoption of the plan of allowing the mother only a shilling a week, and giving her the alternative of the workhouse. Not only has the charge of bastards been diminished, from 184*l*. 17*s*. to 33*l*. 4*s*. 6*d*., but the bastards have not been brought into existence ; as it appears, by the register, that only one has been christened in each year for the last three years. It appears that previously the expense for bastards was 10 per cent. on the gross expenditure of the parish. The above plan Mr. Whately considered must produce a similar or greater reduction all over the kingdom *.

* Mr. Whately gave the following instance in illustration of the immoral tendency of the bastardy laws :—   " A man

. Hitherto I have given portions of the evidence tending to show the common effects of the mal-administration of the poor-laws. I now beg to submit portions of the evidence tending to develope those effects in combination with the effects of common systems of prison discipline and penal administration; for in all the more populous districts, I have found that the bad management of the workhouse and the bad management of the prison, react on each other, and that both exercise a pernicious influence upon the morals and condition of the labouring classes.

Mr. Hooker, one of the former overseers of Bethnal-green, stated that—

" There are now about one hundred and fifty young able-bodied people, of bad character, thieves and prostitutes, who receive relief from the parish. When relief is not given to them immediately they apply, they proceed to Worship-street, and obtain summonses. They will go frequently when they have had relief; and we have reason to believe they have stated that they have had no relief whatever."

Mr. Bunn, one of the present overseers of the same parish, stated,—

" It is quite common for the officers from the police-offices to come to our parish to inquire for bad characters against whom charges are made. The police-officers are well acquainted with their characters. It is the worst characters who generally raise tumults. They repeatedly tell me, that, by being sent to Bridewell, they are sure of getting plenty of food, and shall be sent out with clothes. I do not know what clothes are given to them there: but I have frequently seen them better dressed when they came out of prison, than they were when they were sent in. They

" A man (John Cartland) was engaged to marry a young woman named Bishop. The woman proved to be with child by a man named Hatch. Her disgrace, added to the lover's disappointment, so affected the young man's mind, that he attempted suicide; and after some time offered to enlist for a soldier. At the expiration of two years, having gradually become reconciled to the young woman, he married her, (in spite of her bastard child,) and at a subsequent time, being distressed for money, he appeared before the whole assembled select vestry, and requested the loan of 40s., offering the weekly pay his wife received, for her bastard child, to the parish officers as security for the repayment of the money advanced. This man, whose feelings were at one time so acute that he could not bear to live—not because he was disgraced, but because she was,—now stood before the assembled board of the respectable members of the parish, and without a blush or the apparent consciousness of shame, made his wife's disgrace a matter of bargain. Every instance of bastardy is an instance of the demoralizing effects of the bastardy laws."

frequently dare me to send them to Bridewell. There is no difference between the girls and the men; except that, of the two, the girls are the worst."

Mr. Drouet, the governor of Lambeth workhouse, stated,—

" The great want at present is, as I conceive, the means of a proper classification. We have the worst of characters in the house, which, in fact, constantly serves as a hiding-place for thieves: we have, I dare say, thirty thieves, all of whom have been in prison for robberies and various offences, and who, we have reason to believe, commit depredations whenever they are at large. It is a common occurrence to have inquiries made for particular characters at the workhouse, in consequence of offences supposed to have been committed by them. We also have, perhaps, from twenty to thirty prostitutes in the house. These, the worst characters, can always speak with the best characters; and the forms of the house allow us no means of preventing it. We cannot prevent the thief speaking to the young lad, or keep the prostitute from the young girl who has not been corrupted. There is, unhappily, a strong disposition on the part of such characters to bring others to the same condition. I have overheard a prostitute say to a young girl, ' You are good-looking; what do you stay in here for? you might get plenty of money;' and point out to her the mode. Last October, as an experiment, we sent off eight girls to Van Diemen's Land: they were all brought up as workhouse children, and were incorrigible prostitutes. I have evidence that seven of these girls were all corrupted by the same girl, named Maria Stevens. Every one of these girls had been in prison for depredations. One of them had been three times tried for felonies, having robbed the persons with whom she was in service. Such was the influence which this girl had over them, that they would not consent to go until she consented, nor would they be separated from her, and she formed the eighth of the party. The old thieves teach the boys their ways: a few months ago I took one thief before a magistrate for having given lessons to the workhouse boys, whom he had assembled about him, how to ' star the glaze,' as they call it : that is, how to take panes of glass out of shop-windows without breaking them, or making any noise. In so large a workhouse as ours the youth are never without ready instructors in iniquitous practices. In the spring many of the workhouse boys discharge themselves, and live during the rest of the year, we have reason to believe, in no other ways than dishonestly: we know it in this way, that the most frequent circumstance under which we hear of them is, of their being in prison for offences : but they do not care a rush for the prisons ; for they always say; ' We live as well there as in the workhouse.' "

Mr. Mott, the contractor, in giving evidence on the means of employing paupers in the workhouse, alleges, as one of the great obstacles, the constant liability to depredation.

" Even in these employments, however*, we are subject to continual losses from mismanagement or depredation. One man we lately prosecuted at the sessions for stealing fifty-one shirts, which he was entrusted to take home, and he was sentenced to seven years' transportation, which, by the way, I may observe, was a promotion to a place where he would obtain more food, if not more comfort, than in the workhouse.

" Are you sure of that ?

" I am sure, from conversations which I have had on the subject with the superintendent of convicts, that the convict receives more bread a-day than the pauper. Indeed, it is notorious at Gosport, where I have heard it descanted upon by many of the inhabitants, that the convicts receive one ounce of meat per day more than the soldiers set to guard them. I heard at Gosport, that the convicts being told to do something which they did not like, one of them exclaimed, in the presence of the military guard, ' What next, I wonder! d—n it, we shall soon be as bad off as soldiers.' The convicts ridicule the soldiers ; and I have myself seen a convict hold up some food to the guard, saying, ' Soldier, will you have a bit ?' Yet the operation of this system in gaols and workhouses was pointed out years ago, and it still continues. The convict's labour is proportionably slight.

" Do you find this state of things, as to punishment, re-act upon the workhouse ?

" Decidedly so ; and most mischievously as to discipline and management. The paupers are well aware that there is, in fact, no punishment for them. From the conversation I have had with convicts, it is clear, that confinement in a prison, or even transportation to the hulks, is not much dreaded. ' We are better fed,' I have heard them say, ' have better clothes, and more comfortable lodging, than we could obtain from our labour ;' and the greatest, in fact almost only, punishment they appear to dread, is being deprived of female intercourse. Some months since, three young women (well-known prostitutes) applied for relief at Lambeth workhouse ; and, upon being refused, two of them immediately broke the windows. On the moment, the *three* were given into custody to the police ; but recollecting that only *two* were guilty of breaking the windows, the beadle was sent to state the fact, and

* Sempstresses, &c.

request from the overseer, that the innocent person might be discharged : she, however, declared that she would not be separated from her companions, and immediately returned to the house and demolished two or three more windows to accomplish her desire."

Mr. Benj. Hewitt, keeper of the workhouse of St. Andrew's, Holborn above Bars, and St. George the Martyr, states,—

" I have constant evidence before me that the diet in our house is as good as the majority of labouring men with families can procure for themselves when in work. I believe that the poor in our workhouse live as well as many of the rate-payers. It operates as a powerful stimulus to persons to come into the house. I also see constantly, that many of the labouring classes, having found out that the parish living is no frightful thing, spend all they can. They do not care to save anything for a rainy day; they have no thoughts of the morrow, for they are well aware, that when the rainy day comes, they will be sure to get relief, or admittance to a place of comfort superior to anything their irregular conduct has allowed them to inhabit. Bad character or conduct will not occasion their relief to be forfeited. We have now about one hundred bad characters in the house, many of whom have been the frequent inmates of prisons.

" What is the discipline which you enforce in your workhouse upon these characters, or have you any specific discipline ?

" There is great difficulty in managing the refractory paupers, in consequence of the ameliorated condition of the inmates of gaols, where the allowance of bread is greater than in the workhouses. Many of them have told me, ' Oh, we do not care about the prison; that's where we want to go ; we get more bread there than we can here, and the allowance of meat is the same.' Those who do not say this, prove by their demeanour that they are well-persuaded it is so.

" Have you ever known of any inquiry having been made into the mode of living of independent labourers, with the view of determining, by the comparison, what should be the mode of diet of paupers ?

" I have never known any inquiry of this kind made by any governors or directors under whom I have acted. I think it would be of great importance, that the condition of labouring people should be taken into account, and that a general uniformity of diet should be established in all the parishes. An uniformity of diet would prevent a large proportion of the paupers shifting about, and great expense of litigation. It is most important, too, to diminish the inducement to labouring people coming into the workhouse; and hence the diet should be for able and refractory men, on the lowest possible scale. The progress of pauperism would be abated by proper regulations; and I am certain that the expense of the present paupers maintained by the parishes might be reduced one-quarter for such classes. Similar attention to the diet of prisoners in prisons is requisite, as I conceive, to enable us to maintain discipline in workhouses.

" What influence has your diet and general mode of maintaining paupers had upon the rising generation of paupers or the paupers' children?

" Many of them have left the workhouse with great reluctance. They have frequently cried on leaving it; and I have known them come back to it, when they have been sent out on liking to be apprenticed to respectable persons. They have been dissatisfied with the treatment which those respectable people gave them, as compared with the workhouse treatment. The proposed master has said to me, ' I cannot keep the child, for he seems so unhappy, that it is of no use keeping him.' About two years ago we reduced the diet of the unworthy paupers, amongst which is included the greater portion of the able-bodied. Previous to that time, girls for whom we got places in service were careless about keeping them, as they told their employers that they lived well in the workhouse, and had not so much to do. The girls having thus thrown themselves out of work, were invariably taken into the workhouse again, on the recommendation of the magistrates, to keep them from running the streets. Even now instances of similar misconduct happen, but by no means so frequently. The diet is not at present so low as it might be for these classes."

Mr. Huish, the assistant-overseer of the populous parish of St. George's, Southwark, states—

" It is astonishing that we are so quiet in our workhouse, from what I have heard of the keep of persons in prisons, which is better even than of persons in the workhouses. A short time ago a man named Abbot was refused the amount of out-door relief which he claimed; we told him, ' We cannot give you what you want.' He said that ' He must and *would* have it.' We told him he must get work; he said he could not get work, and would not seek work, he would sooner go into prison. I told him that if he did not take care he would get into prison : ' You have been in prison already,' said I, ' and you would hardly wish to go there again?' ' Indeed I don't care,' said he ; ' I can live better there than I can anywhere out of prison.' ' But if you go on in this way you will get transported.' ' You are mistaken,' said he, ' if you suppose I care for being transported. I know well enough that if I am, I shall be better taken care of, and shall live like a gentleman.' He proved that he did not care for a prison, for he conducted himself so outrageously, that we were compelled to take him before a magistrate, who committed him to Brixton. This was the fourth or fifth time he had been at Brixton on our account. This man had been brought up as a mechanic, in a branch in which, had he been a man of good character, he might now obtain good wages.

"Now this case, with others, affords an instance of what might be done by workhouse discipline. Mr. Hayes, who farms the paupers of several parishes, is a very intelligent man, his mode of action is, to give the refractory hard work, and a spare diet. He will place a man by himself, with nothing but a dead wall before him : he then puts in his hands a certain quantity of oakum, and tells him, " When you have picked that your dinner will be ready for you, and not till then." We sent this man to Mr. Hayes, but he soon got tired of it and left it, and we heard no more of him. This morning I met him coming in the direction·of Billingsgate with a basket of fish on his head, and apparently in an honest employment. We sent three refractory boys to this occupation, and two out of the three preferred going to sea."

Mr. Chesterton, the able governor of the House of Correction for Middlesex, made, at my request, some inquiries into this subject. He stated to me—" I have made inquiries, and caused inquiries to be made of persons, as to their comparative conditions as independent and free labourers, as paupers, and as inmates of the prison. Some of them had been porters, others common labourers; they were all of them strong, able-bodied men, who would probably have the means of earning good wages for labourers of their condition. They seemed to consider that the allowance of food in the prison and in the workhouse was much the same in point of quantity. Two or three (out of about thirty, of whom inquiries were made) said that they found the prison allowance the best. They all acknowledged that they do less work and get better food as prisoners than as independent labourers : but taking into account the irksomeness of the work and the restrictions of the prison, they said that they would rather be independent labourers, if they could get regular work at a shilling a-day. Generally, they appeared to consider that they could live upon a shilling a-day as free labourers. The restrictions in the workhouses in which they had been, were less than those in our prison, and they mostly preferred the workhouse."

This prison, from what I have heard of it, I believe to be in many respects one of the best managed prisons in the metropolis. The statement of the prisoners will of course be received *quantum valeat*.

It is a popular opinion, that " poverty is the mother of crime," or, in other words, that our gaols are filled by "the distress of the times," and not unfrequently by the difficulty of obtaining parochial relief. Previously, and subsequently to my acceptance of the post of assistant-commissioner, I have paid much attention to the subject of the connexion of pauperism with crime, and I can state that evidence is at variance with the popular opinion. The following is an extract from the evidence of Mr. Wontner, the benevolent governor of Newgate:—

" Of the criminals who come under your care, what proportion, so far as your experience will enable you to state, were by the *immediate pressure of want* impelled to the commission of crime? by want is meant, the absence of the means of subsistence, and not the want arising from indolence and an impatience of steady labour ?—According to the best of my observation, scarcely one-eighth. This is my conclusion, not only from my observations in the office of governor of this gaol, where we see more than can be seen in court of the state of each case, but from six years' experience as one of the marshals of the city, having the direction of a large body of the police, and seeing more than can be seen by the governor of a prison.

" Of the criminals thus impelled to the commission of crime by the immediate pressure of want, what proportion, according to the best of your experience, were previously reduced to want by heedlessness, indolence, and not by causes beyond the reach of common prudence to avert ?—When we inquire into the class of cases to which the last answer refers, we generally find that the criminals have had situations and profitable labour, but have lost them in consequence of indolence, inattention, or dissipation, or habitual drunkenness, or association with bad females. If we could thoroughly examine the whole of this class of cases, I feel confident that we should find that not one-thirtieth of the whole class of cases brought here are free from imputation of misconduct, or can be said to result entirely from blameless want. The cases of juvenile offenders from nine to thirteen years of age arise partly from the difficulty of obtaining employment for children of those ages, partly from the want of the power of superintendence of parents, who, being in employment themselves, have not the power to look after their children; and in a far greater proportion from the criminal neglect and example of parents.

" Does any, and what proportion of the average number of criminals who pass through your gaol consist of paupers receiving parochial asisstance at the time of the commission of the offence? —Perhaps one-fortieth : I might say not one-fiftieth."

Mr. Chesterton states, "I directed a very intelligent yardsman, and one who had never I believe, wilfully misled me, to inquire into the habits and circumstances of all in the yard (60 prisoners), and the result was that he could not point out one who appeared to have been urged by want to commit theft." It appears that, in the houses of correction, the proportion of prisoners who have been paupers is more numerous than in the other gaols.

Mr. Richard Gregory, the treasurer of Spitalfields parish, who for several years distinguished himself by his successful exertions for the prevention of crime within that district, was asked—

" We understand you have paid great attention to the state and prevention of crime; can you give us any information as to the connexion of crime with pauperism ?—I can state from experience that they invariably go together.

" But do poverty—meaning unavoidable and irreproachable poverty—and crime invariably go together?—That is the material distinction. In the whole course of my experience, which is of twenty-five years, in a very poor neighbourhood, liable to changes subjecting the industrious to very great privations, I remember but one solitary instance of a poor but industrious man out of employment stealing anything. I detected a working man stealing a small piece of bacon;—he burst into tears, and said it was his poverty and not his inclination which prompted him to do this, for he was out of work, and in a state of starvation.

" Then are we to understand, as the result of your experience, that the great mass of crime in your neighbourhood has always arisen from idleness and vice, rather than from the want of employment?—Yes, and this idleness and vicious habits are increased and fostered by pauperism, and by the readiness with which the able-bodied can obtain from parishes allowances and food without labour."

The effects of the system are increased in particular districts by distress, but I have not found that they are averted by prosperity. It may not be improper to observe in this place, that in America, where many of the circumstances which are here urged as specifics against the malady, such as high wages, and the liberal distribution of land to those who are disposed to labour in cultivating it, are in operation, the poor-law system is attended with similar effects.

By the report of the secretary of state of New York, February 9, 1824, it appears that in the state of New York—

One person in .	220 is a pauper.
Massachusetts, one in .	68
Connecticut, one in .	150
New Hampshire, one in	100
Delaware, one in .	227

In a report made in the year 1825, from a committee on the poor-laws, which sat at Philadelphia, I find the following passages expressive of the conclusions of the committee :—

" Upon the whole, your committee are convinced that the effect of a compulsory provision for the poor is to increase the number of paupers,—to entail an oppressive burden on the country,—to promote idleness and licentiousness among the labouring classes— and to afford relief to the profligate and abandoned, which ought to be bestowed on the virtuous and industrious alone. That the poor-laws have done away the necessity for private charity—that they have been onerous to the community, and every way injurious to the morals, comfort, and independence of that class for whose benefit they were intended. That no permanent alleviation of the evils of the system can rationally be expected from the erection of poor-houses, or from any other similar expedient; and that the only hope of effectual relief, is the speedy and total abolition of the system itself. In this country, where there are no privileged orders, where all classes of society have equal rights, and where our population is far from being so dense as to press upon the means of subsistence, it is indeed alarming to find the increase of pauperism progressing with such rapidity." * * * " We are fast treading in the footsteps of England."

In the fourth report of the Boston Prison Discipline Society, 6th edition, p. 252, there is the following passage on the subject, inserted under the head " Connexion of Pauperism with Crime :"

" This is a subject, too, which we have introduced in this part of our report, because we have become acquainted with the evils of it in consequence of what we have seen in Massachusetts. The state of Massachusetts appropriates, and has done it for many years, about 50,000 dollars annually as a state, besides what is done in the towns, for the support of paupers. In some of the larger towns, the places where they are kept are so constructed and managed that the poor-houses are most corrupt and corrupting. They are nearly as injurious in their influence as the old peniten- tiaries—not in the arts of mischief, but in the low and corrupting vices. There is sometimes not even a separation of the sexes. We might specify large and extensive establishments, which are now what the old alms-house in Boston was a few years ago. And we could give a detail of facts, which have been ascertained from careful examination of witnesses, to which we can only allude in this place, on account of the character of these facts. Suffice it to say, that they are such as to demand immediate attention from the towns and the state. The people of the towns would not counte- nance such things, if they were known, and the state would not

appropriate its thousands annually for the support of establishments, which are nuisances as much as the old state prison. They
are nurseries of vice; they are sometimes introductory to, and
sometimes receptacles from the prison; there is often an alternation
from alms-house to prison, and from prison to alms-house. We
have not stated the facts in detail which are known to us, nor shall
we do it in this place and at this time, but if the character of the
establishment is not altered, from which these facts are gathered,
they will be exposed in their naked depravity. Publicity will
correct the evils, if other means fail."

Mr. Edward Livingston, in his able introduction to the proposed penal code for Louisiana, recommending the establishment
of a house of industry, says that, instead of confining the attention of the legislature, as has been hitherto done, to the means
for the punishment of crimes already committed—

" I draw the attention of the legislature to the means of preventing them, by provisions bearing upon pauperism, mendicity,
idleness, and vagrancy, the great sources of those offences which
send the greatest numbers to our prisons.

" Political society owes perfect protection to all its members, in
their persons, reputation, and property ; and it also owes necessary subsistence to all who *cannot* procure it for themselves. Penal
laws to suppress offences are the consequences of the first obligation; those for the relief of pauperism, of the second; these two
are closely connected, and when poverty is relieved and idleness
punished, whenever it assumes the garb of necessity, and presses
on the fund that is destined for its relief, the property and persons
of the more fortunate classes will be found to have acquired a
security that, in the present state of things, cannot exist.

" This truth has attracted the attention of most civilized nations,
but always making the law of pauperism a distinct branch of legislation, never connecting it with penal jurisprudence, with which
it has so intimate a connexion, has given birth to more bad theory
and ruinous practice, than any other question in government."

With the view of judging of the strength of the influence upon
the labouring population of the mismanagement of workhouses
and prisons, I have endeavoured to obtain detailed information
as to the mode of living of agricultural labourers. In attempting
to make personal inquiries of the labourers in the districts which
I have visited, I found them regard me with so much suspicion,
that it became necessary to obtain the information by means of
persons with whom they were familiar. " This suspicion," an
informant observed, I " ought not to be surprised at, as the independent labourers really believed that mischief commonly followed even well-intentioned interference with their affairs by the

gentry, and they (the independent labourers) did not like to be treated as ' poor,' or as persons to be taken care of like paupers." I have succeeded in obtaining many accounts of their modes of living and expenditure in different places. The following accounts of the actual incomes and expenditures of three agricultural families near Newbury approximate very nearly to the ordinary expenditure of families of agricultural labourers :—

A man, his wife and six children, receive amongst them 13*s.* 6*d.*, which is thus expended at the grocer's shop, paying one week under the other :—

	s.	*d.*
7 gallons of bread	9	11
1 lb. of sugar	0	6
2 oz. of tea	0	8
Soap	0	4
Candles	0	4
Salt, pepper, mustard, vinegar, &c.	0	2
2 lbs. of bacon	1	4
	13	8

A man, his wife, and four children under two years of age, receive in wages 9*s.* and a gallon loaf from the parish weekly, and live rent free in a parish cottage :—

	s.	*d.*
5 gallon loaves	5	7½
1 lb. of lard	0	9
1 oz. of tea	0	4
¼ lb. of sugar	0	2
2 faggots	0	9
Soap and candle	0	3
½ lb. of bacon	0	4¼
½ lb. of butter	0	6
	8	9

A man, his wife, and three children, without parish relief; the man earns 10*s.* a week when in full employment; but occasional want of work reduces the earnings of himself and his wife together to 11*s.*—

	s.	*d.*
½ bushel of flour per week, present price	4	0
¼ lb. of candles .... ditto	0	3½
¼ lb. of soap .... ditto	0	4
Clothing Society	0	5
Needles, thread, &c.	0	6
Butter, tea, and sugar	1	0
Firing per year £3 0 0		
Rent, including house and ¼ of an acre of land } 2 0 0 (this is cheap.)		

Carried forward.....5   0   0 6   6½

$$
\begin{array}{l}
 s. \quad d. \\
\text{Brought up.} \quad 5 \quad 0 \quad 0\ldots\ldots\ldots 6 \quad 6\frac{1}{2} \\
\text{Purchase of pig}\ldots\ldots\ldots 1 \quad 7 \quad 0 \\
\text{Shoes for the family}\ldots\ldots 2 \quad 6 \quad 0 \\
\hline
 8 \quad 13 \quad 0
\end{array}
$$

Making, within a fraction, of weekly expenditure ..3 1¾

9 8¼

From these and several accounts from shopkeepers as to the
quantity of goods which they supply to *classes* of persons, it
appears that, supposing the children of the honest labourer eat
meat, the quantity consumed by each individual does not, on an
average, exceed four ounces each week.   If the head of the family
consumes more, the children must eat less.   Where higher wages
are obtained, it appears, from the statements of the shopkeepers,
that the labourers do not purchase a larger proportion of *solid*
food *.   The excess of meat consumed yearly in the small parish

* On inquiry into the modes of life of the labouring classes, I found some
of them, with comparatively high wages, living in wretchedness, whilst others,
with less wages, live in respectability and comfort.   The effect of economy
is more strikingly marked on comparing the condition of persons of other
classes, such, for instance, as merchants' or lawyers' clerks, with salaries of
50*l.* or 60*l.* a year, with the condition of mechanics earning from 30*s.* to 40*s.*
a week.   The one will be comparatively well lodged, well fed, and respectable in appearance, whilst the other lives in a hovel, is badly clothed, and, in
appearance as well as in reality, squalid and miserable.   Many instances
occur where a clergyman, or an officer on half-pay, maintains a family on
less than 100*l.* per annum.   Mechanics who, during nine months in the
year, earn from 50*s.* to 3*l.* a week in the metropolis, are frequently in the
workhouse with their families during the winter months.   In the course of
my inquiries as to the condition of the working classes, a grocer residing in
the metropolis, in a neighbourhood chiefly inhabited by the lower class of
labourers, observed, that they are the worst domestic economists, and that if
they had the intelligence, they have the means of greatly raising their own
condition.   He stated to me that the working men habitually purchase of him
the smallest quantities of the commodities they want.   They come every day,
for example, for a quarter of an ounce of tea for breakfast.   This they do
though in regular employment, and receiving their wages weekly.   To estimate their loss on this mode of purchasing, he pointed out, that in a pound
of tea they have to pay him, 1st, for the labour of weighing sixty-four
quantities instead of one.   To this loss might be added their own loss of
time in running to and fro sixty-four times to the shop instead of *once*.   2dly,
For the additional quantity of paper used in wrapping up the tea.   The paper
which will wrap up a pound of tea will only wrap up sixteen quarter ounces ;
consequently the purchaser of sixty-four quarter ounces must pay extra for
the wrappers of forty-eight quarter ounces.   Altogether, he considers that
the labouring man pays not less than 6*d.* a pound, or the value of a pound
or a pound and a half of meat extra, for every pound of the low-priced tea he
purchases.   Nor is this the only loss.   He is accustomed to consume the
whole quantity purchased, though a less quantity might often suffice ; all goes

of St. Giles, in Reading, beyond the full allowance to adults in Lambeth parish, has been shown to be 4500 pounds. From hence it appears that the excess beyond a profuse allowance—the mere waste by 62 paupers—in that small parish, would suffice as a year's supply of four ounces of meat per week each to 346 independent agricultural labourers, or to 86 families of four persons in each; or that these 62 inmates of this workhouse (one-third

into the pot; as he will not leave, or, as he calls it, "waste," so small a quantity. And so it is with all other commodities. A pint of beer, for instance, is sent for, when two-thirds of a pint would suffice; a pint not being sufficient, an extra pint is sent for, when a third or two-thirds of a pint would have served. Persons of the middle ranks calculate better, and make larger purchases, and thus " make their money go farther," and are more economical in the use of commodities. Formerly, a very large proportion of the agricultural labourers could only obtain their supplies of tea and other commodities by going four or five miles distant, and the purchases were all made on the market-day, or once in the week; and to this circumstance—this compulsory frugality—it was attributable that the agricultural labourer often lived as well, or better, on less wages than the labourer in towns. But small shops have been established in the villages, and have led the agriculturists to adopt the improvident practices of the labourers in towns, with this addition, that in the country the small shopkeepers give credit. The facility of obtaining parochial relief renders the agricultural labourers improvident. Many of them do not pay, and the shopkeeper endeavours to make up his loss by his charges on those who are less improvident. It is a matter of extensive complaint that the agricultural labourers have now got themselves into the hands of the small shopkeepers, and pay from 25 to 30 per cent. more for the goods purchased in the improvident manner described. It may be observed, that the circumstance of their not having displayed any management with respect to the commodities purchased at the chandler's shop, affords some presumption as to their habitual want of self-control with respect to the commodities supplied from the beer-shops. And the best witnesses declare that this improvidence is fostered, and the probability of amendment excluded, by the system of giving relief to the able-bodied labourers. Mr. Mott, and other witnesses, who have had much experience in maintaining considerable numbers, attest the correctness of the rule—that by adding rent and 20 per cent. as the retailer's profit on commodities, an estimate may be made of the expense at which a single person may live, in the same manner that a number are kept in a workhouse, or in a community of any sort, where the commodities are purchased at wholesale prices. Thus, if at any place, as at Gosport workhouse, the able-bodied paupers are clothed and fed better than most labouring men, at an expense of 2s. 6d. per head, allowing 6d. for the retailer's profit, and 1s. for rent, the allowance to enable an out-door pauper to live in the same manner would be 4s. per week. If the allowances in aid of wages are tried by this rule, it will be found that a large proportion of them are in error, to the extent of 100 per cent. I have found none that were in error less than about 20 per cent. The errors have not a little been fostered by the mischievous application of the word "poor" to independent or self-supporting labourers, as well as to idle and dependent paupers. The witnesses represent, that gentlemen, when endeavouring to determine what wages should be given to " the poor," have had the former class in view, when it was only the latter class which came within their province.

of them children) consumed, in thirteen weeks, as much meat as 738 agricultural labourers are enabled to obtain in the same time by their labour.

The following is the copy of the dietary of the poorhouse of St. Mary's parish, Reading :—

THE QUANTITY OF FOOD CONSUMED DAILY BY EACH MAN.
(In the House—No. 29.)

Days of the Week.	Bread.	Meat.	Vegetables.	Cheese.		Beer.
	lb.	lb.	lb.	lbs.	oz.	Pints.
Sunday . . .	1	¼	1	0	3	3
Monday . . .	1	—	—	0	4	3
Tuesday . . .	1	¼	1	0	3	3
Wednesday .	1	—	—	0	4	3
Thursday . .	1	¼	1	0	3	3
Friday . . .	1	—	—	0	4	3
Saturday . .	1	—	—	0	4	3
Total . .	7	2¼	3	1	9	21

The diet for females and children is exactly the same, except that the beer is only ten pints and a half per week, instead of twenty-one. The child has its ten pints and a half of beer and its two pounds and a quarter of meat, and its seven pounds of bread, &c. weekly, In one of the parishes no meat whatever is allowed to the children, who nevertheless enjoy excellent health. In the course of an examination of one of the London workhouses, where an excessive allowance of meat is made, one of the young able-bodied paupers was asked whether they had a sufficient allowance of food? His reply was that they had not. He was asked what quantity of meat would suffice? He replied that he thought he could eat two pounds of meat a day. Having been bred up in a workhouse, with a stomach habituated in infancy to the diet of an adult, it is scarcely surprising that, when he became an adult, he had a craving and a capacity for a much larger allowance of food. " But judge," said a witness, " what must be the effect of such a diet upon the child of an agricultural labourer, who has never been permitted to taste meat ?" It appears, from all the evidence, as might be expected from classes whose range of mental pleasures is not enlarged by education, that they avail themselves of sensual gratifications with the greatest avidity, and that variations in diet exercise a most powerful influence over them. One ounce of meat a day more or

less makes all the difference between a " good" and a " bad
parish," or a parish that will be sought or avoided by the regular
paupers.

I have thought it advisable to avail myself of an opportunity
of examining the correctness of the statement made by Mr. Mott
with respect to the relative diet of convicts and paupers. I find
that the convicts' superiority is understated.

The fare and general condition of the independent labourers in
the country about Gosport is stated in the evidence of Mr. Drouet
already quoted. The following dietary of the Gosport workhouse
is believed to be nearly as low as that of an independent labourer :—

WEEKLY ALLOWANCE.	MEN.	WOMEN.	CHILDREN.
	lbs. oz.	lbs. oz.	lbs. oz.
Bread . .	5 0	4 3	3 6
Meat . .	1 0	0 11½	0 7
Vegetables .	8 12	7 11	5 6
Pudding .	0 12	0 10	0 8
Cheese :	0 10	0 7½	0 5
Soup and Broth .	5 pints	3½ pints	3 pints.
Gruel, or Milk Porridge	14 pints	10½ pints	7 pints:

The following is the dietary of the Gosport house of correction,
as stated in the Gaol Returns for 1831, p. 101 :—

> Gosport Bridewell and House of Correction.
> Best bread, daily, 1½ lb. .. .. .. ;....weekly 10½ lb.
> Meat .... ;.......;;;......;weekly, 1
> Soup from ditto
> Potatoes............;.;;;...;;....weekly ½ gallon.

By the warrant for the pay of the army, clause 13, it is provided that—

" Soldiers at home, when in barracks or in stationary quarters,
shall be supplied with bread and meat after the rate of three-
quarters of a pound of meat "—[*i. e.* uncooked]—" and one pound
of bread a day for each man, the cost thereof being paid by a
stoppage not exceeding sixpence a day from the soldier's pay; but
if the cost of the bread and meat shall exceed sixpence, the excess
shall be charged against the public."

The following is a copy of the 21st article of the " Instructions
to the Superintendent of Convicts in England," issued from the
office of the Secretary of State for the Home Department :—

" A daily allowance of provisions is to be issued to the convicts
according to the following scheme of diet, a copy of which is to

be kept constantly hung up upon each deck, so that the convicts may always know what they are entitled to receive:—

DAILY ALLOWANCE TO EVERY CONVICT ON BOARD HULKS IN ENGLAND.

Day of the Week.	Barley.	Oatmeal	Bread.		Beef.	Cheese.	Salt.	Small Beer.
			Soft.	Biscuit.				
	lbs. oz.	lbs. oz.	lbs. oz.	lbs. oz.	lbs. oz.	oz.	oz.	Pints.
Sunday . . .	0 4	0 3	1 0	0 4	0 14	—	¼	1
Monday . . .	0 4	0 3	1 0	0 4	—	4	¼	1
Tuesday. . .	0 4	0 3	1 0	0 4	0 14	—	½	1
Wednesday .	0 4	0 3	1 0	0 4	—	4	½	1
Thursday . .	0 4	0 3	1 0	0 4	0 14	—	¼	1
Friday . . .	0 4	0 3	1 0	0 4	—	4	¼	1
Saturday . .	0 4	0 3	1 0	0 4	0 14	—	½	1
Each Convict per Week . }	1 12	1 5	7 0	1 12	3 8	12	3¼	7

" You are to use every possible means to prevent convicts from selling any part of their allowance one to another, or to any other person, and you are to be careful that no other than standard weights and measures are used."

Here within one small locality, we find the honest labourer the lowest in point of condition; the indolent pauper the next step above him; the refractory pauper, or the petty delinquent the next step above the pauper, and nearly approaching to the condition, in point of food, of the soldier; and the convicted felon rising far above the soldier, the petty delinquent, the pauper, or the industrious labourer. But it appears to be true, as declared by the refractory paupers, who proclaim their independence of all regulation, that if they get themselves transported for some more grievous delinquency, that they will receive even better treatment. I was informed by witnesses in Berkshire that several of the agricultural labourers who had been transported for rioting had written home letters to their friends, stating that they had never before lived so well, and soliciting that their families might be sent over to them. I caused application to be made at the colonial office for the dietaries of the convicts abroad, when I received the following extract from the Hobart Town Calendar, for the year 1829, under the head of " Assigned Servants " :—

" By a Government notice, 10½ lbs. of meat, 10½ lbs. of flour, 7 oz. sugar, 3½ oz. soap, and 2 oz. of salt, are laid down as the week's provision for an adult male servant; the supply of tea or tobacco being discretionary. The master is also required to furnish his servant at the rate of two suits of slop-clothing, 3 pair of stock-keeper's boots, 4 shirts, and a cap or hat, per annum. Also the use of a bed, 2 blankets, and a rug, all which are the property of the master. These being supplied, the Government disapproves the supply of money to the prisoner, under any circumstances.

" Female convicts are allowed, upon the same authority, 5¼ lbs. of meat, 8½ lbs. of flour, 2 oz. of tea, ½ lb. sugar, 2 oz. soap, 1½ oz. salt, per week. The annual allowance of clothing being 1 cotton gown, 2 bed gowns, 3 shifts, 2 flannel petticoats, 2 stuff petticoats, 3 pair of shoes, 3 calico caps, 3 pair of stockings, 2 neckerchiefs, 3 check aprons, and a bonnet, not exceeding in the whole cost 7*l.*; also a bed as supplied to males."

In the comparison of the dietaries, some allowances must be made for the want of completeness in the details, as to the strength of the beer and other liquids forming part of them; but these are generally proportioned to the comparative magnitude of the allowances of solid food. The general effect of particular modes of living and gradation of dietaries may be best proved by the declarations and conduct of those who have tried them all.

In consequence of the inquiries I have made on this subject, many of the inmates of the workhouses have been questioned as to their experience. Mr. Hewitt, the master of the workhouse of St. Andrew's Holborn and St. George the Martyr, made separate and close inquiries of several of the paupers in that house who had been in various prisons, and workhouses, and on board the hulks. He has furnished me with several dietaries made up from the statements of the paupers, and I find that they correspond very accurately with the dietaries set forth in the official returns. From the statements and admissions of the paupers, it appeared that they usually knew to an ounce the dietaries of the metropolitan prisons, and the hulks, and of many of the workhouses, of which some one amongst them had made trial. One of the paupers, named James Philby, a stout able-bodied man, (with the exception that he had a club foot,) had been fifteen times in the House of Correction for various misdemeanours. He also acknowledged that he had received relief from the parishes of St. James, Clerkenwell; Chelsea; Bethnal Green; St. Giles, Bloomsbury; St. Dunstan, Fleet-street; St. Andrew, Holborn, above bars; the Liberty of the Rolls; Whitechapel; St. Mary, Newington; St. Andrew, Saffron-hill; Kensington; and St. George, Southwark. He had resided in all these workhouses; he had lived in one workhouse whilst he managed to

s

get relief as an out-door pauper from others, and that too during
the same week. He had also received ' sets up,' or grants of stated
sums for stated periods; from the several parishes. He admitted
that he had, at times, varied his occupation by stealing a little.
One instance was mentioned, where, after he had been liberated
from an imprisonment for stealing a gentleman's great coat, he
went to the owner, and as a favour, offered to let him have his
own coat back a bargain. This pauper, after having received
relief fraudulently from St. George's parish, Southwark, during
twelve years, was prosecuted by them, and his sentence was four
months' imprisonment. This sentence, according to his own
statement, transferred him from the workhouse, where, as an
inmate on a low diet, the allowance was only 134 oz. of food
weekly, to a place where the allowance was 230 oz. From
the statements of these persons, it appeared that the average
dietaries of the workhouses in the metropolis was about 170 oz.
of solid food, whilst in prisons the dietaries were from 200 oz. to
280 oz. of solid food weekly. They admitted that the labour in
the prisons was very often little more than ' mere exercise ;' that
they were always ' very kindly' treated ; but that, as they lived well
enough in the workhouse, they preferred it, because they had
more liberty there, and could get better society when they were
out. ' As to regular work,' Philby said that he could at all times
travel to any part of the country, and live better on the road
than he could possibly do by hard labour.

From the official returns it appears that nearly all the prison
dietaries are twice as good as those of the agricultural labourers ;
and that many of them are much better than the workhouse
dietaries. Although the able-bodied pauper does not *generally*
receive so much *solid* food as the soldier, (he sometimes receives much more,) the pauper is on the whole better kept,
much better lodged, and does less work. The soldiers receive
brown bread of the sort sold in the metropolis to valetudina-
rians as "digestive bread." In no workhouse have I found
the paupers supplied with other than white or wheaten bread ;
nor have I been able to learn that brown bread is used in any
of the prisons. Mr. Hewitt states that the convicts have held up
some of their white bread to the soldiers in derision, using such
expressions as "Look here! *Brown Tommy*" (the name of
soldiers' bread) "is good enough for you, but it will not do for
us." As white bread is supposed to go much farther than the
brown, the allowances to paupers and convicts are in reality
greater than they appear to be from the dietaries.

The family of the pauper is much better kept than the family
of the soldier. In very few poor-houses have I found any dis-

tinction made between the diet of the males and females. In the great majority of the workhouses no distinction is made between the diet of the children and of the adults. From some of the official forms of contract for the transport of troops, it appears that females are allowed, sometimes, only one-half; but, usually, two-thirds the quantity allowed to the males; and that children are only allowed one-half the quantity of females. The latter, probably, approaches to the natural demand for food, and indicates the prevalent extent of waste in the parochial management of the workhouses *.

In most of the prisons one fare is allowed to those who are suspected or unconvicted, and another fare to those who are convicted, the latter having a much larger allowance of better food; usually on the ground that, as they work, or as they may be called upon to work, they need more food†. But the work is

* It is very rarely that any parish officer would venture to enforce, or even to recommend, a reduction of these mischievous allowances. The workhouse-keeper of a large parish stated to me in evidence,—"I once ordered one of the attendants on the paupers to pick up the crusts which he found lying about the dust and the places belonging to the females. In a few days he picked up about half a bushel of crusts which had been thrown away. I contrived that the guardians of the poor should see them, thinking it might suggest to them that the allowance was rather too high, but it produced no effect, and I did not trouble myself again about the matter."

† The variations of diet in the prisons throughout the country appear from the gaol returns to be very great. On referring to the convenient abstracts of the returns published in the Eighth Report of the Prison Discipline Society, (which, in addition to the parliamentary returns, appears to obtain its information from zealous correspondents in every part of the United Kingdom,) it will be seen that the cost of maintaining the prisoners throughout the country varies from 1s. 2d. to 5s., and even 7s. per week per head (p. 59.) In the Coventry city gaol, bread only is allowed, and there are 2¼ per cent. of sick in the year. In other gaols, where the prisoners are maintained at double and treble the cost, there is double and treble the proportion of sick. Where bread alone is given, the daily rations vary from one to three pounds. The variations of charge in the same county are also remarkable. In Suffolk, the food given in the county gaol costs 1s. 9d. per head per week (the food of those at hard labour costs 2s. 11d.); whilst at Woodbridge gaol the cost of food is 3s. 6d.: at the former gaol there were 10 per cent. sick; at the latter, 18 per cent sick. The cost of food at the Wakefield house of correction, Yorkshire, is stated (p. 77) to be 1s. 8¼d., and 6 per cent. of the prisoners are sick in the year; whilst the cost of food at North Allerton is reported to be 5s. 0¼d.; and there are 37 per cent. of sick during the year. In Surrey, the allowance to the prisoners in the Borough Compter costs 1s. 9d. per head per week: in Horsemonger-lane it is 2s. for the unemployed, and 2s. 2d. for the employed. In both these gaols the amount of sick is only 2 per cent. in the year. The food given at Brixton costs 2s. 9d. per week, and the sick amount to 7 per cent. At Kingston, the cost is 3s. 6d., and there are 6 per cent. of sick during the year. In the Cold-Bath Fields House of Correction, which is in a smoky neighbourhood, the prisoners receive a diet of 174 ounces of solid food weekly, and the proportion of sick is 4½ per cent. per annum. At the Guildford House of Correction, a diet of 230 ounces of solid food is given weekly, and the proportion of sick annually is 9 per cent. In general,

declared to be much less than that of the agricultural labourer,
and such as the prisoners do not care for as soon as they become
used to it. The prison work is only ten hours a day : the agricultural labourer works, on an average, twelve hours a day. In
one instance, a reduction of an expensive diet of prisoners was
tried, but it was effected chiefly by the substitution of a diet a very
large proportion of which was liquid, for the previous diets consisting chiefly of solids, and the consequences were injurious.
The health appears, on the whole, to be better in those places
where the diet is moderate, than in those where it is more abundant. Mr. Hewitt states that the reduction of diet mentioned
by him, which was a reduction from a diet consisting of 169 oz.
of solids weekly, to one of 134 oz., was productive of no bad
effects : the paupers maintained on the low diet were as well,
if not better after than before the change; and few of them, comparatively to those who had been accustomed to live on a more
full diet, suffered by the cholera. This witness and several others,
in their evidence with relation to diet, call attention to the fact,
that there are probably some millions of honest men in the three
kingdoms by whom even brown bread is never used as food ;
that the greater part of Scotland is fed with oatmeal, and that
Ireland is fed with potatoes. And the witnesses ask, are Irishmen
a puny race ? Is the arm of the Highlander found weak ? Is the
lesson still to be held out to the honest and independent labourers,
that the food they are content with is not good enough for indolent
and vicious paupers or even for felons ?

The following table, drawn chiefly from official returns, will show
more clearly, at a view, the comparative condition of each class,
as to food, from the honest and independent labourer, to the convicted and transported felon. For better comparison, the whole
of the meat is calculated as cooked.

it appears from these returns, (which, unless they are much more accurate
than the returns to parliament on parochial matters, can only be depended
upon for a rough comparative estimate,) that the smaller and closer the body
having the superintendence, the worse is the management. It is in the
small local gaols that the cost of the diet amounts to as much as 7*s.* per head
per week; and it is stated that it is in these that there has been the least
improvement—" that most of the prisons attached to corporate jurisdictions
are in a state so disgraceful as to corrupt all committed to them."—Eighth
Report, p. 91.

THE SCALE.

I. THE INDEPENDENT AGRICULTURAL LABOURER—
According to the returns of Labourers' Expenditure, they are unable to get, in the shape of solid food, more than an average allowance of

	oz.
Bread (daily) 17 oz. = per week .	119
Bacon, per week . . . . . . 4 oz.	
Loss in cooking . . . 1 „	Solid Food.
— 3——122 oz.	

II. THE SOLDIER—

Bread (daily) 16 oz. = per week .	112
Meat .. 12 .. 84 oz.	
Loss in cooking . . 28 „	
— 56——168	

III. THE ABLE-BODIED PAUPER—

Bread . . . . per week .	98
Meat . . . . 31 oz.	
Loss in cooking . . . 10 „	
— 21	
Cheese	16
Pudding	16——151

In addition to the above, which is an average allowance, the inmates of most workhouses have,—

Vegetables . . . 48 oz.
Soup . . . . . 3 quarts.
Milk Porridge . . 3 ..
Table Beer . . . 7 ..
and many other comforts.

IV. THE SUSPECTED THIEF—(see the Gaol Returns from Lancaster)

Bread . . . . per week .	112
Meat . . . . 24 oz.	
Loss in cooking . . . 8 „	
— 16	
Oatmeal	40
Rice	5
Peas	4
Cheese	4——181

Winchester

Bread. . . . . per week .	192
Meat . . . . 16 oz.	
Loss in cooking . . . 5 „	
— 11——203	

V. THE CONVICTED THIEF—

Bread . . . . per week .	140
Meat . . . . 56 oz.	
Loss in cooking . . . 18 „	
— 38	
Scotch Barley.	28
Oatmeal	21
Cheese	12——239

VI. THE TRANSPORTED THIEF—

10½ lbs. meat per week . = 168 oz.	
Loss in cooking . . . 56 „	
— 112	
10½ lbs. flour, which will increase, } 218——330	
when made into bread, . . . }	

It is declared by the great majority of the witnesses, that any barriers which the vigilance, intelligence, and firmness of any parish officer may interpose between the indolent or the vicious, and the comforts which the present system of workhouse management affords to the worst characters, are almost always broken down by the interference of the magistrates. It is only in one police establishment in the metropolis, that the magistrates do not habitually interfere to order relief without reference to the characters of the applicant. The chief clerk at the Mansion-House, when examined as to the practice of the city magistrates, was asked, " Do you order relief to known thieves if they apply for it?—Yes, Sir, for we cannot let them starve!"

" Do you ever refuse to order relief to be given to prostitutes who declare they are in want of it?—No, Sir; can we let them starve because they are prostitutes?"

Parish officers have, not unfrequently, been reproved by magistrates at other offices for not promptly relieving characters whom those same magistrates have repeatedly committed to prison for felonies and various offences. But the magisterial decisions which have fixed on the parishes such numbers of the characters as those described in the evidence already quoted, appear usually to have been founded on the presumption, that calamitous consequences would ensue to the applicant from the refusal to make the order prayed for. Several magistrates have stated to me, that their position was really one often of great difficulty, from which they would willingly be extricated ; that they feared they did much mischief by their interference ; but they also feared that they would occasion much more mischief by refusing to interfere. It will have been seen, from the preceding portions of evidence, on what state of general knowledge of the means and condition of the labouring classes wages are frequently determined, and adjudications made on questions as to the allowances in aid of wages. Much of the other evidence appears to prove, that the practice in the appeal to the magistrate against the decisions of the parish officers, is not such as to put him in possession of the evidence which may exist in each case to rebut the presumption on which the interference is usually founded. An overseer or a parish officer is compelled to act on evidence of which he is himself commonly the percipient witness and sole depository,—evidence, which, though sometimes slight, amounts to cogent proof, when unanswered by other evidence on the part of the claimant. But in the usual mode of procedure, the parish officer is made a defendant ; his testimony is shut out, and he is often treated as a delinquent, on the mere fact of the refusal to yield relief immediately that it has been applied for. Where magistrates have taken part in the proceedings of parochial boards, they have usually concurred in their decisions; the concurrence being founded on similar knowledge of the facts, which in their position as members of the board were similarly presented to them. The following extract from the evidence of Mr. Waite, one of the parish officers of Whitechapel, with reference to the effects produced by the refusal of Mr. Walker, and the other magistrates of Lambeth-street, to interfere with the decisions of the parish, will, with the other subjoined evidence, serve to exemplify the general statements of the witnesses as to the inherent defects and mischiefs of the existing appeal to the magistrate.

Mr. Waite, in speaking of some applications for relief made by known impostors, stated, that under the former system of that office—

" If relief were not immediately granted to them, they went at once to Lambeth-street, which was close at hand, and they obtained summonses against the overseers to appear and show cause why they were not relieved. Summonses were usually given as a matter of course. One day I received fifteen summonses. An overseer cannot, usually, even in one case, get up evidence to disprove the statement of an applicant, however unworthy the character of that applicant may be, or however satisfactory may be the reasons which the parish officer has for rejecting the application. A large proportion of the applicants were well-known vagrants from other counties. How could we ascertain their past circumstances in order to disprove their statements before the magistrates? For although we might detect their impostures at the board, yet they always went before the magistrates prepared with their stories. Thus, in examining cases of vagrancy at the board, we often found that they gave false descriptions of their routes, and told such contradictory stories as proved that they were impostors. One frequent story with paupers pretending to have come up the road was, that they had that morning come from Chelmsford. I made inquiries about the local peculiarities of these places, and would ask the vagrants, (if they said they came from Chelmsford,) whether they came over any bridge from that town? They frequently replied, that there was no bridge. There is one stone bridge and one wooden bridge at Chelmsford. We have asked them how many churches there were in Chelmsford? Sometimes they would say there was not one, and at other times they would guess it at two or three : the fact was, there was one church. By questions of this description we soon learned whether they were impostors or not. The impostor, when foiled at the board, went amongst the crowd of other vagrants, and was sure to find some one who knew the place, and gave him minute information. He immediately availed himself of the instrumentality of the magistrate, and obtained a summons against the parish officer for refusing to give relief. When before the magistrate, the applicant would be so perfect in his tale as to baffle any skill the parish officer might have, and would make out his case to the satisfaction of the magistrate. Usually they 'explained' away the discrepancies of their previous stories, or stoutly denied that they had previously told the story reported by the parish officers. In order to have met them, it would have been requisite to have instructed a counsel in almost every case; and even then some of the well-practised vagrants were so acute, that I believe they would have baffled any counsel. I may adduce an instance, to show the aptitude of the vagrants and paupers in making use of information and getting up stories. One woman, named Mary Shave, the mother of a bastard child, being refused her 'pension,' went to the police-office and obtained a summons; whilst waiting at the office door, she related her tale to the vagrants in waiting. When the case was called on, a woman made her appearance as Mary Shave; I thought she was not the woman whom I had seen before: I said, 'Are you Mary Shave?' 'Yes,' she said, 'she was *the* Mary Shave, who had the misfortune to be the mother of a natural child, and who had been ill used by the parish officers;' and she made out a circumstantial case clearly to the satisfaction of the magistrates, who ordered her relief, which was immediately given to her. Soon afterwards, the real Mary Shave appeared and substantiated her claim, and she was relieved. The other had made off with the money.

How much did the first or pretended Mary Shave obtain by the fraud committed before the magistrate?—1*s.* 6*d.*

Could she have had a larger sum in prospect?—Not more than 2*s.* 6*d.*

"A few minutes after this second or real Mary Shave had been paid, a third woman made her appearance for the first time, and begged an order for relief from the magistrate: she said her name too was Mary Shave; she was the mother of the original Mary Shave; and she too, on making a good story, obtained relief, having been incited by the ease with which her daughter had succeeded. The entry of this last woman's character is in the following terms :—' Mary Shave, the mother; a widow, aged 36, a notorious impostor; receives from several other parishes, and finds out every charitable institution, and has two children left in the workhouse: she was sent to Clerkenwell by the former overseer.' Mary Shave, the daughter, was an able-bodied woman, but a bad character, and had been dismissed by the magistrates several times, until she had a bastard child, and then she fixed herself upon the parish. These I adduce as instances of the sort of impositions which, though detected and defeated before the board, unavoidably succeeded before the magistrates. These characters, males and females, at the office doors were often so clamorous and desperate, that it became necessary to let me out from the police office by the private door. I have been pursued by them through the streets, and obliged to seek shelter in shops. During twenty-seven years at sea, I encountered many perils in the waves, but these never hurt my mind so much as apparent perils amongst paupers. Had this system gone on, the expenses of our parish must have materially increased, notwithstanding the utmost labour that I or any other officer could have bestowed*.

* Mr. Sergeant, assistant-overseer of St. Paul's, Shadwell, a parish in an adjacent police district, was asked—
" You consider that the decision of the select vestry in matters of relief ought not to be final?"—" I decidedly disapprove of the practice adopted at Lambeth-street, of leaving the poor to the mercy of the parish officers."
" How many cases have occurred during the last year, in which you may have refused relief to applicants, on the ground of their being bad characters, being drunken or undeserving, or, as you believed, not in real want?"— " Perhaps about thirty."
" Were those refusals grounded on a complete knowledge of the characters and circumstances of the applicants?"—" Yes."
" You only refuse in very flagrant cases, and do so in perfect assurance, from the evidence you have before you, that no mischiefs would result from the refusal?"—" Yes."
" Can you give an instance?"—" Some days ago a coal-heaver, named Joseph Somers, applied for relief for himself and his family. I refused it, on the ground that he was in work, and was a general drunken character."
" What was your evidence that he was in work?"—" I had seen him coming home almost every night with the fresh coal-dust upon his face, and with his pipe in his mouth, and frequently reeling under the influence of liquor."
" Did you state your ground of refusal to the magistrate?"—" Yes, I did; and that he was a drunken, dissipated character."
" What did the magistrate say to this case?"—" He told me to relieve the wife and family; and that if I could prove that the husband was at work, a warrant would be granted against him, to show cause why he would not support his family."
" Did you relieve this family?"—" Oh yes."
" Did you attempt to obtain technical evidence of the man's being at work?" —" How was I to do this, Sir? A coal-heaver works one day on one vessel, and one day on another. It would be impossible for me to ascertain what part of the river he was at work at, or what he earned, or to get the people to come to prove it."
" When you say it was impossible, do you mean that it was impossible without an extent of labour which would make the proof cost more than the amount of relief given?"—" No, Sir: simply that it was absolutely impossible."

" Fortunately for our parish, and probably for the other parishes in the district, a different system was soon after adopted at Lambeth-street police-office. The parochial business of the office being left to Mr. Walker, and he having determined not to receive

" Is this a specimen of all the other cases in which relief was refused by you ?"—" Yes."

" Were the decisions of the magistrates similar in the other cases ?"—" Yes; they were nearly the same."

" In the case you have instanced, you would have deemed the evidence of the man's being at work such as you could act upon with safety ?"—" Certainly."

" If such technical evidence is required before a parish officer could be entitled to refuse relief, would relief be often refused ?"—" Certainly not with those characters."

" How many persons have served office as overseers since you have been in office ?"—" About sixteen."

" Of these, how many did you consider were men harshly disposed towards the poor ?"—" I scarcely believe that there was one. In general, their fault was a disposition to excessive liberality or over-indulgence."

" Do you say that they would not have been so disposed, any of them, after the service of their office? after they have become conversant with the characters of the paupers ?"—" Certainly not."

" Do you then think that they would neither allow their annual officers to act with undue severity towards the poor, nor use any themselves, whatever might be their interest in keeping down the rates ?"—" I think they would not."

" Would you expect, in a similar parish, where the annual officers were similarly elected, officers much of the same character as your own ?"—" Yes."

" In the instance you have mentioned as an example of some of the cases you have had before the magistrates, was your knowledge and investigation rendered useless ?"—" Yes."

" The appeal in those instances then is, according to your statement, an appeal from a person who has the best evidence or knowledge which the nature of the case will allow, to a person who has less knowledge, or no knowledge whatever, of the facts (further than of the claimant's own statement), and to whom better evidence cannot be given ?"—" That is a correct statement of the fact."

" Such appeals therefore must, of necessity, be decided by the magistrate without the knowledge of the best evidence of which the case will admit, and therefore probably in many instances erroneously ?"—" Certainly; and the only protection is in giving the paupers work, which, neither in our parish nor in others similarly situated, can be got in sufficient quantity."

" If, then, a board of unpaid officers, elected by the inhabitants, which board was formed, as it necessarily would be, of persons of the character you describe, ' disposed to excessive liberality or over-indulgence, rather than undue severity,' ' whatever might be their interest in keeping down the rates,' were empowered to superintend the general administration of the relief in the parish, and hear and finally decide on the appeals from the decisions of permanent officers such as you describe, do you think it would be an improvement in the administration of relief ?"—" Certainly it would, as they would have better knowledge, and I am sure would act justly and correctly towards the poor, without thinking of the rates. Such persons never do take the rates into consideration in particular cases. If such a controlling body

any appeals from the decisions of the parish officers, who were
the best acquainted with the circumstances of the paupers, we
got rid of a number of this sort of cases, when we found that they
were cases of imposture.

"Had you any riots or any disturbances, when the poor were thus
left wholly at the mercy of the parish officers?"—"No; not so
many riots by far as we had before the alteration. Formerly the
paupers of the worst class were accustomed to swear at us when
we refused them relief, and would say that they would have us
before our masters and compel us to relieve them. I had my windows broken several times, and was constantly threatened and
annoyed at my doors. Since the appeal to the magistrates is
altered, we find the parish materially benefited, and that there is
less bad behaviour on the part of the paupers."

"Did the independent people of the labouring classes—
those who might become chargeable—manifest any sympathy
with the paupers, or evince any disposition to rise for their protection?"—"None whatever: they appeared to be perfectly
satisfied with the proceedings of the parish officers. I received
more praise from independent labourers than from any other
classes."

"From the experience of the change made in your parish, do
you believe that such a change might be made without danger in
the general administration of the poor laws, and the decision of a
select vestry made final throughout the kingdom?"—"Judging
from our own experience, and from my observation of other town
parishes, I have no doubt whatever that the alteration might be
made without the slightest danger in towns, but my knowledge of
the agricultural districts is not such as to enable me to say what
might be the result of the alteration in those districts; though
the course taken by some of the country magistrates as shown in
their decisions certainly appears to me most extraordinary."

"Did charges of oppression, of cruelty, or hard-heartedness,
increase when the final decision was left with the board of parish
officers?"—"No: on the contrary, they decreased."

"Did the paupers go in the way of appeal to the independent
and labouring classes?"—"No; or if they did go, the independent labourers paid no attention them, for we rarely or never
heard any complaints from them of the paupers' treatment. They
did not interest themselves in it."

were established, I think the interference of the magistrates might be very
beneficially removed, for the deserving poor would get better treated, whilst
the drunken, dissolute characters, to whom we are now compelled to give
relief, would not be fastened upon the parish in such numbers. The magistrates now order relief without any reference to character."

" Were not those complaints from the independent labourers more frequent after than before the alteration ?"—" No : the complaints of all sorts were less than before, as it was notorious that the parish generally was in a better state. We had much less crime in the parish, though the New Police (which I think one of the greatest improvements ever established) has, no doubt, greatly contributed to this : but still the old system attracted vagabonds to the parish, who have now left us, and kept many in idleness, which led to pilfering. Some of these people I now see at work in the parish ; the change, I am sure, has benefited the people themselves, for they would commonly spend two or three hours to get a sixpence in charity rather than give an hour's labour to obtain the same sixpence."

" What number of undeserving cases did you get rid of in consequence of this alteration and of your investigations ?"— " About one hundred and fifty, as an immediate consequence of this alteration, but, altogether, including the clearing of the workhouse, (with which the magistrates had nothing to do,) we got rid of about five hundred in the course of two years."

Similar testimony as to the effect of the change of system was given from nearly every other parish within the district, except those in which, as the vigilance of the parish officers presents no barrier, no magisterial interference is required by the pauper, and the change produces no effect. A memorial from the parish officers and inhabitants of Christchurch, Spitalfields, praying that that parish may be included in the Lambeth-street office district, has been prepared for presentation to his Majesty's Secretary of State for the Home Department ; and in consequence of its being understood to be in contemplation to remove the Lambeth-street police-office altogether, a memorial has been presented from the parish officers of Whitechapel, praying that the removal may not be made, as the district would thereby be deprived of the advantages which the change of system has secured to it.

Whilst it is borne in mind that every penny unnecessarily spent on the pauper operates as a bounty on imposture and crime, and a discouragement to industry, forethought, and frugality, the evidence with relation to other positive obstacles created by the administration of the poor-laws to the growth and exercise of these virtues should be taken into account. More evidence has been presented to me on this head than I have been able to record. The following copy of an examination will give a conception of its nature.

Mr. William Hickson, senior, (of Hickson and Son's wholesale shoe-warehouse, Smithfield,) stated—

" As a manufacturer at Northampton, as a tradesman employing workmen in London, and as the owner of some land at Stans-
ford, in Kent, I have had various opportunities of observing the
operation of the poor-laws.

" The general effect of the present system is, to stop the
circulation of labour, and to prevent forethought. I find that
whenever workmen are out of work, they will not shift to places
where work might be got, for fear of losing their parishes. In
this parish, I am one of the Board for the management of the
poor. If, when shoemakers have applied for relief, and stated
as the ground that they have no work, I have told them that
they might get work at Northampton, they have objected on the
ground that the wages were low there ; in fact, I have found that
it is the parochial relief which holds them here ; for I knew at
the same time, that good work was to be had at Northampton.
The present system makes them believe that, when their own
supply of work is interrupted, the parish officers are bound to find
work for them or give them relief ; and that no one is obliged or
ought to leave his parish in search of work. If the other parish
officers, instead of giving money, had joined with me in offering to take such men into the house, they would have gone
for work elsewhere, and got it. One of the men who applied
was what was called a ' don workman,' who would have en-
sured work anywhere, as he had worked for the first houses in
London. Then the settlement law operates in another way to
impede the circulation of labour. If workmen sent to Northampton do not immediately get into work, not having been accustomed to provide against such a contingency, the law relieving
them from the obligation of forethought, they are at once hurried
back to their own parishes by passes. Some time ago a panic
took place, by which the shoe manufactories were stopped, and a
great number of the men thrown out of work. These men, having
saved nothing, were compelled to apply to the parishes. The
parish officers there immediately passed them home to their parishes
in different and distant parts of the country. The furniture
of numbers of workmen was sold, and they with their families,
were transported to their own parishes, some of them on the borders of Wales. Soon after they were sent away the trade re-
vived, and was remarkably brisk, and the labour of these workmen was wanted. Many of them who had been mischievously
sent away at the parish expense, were now brought back at the
parish expense. If these persons had been entitled to relief at
the spot where it was wanted, a great deal of money would have
been saved, and the workmen also would have been spared much
misery.

" The check to the circulation of agricultural labour is too notorious to be talked of. The case of a man who has worked for
me, will show the effect of the parish system in preventing frugal
habits. This is a hard-working, industrious man, named William
Williams. He is married, and had saved some money, to the
amount of about seventy pounds, and had two cows; he had also
a sow and ten pigs. He had got a cottage well furnished; he
was the member of a Benefit Club, at Meopham, from which he
received 8s. a-week when he was ill. He was beginning to
learn to read and write, and sent his children to the Sunday
School. He had a legacy of about 46l., but he got his other
money together by saving from his fair wages as a waggoner.
Some circumstances occurred which obliged me to part with him.
The consequence of this labouring man having been frugal and
saved money, and got the cows, was, that no one would employ
him, although his superior character as a workman was well
known in the parish. He told me at the time I was, obliged to
part with him,—'Whilst I have these things I shall get no work.
I must part with them all. I must be reduced to a state of beg-
gary before any one will employ me.' I was compelled to part
with him at Michaelmas—he has not yet got work, and he has
no chance of getting any until he has become a pauper; for,
until then, the paupers will be preferred to him. He cannot get
work in his own parish, and he will not be allowed to get any in
other parishes. Another instance of the same kind occurred
amongst my workmen. Thomas Hardy, the brother-in-law of the
same man, was an excellent workman, discharged under similar
circumstances; he has a very industrious wife. They have got two
cows, a well-furnished cottage, and a pig, and fowls. Now he
cannot get work because he has property. The pauper will be
preferred to him; and he can only qualify himself for it by becoming a pauper. If he attempts to get work elsewhere, he is
told that they do not want to fix him on the parish. Both these
are fine young men, and as excellent labourers as I could wish
to have. The latter labouring man mentioned another instance
of a labouring man in another parish (Henstead) who had once
had more property than he, but was obliged to consume it all,
and is now working on the roads.

" Such an instance as that of William Williams is enough to
demoralise a whole district. I say, myself, that the labouring
man who saves where such an abominable system prevails, is
foolish in doing so. What must be the natural effect of such a
case on the mind of a labouring man? Will he not say to himself, why should I save? Why should I diminish my present
scanty enjoyments, or lay by anything on the chance of my
continuing with my present master, when he may die, or the

means of employment fail him, when my store will be scattered to waste, and I shall again be made a pauper like William Williams, before I can be allowed to work for my living? This system, so far as relates to the circulation of labour, I am firmly persuaded, can only be put an end to by utterly abolishing the law of settlement, and establishing a uniform national rate, so as to allow a man to be relieved at the place where he is in want, instead of his being pinned to the soil."

The above are instances where the labourers would gladly have removed if they could before they became paupers; but in the evidence there is another and more numerous class of cases, where the agricultural labourers would not remove if they could. The Rev. R. R. Bailey, Chaplain to the Tower, who has had extensive opportunities of observing the operation of the poor-laws in the rural districts, states,—

" I consider that the present law of settlement renders the peasant, to all intents and purposes, a bondsman: he is chained to the soil by the operation of the system, and it forbids his acquiring property, or enjoying it openly or honestly. I am of opinion that management by hundreds, instead of by parishes, would greatly benefit all classes. Very frequent instances have occurred to me of one parish being full of labourers, and suffering greatly from want of employment, whilst in another adjacent parish, there is a demand for labour. I have no doubt that if the labourers were freed from their present trammels, there would be such a circulation of labour as would relieve the agricultural districts."

Can you give any instances within your own knowledge of the operation of the existing law of settlement?—" I was requested by Colonel Bogson, Keagrove House, to furnish him with a farming bailiff. I found a man, in all respects qualified for his situation; he was working at 9s. a week in the parish where I lived. The man was not encumbered by a family, and he thankfully accepted my offer: the situation was, in point of emolument and comfort and station, a considerable advance; his advantages would have been doubled. In about a week he altered his mind, and declined the situation, in consequence, as I understood, of his fearing to remove from what was considered a good parish to a bad one, the parish to which it was proposed to remove him being connected with a hundred house, in which there is more strict management. I was requested by a poor man, whom I respected, to find a situation for his son, in London: the son was a strong young man, working at that time at about eight shillings a week: I eventually succeeded in getting him a good situation of one guinea per week, in London, where his labour would have been much less than it was in the country; but when the period arrived

at which he was expected in London, he was not forthcoming.
It appeared he had altered his mind, and determined not to take
the place ; as I understood, his reason for refusing to accept it
arose from a reluctance to endanger his settlement in his parish.
Such are the instances which are continually presented to my
observation, with respect to the operation of the present system
of settlement."

" I am certain that the poor labourers of those parishes with which
I have been connected in the country are fully aware that it is
not their interest to advance their condition by the acquisition of
property. I once congratulated my bailiff on the prospect of his
inheriting, by his wife, a little real property; he replied, ' It
would be of no use to me, sir ; for I should be less able to get
employment, and could obtain no relief until it was all spent.'
When the gentlemen and clergy in the neighbourhood of Henly
contemplated the establishment of a savings-bank in their neighbourhood, I thought it my duty to address the young men on the
subject, after morning service, and urge upon them the propriety
of saving for their protection against the contingencies of sickness
and old age. They listened to me very attentively. One or two
persons asked me whether I honestly thought it would not be for
the benefit of the parish more than themselves if they saved ? I
was startled by the inquiry, but, on consideration, I found that
I really could not state that it would be for their benefit to save.
The decided conviction of the whole body of the labourers was,
that any saving would be for the benefit of the parish and the
farmers, and not for the benefit of the individuals saving."

In nearly every parish where bodies of Irish labourers are
located, the evidence as to the cause of their location is of the
following tenor :—

Mr. Joseph Whittle, one of the guardians of the poor and overseers of the poor, in the parish of Christchurch, Spitalfields, stated—

" In our parish it is a very rare thing to find any labouring men
working for less than twelve shillings a week : indeed, the average
rate of wages throughout the year is not less than from fifteen to
twenty shillings a week. A man could not be obtained to work
job work at less than three shillings a day.

Are there many Irish labourers in the parish ?—" Yes ; there is
a great proportion of them, and especially about Spitalfields
Market."

Do they usually receive the average wages you mention ?—
" Yes ; they do."

Why are English labourers not employed—or why are Irish
labourers preferred ?—" Because English labourers are not to be

had for love or money to perform the labour. I am sure, from my knowledge of the circumstances of the place and the employment, that there is not a sufficient supply of English labourers to take the work at any such wages. I believe the wages must be doubled to attract a sufficient supply of English labourers from other sources in the metropolis."

Are you not aware that, within a day's walk from any part of the metropolis, there are to be found English labourers working as hard, or much harder than any other class of workmen, for wages of about one-half the amount of those received by the labourers in the metropolis?—"Yes; I am acquainted with all the agricultural districts within twenty miles round the metropolis, and I know that is the case."

Why do not whatever superabundant labourers there may be in those parishes, remove and avail themselves of the demand for labour now supplied by Irishmen?—"Thousands of instances may be given, where the labourers will not stir for fear of losing their parishes. I think the law of settlement is the great means of keeping the English labourers confined to their parishes. It appears to them to be like running away from their heirlooms, or their freeholds. I am sure, from my own knowledge of the Whitechapel and other adjacent parishes, that there are not enough of English labourers to be had for such wages to perform the labour. Seven-tenths of the cases of alleged distress relieved are cases of imposture."

Mr. T. J. Holland, some time vestry-clerk of Bermondsey, stated,—

"There are great numbers of Irishmen employed in our parish ; but they are only employed because English labourers cannot be got to do the same work for the same wages.

And what sort of wages are those ?—"Not less than from ten to fifteen shillings a week. An English labourer might live upon this. But English labourers would have more wages, if they were to be had for the work, because they are worth more. I have heard a saying amongst the employers of these labourers, that an Irishman must always have his master over him. An English labourer does not require so much superintendence."

Why is it that, in your district, the English labourers have not taken the employment?—"I fear that the facility of obtaining parochial relief indisposes them to exert themselves or seek about to procure employment, or to take the labour which is given to the Irish."

Several witnesses state that the average wages of a labourer in the metropolis are not less than eighteen shillings a week, and that Irishmen obtain these wages under such circumstances as those stated. Some divisions of labour are now occu-

T

pied exclusively by Irish labourers, chiefly from custom and from the first demands having been supplied by their predecessors. And it is feared by witnesses conversant with labour markets, that whenever new demands for labour arise, they will occasion the location of additional numbers of this class of labourers.

Mr. Huish states that, "unless an alteration of the English poor-law takes place, I fear that the Irish labourers will obtain a more extensive footing in England than they now have : indeed, they will be sure to do so, because the present system keeps the English labourers shut up in their parishes."

———————

The foregoing evidence displays some of the corrupting circumstances operating on the classes by whom relief is received. The following examination is exemplificative of the corruption of those by whom relief is administered :—

Mr. Wm. Hickson, jun., of the firm of Hickson and Sons, wholesale shoe-warehouse, Smithfield. "On Tuesday, Dec. 23d, 1828, two persons came into the shop, and asked to see some shoes, and gave an order. They represented that they were parish officers of St. Leonard, Shoreditch. They then fitted on four pairs of shoes, of a superior quality, for themselves. The wholesale price of these shoes was 6s. 6d. each pair, the retail price was 7s. 6d. It is a custom in the trade, when any agent or other person gives a wholesale order, to allow him to have shoes for himself at the wholesale price. Thus, when we have received an order from a merchant, we allow the clerk who brings the order, if he wants to purchase anything for himself, to have the benefit of the wholesale price. The parish officers, however, in this instance, told me that I was to charge eighteen pairs of shoes instead of twelve (the number to be delivered), and that the money to be obtained for the six pairs not sent in was to cover us for the four pairs of the better sort of shoes supplied to them. I was very much surprised at this proposal, and I requested them repeatedly to state the manner in which the goods were to be sent in, and how they were to be entered, when they gave me instructions."

Was all this done in an ordinary business way, as if such a mode of dealing were familiar to them?—" Quite so, to one of them especially."

And you sent in the goods?—" Yes. I made the following entry of the transaction in the day-book :—

St. Leonard, Shoreditch.	*Dr.*		
18 Pairs men's shoes, at 4s.	£3	12	0
36 Ditto women's, at 3s. 2d.	5	14	0
	£9	6	0

12 Pairs of men's shoes sent instead of 18, and 4 pairs of best wax fitted on the two churchwardens or overseers, who instructed us to charge 18 pairs, instead of 12, to cover us for the 4 pairs.

W. E. Hickson.

" We then sent information of the fact to one of the members of the board, that he might take such steps upon the matter as he thought necessary."

Have you any reason to believe that such transactions have been or are common in other parishes, in the supply of goods on account of the parish?—" In some parishes we believe they are common. We have supplied many other parishes in which similar irregularities have never occurred. In one instance, an overseer came to us, and promised us a large order for the parish, if we would allow him a commission of two and a half per cent., which we declined."

Was this offer made in an ordinary manner?—" Yes, he appeared to consider it as a fair mode of trade. We had another instance in which we supplied about a hundred pairs of shoes, not to a parish, but for a charity-school. The treasurer of that school ordered these shoes to be sent in to a small shoemaker, who sent them in to the school as from himself. We afterwards heard that he had charged a profit of a shilling a pair on these shoes, with the knowledge of the treasurer of the charity."

Was this transaction conducted in a clandestine manner by the treasurer of the charity?—" No ; he stated his object to be to serve this tradesman, and that to do this he gave the order to him."

Have you any reason to believe that this is a common mode of persons in such situations serving friends who are tradesmen?— " Yes, I believe it is very common. It is not in such instances as these usually done from what are called mercenary motives, but they think they are justified in serving their friends at the expense of those unknown people, the public. On the other hand, I have seen instances, where grievous sacrifices of personal interests have been made by parish officers to enable them to perform their duties properly. The remedy for these things would be, to place the administration of parochial money in paid responsible agents. From our observation as tradesmen, having had to do with many cases of bankruptcy, we can state (whatever attorneys may state,) that the greatest benefits have resulted from taking the administration of bankrupts' effects out of the hands of tradesmen, who lost immense sums by jobbing, but more generally by neglect, and employing official assignees. I cannot speak as to the general constitution of the Bankruptcy Court, but I think that this appointment of respectable people, whose express business it is to attend to the administration of bankruptcy effects, is one of the best things that Lord Brougham has done for the country. I have no doubt

T 2

that similar results would follow from the appointment of respectable and responsible persons to administer parochial affairs."

Whilst parish officers are subjected to various descriptions of temptations in the performance of their duty, they have also another class of interests—the interest in obtaining popularity—to contend with. Mr. Crook, the parish officer of St. Clement Danes, stated that, " at present, a tradesman is often liable to injury if he administers relief impartially. I may state an instance of this: Mr. Rex, the keeper of a spirit-shop in Clare-street, Clare-market, served the office of overseer: during that service he found, amongst the applicants for relief, many of his own customers, who were drunken and dissipated. He censured them for their profligate habits, and the indulgence in spirituous liquors. He was ruined in his business; in consequence, as it was considered, of this mode of conducting himself as an overseer."

Mr. Richard Gregory, in his evidence, details some of the cir-cumstances which, in the town parishes, commonly govern the choice of the permanent and annual officers to whom the difficult task of administering the poor-laws is confided :—

Have you considered of any measures or proposed any for arresting the progress of relief?—" In the first place, I am sure that no improvement can take place in the administration of the poor-laws so long as it is left to parishes, or to such persons as the present unpaid annual officers. These officers have not, and never can have, the requisite ability; nor will they sacrifice their own time and interests to attend to the affairs of others. It is a thing morally impossible to have clever and able men willingly devote their time to the performance of such public duties without pay."

Might not paid and responsible officers be elected by the parishioners?—" No; I think you would never get such offices well filled unless it was by accident. The people have no conception of what sort of men are requisite to perform properly the duties of a parish officer.—If such a situation were vacant what sort of a man would apply for it? Why, some decayed tradesman; some man who had got a very large family, and had been ' unfortunate in business,' which, in ninety-nine cases out of a hundred, means a man who has not had prudence or capacity to manage his own affairs ; and this circumstance is usually successful in any canvass for a parish situation to manage the affairs of the public. Men who have before been in office for the parish would obtain a preference."

—And what sort of men are those who would be likely to be at liberty to accept a vacant situation ? " The situations of overseer and churchwarden are by some considered situations of dignity, and dignity always attracts fools. I have known numbers of small tradesmen who were attracted by ' the dignity of the office,' and succeeded in getting made overseers and churchwardens. Their elevation was their downfall. They have not given their minds to their own business as before. The consequence of this was that they have lost their business and have been ruined. Now and then a good man of business will be desirous of taking office when he thinks he is slighted, or has had an affront put upon him by being overlooked; but in general, any man in decent business must know, if he has the brains of a goose, that it will be much better for him, in a pecuniary point of view, to pay the fine than serve. I could name from fifteen to twenty people in our parish, who have been entirely ruined by being made churchwardens. These would be the people who would succeed best in parochial or district elections, for the people would say of any one of them, ' Poor man, he has ruined himself by serving a parish office, and the only recompense we can give him is to put him into a paid office.' This always has been the general course of parish elections, and I have no doubt would always continue to be so. There is infinitely more favouritism in parish appointments than in government appointments. In appointments by the government there is frequently some notion of fitness; but in the case of parish appointments, fitness is out of the question. When I was the treasurer of the watch department of the parish, I took great interest in the management of the police of the district, and determined to make it efficient. You would conceive that the inhabitants would have been so guided by their own apparent interests, as to get active men appointed, but I had solicitations from some of the first and most respectable houses in the parish to take their old and decayed servants and put them on the watch. I had also applications from the parish officers to put men upon the watch who were in the workhouse. As I was determined to make the police efficient, I resolutely resisted all these applications. My opinion is, that the management should be entirely under a central authority, which should divide the country into districts. The whole of the county of Middlesex, including the city of London, should be included in one district. If there had been a government management, the abominable practice of making allowances in aid of wages, which together with the improper interference of the magistrates has been so ruinous in the parishes of Bethnal Green and Spitalfields, and Christchurch, would never have been permitted. We should never have had, as we have had, silk masters, who have made rapid fortunes by giving their men low wages, and driving them on the parish for the rest of their means of subsistence."

Such being the frequent character of the appointments even to permanent offices, the following are exemplifications of the qualifications, in activity, acuteness, especial knowledge, and firmness, requisite for the dispensation of relief to the poor under the present system.

Mr. Brushfield, a tradesman, residing in Spitalfields, and one of the parish officers of Christchurch, Spitalfields, states:—

" The first day I was in active office, (25th May, 1831,) a woman named Kitty Daley came to me for relief on account of the illness of her child—she came without her child. I knew this case, as the doctor had said that something ought to be given to her on account of the child being ill of the small-pox. I gave her sixpence to serve until I had an opportunity of visiting her. In the course of the day, between the hours of ten and two o'clock, about forty or fifty applications were made to me for relief. Usually it is the practice of the parish officers to give away money on the representation and the appearance of the parties; indeed it is scarcely possible for a tradesman who has a retail shop to avoid giving away considerable sums of money; as the applicants excite the sympathy of his customers, and if he does not comply with their demands, they (the paupers) may and do raise mischievous tumults, and injure his business by their clamours and obstructions. They did injure my business in this way, and must injure the business of any man who does his duty. However, I determined to give no relief on the mere representations of the parties. I, therefore, took down the names and addresses of the applicants for the purpose of visiting their residences. In the course of the forenoon three women came to request relief, and each brought in her arms a child, which she said had the small-pox. The child was muffled up very carefully. One woman showed me the arm of the child; the other showed me the face of the child which she had; the third gave me a glance of the face of the child which she had. It appeared to me strange that there was so much small-pox about; but when I saw the face of this third child, it immediately struck me as being the same child that had been shown to me before, though it was now in a different dress. On visiting the places where the parties said they resided, it was found that about one-third of their statements of residence were falsehoods; no such persons were to be found. The names of some on the list were immediately recognized by the beadle as ' overseer-hunters,' —persons who make it their business to seek out and impose upon new overseers. Ultimate relief was not given to more than about twenty; the remainder, after much exertion, (which had never been undertaken before,) having been ascertained to be cases of imposition. Few tradesmen who had the inclination would have had the time to go through the same investigation, which, I dare say, was even then very imperfect. I found nowhere the three mothers who had each come with the infant afflicted with the small-pox ; but on visiting the residence of Kitty Daley, there I found the very same infant I had last seen, and it was dressed in the same dress. She did not deny the fact, that it was the same child that had been brought that morning in three different dresses by three different women. I accordingly gave her no relief.

" Subsequently I pursued my investigations into the cases of other applicants for relief, and struck off many cases of fraud.

" My general mode of investigation was, not to make inquiries elsewhere, but to visit the residences of those persons I suspected (which by the way was most of the paupers) first on the Saturday, and next on the Sunday. On Saturday they expect us, and I had generally some cause to doubt the appearance of their dwellings on that day. In general, those who wished to impose upon us overcoloured the picture, and certainly the pictures they drew were often very appalling. One Saturday, one of the churchwardens accompanied me, and we visited ten places : the scenes of distress were quite frightful ; there were two cases which appeared to be cases of extreme misery. In one house, that of a man named Bag, a man with a wooden leg, residing in Pelham Street, we found him there sitting as if sunk in despair ; he said he had no work, and had had no food that day, or since the evening before. His wife was afflicted with a bad leg ; she was in bed, and stated that she had not been able to get out of bed for six weeks. The room was in a miserable plight, dirty and wretched. I looked into the cupboard and found no provisions there ; the appearance of the place was such, that the churchwarden could not forbear giving the man some pecuniary relief at once. The other case was one of a man named Ansler, of Red Lion Street, who had for some time before been chargeable to the parish as an out-pauper ; we found the appearance of the place most deplorable. There was no appearance of food or comfort, and the children were ragged, dirty, squalid, and wretched. I told the wife to tell the husband to apply to me for relief in the evening, when I would give him relief, as I intended to do, being fully convinced of the necessity by the extreme misery which I had witnessed. The husband and wife came together to my house in the evening; I expressed my regret that they should be obliged to come to the parish, and asked if the husband had no prospect of getting work, he declared he had neither work nor any prospect of getting any at present. I judged by his appearance that he had been drinking, and said,—' Well, call upon me in the morning, and I will see what I can do for you.' They said they were very much obliged to me, and went away, apparently quite pleased, although according to their representations they were absolutely in a state of starvation.

" On the Sunday morning, I renewed my visits to most of those whose residences I had visited on the afternoon previous. The first case I visited was that of this man Ansler: I went at about nine o'clock in the morning; I opened the door, and then knocked, when I found they were in bed. I saw the wife jump out of bed, and in great haste she ran to a table which was standing in the middle of the room, and cover it over with a cloth; but in her haste to get away and in her confusion, she pulled the covering off, and exposed to my view—a large piece of beef, a piece of mutton, and parcels of tea, sugar, bread, butter, &c. The man called from the bed, ' B——t 'em, never mind them; you know they belong to your father.' I told them that was enough, and immediately left the place: they have never applied to the parish for relief since.

" When I visited the house of Bag, I found Mrs. Bag out of bed and at her breakfast; she had her tea and he had his coffee; I saw a neck of mutton on one shelf, and two loaves on another shelf of the cupboard, which was empty on the day before. I went into his workshop (he was a silk-dresser), which I found full of work. The man swore horribly, and I left the place: I do not know that he ever again applied to the parish.

" My impression now is, that nearly the whole of the cases which we had visited on the Saturday were found to be each partially or entirely similar cases of imposition. This man Bag must have concealed his work under his bed, and idled away the whole of the Saturday in order to make up the miserable scene which we first witnessed. In some other instances we have found the provisions actually concealed between the sheets or blankets of their beds. Such instances were frequently presented on other visits. I found it necessary in entering their dwellings, and in going up any common staircase, not to make the least noise,—to approach them by stealth; or the scrutiny would have been defeated. I think in all cases where the door was fastened the parties were impostors. At those places where the door was fastened it was necessary to kick very gently at the bottom of the door—as if it were a child at the door. A knock or a tap as from a man would have been the signal for preparation or disguise. In one recent visit made to a number of applicants, every one was found to be a case of imposition. It is quite common to find the applicants full of work in cases where they have declared they had no work whatever, and were starving. In one case I went up gently and opened the trap-door of a warper's loft, and found him deeply engaged with work of the best sort.

"Taking our own board of guardians as a sample, I should say that if they err at all it is on the side of humanity. My own impressions with relation to pauperism have been the result of experience. I took office with the popular belief that the poor were exceedingly oppressed and maltreated, and that overseers and parish officers were made of cast-iron,—men without hearts or sympathies; and I was firmly determined to make the poor comfortable. The first time I sat at our board I shed tears at the representations which were made, and I thought that our chairman (who was an experienced and judicious officer) was extremely severe. I have seen others of my colleagues shed tears at the first cases which were presented to them ; and these cases I have afterwards discovered to be such as I have already described. My conviction now is, that by far the largest proportion of pauperism is the result, not of unavoidable distress or of maltreatment, but of improvidence, influenced by the facilities which the system holds out to individuals of being well provided for without work. This system can, I think, only be checked by an improved system of administration by efficient officers. Persons in the situation of tradesmen cannot be expected to devote themselves to the performance of these duties, sacrificing their own interests and affairs. I am not sorry to have served the office of overseer, as it opened to me a new and very extraordinary view of mankind ; but with regard to my pecuniary interests, I had better have paid at least a hundred pounds than have served the office. I certainly believe that the best and most just means of relief would be by a national rate, and, if it can be devised, by a system of national management. One great effect of making the management national would be the prevention of the partiality shown in the distribution of relief, as where a pauper went to the same chapel as the distributors. There is often striking partiality exhibited in this respect."

Some witnesses have declared that they thought no alterations of the poor-laws would be necessary provided a " proper officer" was chosen to administer relief in each parish. These witnesses admitted that the indispensable qualifications of a proper officer were, that he should be a man, first, of remarkable intelligence; secondly, of remarkable activity; thirdly, of remarkable firmness; and, fourthly, that if he were an unpaid officer, he must be also a man of remarkable disinterestedness, ready to sacrifice himself to the performance of his duty. Several witnesses admit, or state as indispensable, such qualifications as, that he must be a man who, in the adjudication of relief, habitually "estimates all the consequences, meaning the consequences which are remote and contingent, as well as those which are direct and collateral; he must be a man of "great penetration," *i. e.* capable of at once detecting fraudulent rapacity, when it wears the mark of indigence; he must be a man of "great firmness," to withstand the demands even of real indigence, where, by yielding temporary relief, he would propagate permanent misery; he must be "regardless of popularity," ready, in the performance of a thankless duty, to incur the curses of the profligate, the censures of the sentimental, and the enmity of the powerful. He must be a man not of narrow sympathies, governed by the appearances of misery before him, whether those appearances be real or assumed; but one whose sympathies include the industrious and prudent classes and the poorer rate-payers, from the produce of whose labour the relief which he has the gratification of administering is to be made up. It has further been declared, that it is necessary that a succession] of such officers should be obtained: as a single manager, rendered profuse or negligent by indolence or ignorance or ill-judged humanity, may be enough to spoil the industry of the whole of a parish, and plant such a habit of profusion as a man of firmer temper and more correct views (when such a one may happen to take his place) may attempt in vain to eradicate. The witnesses, though they admitted that the poor-laws can be well administered only when there shall be, *at least,* one such officer in every parish in the kingdom, when asked to point out one such in their own parish, who could be had for payment or otherwise, failed to do so. They were somewhat surprised when they were informed that since there are 14,640 parishes, or places supporting their own poor, in England and Wales, they had declared that, on their theory, the poor-laws could only be safely administered, when at least 14,500 men of remarkable intelligence, remarkable activity, remarkable firmness and disinterestedness, were found to administer them.

———

Finding in the course of my inquiries with relation to the administration of out-door relief in the metropolis, how little was usually done in the way of inquiry or investigation as to the merits of the cases relieved, by the greater proportion of those who are engaged in the *compulsory* service of parochial offices, it appeared desirable to ascertain what lights for improvement might be obtained by a collateral inquiry into the modes of administering and investigating the cases of the poor of the distressed districts, by *voluntary* associations, conducted by individuals pre-eminent for their active benevolence, with whom no labour or personal inconvenience formed obstacles to their zeal for the alleviation of misery. Whilst I was preparing to obtain information from these sources, I received from those witnesses who were examined on the subject of the parochial administration, such evidence with relation to the common operation of voluntary charities in various ways for which I was not prepared, and such statements of their effects on the progress of mendicity and pauperism, as appeared to render this inquiry absolutely necessary for the direct objects of the commission. The district of Spitalfields is one, perhaps, where voluntary charities are more numerous and powerful than in any part of the kingdom. The Rev. William Stone, the Rector of Spitalfields, was pointed out by several benevolent individuals as admirably qualified to give information with relation to them. I submit the whole of his examination as part of this selection.

SPITALFIELDS—Evidence of the Rev. William Stone.

" I have superintended the parish of Christ Church, Spitalfields, about three years and a half. During that time I have taken an active part in all the leading charities in the district, and I have given my support and subscriptions to others in which I do not take an active part. During the last year I have been accessary to the distribution of above 8000*l.* I would specify amongst others the following sums :

	£.	*s.*	*d.*
In soup (from the Soup Society) .	3803	5	1
Spitalfields Association . . .	2169	11	0
Blanket Association . . .	294	2	8
Wheeler Chapel District Visiting Society .	536	17	4
Benevolent Society	1238	12	6

" This, viz. 8000*l.*, when the soup society is open, may be considered as the lowest average proportion of charity distributed for a year. The *district* commonly known under the name of Spitalfields, is to be distinguished from the *parish of Christ Church* Spitalfields, which is but a part of it. The distributions of voluntary charity are rather *local* than *parochial. All* persons co-operate in every charitable institution without regard to rank or sect.

" In the course of my experience in this district, I have observed many facts with relation to the operation of these distributions of voluntary charity, which have materially changed my views and led me to doubt whether the district is ultimately benefited by them."

Will you have the goodness to state some of the particulars to which you advert as having tended to modify your first opinions? —" In the first place, I can distinctly prove the migration of people from other parishes into this district upon the opening of the soup society. It may be stated that this society is conducted in the following manner. The subscribers are allowed tickets in proportion to the amount of their subscriptions. (I have an unlimited supply.) These tickets entitle the bearer to excellent meat-soup on the payment of a penny, but sometimes so little as a half-penny a quart. The tickets are so distributed as to allow two, three, four, or more quarts to a family, in proportion to the number of members. To a single man about one quart is given. The following statement comprehends all the expenses of the society :

Amount expended for meat	.	2854	10	8
ditto	grain . .	801	18	0
ditto	coals .	113	18	0
ditto	onions . .	51	2	0
ditto	salt and pepper	50	19	11
ditto advertising and printing	155	8	8
ditto	wages .	233	0	0
ditto	repairs, &c. .	52	7	10

£3803 5 1

" The receipts at the bankers from the commencement in January, to the close in June, 1832, have been 4280*l.* 3*s.*, of which we deduct 1359*l.* 10*s.* 3*d.*, for copper taken for soup, leaving a net balance of subscriptions, 2920*l.* 12*s.* 9*d.* The weight of meat bought by the society was 133,083 lbs., and the number of quarts of soup made and distributed amounted to 467,377.

" As an example, I may state the case of one woman who had the misfortune to be residing at the time without the precincts of the charitable district. She observed to me, ' Will I not come and live in your good parish, where the kind gentlefolks give away bread, and coals, and potatoes, and soup?' She was amongst us soon after as an applicant. A person of great experience in the district, speaking to me on the subject of these charities, ventured to intimate some doubts as to their tendency, and declared he could prove that the rents of lodgings within the district were raised on the opening of the soup-house, and the commencement of other local distributions. It was held out as an advantage to the tenants, that they were within a stone's throw of the soup-house. Some of the butchers in the district, though reluctant to observe upon it to myself, have declared that, immediately upon the distribution of soup being commenced, though the population has increased, a perceptible cessation of the demand for inferior pieces of meat takes place. There are complaints made by these tradesmen of the diversion of business, and of the injury done them by the sudden withdrawal of customers, who before could and did pay for the meat. I might, I believe, say, that there is a reduced demand for other sorts of provision *."

And to what class of persons are these soup distributions chiefly made?—"Undoubtedly, very many severe cases of distress are relieved by it; many cases where no other relief would be available; and it must be observed with respect to this charity, that being opened only occasionally, it cannot be regularly calculated upon, and is on that account not so liable to abuse. But I nevertheless believe, that for the time during which it is opened it is productive of the mischiefs to which I have adverted."

What is the nature of the Spitalfields Association?—"It consists of a number of individuals who visit the poor at their own houses, and who relieve them by tickets on certain tradesmen for coals, bread, and potatoes, originally gratuitously. But the last time we distributed (this being an occasional charity), I contended that we ought to diminish the chances of imposition by requiring some portion of payment from the objects; and accordingly it was provided that those who received tickets should pay threepence for the quartern loaf, fourpence for the half-hundred weight of coals, and threepence for the thirty pounds of potatoes. I believe that this regulation had the effect of diminishing the amount of imposition. We certainly were thereby enabled to continue our distribution longer than we otherwise could have done."

Is this Charity subject to much imposition?—"I will give you the following case as an instance; I received a note from No. 9, Crispin-street, Spitalfields, stating, that a young woman had just been confined of her fourth child; that she had absolutely not the necessaries of life in that delicate state of health, and begging me to come and save her from starvation.—The note was well written, so well that I was struck with it. When I went

* Similar evidence is given from the other parishes, where the voluntary gifts are considerable. Mr. Booker, the assistant-overseer of the parish of St. Botoph's, Bishopsgate, stated, " Our gift-coals are about forty chaldrons in the year, which are distributed in December, January, and February, to persons resident in the parish. During that time the business of the small coal-dealers was at a complete stand still, and they complained that they lost the best portion of their *ready-money* customers. This year, in consequence of these complaints, a new practice has been established, of distributing these coals by tickets on the various retail dealers in coal in the parish : the tickets are equally allotted among these retail dealers resident in the parish. No doubt we might obtain the coals cheaper by contract, but the poor do not complain, and the practice gives satisfaction to the retail dealers, some of whom have large families, and are as badly off as the paupers themselves."

to the house, I found on making inquiries, that the note had (as is common) been written by the landlord not by the husband. There I found the young woman (the name of the parties was Cartwright) who had certainly been delivered but a few days. She stated, that her husband had been for a long time without any employment whatever, that he refused to eat any portion of her or her children's meals for fear of depriving them of subsistence, and that, in fact, he left the house every morning in a state of desperation. On inquiry, I found I was not the first charitable person that had been applied to. She had been visited by some Quaker ladies attached to a charity in the neighbourhood, who, among other means of relief, had procured them some of the tickets of our Association : three of those tickets were immediately produced. It was evident from their dirty appearance, that they had been in their possession some days. I expressed surprise that these tickets had not been used as the applicants were in a state of starvation. The reply to this was, that they had not the 10*d*. to pay for the three tickets for coals, bread and potatoes. It being a case of sickness and strongly attested by the landlady, I deviated from my usual practice, which is not to give money. I provided them with a nurse, who did every thing for them. I visited them personally every day and sometimes twice, and I supplied them from time to time with these tickets, giving them money, and in some instances, as much as 2*s*. at a time. I afterwards discovered on the testimony of the nurse, whom I myself employed, and who was interested in keeping up the employment, that the husband was during this time frequently drunk, so much so, that on one occasion, when bringing physic for his wife, he had fallen down and broken the bottle; and that in the last instance of my giving him tickets for bread, and also money to the amount of 2*s*., and after strongly but very kindly expostulating with him on the past improvidence of his life, he left me and expended the 2*s*. in mutton-chops, ale, &c., and on the following morning importuned me, through the nurse, for a loaf. The wife might unquestionably have sustained inconvenience, and probably did so; but no wonder that she should, when the money given was all spent in liquor and mutton-chops. I might have stated that this man was a smith, of about thirty years of age ; his wife was a very young creature; he had married several years before, not having saved any thing beforehand; but when, as he stated to me, his wages were not less than 30*s*. a week, and continued to be so for some years after his marriage. On his own admission, he might, without any sacrifice, have saved 10*s*. a week during that time, to provide for the foreseen contingency for which it was now requisite to provide by charity.

" I may add, that this instance was accompanied by another, of the way in which these impostures are supported by others. A woman came in from an adjacent room (she was a lodger in the same house) with a cup of tea, and stated that all the poor creature had had was a cup of tea which she (the witness) had given her. She drew me into her own room and made another application in her own behalf, making the aid given to imposture support her own claim."

Have you observed many instances of this sort of marriages ?— " Unhappily they are fearfully increasing, the increasing recklessness of the labouring classes appears to me quite appalling. Whilst resident in the adjoining parish of Bethnal-green, I visited a poor family; the father and mother were in great want, in fact, the only subsistence which they had for some weeks was procured by a soup ticket, and some occasional advances of money from myself. Early in the following winter, being then resident as rector in my present parish, I was applied to by the mother of the same family who had then become resident in Vine-court, in my new parish. She applied to me partly for relief for herself and family, but more professedly on behalf of her eldest son, which son was one of the children relieved by me in the preceding winter. Without any provision, further than the scanty wages which he got on obtaining a little work, he married a servant girl; and the object of the present call was to provide her with a nurse on the delivery of an eight months' child, and ' any other relief that I could give them in a state of total destitution.'

" I have been compelled to pay great attention to the subject, and I have seldom given relief in any case without inquiring into the previous history of the family. Although in some instances the husbands at the time of the marriage and for a long time previous had been receiving high wages (as from 2*l.* to 3*l.* a week), although these wages had been received for years before the marriage as for years after; yet neither for the marriage, for sickness, nor for any other known casualty had any provision whatever been made. All came upon the parish to provide for every casualty, or sought relief from voluntary charitable associations. I do not think, during the three years and a half that I have been in my present parish, I have met with one instance of severe distress which was not to be traced immediately or remotely to some improvidence— the great improvidence being marriage, I mean a marriage contracted without the means either in possession or in reasonable expectation of providing for four children as the result of the marriage. It has come within my observation also, that parishes, by a most miserable and short-sighted policy, get rid of one pauper by creating ten—instances have come to my knowledge where the parties coming to be married have entered the church with hardly clothing."

Do voluntary associations, such as these you have mentioned, become subservient to such improvidence?—" Inasmuch as our visitors are persons actuated purely by benevolent feelings, they administer their relief with reference to the amount of actual distress in each individual case; and as that will commonly be in proportion to the number of the children and the past improvidence of the parents, I can have no doubt but that they ultimately, though indirectly, and certainly unintentionally, tend to promote these improvident marriages. The benevolent and very excellent persons with whom it is my happiness to act, are precluded by the circumstances of the case and the pressure of the immediate distress from investigating the causes."

How does the last charity you have mentioned, the Spitalfields Association, operate with regard to the traders who deal in the commodities dispensed by the association?—" It is equally complained of by the smaller tradesmen who supply the poor, that it deprives them of actual money customers, that the class of poor who deal with them are thus withdrawn, and that the profit of the commodities dispensed by the charity is diverted from themselves to a few, and those often wealthier tradespeople with whom the poor do not themselves generally deal."

What is the operation of the Blanket Association?—" This association is occasional in severe seasons; but it has been more or less open each year, from the year 1827, when it was instituted. The chief object is to lend the blankets for the winter months, to be returned in May."

What proportion are actually returned?—" I think about one-third; but those who return them come the next year, and it is common with those who come the following year to intimate, that they consider they have a claim, first of all, for having had blankets before, and secondly, for having returned them."

Then the other two-thirds are made away with?—" We have received proof that in some instances they have been pledged. We had it in contemplation to prosecute a pawnbroker in our neighbourhood, for having received a blanket in pledge, that blanket having the stamp of the Association; but we were told that our prosecution would not succeed, and we abandoned it."

Will you state what is the operation of the Benevolent Society?—" It is in its designs intended to relieve the peculiar distress of the district, in cases of sickness, and especially the cases of lying-in women. It is discretionary with the visitors to give money, and they have boxes of linen to bestow on lying-in women. They also give blankets, and that too in other cases than those of lying-in women."

What is the operation of this charity?—" The other day I had occasion to make inquiries of a person, who has the distribution of the commodities for which orders are given, as to the sort of persons who applied for relief, whether they saw the same persons repeatedly? I was assured, that the same persons (with the addition of others) invariably applied for relief, with the confident expectation of obtaining it. Within the last few days a woman applied to me, as having the disposal of an annual parish gift of coals; she stated to me as a reason for my compliance with her petition, that she had been considered a worthy object by the conductors of other charities in my parish; that she had been visited and relieved with the box of linen by the Benevolent Society, during no less than five successive confinements; and she was confident, that the same charity would be extended to her on any future occasion."

Would this argument, do you think, be deemed cogent by the usual administrators of the charity?—" I believe it to be one which, so far as I have observed, is too commonly acted upon."

Do you find it urged by the regular applicants, in such a manner as to lead you to believe that they commonly find it successful?—" Without exception they urge the same plea to myself in that expectation."

Have you made observations on the general effects of this last sort of distribution; namely, the provision for the lying-in women?—" I have observed, that its effects have been to paralyse provident habits; that it has tended to make these females calculate upon it, and to neglect making due provision for an event, which must have been sufficiently foreseen. This tendency I can state from extensive observation. A person, most intimately connected with this charity, has expressed regret, that all the charities of the district were not under the management of one superintending committee, as the objects there relieved were, to her knowledge, successful applicants to the various other charities in the district."

What is the Wheeler Chapel District Visiting Society?—" It is a society formed for the purpose of making a religious visitation; but as its members observe, in the course of their visitation, much temporal distress, they cannot avoid uniting temporal relief to religious exhortation. The parish is subdivided into two districts, and these districts are again subdivided into sections, and to each section are appointed one or two, or more visitors. Their visits are made once in every week, or fortnight, or as often as their time and occupations will allow. I should say that the design of this society is extremely good; the more so, as it does not originally contemplate temporal relief. I conceive, that one of the great things wanted in the present day, is a more frequent and acknowledged friendly intercourse between the various classes of society. I am satisfied that it would produce most satisfactory results to all parties. I find the labouring classes are extremely well disposed to receive instruction, and communicate with other classes."

What is the practical operation of the visits of the members of this society, as regards temporal relief?—" I regret that I cannot give so favourable a testimony as to the operations of the society, viewed collectively on this head, as on the other. The visitors being chiefly engaged in religious discussions, are I find, in some instances, too apt to be carried away by their religious feelings, and to be less strict than is necessary in their judgment of the amount of the actual and unavoidable want and distress. These visitors form, as it were, the connecting link between the various charities: they tell the poor whom they visit, and who state they are in want of relief, where and how to apply for it; and, moreover, the visitors personally exert themselves, and aid the applications which they have recommended. They commonly have in their hands tickets, or have access to recommendations through various subscribers to other charities, such as the Lying-in Hospital, the Welch Dispensary, the City Dispensary, the London Dispensary, the Institution for the Diseases of Children, the Rupture Society, the Ophthalmic Infirmary, the City of London Truss Society, the Blanket Society, and the Spitalfields Association, for the distribution of coals, bread and potatoes."

Are there no other modes of relief within the means of this society?—"Yes: I cannot recollect the whole. Besides the medical charities which I have mentioned, there is the Royal Maternity Society for delivering poor women at their own houses; there is the parish apothecary; there is also gratuitous medical assistance given by medical gentlemen in the parish, when applied to for that purpose; they have also access to the great Fever Hospital at St. Pancras; there is also an association called ' The City Kitchen,' which distributes potatoes, coals, &c. at a reduced price; there is the Educational Clothing Society, which is formed chiefly for the purpose of lending clothes, to enable children to attend schools, and adults to attend church."

Do they lend a suit of clothes for the one day, or how is the operation of returning the clothes conducted?—" In several parts of the district there are appointed depôts for clothing, generally the houses of some members of the committee, &c. The Sunday suit is taken from thence on Saturday evening, and returned on Monday morning."

Cannot you adduce any instance of the deceptions to which the visitors of the District Visiting Society are liable?—"A case came within my own knowledge. It was that of a woman, who stated that being utterly incapable of obtaining work in London, her husband was traversing the country in quest of employment. In the mean time she was left with four children without any means of subsistence: she had of course applied to the parish; but could obtain no relief. I was myself aware of the real circumstances of the case; for upon an investigation made long before, I discovered that the husband had even from the time of his marriage been assisted by the parish. In one instance, during an alleged inability to procure work as a weaver, he had been, as the parish officers called it, 'set up,' or provided with the means of obtaining a livelihood in another way. But, soon after this, he continued his occasional absences from his wife, and the parish had found no means of providing against the consequences of the profligacy of the man, and the deceitfulness of the woman. The visitor had not himself resorted to any means of obtaining correct information; and continued his visits and occasional assistance without any knowledge of the real circumstances."

Would the visitor in all probability also have distributed recommendations or tickets to this same individual?—"Unquestionably the visitor would have acted only upon the evidence obtained within the room itself, which is none at all."

Do you find many of the visitors competent to form a correct judgment as to the real wants of the poorer of the labouring classes?—"I think that visitors are frequently mistaken *; they are too apt to take into the houses of the poor their own standard of the value of money, and apply their own scale of personal and domestic comfort to *their* condition. I have known a visitor of our charities give an order for four bushels of coals, as the lowest proper amount of relief, to a person of a class in which they obtain their own supplies only in pecks, or even in half pecks. Articles of clothing are sometimes distributed to persons of a class who themselves consider, or at least treat them, as luxuries. When I first went into the parish, I viewed with great pain children without shoes or stockings, considering that they were sufferers; but

* Mr. Hewitt, the master of the workhouse of St. Andrew, Holborn, and St. George the Martyr, stated, "I am satisfied that the in and out-door paupers of this metropolis get by far the greater share of the charities in and about London, or else the greater part of them could not consume so much tobacco and other things, and return home intoxicated, and money in pocket." What evidence have you that they obtain money from the charities?—"I have searched them, and found not only money but charity-passes showing from whence they came, and tickets and other things belonging to the different voluntary charities."

u 2

subsequent observation has shown me that it was not so to the extent I first imagined.   The children in this condition I found in as good health as others; and, except in the winter, when subject to chilblains, sustaining no apparent inconvenience.

" With regard to the relief to be given in money, I have often been amused at the declamation in newspapers against parish officers, who, when an application for casual relief was made to them by a labouring man, ' only gave him a shilling.'   Now, although to a person in the middle or higher ranks of life this is a very trifling sum, yet I have known it to constitute one-fifth of the weekly expenditure of a person dependent upon her own earnings.   I should be sorry indeed to deny the poor any increase of comforts; but I believe that the gratuitous bestowal of them by our visitors often provides them with an article not in itself absolutely indispensable, and which would be better provided by their own exertions.   In many instances, where I have felt myself prompted to give the poor assistance of this kind, I have, on second thoughts, withheld it, from fear of the precedent which it would establish, and of the effects to be anticipated from that precedent, in creating an expectation on the part of the poor that relief would be given without work.   When a boy has come to my school ill-shod, I have felt strongly inclined to give him a pair of shoes or stockings, and should have done so, had I not been well convinced from experience that by my doing it in this particular instance, in a few days a number of other boys would have come without shoes or stockings."

Do you speak from experience, or from conjecture?—" Indeed it was positive experience that induced me to draw back.   I have given shoes and stockings to boys, and I have found that, in a few days, an increasing number of applications from other parents for shoes and stockings for their children has been the consequence."

Do you not think that the parents who send their children to schools are of the best of the working classes?—" Certainly I am disposed to think them so."

How do you find the administration of these charities bear upon the administration of the poor-rates by the parochial authorities? —" In the first place, it is assumed, I think, as a general principle, that the relief of the poor by the charities ought not to interfere with the parochial relief, and should be regarded as entirely independent of it.   Thus it is considered that, although a family may be relieved with soup by the Soup Society, the amount of the claims upon the parish for relief is not thereby diminished."

Is it not then considered that the one mode of relief should in any way be administered in co-operation with the other?—" So little so, that no tickets are ever given by the Soup Society to the parish officers.   A case was detected in which a visitor placed a few tickets in the hands of an overseer : this fact was brought forward and severely condemned at the ensuing meeting of the Soup Committee."

And is the same principle of administration adopted in each of the other charities, with the management of which you are intimately acquainted?—" I believe with each of them."

Do the administrators of charities and the parish officers often interfere with one another?—"In point of fact, they never come in contact with each other ; but I regret to state, that there is much jealousy between them, and that, whilst the parish officers accuse the visitors of weakness, the visitors charge the parish officers with cruelty : one of the consequences is, that the officers are checked in the performance of their duty.   I have had it deliberately hinted to me by tradesmen serving the office of overseers, that my opinions respecting the merits of applicants for charity have been at variance with their own : their manner evidently betraying apprehension that I had formed an unfavourable judgment of their humanity.   Without doubt, a tradesman in the situation of an overseer would not like to render himself obnoxious to one known to take an interest in the condition of the poor.   I have known instances in which the censures of the parish officers by visitors have been strong and unmeasured."

Do you find, on the whole, the feeling of reluctance to have recourse to parochial relief increasing or diminishing in the district in which you reside?—" Diminishing fearfully; though I am bound to say that it is not yet entirely eradicated.   I have been astonished and grieved to observe how persons of comparative respectability almost naturally resort to the poor-rates as a legitimate and inexhaustible fund for relief.   The other day, a widow who carries on a good business as a dress-maker, and had with her husband been for years in a situation of life to have enabled them to put by ten shillings a week or more, having sustained some temporary injury to her finger, was about to apply to the parish for relief.   At this very time she admitted that her business was extremely good, and that her chief difficulty was this temporary inability to continue it.   At this very time too she had two daughters provided for in good situations as household servants.   To my own knowledge, one of them, the younger of these daughters, might have had an advance of her quarter's wages.   It was suggested as a natural expedient, that the daughter, being so competent, should afford her this temporary assistance.   This, however, was not the object of the applicant—she preferred throwing herself upon the parochial fund, that she might enjoy that allowance over and above the supply from more natural sources of relief. I could multiply such instances, all of which have tended to convince me that the poor regard the parish rate as an exhaustless fund, by refusing to partake of which they shall only be doing an injury to their own families without benefiting any other party. I have expostulated with them on the impropriety of drawing this relief from the pockets of a class of people who, like the poor rate-payers of our district, are in little better, if so good, circumstances as themselves."

Do your observations lead you to believe that the present system of administering voluntary charity tends to create the distress which it proposes to relieve?—" I feel convinced that it does. With regard to the *standing charities*, that is, the charities which are in perpetual operation, the fact is unquestionable: I have known numerous families in which it is thought utterly unnecessary to provide for many regular and incidental expenses, from a confident expectation of assistance from these institutions."

Do you believe it relieves *all* the distress which it creates?—" By no means. For instance, I have known cases in which the unavoidable disappointment of the expectations held out by the *Lying-in Charities* has reduced poor women to the most cruel extremities. I know too that the *occasional* charities attract multitudes, who always become burthensome to the parish as *casual* poor. This is remarkably the case with the Irish. Armies of this degraded and almost brutish populace refuse to leave our neighbourhood *on account of the charities*. And yet, notwithstanding these means of relief with which, from their superior pretensions of misery, they are extraordinarily favoured by our visitors, they are frequently in so destitute a condition as to render it impossible for our parish officers to refuse them relief. I have had so much experience of this fact in my parish, and feel so persuaded of the impossibility of improving the moral or temporal condition of an indigent Irishman, that I almost sicken at the sight of one *."

---

* The following are examples of the evidence from other parishes, where the amount of money distributed in charity is considerable.

The Rev. E. J. Tyler, the Rector of St. Giles', Middlesex, examined:—

Have you observed any influence upon the Irish labourers by the charities in your parish, or in any other part of the metropolis?—"I am persuaded that the certainty of being either supported by alms or parochial assistance during their stay, should other means fail, or at all events of being returned to their country at the public expense, forms an inducement for vast numbers to come over from Ireland on the chance of what they may obtain, who would not otherwise leave their native country. It is known that many pregnant women come over for the express purpose of being admitted into some charitable institution for their confinement, with the certainty, at least the great probability, of receiving more from the bounty of individuals on their recovery."

Colonel

Will you describe the operation of the various charities, which

Colonel Page writes to me thus :—"I hope you will notice in your report the large charities bequeathed in Newbury, as a very principal cause of the high poor's-rates. Everybody is anxious to obtain settlements by servitude or renting in that parish, in order to obtain the chance of benefiting by the numerous charities."

Mr. Thorn, assistant-overseer of St. Giles', Cripplegate, examined. Have you any monies to dispense in charities within your parish?—" We have about 1,600*l.* per annum available to be given to the poor in our charities, according to the directions of donors. For the most part, the donations consist of bread, fuel, and clothing."

What is the effect produced by the distribution of these donations?—" We find that, a few weeks previous to the gifts being distributed, the people leave their work in search of them. There are always a great many more seekers of gifts than finders. Most of them by leaving their work neglect their families, and become really necessitous : those who are disappointed are irritated, and then demand relief as a right, the parish being called upon to make good their loss. Even those who have received relief always say, when they come to us afterwards, ' that, though it was very true they had received the gift, yet it had done them no good ; they had lost so much time, and they had got into debt.' We employ some of the out-door paupers in carrying home the gifts of coals, and pay them liberally for doing so. These men, when they apply for relief, and are told, ' Why, we gave you money the other day!' say, ' It is very true; but then we were in debt to our landlord,' or the chandler-shopkeeper, ' and we were compelled to pay him when we returned from labour ;' so they always calculate on the relief. After every season for the distribution of the gifts the applications for parochial relief are more numerous."

During the time when the gifts are distributed, are the demands on the poor's-rate reduced?—" Not at all : in fact, when the effects of these charities are examined, as shown in our parish, it will be admitted by the most prejudiced person that they are a curse rather than a benefit. They were a great deal worse formerly, when settlements were to be obtained by forty days' residence in the parish, as it led numbers to endeavour to obtain settlements with us. I am sure that our parish has been considerably injured by them. I have long been of opinion that it would be of great advantage to have the funds of these charities applied directly in aid of the poor's-rates."

Mr. Richard Gregory, treasurer of Spitalfields, examined. You have had, from time to time, assistance from Government in your parish. What have been the effects of those donations?—" That they have done great mischief by causing paupers to come from all parts of the kingdom, for the purpose of sharing in the relief; and when they have once come there, they have invariably stopped there."

Do you believe that such donations have a tendency to create distress of the kind which they propose to relieve?—" I do ; for there are numbers who would waste a whole day to obtain 6*d.* by charity, rather than work two hours to obtain 6*d.* by honest industry. I have seen in our own district abundant instances of this."

Do you believe that they relieve all the distress which they create?—" Always when there has been a donation of these sorts, we find that the parish burdens increase; these burdens continue, but the donation goes away. Some years ago we received a large donation from the Government, and I do not believe that the parish has got the better of it to this day ; for it made paupers, and attracted vagabonds from all parts."

are actually available in your parish, as exemplified in the case
of an individual, beginning with his birth, under the superintendence of the Royal Maternity Society?—[The Rev. Gentleman
requested time to make the answer, and he returned it in writing.]
" —*My own personal observation* enables me to describe the process as follows :—

" A young weaver of twenty-two marries a servant girl of nineteen—and the consequence is the prospect of a family.   We
should presume, under ordinary circumstances, that they would
regard such a prospect with some anxiety; that they would calculate upon the expenses of an accouchement, and prepare for
them in the interval, by strict economy and unremitting industry.
No such thing.—It is the good fortune of *our* couple to live in
the district of Spitalfields, and it is impossible to live there without witnessing the exertions of many charitable associations.   To
these, therefore, they naturally look for assistance on every occasion.

" They are visited periodically by a member of the " *District
Visiting Society.*"   It is the object of this society to inquire into
the condition of the poor, to give them religious advice, and occasional temporal relief, and *to put them in the way of obtaining
the assistance of other charitable institutions.*   To the visitor of
this institution the wife makes known her situation, and states her
inability to meet the expense of an accoucheur.   The consequence
is, that *from him,* through *his recommendation,* or *under his directions* she obtains a ticket either for " *the Lying-in Hospital,*" or for
" *the Royal Maternity Society.*"   By the former of these charities she is provided with gratuitous board, lodging, medical
attendance, churching, registry of her child's baptism, &c. &c.
By the latter she is accommodated with the gratuitous services of
a midwife to deliver her at her own home.

" Delivered of her child at the cost of the " *Royal Maternity
Society,*" she is left by the midwife—but *then* she requires a
nurse, and for a nurse, of course, she is unable to pay herself;—
a little exertion, however, gets over this difficulty—she sends to
the *district visitor,* to the *minister,* or to some other *charitable
parishioner,* and, by their interest with the *parish officers,* she
has, at last, a nurse sent to her from *the workhouse.*   But
still, she has many wants—and these too she is unable to supply at her own expense.—She requires blankets, bed and body
linen for herself, and baby-linen for her infant.   With these she
is furnished by *another charitable institution.*   Soon after her
marriage she had heard one of her neighbours say, that she
had been favoured in no less than *five* successive confinements
with the loan of the " *box of linen*" from the " *Benevolent So-*

ciety." She had, accordingly, taken care to secure "*the box of linen*" for herself, and during her confinement she receives occasional visits and pecuniary relief from a female visitor of the charity. By her she is kindly attended to, and, *through her* or "*the district visitor,*" she is provided, in case of fever or other illness, with the gratuitous services of the *parish apothecary*, or of some other *charitable medical practitioner* in the district.

"At the end of the month, she goes, *pro formâ*, to be churched; and though, perhaps, the best-dressed female of the party, she claims exemption from any pecuniary offering by virtue of a *printed ticket* to that effect put into her hands by the midwife of " *the Royal Maternity Society.*"

"The child thus introduced into the world is not worse provided for than his parents. Of course he requires *vaccination*, or, in case of neglect, he takes the *small-pox*. In either case he is sent to the " *Hospital for Casual Small-pox and for Vaccination*," and by this means costs his parents nothing.

" He has the *measles*, the *whooping-cough*, and other morbid affections peculiar to childhood. In all these instances he has the benefit of the " *City Institution for Diseases of Children.*"

" Indeed, from his birth to his death, he may command *any medical* treatment. If his father is a Welshman, he applies to the " *Welsh Dispensary*"—if not, or he prefers another, he has the " *Tower Hamlets Universal Dispensary,*" " *The London Dispensary,*" and the " *City of London Dispensary.*" In case of *fever*, he is sent to the " *Fever Hospital.*" For a *broken limb* or any *sudden* or *acute disorder*, he is admitted into the " *London*" or other " *Public Hospital.*" For a *rash* or any specific disease of the *skin* or *ear*, he is cured at the " *London Dispensary.*" And for all morbid affections of the *eye*, he goes either to the same charity or to the " *London Ophthalmic Infirmary.*" In case of *rupture*, he has a ticket for the " *Rupture Society*" or for the " *City of London Truss Society.*" For a *pulmonary* complaint, he attends the " *Infirmary for Asthma, Consumption, and other Diseases of the Lungs.*" And for *scrophula*, or any other disease which may require *sea-bathing*, he is sent to the " *Royal Sea-bathing Infirmary*" at Margate. In some of these medical institutions, too, he has the extra advantage of board, lodging, and other accommodations *.

* The managers of benefit societies and savings banks complain, in some instances indirectly, and in others directly, of the effects of the eleemosynary relief for such casualties as those institutions (and benefit societies especially) afford effectual means of providing for by easy insurances. It is urged by some witnesses that, although a person in work may not be able to raise money to pay for the relief of unforeseen casualties at the moment when that

" By the time the child is eighteen months or two years old, it becomes convenient to his mother to *"get him out of the way;"* for this purpose he is sent to the *"Infant School,"* and, in this seminary, enters upon another wide field of eleemosynary immunities.

" By the age of six he quits the *" Infant School,"* and has before him an ample choice of schools of a higher class. He may attend the *Lancasterian School* for 2d. a week, and the *National* for 1d., or *for nothing.* His parents naturally enough prefer the latter school,—it may be less liberal in principle, but it is lower in price. In some instances, too, it is connected with a *cheap clothing society ;* in others *it provides clothing* itself to a limited number of children. And in others, again, it recommends its scholars to the governors of a more richly endowed *clothing charity school.* To be sure, these are only *collateral* advantages. But it is perhaps excusable in a parent delivered by the *" Royal Maternity Society,"* to value these above any of the more obvious and legitimate benefits to be derived from a system of education.

" A parent of this kind, however, has hardly done justice to herself, or to her child, till she has succeeded in getting him admitted into a, school where he will be *immediately* and *permanently* clothed. This advantage is to be found in the *" Protestant Dissenters"*—in the *" Parochial,"* or in *" the Ward Charity School ;"* and she secures him a presentation to one of these, either by a recommendation from *" The National School"*—by the spontaneous offer of her husband's employer—or by her own importunate applications at the door of some other *subscriber.* It is true, some few industrious and careful parents in the neighbourhood *object* to putting their children into these charity schools. With more independence than wisdom, they revolt at the idea of seeing their children walk the streets for several years in a *livery* which degrades them, by marking them out like the *parish paupers* of former days, as the objects of *common charity.* But

relief is needed, yet he might be called upon to pay for it by instalments after he is convalescent and has returned to work. The trustees and managers of the Marylebone savings bank state—

" We are of opinion that, if the facilities given to the able-bodied of obtaining parochial relief or public charity (and we are induced to lay much stress upon the latter) were removed, the number of members of such institutions as ours would be increased.

" We are unable to state in what proportion the increase would take place ; but we think that, wherever any considerable number of a class of labourers and others are found to be depositors in banks for savings, almost all such persons might follow their example, and probably would do so, were they not encouraged in their thoughtless and improvident habits by the expectation of obtaining relief from some established public charity in almost every circumstance of difficulty or distress to which they can be exposed."

the parent in question has no such scruples—she has tasted the *sweets*, and, therefore, never feels the *degradation* of charity. She is saved the expense of clothing her own child herself; and she observes that almost all her poor neighbours, like the dog in the fable, have come to think what is really *disreputable* to be a *badge of distinction*. She knows, too, that most of the "*gentle-folks*" who support these charities openly proclaim (Oh monstrous absurdity!) that they were more especially designed for "*an aristocracy among the poor*."

"It is possible that she may not *succeed* in getting her child into a *clothing charity school*—it is more than possible, too, that she may find a more *profitable* employment for him than attendance at the "*National;*" she may keep him at home all the week to help her nurse her fourth and fifth babies, or she may earn a few pence by sending him out as an errand boy. Yet even under these circumstances she does not necessarily forego the means of getting him an education, or a suit of clothes for nothing: *even then* she can send him to one of the innumerable "*Sunday schools*" in the neighbourhood; and for clothing, she can apply to "*the Educational Clothing Society*." "The object of this society is the lending of clothing to enable distressed children to attend Sunday schools." *Only*, then, let *her* child be "*a distressed one*," and he is provided by the "*Educational Clothing Society*" with a suit of clothes which he wears *all the Sundays* of one year, and, in case of past regular attendance at school, all the *week-days* of the next. The *Sundays* of the second year, he begins with a new suit of clothes as before.

"The probability, however, is, that, by the time the boy is eight or nine years old, his mother *does* succeed in procuring his admission into the "*Clothing Charity School:*" and there is the same probability that she will *continue* him in it; she has strong reasons for so doing—for she knows that he will not only be clothed and educated at the expense of the *charity*, but that, when he is fourteen, that is, when he has remained five or six years in the school, he will be apprenticed by it to some tradesman, with *a fee* varying in the different schools from 2*l.* to 5*l.*

"At fourteen, accordingly, the boy is put apprentice by the charity to a weaver, and at the expiration of the usual term, he begins work as a journeyman. He has hardly done so, before he proposes to marry a girl about his own age. He is aware, indeed, that there are difficulties in the way of their union; and that, even on the most favourable supposition, their prospects in life cannot be considered flattering.—He has saved no money himself, and his intended is equally unprepared for the expenses of an establishment. He knows that, working early and late, he can

earn no more than 10*s.* a week—that, in case of sickness or
the failure of employment, he may frequently be deprived even of
these—and that his own father, with a wife and seven children,
was in this very predicament but the winter before; nevertheless,
" *nature intended every one to marry* ;" and, in the case of himself and his beloved, " *it is their lot to come together.*" On these
unanswerable grounds he takes a room at 2*s.* a week, and thus
utterly unprepared, as he appears, either for the *ordinary* or con-
tingent expenses of a family—he marries.

" We may suspect, however, from the result, that he is not so
rash and improvident in this conduct, as, *upon an ordinary calculation*, he must appear to be.

" Within a few months she has the prospect of a child—and a
child brings with it *many expenses*,—but no matter, *he* need not
pay them—for in *his* neighbourhood he may fairly calculate
upon having them paid by *charity*. Charity never failed his
mother in her difficulties—and why, *in precisely the same difficulties*, should it be withheld from *him* ? In the case of his wife,
therefore, as in that of his mother, the " *Lying-in Hospital*," or
the " *Lying-in Dispensary*," or the " *Royal Maternity Society*,"
provides the *midwifery*, &c.—The " *workhouse*," the nurse. The
" *Benevolent Society*," blankets, linen, pecuniary relief, &c. The
" *parish doctor*"—the " *Dispensary doctor*," or some other " *charitable doctor*," extra drugs and medical attendance. By a little
management, he may avail himself at the same time of *several*
obstetric charities—and be visited successively by Churchmen,
Quakers, Independents, Wesleyan Methodists, Calvinistic Methodists, Huntingdonians,—in fact by the *charitable associations* connected with every church and chapel in the neighbourhood.

" He now finds that his earnings are precarious—and that, even
at their utmost amount, they are inadequate to the support of his
increasing family. But his father's family was for years in the
same circumstances—and was always saved by *charity*. To charity, then, he again has recourse.

" He hears, that twice a year there is a *parish gift of bread*.
From some vestryman, or from some other respectable parishioner,
he obtains a ticket for a quartern loaf at Midsummer and at
Christmas. There is also a *parish gift of coals*. By the same
means he every Christmas gets a sack of coals. Indeed, by im-
portuning *several* parishioners, and by giving to each of them a
different address, or the same address with different names, he is
sometimes so fortunate as to secure *three* sacks instead of one.
On these periodical distributions he *can confidently depend*; for
most of the parishioners dispose of their annual tickets to the same
poor persons from year to year, *as a matter of course;* and others,

who are more discriminate, invariably find, upon renewed inquiry, that their petitioners are in the same state of apparent indigence or destitution. Under these circumstances, our applicant soon comes to look upon his share of the *parochial bounty* as a legitimate and certain item in his yearly receipts.

" But this is only a slight periodical relief. He wants *more loaves* and *more* coals, and he has the means of obtaining them. If the weather is severe, the " *Spitalfields Association*" is at work, and for months together distributes *bread, coals, and potatoes.* The " *Soup Society,*" also, is in operation, and provides him regularly with several quarts of excellent meat soup at a penny, or, sometimes, even a halfpenny a quart. At *all* times several " *Benevolent Societies*" and " *Pension Societies*" are acting in the district; and from these he receives food or pecuniary relief. He may apply too, during the temporary cessation of any of these charities, to the charitable associations of the different religious denominations, to the " *District Visiting Society,*" to the Independents' " *Visiting Society,*" to the " *Friend in Need Society,*" to the " *Stranger's Friend Society,*" to " *Zion's Good Will Society.*" He may even be lucky enough to get something from all of them.

" If his bedding is bad, he gets the loan of a blanket from the " *Benevolent Society,*" or from the " *Blanket Association ;* " or he gets a blanket, a rug, and a pair of sheets from the " *Spitalfields Association.*" The last of these charities supplies him with a *flannel waistcoat* for himself, and a *flannel petticoat* for his wife. In one instance, it furnishes his wife and children with *shoes and stockings.*

" Thus he proceeds from year to year with a *charity* to meet every exigency of health and sickness. The time at length arrives, when, either from the number of children born to him, under the kind superintendence of the " *Lying-in,*" the " *Royal Maternity,*" or the *Benevolent Society ;* " or from a desire to add a legal and permanent provision to the more precarious supplies of voluntary charity, he solicits *parish relief;* he *begs* an extract from the parish register, proves his settlement by the *charity-school indenture of apprenticeship,* and quarters his family on the parish, with an allowance of five shillings a week. In this uniform alternation of voluntary and compulsory relief he draws towards the close of his mendicant existence.

" Before leaving the world, he might, perhaps, return thanks to the public. He has been *born for nothing*—he has been *nursed for nothing*—he has been *clothed for nothing*—he has been *educated for nothing*—he has been *put out in the world for nothing* —he has had *medicine and medical attendance for nothing ;* and he has had his children also *born, nursed, clothed, fed, educated, established*, and *physicked for nothing*.

" There is but one good office more for which he can stand indebted to society, and *that* is his burial. He dies a parish pauper, and, at the expense of the parish, he is provided with shroud, coffin, pall, and burial-ground; a party of paupers from the workhouse bear his body to the grave, and a party of paupers are his mourners.

" I wish it to be particularly understood, that, in thus describing the operation of charity in my district, I have been giving an *ordinary*, and not an *extraordinary*, instance. I might have included many other details; some of them of a far more aggravated and offensive nature. I have contented myself, however, with describing the state of the district as regards charitable relief, and the extent to which that relief *may be*, and actually *is* made to minister to *improvidence and dependence*."

Have you any other remarks to make respecting either the administration of the poor-laws, or the distribution of voluntary charity, in your district?—" The testimony which I have now given makes me anxious to guard it from misinterpretation. It is certainly at variance with my former sentiments on the subject; and it may appear to be so with my present practice in the distribution of charitable relief; 1 would, therefore, add a few observations:—

" I entered upon my parish in 1829, with an earnest desire and solemn resolution to discharge its duties to the satisfaction of my conscience. I entertained the common notion respecting the necessity and application of charity. I made up my mind to sink all religious distinctions; and as the clergyman of the establishment, to conciliate and unite with all parties, for the relief of a numerous and distressed population.

" Before the expiration of the first year I was struck with the observation of many such facts as those detailed in the course of my evidence, and I then began to suspect the general tendency of our charitable distributions. I found that charity was, in this district, *reduced to a system;* that the immense sums expended in voluntary relief were, in effect, a *second poor-rate ;* that they were calculated upon in much the same manner by, at least, a large proportion of the poor; and that, like the poor-rate, they produced no perceptible or permanent diminution of distress. I found that an active clergyman in this district must ' leave the word of God and serve tables;' must be, in fact, no better than a *perpetual overseer.* The same applicants for charity presenting themselves from month to month, and from year to year, in the same state of apparent wretchedness, and with their numbers swelled by crowds of others, satisfied me that the utmost imaginable exertion of the charitable must prove utterly ineffectual for the relief or prevention of the most aggravated misery.

" I give it, then, as my decided and mature conviction, that without a change in the habits of our population, *no amount whatever* of charitable relief, whether raised by voluntary subscription, or by compulsory assessment, will ever meet the demands which will be made upon it. I feel confident that, had we millions, where now we have thousands of money to dispose of, we should only have millions instead of thousands of applicants. The root of all our evils is the universal prevalence of a profligate and *brutish* improvidence. The poor of this district are utterly *reckless of the future;* and even when they are not, in the common acceptation of the term, *vicious,* they are wicked enough to propagate misery at the very moment that they are petitioning for its relief.

" Inasmuch, then, as the distribution of charity, whether voluntary or compulsory, mitigates the *natural* consequences of improvidence, and tends to dissipate the apprehension of those consequences from the minds of the poor, I believe it to be unquestionably *prejudicial* to our district. It is under *this* conviction, and in *this* sense, that I have given the preceding testimony.

" Cases, however, of aggravated, and humanly speaking, unmerited suffering, are to be found, of course, in this district, as well as in others; and it is to these that I would confine the application of voluntary and compulsory charity.

" With regard to the poor-laws, then, I would have their operation brought back, as nearly as possible, to the original principle of the 43d Elizabeth, the principle, namely, of relieving none but the aged, infirm, and impotent. I would wish to see the visitors of charitable societies administer *their* relief also as much as possible upon the same principle. But, I would hope, at the same time, that every plan, whether of the legislature for the improvement of the poor-laws, or of individuals for the better distribution of voluntary relief, might be such as would tend to the ultimate discontinuance of almost all purely *eleemosynary* assistance.

" As the case now stands, both parish officers and benevolent visitors are, *in general,* quite incompetent to the proper administration of relief. I have known overseers, who made *no* inquiry whatever into the condition of the poor; and I have known a benevolent visitor boast of having, in one week, visited one hundred and seventy-four poor families, besides attending to his own counting-house. I can hardly say which, in my opinion, was the more mischievous to society.

" Experience in this district has taught me that the beneficial administration of relief requires·persons of enlarged views, extensive information, and long experience. Benevolent visitors, espepecially *females*, seldom possess *any* of these qualifications; and parish officers, under the present system, cannot, in general, be more competent to a satisfactory discharge of their arduous duties.

" I should very much regret any act of the legislature which would increase the amount of funds to be distributed among the poor of any given district. *With this understanding*, I should approve of a national rate, or enlargement of districts. I should rejoice especially at any regulation by which the administration of the poor-laws would be placed in more competent hands than it is at present, whether the instruments selected for that purpose were the most intelligent inhabitants of the district itself, or persons appointed by government, with a reference solely to their qualifications for the office."

The officers from the small parishes declare in their examinations, as to the expense of the keep of the paupers, the application of labour, and the maintenance of discipline amongst them, that their parishes have not the means to obtain more efficient management; that whilst the classes of their paupers are as varied as those of the paupers of larger parishes, they have not funds, or in any respect the means, to obtain the requisite superintendence and separate management. Nearly all the witnesses from the larger parishes, whom I have examined with relation to the state of their parishes, ascribe their demoralisation to the want of adequate means of classification; and declare that any system, if it be efficient, must furnish those means. Mr. Mott is the witness of the most extensive practical experience I have met with; and as his evidence embraces the chief points of consideration, with respect to the management of poor in large and small districts; and is enforced by other witnesses of great practical experience, I have thought it my duty to submit for consideraon the whole of his examination.

Evidence of Mr. Charles Mott, Contractor for the Maintenance
of the Poor of Lambeth.

" I have for the last twelve years given my entire attention to the subject of the maintenance of the poor in workhouses."

Were you not connected with parochial management before that period?—" No; I was brought up in a merchant's house (that of Baring, Mair, and Co.), from which I entered into business on my own account. Whilst I was a shopkeeper, some rates were applied for, which I thought exorbitant, which induced me to investigate the management of the parish; and, in consequence of that investigation, the rates were greatly reduced. From what I then saw of the general parochial management, it occurred to me that I might serve myself whilst I served the public, by contracting for the management of the paupers, as well or better than.they were then managed, and at a cheaper rate. I soon after availed myself of an opportunity of contracting for the maintenance of the poor of Newington parish, and also of the poor of the parish of Alverstoke, which comprehends the town of Gosport. I am now in the third year of my contract for the management of the poor of Lambeth. I have just now concluded a contract to maintain the poor of that parish, from the 25th November, for three years to come.

" I am the principal proprietor of the Peckham House Lunatic Asylum; and in that capacity I have transactions with about forty parishes.

" At Gosport the average number of the in-door paupers is about 240; in Newington, they average about 270; in Lambeth, about 700. My contract for the maintenance of the poor of Lambeth is at 3s. 11d. per head,—men, women, and a few children,—ablebodied, decrepit, impotent,—all included.

" This includes all the expense of the establishment, except rent and taxes. The parish agrees to keep every article in repair, except bed, bedding, and clothing, which I find altogether; and I pay a per centage for the use of them, which about covers the current expenses. I did contract on the same terms for Newington; but I gave it up for Lambeth parish, the latter being much larger, and I having a lunatic asylum and other business to attend to. It was publicly stated a few days ago in Lambeth vestry, that the contracting system had saved them 3000l. per annum for their in-door poor, during the two years the contracts had been in operation. The gross sum paid to me during those two years was between 6000l. and 7000l. a year. In round numbers the saving may be stated as about one-third. The diet is generally precisely the same, and indeed better."

To what circumstances do you attribute this great difference between parochial management and contract management?—" I should say principally to the different descriptions of food being given out in more exact proportions. A man who serves out food for the parish has no interest, or no sufficient interest, in distributing the food. However exactly the proportions may be prescribed, it will make very little difference to a parish officer, whether or not he gives half an ounce more to each individual. Now in Lambeth workhouse, 700 half ounces, wasted three times a day,

x

would make a very formidable difference. When I first took the Newington contract, I found the scales at the workhouse nearly an ounce deficient in the balance. This arose from an accumulation of filth in the scale appropriated for the weights; whilst the scale in which the provision was placed, had been taken out and daily scoured, perhaps with brick-dust. I found when I took the contract, that by this same process of scouring, the scales at the Lambeth workhouse had been disturbed to the extent of about half an ounce. This made a difference of about 50 lbs. of meat a week, or upwards of 300 stone weight in a year. I find it necessary to have the scales taken care of, and adjusted with nicety, annually, by a scale-maker, and daily by the parties using them. The person who had held the contract before me, at Newington, had ruined himself by it, though receiving 4s. 8d. per head. His ruin I have no doubt was occasioned by mismanagement, chiefly of the sort I have mentioned.

" A contractor, for his own interest, will attend more closely to such points than any parish officers, however well-intentioned, can be expected to attend to the interests of others.

" Another great point in favour of contract management is, that the contractor is unlimited in his markets, and that there is no favouritism or corruption on the part of tradesmen. It is notorious that there is great partiality in the parochial dealings; and officers have been known to supply goods in other names. It is also notorious, though difficult to substantiate the fact, that tradesmen give gratuities, per centages, and allowances of some sort or other, to the officers whose duty it is to examine their goods and accounts. A contractor is not so much exposed to this loss as the parish. In saying this, I wish to guard myself against being supposed to refer, in the slightest degree, to the officers of Lambeth or Newington parishes; for I can bear testimony to the respectability of those officers, and the very correct manner in which the parish affairs are conducted: any faults that exist there are attributable entirely to the system, and not to the officers. Again: if proper persons are not appointed to manage the cooking (which they seldom are by parishes), great loss may be occasioned by improper cooking. In some parishes, for example, it is quite common to put all the joints, small and large, into the copper, and boil them the same length of time; the smaller joints are consequently boiled too much. With the quantity of meat used in Lambeth workhouse, there might be a difference of four or five stone in the consumption of meat for one day, for that number of people. In receiving bread from bakers in a hot state, five per cent. is lost by the parish from the evaporation : for this reason parish bakers always send in their bread hot to the workhouse, where they can. We bake our own bread, and bake it of a size to save time and loss from cutting up: we also adjust the quantities better, and prevent waste. I remember that at Deptford parish, some years ago, the parish officers having to make a Christmas pudding for 150 or 160 persons, the manager made upwards of a hundred weight more of pudding than was wanted for the number of people*.

"It is only by persons who have a direct personal interest, that the small savings, which make the difference between economical and extravagant management, will be carefully attended to. Unless the extravagance is very gross indeed, as in the last instance, annual parish officers cannot see it. In the first instance, the scales had been going for many years as I have described, without the source of loss having been dreamt of by the overseers."

You have stated that the poor of the Lambeth workhouse are now advocates for the supply and management of the workhouse by contract. Will you have the goodness to explain the causes of the popularity of the contract management?—"In the first place, the poor people admit that their food is better. I have heard them say that their soup is much better—that their bread is better; in short, that their supply of provisions is generally much better. But the main cause is, perhaps, that they are more quickly and comfortably served with food than they were formerly, which is done with more skill and discipline. On the old system it was expected that the master should serve out the meat himself. I believe it formerly took two hours and a half, and sometimes three hours, each of the three meat-days in the week, to weigh and serve out the meat for dinner only. I may say also, I believe, that a large proportion of the meat was kept boiling whilst the one portion was being served out. It is unnecessary to specify the consequences of this to those who were the last served: the bell being rung at the commencement of the dinner, all the inmates struck work, and considered themselves free until the conclusion of the dinner : that would be a loss of labour, were their labour worth anything, and the people kept waiting in idleness and discontent. At Lambeth it requires

* Mr. Hewitt, the master of the workhouse of St. Andrew, Holborn, and St. George the Martyr, has proved that, during the first year of his services in that workhouse, which contains on an average four hundred and fifty paupers, a saving was made in the consumption of articles of food to the amount of 442*l.* 1*s.* 5*d.* per annum. The saving was effected by attention to details such as those described by Mr. Mott. The consumption of bread was diminished per annum upwards of 91 cwt., butter 13 cwt., cheese 10 cwt., beer 104 barrels, coals 12 chaldrons, candles 55½lbs., soap 11 cwt., oil 18 gallons, and milk 16 quarts per day ; the rations remaining the same, and the number of paupers having increased. In most workhouses the old modes of providing for the paupers continue.

x 2

two persons to cut, and four or five of the inmates as assistants.
By the system which I have used, the dinners are served commonly within one hour. When the change took place, nothing
could exceed the astonishment and gratification of the inmates
on having their meals supplied so comfortably."

How do you account for the extreme unpopularity of contractors,
or what are called the farmers of the house?—" The complaints of
the abuse of the contracting system are certainly too well founded;
and it is undoubtedly liable to great abuse where character is not
taken into account, and proper securities imposed. A contractor
who is not properly chosen or made responsible, as he ought to
be, will supply many of the articles very indifferently; he will
give to the paupers money instead of other articles. Thus the
people can do without butter, and the contractor having to supply
butter, which, perhaps, would cost him 84*s.* per cwt., pays the
poor perhaps at the rate of about 56*s.*, getting thus about 50 per
cent. In this way, too, the paupers frequently sell their meat,
bread, and other provisions."

How is the money thus obtained by the paupers spent?—
" Principally in gin and other liquors."

Which liquors are drunk in the house?—" Yes. They are
brought into the house by the nurses and other such people."

Then it is to be presumed that this system of purchasing food
of the paupers is an inlet to other disorders in the management
of the house?—" Decidedly so, for the contractors must wink at it.
Disturbances are thus bred in the house, independently of the
dissatisfaction created in the better class of paupers. Then again,
as the contractor, by his conduct, declares the food to be saleable,
he cannot well hinder them selling it to others. Food is consequently sold to people out of the house, as well as amongst the
paupers themselves; and much peculation and misery is necessarily occasioned. I may also mention another cause of the
unpopularity of the contracting system, that when a contract
is taken for the management of the workhouse, the liability of
the parish to the tradesmen ceases. Tradesmen very frequently
supply goods for consumption in the workhouse, from the belief
that they are making the supply on the responsibility of the
parishes. A contractor may be a man of straw as regards the
tradespeople, and yet be bound in good sureties as regards the
parish; for the sureties only undertake that he shall perform his
contract, or make the requisite supply of goods to the parish; not
that he shall pay for those goods to the tradespeople. The contractor whose management of the scales I have mentioned, failed
twice, and occasioned very considerable loss to the tradesmen
during the time of his holding the contract. The parish did not

lose a shilling. This same man has repeatedly since got other contracts for other parishes, which I can only account for from the ignorant eagerness of parishioners to snap at the lowest-priced contracts that can be offered, without regarding the consequences. This person now contracts at very low prices, the means of supplying which must be obvious to persons of experience."

Several parishes have tried contract management, and abandoned it. Are you acquainted with any instances, or can you assign the general cause of the abandonment?—" I do not know particular instances sufficiently well to speak about them; but I have no doubt that the failure arose from the parish not having given a remunerating price, or paid attention to the character of the contractor for integrity and ability. The fact is, these parishes have tried *bad* contract management, and having found that strict parochial management was *less bad*, they have immediately concluded that parochial management was *the best* possible. When the contract with my predecessor at Newington had closed in the manner I have stated, it would have been very natural to conclude that contract management had been properly tried, and that nothing was so good as the management of annual officers, or persons who gave no special attention to the subject."

Has the size of parishes any effect on the character of contractors?—" I do not hesitate to say a very considerable effect. In the larger parishes, the management is not only much more economical, but much more respectable, though still liable to great abuses. A very large proportion of the parishes are far too small to render it worth the while of any respectable contractor or capitalist to attend to them. I should say that it would not be worth while for any respectable person to give attention to a parish where the inmates were less than two hundred in number. They cannot be attended to. A respectable person ought, I think, to get for his labour in the management of two or three hundred persons (if he attends to them properly) as much as a parish must pay for the keep of fifty persons. A small parish must either pay largely for the keep of their small number of poor, or the poor must be badly managed and defrauded, and the small contractor will pay himself by malversation. In the large parish, where the contractor must, by the Act of Parliament, give proportional securities, that circumstance alone ensures very considerable responsibility. I am compelled to give sureties to the amount of 30,000*l.* to the parish officers of Lambeth. This again I may notice, as a circumstance which might operate mischievously by narrowing the competition; for I think a much smaller sum would be ample security to the parish, while it would enable a greater number of respectable men to supply the parish, or compete for the contract. The smaller parishes are also more liable to intrigues between the contractor and the parish officers."

The average number of paupers in the workhouses throughout the country is, say, fifty poor in each workhouse. Now, suppose that if, instead of the seven hundred in-door poor of Lambeth parish being kept in one workhouse, they were kept in fourteen distinct establishments, can you form an estimate of what would be the expense per head of the poor thus kept?—"Would you wish to have an estimate inclusive or exclusive of the expense of superintendence?"

It is to be presumed that, in so large an establishment as that of Lambeth parish, superintendence is procured of a degree of ability much higher than that which is obtainable for 40*l.* per annum and board, or 60*l.* for a man and his wife—the average salary paid to the master of ordinary workhouses?—"My experience has shown me that not only is much ability requisite for such management, but that the person having immediate superintendence of the details of the establishment should have an interest in its good management. For this reason, I have taken the contract in conjunction with Mr. Drouet, a person of respectability—a remarkably active man, who resides in the house, and devotes his whole time and attention to the management."

Let it be assumed in the estimate requested of you as to the comparative expense of large and small workhouses, that 40*l.* per annum is paid for the management of each establishment.—[The witness took time to consider this question, and has sent in the following answer in writing.]—"Supposing the poor to have precisely the same food, clothing, &c. in fourteen small houses, fifty inmates in each, as they do in one large establishment containing seven hundred persons, it would make a difference, as near as I could calculate, of about 7*d.* or 8*d.* per head per week; that is to say, where the seven hundred would cost 3*s.* and 11*d.* per head, the small houses would cost 4*s.* 6*d.* or 4*s.* 7*d.* per head. This, it must be obvious, would not be occasioned by the difference in the food, but principally from the saving in the superintendence and other details of management. The large establishment would not only make the difference of 7*d.* or 8*d.* per head in the cost of maintenance as compared with the small ones, but would leave also, if conducted to the best advantage, such a remuneration, as would render it worth the attention of a clever, active person to undertake the management. Some parishes have been misled by this difference; and from an erroneous opinion that small numbers can be maintained in the same ratio as a large number, have let their poor to some needy adventurer at a price at which it is impossible justice could have been done; and hence arises the objection to the system. If the character and the competency of contractors are not made the first consideration, I see nothing to prevent the contracting system becoming ten times worse in its effects than the worst parish management. And here let me observe, that I am not here as an advocate of this or that system, but to speak to the facts within my own knowledge, and offer whatever opinion you may please to ask of me. The facts will speak for themselves. I beg also to add, that I consider myself, in a great degree, a disinterested witness, as I have now many engagements on my hand; and it is very improbable that I shall take any other contract after the expiration of the present Lambeth contract. On this account I shall not renew the Gosport contract, which I have held for the last ten years."

The city of London within the walls, comprehends a population of 55,000, whose poor are relieved and managed in 96 parishes. Lambeth comprehends a population of 87,000, and the administration of relief to the poor is managed by one establishment, and the money raised for the purpose is collected on one rate. What do you consider would be the effect of the subdivision of Lambeth into 96 independent parishes, each managing the poor independently of the rest; or each exercising the right of assent or dissent from any combined management in the same way as each parish belonging to the incorporated hundreds?—" The chief effects which appear to me to be likely to ensue are, that we should have ninety-six imperfect establishments instead of one : ninety-six sources of peculation instead of one : ninety-six sets of officers to be imposed upon by paupers instead of one set : ninety-six sources of litigation and of expense for removals and disputed settlements instead of one, and ninety-six modes of rating instead of one."

The witness referred to the returns of parochial expenditure and stated, " It appears that the 96 city parishes (many of which are extremely wealthy and lightly burthened with poor) with a population of 55,000, expended for the relief of the poor in the year 1831, 64,000*l.* Lambeth, with 32,000 more people, and many densely-peopled districts containing very poor people, expended on the relief of the poor only 37,000*l.* during the same year. In the wealthy parishes of the city of London, the money paid as poor's-rates amounted to 1*l.* 3*s.* 3½*d.* per head ; whilst in Lambeth the amount paid is 8*s.* 6*d.* and a fraction per head. I believe that the individuals relieved are much more numerous in Lambeth than in the city of London. They were so formerly, and I believe they are so now. The adults of Lambeth parish are now supported in the workhouse at 3*s.* 11*d.* per head ; whilst in the city of London, the greater proportion of all

classes of poor, including children, are farmed out at an expense
of from 4s. 6d. to 7s. each, whilst the expense of those maintained in the small city workhouses varies from 5s. to 8s. per
head per week for all classes." *

Do you think this statement gives a fair view of the merits of
management in small as compared with large town parishes?—
"It never occurred to me to make any comparison of this kind
until it was suggested by the question; but my impression is that
it does afford a fair comparison. The management of the poor
in incorporated hundreds is undoubtedly superior to the management by independent parishes; but still the good of the hundred
management is much diminished by the numerous sets of officers,
and quarrels and conflicting interests of the separate parishes."

It has been suggested that, for the purposes of classification, the
present workhouses of a town might be brought under a central
management—that in a town in which there are at present five or
six workhouses, each of these workhouses might be appropriated
to the reception and treatment of one class of paupers; that one
house might be made to contain all children, another all the able-
bodied females, another all the able-bodied males, and so on—
Now, do you think that a system of combined management of the
paupers in these distinct houses might be conducted in such a
manner as to reduce the total expenditure for the maintenance of
the paupers of that town?—"With respect to superintendence, there
would be some additional expense; but that would, I think, be
more than counterbalanced by the increased number of the poor
maintained. The bread, for instance, might be supplied from one
common bakehouse. This of itself would be a considerable saving. In small establishments you generally lose more than you
gain by baking in the house, as you cannot get it done by the
paupers without great waste, and the consumption is not enough
to make it worth while to employ a regular journeyman baker.
In Newington, the consumption of bread was not enough to keep
a baker employed; whilst at Lambeth, by baking fourteen or
fifteen sacks a week, we have ample employment for one journeyman and assistants in the house. The greater part of the other
food could be supplied from one common kitchen, and conveyed to
the houses hot. In most workhouses there are persons who,
though they cannot be trusted with the management of anything

---

* On examining the answers made to the queries forwarded by his Majesty's commissioners, this statement appears to be strictly accurate. Several
witnesses, who are respectable paid officers of the parishes within the city of
London, have strongly represented the evils of the existing system of administering the poor-laws by numerous petty establishments; and have urged
the expediency of the legislature prescribing some system of combined management.

themselves, may be usefully employed under an intelligent super-intendent. In fact, I see no more difficulty in managing so many establishments in a town than there is in managing five or six wards of one house. Indeed, I believe the trouble of management would be greatly reduced by means of the classification, which would be of great value, by enabling you to put the refractory by themselves. It is a very few of these who occasion the constant necessity of the presence of a superintendent. I think that, if Mr. Drouet had the means of locking up or separating in any way about half a dozen refractory males, or as many females, in Lambeth workhouse, who are always ready to throw the whole establishment into a state of confusion, he might leave the place with the greatest security, to attend to other departments, where there was anything going on to require the attendance of a director."

We find from the returns of a number of the workhouses sent to us, that in very few is there any distinction made between the rations for children and for adults, or between males and females. Would such a combined system as that alluded to enable you to make a better adaptation of dietaries?—" Most certainly, and that without exciting the jealousies which are created by different scales of diet being served in one house, where the different classes run a good deal one into another. There might be more economy in the diet of children, and of the poor in general, whilst the old and infirm, and proper objects, might be indulged with some com-forts, without exciting dissatisfaction amongst others. It is for the sake of peace, as well as saving trouble, that the dietaries of parish workhouses are generally uniform. Many parish officers would prescribe a more appropriate diet for the idle and the vicious, if they did not see that they would thereby make deserving objects suffer."

You are then of opinion, that the management of a combina-tion of workhouses may be as economical as the management of the same number of paupers in one workhouse?—" Yes; and ra-ther more so on an extended scale; because I find that the cost of maintenance decreases as the numbers increase. With reference to the Lambeth workhouse, I have calculated that one thousand persons might be maintained at 300*l*. per annum less than seven hundred persons; and, by the same rule, two thousand persons, in two different houses, one thousand persons in each, might be main-tained for 1000*l*. per annum less than one thousand persons in two houses of five hundred each. In fact, the saving may be estimated at 1*l*. per head per annum. If I were competing for a contract, I would on these data take a reduced sum in proportion to the number; judging from my own experience at Newington and Lambeth, I should say that one active individual, sufficiently interested, might superintend the establishments for two thousand persons."

If such a system of combined management were established, do you think that local authorities or visiters might be intrusted with the power of modifying the dietaries?—" I am decidedly of opinion that no such authority can be beneficially exercised, even by the local manager and superintendent of any place; whatever deviation there is in the way of extra indulgence has a tendency to extend and perpetuate itself which cannot be resisted. If you give to particular people an extra allowance on special grounds, all the rest will exclaim, 'Why should not we have it as well as they?' and too often they get it. That which was only intended to be the comfort of the few, and as an exception, at last, one by one being added to the list, becomes the general rule; and when once established, there are few annual officers who will interfere to abridge the accustomed allowance, or get themselves stigmatized as ' oppressors of the poor.' I may mention, as an instance, that about two years ago Mr. Randal Jackson, one of the county magistrates, visited Lambeth workhouse, and humanely distributed some small parcels of tea to several of the old inmates; and, at the same time, suggested the propriety of allowing to several of the old and deserving inmates a trifle per week for such comforts (tea and sugar). I remonstrated with some of the officers against the adoption of this proposal, as I well knew from experience that it had a dangerous tendency. The answer was, that they could not do otherwise than fall in with the suggestion of such a person. They have ever since allowed ninety-five old inmates 6d. each per week in addition to their allowance of food. Now the very worthy and humane individual, when he recommended an allowance to 'a few' old persons, could not have thought of the extent of the alteration (apparently so trifling and unworthy of consideration), or he would have seen that it would amount to between one and two hundred pounds per annum; a charge that would be perpetuated on the parish, and would, to sustain it, have required an endowment of nearly 4000l., had the benevolent individual said, ' If the parish do not do this, I will.' In this way alterations in detail, which appear trifling, make in the aggregate very large sums. Humane individuals rarely calculate upon the tendency or aggregate effect of such alterations; the extension of this indulgence is at present checked by the contract management, but had the workhouse been under the old management, the probability is that the indulgence would have been extended to the greater proportion of the inmates. In the way exhibited in this instance such alterations are made without exciting any inquiry; while, if a new school had been to be established, requiring between one and two hundred pounds per annum from the parochial revenue for its maintenance, the whole parish would have been agitated to consider the propriety of it."

Have you not found that one cause of pauperism is occasional sickness, which compels independent labourers to come into the workhouse during the continuance of that sickness, and thus introduces them and their families, for the first time, to parochial relief?—" This is a very great cause, the existence of which I have long regretted; for the comforts received during their sickness, and the general mode of living which they observe in the workhouse, are such as to induce them to remain a long time, and offer very strong temptations to them to throw themselves upon the parish entirely on the first opportunity, of which they are sure to avail themselves. I have long considered it would be desirable to procure separate establishments for the treatment of the poor who fall sick *."

Has it ever occurred to you, that by means of a central administration of the parochial funds of a town, and a combination of workhouses, such as that mentioned, one of the existing houses might be appropriated exclusively to the reception of the sick ?—" In the central government of the poor of a district such a provision would certainly enter into the plan; but although it has never occurred to me, yet it would be obviously of great advantage. Whilst very good provision is made in our parish, and, perhaps, in other larger parishes, for the treatment of the sick poor, in the small country workhouses the treatment of the sick is commonly very wretched, as they have no constant attendance, and in every emergency the doctor must be sent for, frequently at two or three miles distance. It is also common, that in consequence of the great distance, the doctor prescribes and sends medicines on the report of the messenger, and without seeing the patient. If one house were appropriated in the manner stated for the sick of a district, and a portion of each separate expenditure were collected together, and systematically applied, a hospital for the poor might be maintained without any additional expense. And whilst the sick would be better treated, without being tempted to remain paupers, all the advantages of a medical school would be derived for the district."

* Mr. Lee, the master of St. Pancras workhouse, states, "We have on an average about one hundred and fifty patients in our hospital and in the workhouse. A large proportion of these are independent poor. When the independent poor come into the workhouse and see how well the paupers live, it is very difficult to get them out of it. For this reason I have always thought our hospital, though maintained with the best motives, produces very bad effects. The larger proportion of our paupers are hereditary paupers : the hospital affords an inlet from the dependent paupers. It would be very beneficial if the hospital were a separate establishment.

From the statements of medical men in the metropolis, and
also of such persons as Dr. Kay of Manchester, it appears that,
in consequence of the want of drainage of certain districts, and
the crowded and dirty state of the habitations, there are some
neighbourhoods from which disease is never absent—Have you
observed similar effects in the parishes with which you are acquainted?—" I have observed it, not only in Lambeth, but in all
crowded neighbourhoods: and, seeing how large a source of unavoidable pauperism this is, I have long regretted that the proprietors of these small houses were not compelled to keep them in
a proper state.   An independent labourer may be industrious and
provident, and yet both he and his family may be subjected to a
fever, or other disease, and thrown upon the parish, in consequence
of want of drainage, and filth, and other causes, which he has no
means of removing."

So that, looking merely to the poor-rates, it would be good
·economy to pay attention to drainage and the enforcement of sana-
tary regulation?—" I think so; and that it would be attended with
great benefit.   Some neighbourhoods are so constantly the seats
of particular diseases, and sources of pauperism from that cause,
that if assistant-overseers, and others accustomed to visit the
abodes of the poor, were asked for cases of those diseases, they
could direct you to particular places where you would almost be
sure to find the disease at work.   I remember that, one winter,
when the weather was very severe, the beadles of Newington
parish were directed to pay particular attention to the sick out-
door poor.   They went at once to some courts in Kent-street, as
a matter of course, without making any inquiry (just as a game-
keeper would go to a well-stocked preserve); and returned with
two coach-loads full of most deplorable objects, the victims of
frightful disease."

What has been your experience on the subject of the employment of the poor in the workhouse?—" The great difficulty, as it
appears to me, is the obtainment of employment for the paupers
which does not interfere with the regular labour of people out of
doors.   I have had two manufactories: I have had, perhaps, a
dozen looms at work at a time; and I used to manufacture all the
sheeting and linen and cotton goods required for the consumption
of the workhouse.   But I found manufacturing in the workhouse objectionable on several grounds.   In the first place, with
regard to returns, you can rarely get anything to pay the expenses,
because, with paupers, you cannot enforce from them that regularity (although you give them a proportion of the price of the
work) and attention to small savings which a manufacturer can
enforce from paid workmen.   These small savings make the profit

of the manufacturer. Then, machinery has made such progress, that, unless the workhouse was formed into one immense manufactory, I do not believe that, if the raw material were given to the parish, any return could be obtained for pauper labour. Both with the adults and the children, there is great loss in teaching them the trade. Besides this, you must get a paid superintendent; for I never knew a pauper who, even if he were well acquainted with any branch of manufacture, could be depended on as superintendent of a department. If you educate the children to a trade or manufacture conducted by a parish, you give the contractor, or the workhouse-keeper even, a motive to keep them upon the parish, or not to put them to independent occupations Being thus kept in the workhouse, they contract various bad habits. If they are kept until they become adults, they are too old to submit to the drudgery of apprenticeships, and can very seldom get employment, as they are mostly unfitted for any. When I had the Newington contract, I found there two lads, upwards of seventeen years of age each. They had both been found expert weavers for the workhouse, and had been kept in by the former contractor. The overseer proposed that they should be ejected. I pointed out the improbability of their being able to get into any employment; for it was notorious that no manufacturers would employ them, on account of their not having served a regular apprenticeship. The overseers, however, insisted on their being sent out of the house. One of them, named Porter, died in about a month, not having obtained a day's employment, after having lived in very great misery. The other, named Giles East, got little or no employment; and in less than three months committed an offence for which he was executed. The parties who had expelled him from the house were called upon to prosecute him for the offence. All these consequences I consider to be the results of the system, though the incidents were more strikingly marked in those cases than in others."

Have you retained no descriptions of labour in your establishments?—" We have retained several descriptions : for the women, coarse needle-work, cotton-winding for the tallow-chandlers, sorting hairs for the brush-makers : for the men, door-mat making, knotting yarns for spun yarn and cord for the bottoms of mats, coarse kinds of twines, picking oakum. These are descriptions of employment that may with little difficulty be obtained, without affecting, to any extent, the labour of the inhabitants." [Here Mr. Mott adduced in evidence instances of the mischievous effects produced by want of secondary punishments, which have been quoted in p. 239.] " I will merely observe further that a contractor is worse off, as to the maintenance of order, than other persons—

the jealousy with which he is viewed, and the credit given to all
the statements of paupers, preventing him from using the little
power which he has.   It is, however, necessary that some ready
and efficient punishment should be available to whomsoever is
intrusted the application of pauper labour."

It has been stated to us that in St. Paul's, Covent Garden,
the paupers have been usefully employed in cleansing the
streets more frequently than would be done by the contractor.
Do you not think that much labour of that sort might be found
for the paupers?—" The mischief is, that the superintendence of
the paupers and the application of their labour, and the management of the roads, are usually under distinct trusts.   In most
cases the surveyors do not like to be troubled with paupers.   Arrangements might, I think, be made, to render the greater proportion of the road-labour available for the purpose of employing the
poor.   But this could only be by a union of management of
large districts, in which there would always be a large stock of
pauper labour available, and in which there could be skilful
management."

Have you observed that, in the smaller agricultural parishes,
one main difficulty in the way of the employment of the paupers
is the want of permanent superintendents of adequate skill to
direct their labours?—" Yes, and the cause is obvious, in the want
of sufficient extent of the parish to pay a competent person, and
the want of a sufficient amount of disposable labour to make it
worth while to employ such a person, even if the parish could
afford it."

A second cause of the idleness of paupers in the smaller
parishes, is stated to be the division of authority amongst overseers: how have you found this operate?—" I have seldom observed the overseers agree about the employment of the paupers
in any one new mode, even if the surveyors of the roads could
be got to agree with the overseers.   The want, on the part of the
overseers, of an adequate pecuniary interest in the success of the
management might, I think, be placed as the first cause of the
want of success in the employment of labourers in most of the
smaller parishes; the next is the want of capital for the purpose.
I have the means of knowing the pecuniary condition of a number of parishes, and I know few instances in which they are not
constantly in debt."

Do you think that the evils of the present system are in a process of correction?—" In the larger parishes, where there is a more
respectable and intelligent superintendence, there has lately been
some check to the increase of allowances and temptations; but
I believe that in the great majority of the parishes the evils of
the system go on increasing."

Have you observed the operation of the advantage given to paupers over independent labourers?—" It is too notorious. When the working men who have never been in the habit of obtaining parochial relief, get into the workhouse by any accident, they are only to be got out with the greatest difficulty : the parish-officers are forced to bribe them out. The workmen say they cannot go out unless certain sums are given them to ' set them up.' Scarcely a week passes in which three or four bargains of this sort are not made; but after having seen what sort of a place they have to fall back upon, they commonly spend the money and return in a few days. A family, consisting of an agricultural labourer, his wife, and six children, some time since came into the Newington workhouse from Norfolk. Before they were classed with the other paupers, they were allowed to dine by themselves. When the regular rations were served out to them, they were all in astonishment at the quantity ; the man had never before been in a workhouse, and he especially was amazed : when the food was first taken in, he asked the person who served it how much of it was intended for them ? and was lost in astonishment when he found that they were allowed the whole of it. He declared that he had more meat to divide amongst his family in one day, now they were paupers, than he had been able to obtain for them during several months, when he was an independent labourer ; and he repeated afterwards, that during the whole of his life he had never lived so well as he lived in the workhouse. It is unnecessary to observe that we had the greatest difficulty in getting this family out of the workhouse. Girls who are sent out from the workhouse to situations, commonly quarrel with their employers, and throw themselves out of place, on the ground that they are worked harder than in the workhouse, and are not kept so well, though they are, as well as their employers, in the middle ranks of life, and are required to work no harder than many of the wives of industrious tradesmen. On Christmas-day, when the customary allowance, consisting of seven ounces of cooked roast-beef, clear of bone, one pound of potatoes, one pound of plum-pudding, and a pint of strong beer, exclusive of their bread and other daily allowances, was served out at Lambeth workhouse, one of the collectors happened to be present, and he remarked on the goodness of the quality as well as on the quantity of the provisions. I asked him whether there were not a great many persons, from whom he collected this rate, who were not able to procure such a dinner for their families? His reply was— ' Hundreds.' "

What proportion of those who partook of this superior fare

you have mentioned, do you consider deserving objects?—
" If by deserving objects is meant those who have not been
reduced to want by idleness, improvidence, or vice, but by unavoidable circumstances, I should say, certainly not one-fifth.
Some few years back I endeavoured to trace the causes of the
paupers becoming chargeable, and I found that, in nine cases
out of ten the main cause was an ungovernable inclination for
fermented liquors."

Over how many cases did your inquiries extend?—" I was
then the contractor for Newington workhouse;—the number of
the cases I took was upwards of three hundred. The inquiry
was conducted for some months, as I investigated every new case
that came under my knowledge. All my subsequent observations
have strengthened the conclusions from these cases."

What proportion of these cases arose from failure of employment?—" Not one in twenty."

In the course of that investigation, did you trace any effects
as resulting from the absence of education?—"As to moral or
religious instruction, I observed a very marked and lamentable
deficiency; for, out of three hundred, there were, I think,
two professing the Catholic faith, about twenty Methodists,
and, with the exception of about fifteen idiots, or persons of
imbecile mind, the rest, though they professed to be ortho-
dox, yet might be termed " anything-arians." They had the
liberty of attending divine service, or of going out to any other
place of worship; but I found that the majority of them who
availed themselves of this privilege never went to any place of
worship, but followed vagrant habits. Those who have had edu
cation I have always found more easily manageable; and, certainly, the most desperate characters have been the most completely
uninstructed. No one can feel more strongly than I do the utility,
the absolute necessity, of a general education; but it must be of
a better description than that now commonly given before it can
have the desired effect. It is forgotten that reading and writing
are not of themselves knowledge, and will not of themselves
make a man moral. Amongst the number of persons whose
cases I investigated were several of an education far above the
average; and I had one person under my care, named William Jones, who was the cousin of an eminent barrister, and the
son of a clergyman. This person was very learned, and, for the
purpose of keeping up his knowledge of the languages with which
he was conversant, he used to keep a journal of each day's transactions, and the account of each day was kept in one of the seven
different languages with which he was the most familiar. He
was sent to my charge at the workhouse as a victim to the habit

of drinking. His journal contained very accurate accounts of his own aberrations; and yet, notwithstanding the calamitous consequences which he himself noted and commented upon justly, he could not refrain from indulgence. On one occasion, after he had been for some time debarred from liquor, he, by some means or other, got some drink, but he was nevertheless sober, and capable of reasoning collectedly, when he came to me, and begged permission to be allowed to go out of the workhouse, for he said he could not bear abstinence any longer. I told him I could not make the house a prison, and that if he, when sober, went out, I would not receive him back again. He still besought me, and I gave him half an hour to consider of it. At the end of the time he came again, and, finding me still adhering to my resolution, said he was extremely sorry, for he must go; he could not resist having some more liquor, 'if it was to secure him a crown of glory.' I was obliged to allow him to go; and in the middle of the next day he was brought back in a state of beastly intoxication, and nearly naked; his clothes having been disposed of to obtain the means of indulging his propensity. I refused to pay the coachman, or receive him again. I afterwards learned that the coachman, after having driven him about to respectable persons, his family connexions, to obtain payment, drove him to Union Hall, where the magistrates committed him to Kingston house of correction. Since then I have not seen him. Such instances among educated people are not common."

Do you think that anything may be done in the way of education for the present mass of adults of the working classes?— " It is not possible to say what *might* be done; but I have not seen any system of direct education from which I could anticipate any material benefits as regards the adults. No time, however, should be lost with children."

But although nothing could be expected from any influence of education upon adults, have you not observed circumstances mischievously influencing their habits which may be removed or altered?—" Yes; I am glad to have an opportunity of stating, that I have observed such circumstances, and have often regretted the extreme facility with which the means of gratifying the propensities to drink and other indulgences are afforded by the system on which the pawnbroker's business is at present carried on. In the course of my experience and investigations, I have had many thousands of duplicates of articles pledged by the poor; and I have found that nearly all the articles pledged by these classes are at sums from 3*d.* to 1*s.*, and not exceeding 1*s.* 6*d.* each pledge. It is notorious to those acquainted with the habits of the people, and it is indeed admitted by the paupers themselves, that nine out of ten of them are pledged for liquor. The immense proportion of those pawnings were by women, and chiefly of articles usually deemed essential to their use or comfort, such as handkerchiefs, flannel-petticoats, shifts, or household articles, such as tea-kettles, flat-irons, and such things; these articles being always in requisition, they are usually redeemed in a few days, and very frequently the same day. I made a calculation of the interest paid by them for their trifling loans, and found it to be as follows:

A loan					if redeemed same day, pays int. at rate of		if weekly
3d.	.	.	.	.	5200 per ct.,	. .	866 per ct.
4	.	.	.	.	3900	. .	650
6	.	.	.	.	2600	. .	433
9	.	.	.	.	1733	. .	288
1s.	.	.	.	.	1300	. .	216

What is the remedy you proposed for this system?—" An enactment that no pawnbroker should be allowed to advance a less sum on any article than 2s. 6d. From some conversation which I have had with one very respectable pawnbroker, I am led to believe that the most respectable of that body would not object to such an alteration. It is to be observed, that the Pawnbroker's Act allows them to charge the same interest, namely, 20 per cent. on a loan of 3d. on a pledge for a day as it does upon the loan of 2s. 6d. for a month; I think it probable that the legislature never conceived that any pledges would be made for less sums than 2s. 6d. The facility of obtaining the means of indulgence is also a facility for disposing of the produce of petty thefts, and a temptation to them. After a general examination of the pauper's clothing account, finding a large proportion of the articles missing, I have next seized all the duplicates we could find on their persons or in their boxes, and on sending round to the pawnbrokers we were sure to find a great proportion of the missing articles. Here, it may be observed, there was no real want. I might have added, as one of the advantages of contract management, that the contractor is necessarily compelled to take greater care of the stock in the house, which under other management is inevitably plundered extensively."

Have you observed any bad effects produced by facilities given to contract debts, operating on the improvident habits of the poor?—" Yes, very bad effects indeed, and this is one point on which I am glad to have an opportunity of speaking. I am well informed, that credit is given to poor people on the knowledge on the part of the creditors, that they have a sort of security on the parish rates. They know that when the head of a family appears likely to be thrown into prison on the judgment of one of the small debt courts, the wife and family immediately apply to the parish for relief, and the parish officers too often assist in paying the debt in order to get rid of the burthen of the wife and family. I can hardly trust myself to express my feelings with relation to what I have heard, and the instances I know of the oppression and cruelty practised by these small courts, where the judges are frequently small shopkeepers directly interested in the decisions*."

Have you thought of any remedy for these abuses?—" I have thought that at all events, a limitation of the powers of such courts to distrain on the goods of the debtor where he had any, would prevent credit being given to the mischievous extent to which it is now given to persons who have no self-control and no means of paying the debts they contract. The suppression of the power given to these petty courts to imprison the person, would be one of the greatest boons that could be conferred on the labouring classes, and would at the same time afford very great relief to the parishes."

Do you think the remedy might go any farther with advantage? or that there would be no bad effects from depriving the creditor of his remedy where there are not goods?—" I certainly consider that the remedy might be carried farther. I think that the effect would be, to prevent credit being given to the thoughtless and improvident, whilst the honest and industrious man would receive all the accommodation *upon honour* that he has before been in the habit of receiving or could require. The tally-shops and the chandler's-shops in districts which furnish a large proportion of the business of these courts, have had a most mischievous effect in fostering habits of improvidence amongst the labouring classes †."

Have you formed any opinion as to the expediency of increasing or maintaining the duties on fermented liquors, as a means of abating their consumption?—" I have not considered that subject, and I do not, therefore, feel myself competent to express any opinion upon it."

Have you considered what is to be done in giving additional

* The fees of these courts are flagitiously high in proportion to the debts.
† On referring to some parliamentary returns of the number of prisoners committed to Whitecross-street and Horsemonger-lane prisons on process out of the courts of request, it appears that, in the year 1829, there were nine hundred and thirty-two prisoners committed to the latter gaol, and confined during periods from one to one hundred days; that the aggregate amount of debts for which these nine hundred and thirty-two prisoners were confined, was 1,900*l.*, and the aggregate costs 574*l.*; that, during the same year, one thousand five hundred and sixty-three persons were confined in Whitecross-street prison during similar periods, and that the total amount of their debts was 2,071*l.*, of the costs 746*l.* The return from this prison states that "there are, upon an average, about seventy-five prisoners on process out of the courts of request constantly in the above prison; and their food, firing, bedding, medicine, &c., are estimated to cost annually 422*l.* 14*s.* 4*d.*"

facilities for the formation of frugal habits by the improvement of
Friendly Societies and Savings Banks?—"They are inestimable
institutions, which, it appears to me, are susceptible of great improvements; I have no doubt that if the inducements to improvidence were removed by the reform of the present system of poor-
law management, they would be immensely resorted to. Something should certainly be done to give additional securities to
benefit societies. It was only on Friday last, a person in middling
circumstances stated to me, that a benefit society to which he had
contributed for some years, to the amount of upwards of 120*l*.,
had been broken up from bad management, and that his proportion of the fund, when distributed, only amounted to 3*l*. He was
thus deprived of the saving which was probably his only resource
against pauperism. It would be a very great advantage and
inducement to save, if annuities, adapted to the circumstances of
the labouring classes, were provided with government security.
But the legislation on these subjects has hitherto been peculiarly
blundering and unfortunate, and if there is any further interference, it should certainly be with greater caution, and by
persons of superior knowledge and abilities."

What proportion of the paupers under your charge do you
believe to have had a surplus of wages beyond what was requisite
for a comfortable subsistence, a surplus which they might have
put by, (had there been adequate inducements,) to guard against
the destitution by which they were pauperized?—"I might have
mentioned, when stating the results of my investigation of the
causes of pauperism in the three hundred cases, that the greater
number of the men admitted, that they had long been in the
receipt of good wages, from which they might have saved, and
expressed their regret at their improvidence; as they might, if
they had been careful, have kept themselves from the parish.
Here again the practice of taking pledges to meet occasional
wants interferes to check provident habits. We know that the
wants which small loans are obtained to relieve are not important,
and that the people would often have to meet them if the pawnbrokers were not so open."

From the whole tendency of your evidence, as to the superiority of the larger parishes over the small ones, it is to be
presumed, therefore, you consider that, for the same reasons,
county management affords better means of diminishing the evils
of pauperism than the larger parishes?—"Precisely so."

Does your observation enable you to give any opinion on the
further subject of a central or national management under some
central authority, as compared with a county management?—
"I do not speak from any speculation, but from a close attention

to the subject; for the opinions which I entertain have been forced upon my mind by the facts which have come under my own observation. I have long concluded that any efficient management must differ materially from the present system. I have seen sets of officers succeed sets; I have seen a great many plans and systems suggested and tried; I have seen them tried by officers of the highest respectability and intelligence, and the little good derived from the practical operation of their plans utterly defeated by their successors, who, though equally honest, come into office with different opinions and views. Here and there an extraordinary man will come into office, and succeed very satisfactorily. But when he goes, there is generally an immediate relapse into the old system. His example works no permanent change in his own parish, still less is it attended to in the adjacent parishes. In short, I am quite convinced from all my experience, that no uniform system can be carried into execution, however ably it may be devised; nor can any hopes of permanent improvement be held out, unless some central and powerful control is established. The present vicious system is so rooted in the habits of the people, that I do not think that it would be in the power of the existing parish officers to alter it. However determined they might be to do so, in a very large proportion of cases, they cannot act or make any improvement; for they are even now obliged to yield relief to the worst objects under the influence of fear. I know that, in many parishes, the officers are very much gratified by the exercise of power, and would very reluctantly yield to any interference with what they call ' their privileges;' but still I would say that the good sense and respectability of the country would overcome all ignorant and selfish opposition of this sort. Ignorant or interested persons talk about the advantages of people applying their money and managing their own affairs, in opposition to any plan of central management; but however great the mismanagement of this or any other government that I have ever heard of may be, there never was a tax so harshly and vexatiously levied, or so badly and corruptly expended, as the tax raised for the relief of the poor. It is the only one raised and appropriated immediately by the payers themselves, and it is in every respect the very worst."

Be so good as to specify some of the advantages which you think would be attainable from a central management?—" In the first place, (setting aside the superior economy and skill of the establishment for a central management,) one great point I have always considered would be in obtaining a uniformity of diet throughout the country. At present there are scarcely two parishes that agree either as to quantity or quality: the cost in some being as low as

2*s*. 6*d*. per head per week, whilst in others it is as high as 6*s*. or 8*s*. They only agree in this, that they are all much better than the diet obtained by the greater proportion of working men out of the house. I have examined many parochial diet tables, and I do not know any place except Gosport where the diet is so low as that of the independent labourer."

To what do you ascribe the difference between the parishes in their diet?—" In the parishes where the lower contract is taken, articles which are there considered luxuries, or at least not absolute necessaries of life, are omitted. The following is a copy of the dietary for Lambeth, where the contract is at 3*s*. 11*d*. per head per week: in Gosport, I take the contract at 2*s*. 8*d*. per head per week.

MEN AND WOMEN.		
	Breakfast and Supper.	Dinner.
Monday .	Bread 13 oz. {2 oz. Cheese or 1 oz. Butter	1 Pint Leg of Beef Soup
Tuesday .	Ditto {1 Pint Milk Porridge, ditto	1 lb. Rice Pudding
Wednesday .	Bread 13 oz. ditto	7 oz. Boiled Beef & Vegetables
Thursday .	Ditto ditto {1 Pint Milk Porridge ditto	1 Pint Leg of Beef Soup
Friday . .	Bread 13 oz. ditto	7 oz. Boiled Beef & Vegetables
Saturday .	Ditto {1 Pint Milk Porridge ditto	1 Pint Leg of Beef Soup
Sunday .	Bread 13 oz. ditto	7 oz. Boiled Beef & Vegetables

One Quart Table Beer per Day.
Extra for the Sick, Mutton and Broth, Beef Tea, Wine, Porter, Milk, &c., or whatever is directed by the Visiting Apothecary.

FIVE EXTRA DINNERS.

EASTER—Legs of Mutton 7 oz. with Baked Potatoes, and 1 Pint of Porter each Person.
WHITSUNTIDE—Ditto   ditto   ditto.
BEAN FEAST—Bacon 7 oz. with Beans, and 1 Pint of Beer each.
PEA FEAST—Bacon 7 oz. with ½ Pint of Peas, and 1 Pint of Porter each.
CHRISTMAS DAY—Roast Beef 7 oz. with 1 lb. Potatoes Baked, 1 lb. of Plum Pudding, and 1 Pint of strong Beer each.

See the Gosport dietary, page 253.

Are the paupers of Gosport as well satisfied with their diet as the Lambeth workhouse inmates are with the diet given them there?—" Yes; they are even better satisfied."

Then do you find that the conceptions of this class of people, as to which they ought to have, rise in proportion to what is given them?—" Precisely so; it is a settled thing; there can be no doubt of it. This may always be seen in those places where there is any considerable distribution of coals, clothes, or other things, from benevolent societies or individuals. It is universally the case, that there is in those places much more discontent and disorder than in those places where no such gifts are distributed."

What advantages do you expect to result from an uniformity of diet?—" In the first place, it would do away the strong temptation which paupers now have to remove from what they call ' bad parishes' to others which they call ' good parishes,' or from good parishes to better, or to stay in good parishes, instead of seeking work elsewhere. If there were uniformity of diet and other treatment, it would make no material difference in which parish a man was kept. There would not be, on the one hand, the mischievous shifting, and, on the other hand, the mischievous continuance that there now is. Frauds in settlements, and the attendant expenses, and the expenses and trouble of removals, would be materially lessened. The necessity of uniform diet, and the important effect which it has upon the administration of the poor-laws, it appears to me has never yet received the attention which it deserves. It would be more especially available against the most dangerous and fearfully burthensome part of the system, the money payments to the out-door poor. Uniformity of diet and management would also enable every parish to know what the cost of the poor ought to be, and would enable them to detect many frauds. When the diet varies, you have no means of doing this, and no two diets agree. At present, people say the expenditure in our parish is so much per head, whilst in such another parish it is so much less, without at all considering the difference in diet, or other local circumstances, all of which you must consider before you can decide whether the pecuniary management of parishes is comparatively good or bad. It would save the parishes and parish-officers from those bickerings, and the ill feeling which is occasioned by this hidden cause of the expense of their poor. It is a very common thing for parishes to look at the great number and expense of the poor, and, without taking into account the dietaries and other local circumstances, to compare them with other parishes, and attribute fraud or mismanagement to officers, who have really managed as well as the system will permit. A prescribed uniformity of diet would also check the tendency which there is at present in parochial management to a constant increase of diet and accumulation of comforts, from the interference and influence of humane but mistaken individuals. Parishes are always subject to such influences as I have mentioned, with reference to the interference of Mr. Randal Jackson, and such benevolent individuals, who cannot from their position be expected to see that every comfort bestowed on the idle is a bounty to the improvident, and an injury and cruelty to the industrious."

From this statement, it is to be presumed you contemplate the discontinuance of all pecuniary out-door relief, or the rendering that relief also uniform?—" I am certainly of opinion, that if out-door relief is given at all, it should be given in kind, as I have found, on investigating the cases, that such relief is not applied to the purposes contemplated in nine cases out of ten; but if a cautioned system of workhouses, under a central management, could be established, then the out-door management might be usefully discontinued. A large proportion of the applications for out-door relief are made, first, in the confidence that there is not room in the workhouse for one-third of those who insist upon relief; and secondly, that from the keep in the workhouse being extravagant, the parish-officers will prefer giving any single applicant, and much more any family, a weekly pension to taking them into the house. Men serve during their lives in the army, or the navy, and sustain wounds and extreme hardships; and are, nevertheless, obliged to maintain during all that time a good character to entitle them to a pension of sixpence a day; whilst you will find, that in the metropolis thousands of thieves, prostitutes, and all over the country tens of thousands of the worst characters, obtain weekly allowances, or pensions, as ' their right,' immediately that they demand them. If all were taken into the house, and the diet for the able-bodied pauper were what it ought to be, the same effects would follow that are noted in an account of the establishment of several workhouses published in 1725. " Very great numbers of lazy people, rather than submit to the confinement and labour of the workhouse, are content to throw off the mask, and maintain themselves by their own industry. And this was so remarkable here, at Maidstone, that when our workhouse was finished, and public notice given, that all who came to demand their weekly pay should be immediately sent thither, little more than half the poor upon the list came to the overseers to receive their allowance."

You propose, then, that the diet, besides being uniform in amount, should be uniformly reduced in quantity and quality?—" I do. The national diet should be low, even to all classes. The wealthy, and all those who had the means, would then have an ample opportunity of exercising their benevolence, by adding, by voluntary contributions, to the comfort of deserving poor. As to the food and clothing of the undeserving, the advantage of relief in kind is as a check to misapplication. But even if the officers had sufficient fortitude to carry such a regulation into effect, it would not do for them to say, ' We have determined to alter the allowance.' They must be enabled to say, ' We cannot help it; we are compelled to do it;' and it must be apparent that this is really the case. The controlling power must be strong, and be at a distance. It is only by some such system that the condition of the pauper can be reduced to that of the independent labourer, which is the grand effort to be made; for if it is not made, you will surely have the independent labourers place themselves in the more advantageous condition of paupers, which they have now the means of doing."

You are, of course, aware that such extensive changes are not free from danger, and have considered it?—"I have, and I am well aware that any sudden change might be attended with much mischief; not from the in-door poor, who might, without difficulty, be gradually brought to submit to regulations, but from persons in the habit of receiving out-door relief in money, the system now being so much interwoven with their habits. The first thing to be done would be obtaining uniformity of management, and then of diet. The next would be the gradual reduction of the relief, penny by penny, and ounce by ounce. The very old, who have been brought up under the present regulations, might be allowed to continue, so long as they lived, in the enjoyment of the same comforts. All new applicants should, however, at once be subject to the new and strict regulations."

Have you had, within your own observation, an instance of the reduction of the allowances to a whole body of paupers?—"Yes; I recollect, about ten or eleven years since, the officers of the town of Maidstone were induced, from the great cost of the poor, (which had increased, I think, to 7*s.* or 8*s.* per week each,) to set on foot some inquiries. The result was, that the officers reduced the diet; and after enforcing the alteration for about two months, they contracted with a person to keep the poor for about 3*s.* 3*d.* per head. They have continued the contracting system ever since."

Were there any riotings or burnings?—" No; the disturbance was scarcely of a nature to be noticed, or more than the workhouse-keeper himself could easily control. They soon settled down into the reformed system very quietly. And I believe that the contractor, who was an intelligent man, obtained more work from the poor of that parish than could be expected from most parishes of that extent."

Might not such general regulations as those to which you have alluded be prescribed by Act of Parliament?—" No, certainly not. The regulations of any system must be very numerous; and though they may be uniform, it would be necessary to vary them from time to time; and unless parliament was to do nothing but occupy itself with discussions on details of workhouse manage-

ment, it would be impossible to effect any great alteration in that
way. A great many regulations, however ably devised, must be
experimental. Here unforeseen and apparently unimportant details might baffle the best plans, if there were not the means of
making immediate alteration. Suppose a general regulation were
prescribed by Act of Parliament, and it was found to want alteration ; you must wait a whole year, or more, for an Act of Parliament to amend it, or the law must be broken. A central
authority might make the alteration, or supply unforeseen omis-
sions in a day or two. Besides, a central board or authority might
get information immediately on the matters of detail. If they
had, for instance, to settle some uniform diet, they could at once
avail themselves of the assistance of men of science, physicians or
chemists ; but you would find that Parliament, if it could really
attend to the matter, and would do anything efficient, must have
almost as many committees as there are different details. If there
were a central board established, and it were easily accessible, as
it ought to be, persons in local districts would consult them or
make suggestions, who would never think of applying to Parliament. Who would think of applying to Parliament to determine
whether four or five ounces of butter should be used as a ration
in particular cases, and whether the butter should be Irish or
Dutch? or, if Irish, whether Cork or Limerick : or to determine
whether the old women's under-petticoats should be flannel or
baize, and how wide or long ? And suppose the petticoats laid
down by Act of Parliament are found narrow, are the poor old
people all over the kingdom to wait a whole year before they can
have them altered ? Yet on details of this sort, beneath the dignity of grave legislators, good or bad management would depend."
    You then think it would be practicable for one central authority
to control the management of the poor, and all their details
throughout the kingdom?—" Yes, I do : quite as easily, and indeed much more easily, and much better and cheaper than the
barracks and dockyards are managed throughout the kingdom. I
cannot speak confidently of the management of those establishments; but I believe they are not under the uniformity of system,
of which I think the system of management for the poor susceptible under a central control."
    Do you consider a central board more eligible than any system
of immediate action of the government ?—I do : for while it would
save the time of government for the performance of its other duties,
a central board would, I think, excite less discontent, as the people
would consider that they had still an appeal to the government
or the legislature."
    Do you not think it practicable to bring parishes to the volun-

tary adoption of any uniform regulations when their importance is proved to them?—" I certainly do not think it practicable. I think it utterly impossible to bring the twelve or fourteen thousand parishes in England and Wales to one mind upon any one subject, however clear the evidence may be; much less so to act with uniformity in any one point. The Commissioners must be well aware that great frauds are committed by paupers in the metropolis receiving relief from different boards on different board days. I have known instances of paupers receiving pensions from three or four different parishes. It was proposed some years ago, and it has been proposed from time to time, to remedy this evil, which all the parishes are aware is very great, by one simple but effectual expedient, which it would be very easy to adopt; namely, by all the parishes paying on the same day; but they never could be got to do this. Individual conveniences prevented the remedy being applied; and the system of fraud still prevails, and will continue to prevail, so long as the present management prevails. Now, if the parishes in the metropolis cannot be got to act in concert for the suppression of an evil which affects only one part of the system, I think it will be seen that I am justified in my opinion, that any reform or co-operation in the country is quite hopeless without the establishment of a strong central management; nothing else will check the system. This has been my opinion for years; and I am confident that all the evidence will confirm it."

Have you ever formed any opinion as to the appointment of such a central authority, whether it should be by popular election or otherwise?—" Certainly not by popular election or delegation; for the requisite qualifications would not generally be appreciated; and we now find, that in the appointment of the permanent and more important parish officers, even where the electors have a direct interest in the appointment of persons of ability, they rarely take the peculiar qualifications into consideration, but vote from a desire to serve a friend or a favourite. It may be objected that this would, in some degree, be the case if the appointment of a central authority were with the government; but it could hardly fail to be so in a much less degree. In my opinion, the best mode of getting an efficient central management would be to concentrate the responsibility for good management in the chief of the new department, and allow him to select his assistants."

Have you formed any opinion as to the probable saving to be effected by a central and efficient management?—" I should say, at least one half of the amount of the rates. This is shown by the instances where very imperfect trials of better systems have been made. I consider, too, that the progress of the evil may be checked, and additional benefits conferred on the deserving classes, and, indeed, on the undeserving, as it would be a benefit to them to subject them to the obligations of regular industry. The question of settlement would, under a national or central management, become a matter of very minor consideration. I think the parish rates might be settled amongst themselves. Any objection on the part of the less heavily burthened parishes to unite a management with those more heavily burthened, might be safely met by a guarantee that their rates should not be increased beyond the average amount for a given number of years past, say six or seven; whilst, on the other hand, they should have the benefit of any reduction. I state my opinions on this subject, and the importance of a change, with great earnestness; for having some stake in the country, I have long observed the accelerated progress of the system with great anxiety, as I see clearly that the same state of things, of which you have an example in Bethnal-Green, will, sooner or later, overtake the other parishes; the pauper population becoming too great for the industrious classes to bear; industry paralysed; rents diminishing; property absorbed, and all sinking down to a pauper level."

The following extracts will afford examples of the progress of the system in those districts where it is the most in advance.

Mr. Burm, one of the parish officers of Bethnal Green, examined.

What is the condition of the property in your parish in consequence of the burthen of the poor-rate?—" I believe there are now about 500 houses unoccupied. There are parts of whole streets where the leaseholders would be glad to give up the houses, some of them six-roomed houses, if they could get rid of them. In fact, such property is rapidly becoming absorbed. The landlords are complaining bitterly that the number of those who pay rent is very rapidly diminishing."

Mr. Farr, of the parish of Mile End New Town, examined,—
What is the effect of the increasing burthens of the poor's-rate within your district?—" I think that every ninth house is now empty, and the proportion of empty houses is increasing rapidly. We have two whole streets in our small parish, in which the houses are almost entirely empty. There the property is entirely destroyed. If there are two or three occupants in them it is as much as there are. The shopkeepers are sinking rapidly, and they must soon go. The whole value of the property in the neighbourhood is wonderfully depreciated."

Mr. Thomas Single, of Mile End Old Town, says, " I hear it

very frequently said in the parish, that it would be a very excellent thing, if the Government would take the parish affairs in their own hands, for the inhabitants see no chance of the pesent rates being reduced under the present system. Some regulating power should be established.

Would not even this regulating power be deemed an obnoxious interference?—" It might be unpopular for a short time, as the new police was (which in our district and most others now gives general satisfaction). I consider it a very necessary interference for the protection of the good order of society, against the worst misgovernment. I think it necessary for the protection of property, which is now giving way, and must continue to give way under the pressure of pauperism. Rents are now much reduced in consequence of the heaviness of the rates. We have 800 empty houses in our parish, and persons are constantly leaving it to go to other parishes where the rates are lower. As the owner of houses, I can speak to these effects from my own knowledge."

In every district the discontent of the labouring classes appeared to me to be proportioned to the money dispensed in poor's-rates or in voluntary charities. I found the able-bodied unmarried labourers discontented from being put to a disadvantage as compared with the married, and from other effects of the system. The paupers were discontented, apparently from their expectations being raised by the ordinary administration of the system, beyond any means of satisfying them. They, as well as the independent labourers, to whom the term poor is equally applied, are told that under all circumstances they have A RIGHT to have subsistence provided for them. I found that verbally they were instructed that they had a right to a " *reasonable* subsistence," or " a *fair* subsistence," or " an *adequate* subsistence." When I have asked what " *fair,*" or " *reasonable,*" or " *adequate* " meant, I have in every instance been answered differently ; some stating they thought it meant such as would give a good allowance of " meat every day," which no poor man should be without; although a large proportion of the rate-payers do go without it. It is abundantly shown in the course of this inquiry, that where the terms used by the public authorities are large and vague, they are always filled up by the desires of the parties benefiting, and the desires always wait on the imagination, which is the worst regulated and the most active and vivid in the most ignorant of the people. In Newbury and Reading, the money dispensed in poor's-rates and charity is as great as could be desired by the warmest advocate either of compulsory or of voluntary relief; and yet, during the agricultural riots, the inhabitants in both towns were under strong and well-founded apprehensions of the rising of the very people amongst whom the poor's-rates and charities are so profusely distributed. The Spitalfields Benevolent Society, in their thirteenth report, state that " Many of the poor are very thankful for the relief afforded, and in some instances they give striking proofs of gratitude. There is often found also a degree of sympathy one with another. In general, however, the experience of the society lamentably proves that poverty has, of itself, no tendency to renew the heart." Other benevolent persons, though reluctant to yield to the evidence, express their bitter disappointment at the results of their efforts. The police inspectors concur in stating, that the paupers entertain the most exaggerated conceptions of the funds provided for them ; and " that wherever their expectations in this respect are opposed, they consider themselves defrauded by the overseers ; that their outbreakings of violence arise from an opinion of the inadequacy of supplementary relief, which inadequacy they charge to the supposed cupidity and mercenary tricks of those to whom the management of the POOR's funds is confided*." Those who work being called poor, though receiving good wages, are of course entitled to a share of the " poor funds." Whatever addition is made to allowances under these circumstances, excites the expectation of still further allowances ; increases the conception of the extent of the right, and ensures proportionate disappointment and hatred if that expectation is not satisfied.

On the other hand, wherever the objects of desire have been made definite, where wages upon the performance of work have been substituted for eleemosynary aid, and those wages have been allowed to remain matter of contract, employment has again produced content, and kindness become again a source of gratitude.

" During the agricultural riots there was no fire, no riots, no threatening letters in Cookham parish. In the midst of a district which was peculiarly disturbed, Cookham and White Waltham, where a similar system of poor-law administration was adopted, entirely escaped, although in Cookham there are several threshing-machines, and the only paper-mill had, at the time of the riots, been newly fitted up with machinery†."

I cannot close my report without soliciting attention to further evidence of the superior condition of the independent labourers, as compared with the condition of those out-door poor who receive parochial or charitable aid, though sometimes obtaining

---

* Evidence of T. Y. Smith, Police-superintendent of the K. Division.
† Evidence of Mr. Whately.

more money. In every district, I have found that their condition is
distinct and superior. The following testimony from Mr. Miller,
of St. Sepulchre's, is corroborated by the testimony of other witnesses in the metropolis.

" In the course of my visits to the residences of the labouring
people in our own and other parishes, I have seen the apartments
of those who remained independent, though they had no apparent means of getting more than those who were receiving relief
from the parish, or so much as out-door paupers. The difference in their appearance is most striking; I now, almost imme--
diately on the sight of a room, can tell whether it is the room of
a pauper or of an independent labourer. I have frequently
said to the wife of an independent labourer, ' I can see, by the
neatness and cleanliness of your place, that you receive no relief
from any parish.' ' No,' they usually say, ' and I hope we
never shall.' This is applicable not only to the paupers in the
metropolis ; but it may be stated, from all I have seen elsewhere,
and heard, that it is equally applicable to other places. The
quantity of relief given to the paupers makes no difference with
them as to cleanliness or comfort; in many instances very much
the contrary. More money only produces more drunkenness.
We have had frequent instances of persons being deprived of
parochial relief from misconduct or otherwise, or, as the officers
call it, " choked off the parish," during twelvemonths or more,
and at the end of that time we have found them in a better condition than when they were receiving weekly relief.

The following is an extract of a letter, with which I have been
favoured by the Rev. H. H. Milman of Reading.
" Another important question you suggested was, how far
there is a marked and manifest difference between the pauper and
independent part of the labouring population ; between those who
are habitually supported, either wholly or in part, by the parish
funds, and those who maintain themselves by their own industry.
How far habits of idleness, intemperance, or mismanagement
may have been the original causes which have reduced the lowest
of our paupers to parochial support; and how far the dependence
upon such support may have formed or confirmed such habits, it
may be difficult to say. With the exception, however, of decent
persons reduced by inevitable misfortune, as is the case with
some of our manufacturers, whose masters have totally failed, and
who are too old or otherwise incapable of seeking elsewhere their
accustomed employment, I should state, in the most unqualified
manner, that the cottage of a parish pauper and his family may

be at once distinguished from that of a man who maintains himself. The former is dirty, neglected, noisome; the children,
though in general they may be sent to school at the desire of the
clergyman or parish officers, are the least clean and the most
ragged at the school: in short, the degree of wretchedness and
degradation may, in most instances, be measured by the degree in
which they burthen the parish: unless some few tenements inhabited by the lowest, and usually the most profligate poor—the
refuse of society, the cottages in my parish which it is least
agreeable to enter are those of which the rent is paid by the
parish, in which the effect of our exertions and of the liberality of the landlords to cleanse, on the alarm of cholera, was
obliterated in a very few weeks. The worst consequence, however, of regular maintenance from the parish-funds shows itself in
the character and demeanour of the young lads who have grown
up in such families. They have been accustomed to live in idleness, and in perpetual strife with the overseer, whom it is their
constant endeavour either to browbeat by insolence, weary by
importunity, or overreach by cunning. They have never felt,
they cannot feel the shame or degradation of pauperism; they
are utterly insensible of the honest pride of independence. The
only security to the parish is that they are in general of dissolute
habits, which in the town they can gratify, and are not so much
inclined, or are not so often compelled, to early marriages as
youth of a similar description in the country parishes."

" It would be a great point gained if there could be some line
drawn, some distinction made, which could be impressed upon the
feelings of the poor themselves, between those who are reduced
by real misfortune or by providential affliction to subsist on alms,
and those who are maintained as parish paupers. I cannot but
think that the establishment of two such establishments as I suggested might tend to draw this line of separation. The *poor-house*
should be a place of *comparative* comfort; it should be liberally,
though economically maintained; it should be a refuge from the
evils and miseries of life; it should be what the law of Elizabeth
contemplated. The *workhouse* should be a place of hardship, of
coarse fare, of degradation and humility; it should be administered with strictness—with severity; it should be as repulsive as
is consistent with humanity, for it is most evident that humanity
is far more concerned in using every method to incite the labouring classes to depend upon themselves, than to depend upon
parochial assistance. Where the industrious man can with difficulty obtain subsistence, it is most unjust, as well as most detrimental to the moral being of the individual, to encourage him in
idleness by the gratuitous offer of a better, at least of a sufficient

subsistence. Though I must acknowledge that I have considerable misgivings as to the practicability of drawing this line between
the poor and the paupers;—could it be done, it might materially
conduce to giving a right direction to those sympathies which at
present disturb the more rational consideration of the subject. We
feel for the old, the infirm, the disabled, the sick, the providen-
tially afflicted, and are anxious that no diminution of their comforts
should take place; while the able-bodied, though capable of work,
and only prevented by their own indolence or habits of dependence
from finding it, creep in, as it were, beneath the shelter of our
compassion, under the general denomination of the poor. There
would be much less objection with overseers, with magistrates,
and with the country at large, if the real objects of Christian
charity were thus exempted from the struggle, and set apart as
acknowledged objects of national care; of course strict attention
would be necessary that even this portion of public bounty should
not be extended to those who have relations, whose duty it is, and
who have the power, to contribute to their support. The doors
even of this asylum should be jealously watched, and opened only
after strict investigation of each case."

In the instances of individuals, as well as in several whole
parishes, wherever the influence of the present system has been
removed, the rise of the condition of the people has been proportionate to the removal of that influence or their previous
depression. In Cookham, where the change was the most extensive, the parochial expenditure was reduced from 3133*l.* to 1155*l.*
and the general condition of the labouring classes improved.
Mr. Russell, the magistrate of Swallowfield, stated to me, that
in riding through Cookham he was so much struck with the
appearance of comfort observable in the persons and residences of some of the labouring classes of that village, that he
was led to make inquiries into the cause. The answers he
received, determined him to exert his influence to procure a similar change of system in Swallowfield.

In Swallowfield, where it was partially effected, the rates
were reduced from 9*s.* and 10*s.* in the pound to 5*s.* 8*d.*, and
during the last year to 3*s.* 8*d.* in the pound. When I was there,
one of the witnesses stated, that the demand for labour had increased : that he had himself that day gone in search of a young
labourer, and not being able to find one to perform his labour, he
should be *obliged* to seek one out of the parish, an event which he
did not remember to have known occur before.

In every parish a " foreigner," namely, a labourer who has no
immediate resource from the parish, is considered the best

workman, the best-conducted man, and the most respectable in every respect. (See note on Mr. Cottrell's evidence, p. 208.)

It appears to me that the inferences to be drawn from the large body of evidence which I have now stated, and from the much larger body which I shall state in my final report, are these :—

1. That the existing system of poor-laws in England is destructive to the industry, forethought, and honesty of the labourers ; to the wealth and the morality of the employers of labour, and of the owners of property ; and to the mutual good-will and happiness of all. That it collects and chains down the labourers in masses, without any reference to the demand for their labour : That, while it increases their numbers, it impairs the means by which the fund for their subsistence is to be reproduced, and impairs the motives for using those means which it suffers to exist : And that every year and every day these evils are becoming more overwhelming in magnitude, and less susceptible of cure.

2. That of these evils, that which consists merely in the amount of the rates, an evil great when considered by itself, but trifling when compared with the moral effects which I am deploring, might be much diminished by the combination of workhouses, and by substituting a rigid administration and contract management for the existing scenes of neglect, extravagance, jobbing, and fraud.

3. That, by an alteration, or even, according to the suggestion of many witnesses, an abolition, of the law of settlement, a great part, or, according to the latter suggestion, the whole of the enormous sums now spent in litigation and removals might be saved ; the labourers might be distributed according to the demand for labour ; the immigration from Ireland of labourers of inferior habits be checked, and the oppression and cruelty, to which the unmarried labourers, and those who have acquired any property, are now subjected, might, according to the extent of the alteration, be diminished, or utterly put an end to.

4. That, if no relief were allowed to be given to the able-bodied, or to their families, except in return for adequate labour, or in a well-regulated workhouse, the worst of the existing sources of evil, the allowance system, would immediately disappear ; a broad line would be drawn between the independent labourers and the paupers ; the number of paupers would be immediately diminished in consequence of the reluctance to accept relief on such terms ; and would be still further diminished in consequence of the increased fund for the payment of wages occasioned by the diminution of rates, and would ultimately, instead of forming a constantly increasing proportion of our whole population, become a small, well-defined part of it, capable of being provided for at an expense less than one-half of the present poor-rates.

5. That the proposed changes would tend powerfully to promote providence and forethought, not only in the daily concerns of life, but in the most important of all points, marriage.

And lastly, that it is essential to the working of every one of these improvements, that the administration of the poor-laws should be entrusted, as to their general superintendence, to one Central Authority with extensive powers, and, as to their details, to paid officers, acting under the consciousness of constant super-intendence and strict responsibility.

COUNTY PALATINE OF LANCASTER.

My Lords and Gentlemen,

In compliance with your letter of the 5th instant, I have the honour to lay before your board some details touching the administration and operation of the poor-laws in Lancashire.

The pressure of the poor-rate on property in this county varies considerably; ranging from $10\frac{1}{2}d$. in the pound on the rack-rent, in West Derby township, near Liverpool, where the rates are commonly lowest, to 6s. at Padiham, in the agricultural and weaving district, where the rates are commonly highest. In the agricultural districts, the poor-rates average from 1s. 6d. to 2s. in the pound, in the southern; and from 2s. to 2s. 6d. in the pound, in the northern parts of the county. In Liverpool last year the rates were 1s. 9d.; the manufacturing towns probably average 3s.; and in the country districts, with a mixed weaving population, the rates vary from 3s. to 6s. in the pound. The county-rates, which of course must be deducted from the poor-rate, varied last year from 3d. to 5d. in the pound in the several hundreds; so that by deducting 4d. from the rate in every instance, a close approximation may be made to the proportion of the rate applicable to the relief of the poor.

The poor-rates have been greatly augmented by the transition from hand to power-loom weaving. This vicissitude affects the whole of the Salford and Blackburn hundreds, which comprise three-fifths of the population of the county, and is partially felt in the other hundreds. The county places in the hundred of Blackburn suffer more than the manufacturing towns, where the various demands for labour enabled many weavers to choose other occupations; and the power-looms coming into extensive use, by giving employment to their children, alleviate, in a great degree, the evils they had occasioned. The country weavers have no such resources, and their weaving being frequently of the coarsest and commonest description, the rate of their earnings is more reduced. Thus, in the neighbourhood of Burnley, an average hand-loom weaver cannot at present earn above 4*s.* 6*d.* a week, although a Manchester or Preston weaver may earn 6*s.* or 7*s.* weekly.

This depression of wages, and the difficulty of obtaining employment, especially for the older weavers, whose habits were fixed, has led to a general practice in the weaving district, of making an allowance to able-bodied weavers with more than two children under ten years of age. There is no fixed scale for this allowance; but the practice is to make up the earnings of the family to 2*s.*; or, in some places, to 1*s.* 6*d.* a head. This course certainly is an approximation to the payment of wages out of the poor-rate; but there are some material distinctions between the case of the weaver and the case of the agricultural labourer: the agricultural roundsman has no spur to exertion, nor interest to please the farmer, who is his master only for the day, consequently his habit of industry is relaxed and destroyed; on the other hand, as the weaver always works by the piece, and the current rate of wages is well known, it is easy to calculate what he might earn if industrious, and the parish allowance is apportioned accordingly; so that, if he is indolent, he suffers for it; if he is industrious, he reaps the benefit of his exertions; and the fact unquestionably is, that the weavers are stimulated beyond their powers under the allowance system. Again, the farmers often contrive, by the management of the parish funds, to depress the rate of wages below the natural level; but the manufacturers in this instance have not taken a similar advantage, nor has the rate of wages of the hand-loom weavers sunk lower than was to be expected, as the natural result of an invention which compelled them to compete with the prodigious power of steam.

The weavers thus receiving parochial relief are usually in a state of great destitution; their houses bare of furniture; their children half clad; their food chiefly potatoes, oatmeal porridge, and milk, with the addition of oat-cakes, in the north of the county; a herring, or a little bacon, is added on Sundays, and the women have a little tea, coffee, and bread. Butter, beer, and meat, are luxuries beyond their reach; even sliced onions, fried with lard, and added as a seasoning to the potatoes, are too dear for common use. The weavers themselves usually have a lean and hungry look, and frequently assert that they do not get victuals enough. They are perfectly aware of the hopeless condition of their employment, and are extremely patient under the privations they undergo.

To this general description, verified by extensive inquiry, and frequent visits at their houses in various parts of the county, I shall add some particulars, collected for the Board of Health at

Preston, in December, 1831, by Mr. James Harrison, surgeon, which will give a more accurate notion of the condition of the weavers there. Their correctness may be depended on, as they were collected with great care.

" The district of the town I visited, according to the parish books, contained 439 houses; these houses were almost all visited, and a register of the state of 243 families was preserved. These families were found to comprise 1287 individuals, on an average 5·29 individuals for each family. The weekly income* of these 243 families was 144*l*. 4*s*. 9*d*., making 11*s*. 10½*d*. for each family, or 2*s*. 2½*d*. for each individual.

" Of the 243 families, 139 were hand-loom weavers. These 139 families contained 634 individuals, or 4·56 to each family. The weekly income of these 139 families, including the parish allowance when made, was 73*l*. 3*s*. 3*d*., which makes, on an average, 10*s*. 6½*d*. for each family, or 2*s*. 3½*d*. for each individual. From the 10*s*. 6½*d*., however, we ought to deduct 2*s*.† a week for looms, paste, brushes, candles, &c. which are expended in the production of their manufactures, and from which expense most other operatives are exempt. This will leave 8*s*. 6½*d*. a week, on an average, for rent, taxes, fuel, clothes, food, &c. for 4·56 individuals, or about 1*s*. 10½*d*. for each individual. Thus, though the hand-loom weavers in this district were receiving above the average income of other operatives, yet in reality their available income was considerably less. There is another disadvantage under which these operatives labour: they are obliged to have workshops attached to their houses, and are therefore compelled to pay a higher rent than other labourers. In many instances I found the weavers paying 2*s*. 6*d*. a week for the rent of their houses, while few of the other classes of operatives paid more than 2*s*. or 2*s*. 3*d*. per week for house rent. If then we deduct 2*s*. 6*d*. from 8*s*. 6½*d*., the net average income of a weaver's family, we shall have 6*s*. 0½*d*.; from this again we must take 3*d*. a week for direct taxes, and 7*d*. for fuel, which will leave 5*s*. 2½*d*. a week for the food and clothing of 4·56 individuals, or about 1*s*. 1*d*. a head. This is the average, and of course there were many below this statement.

" Taking 58 of the poorest families out of the 243, I find they contained 318 persons, or 5·48 individuals to each family. Their weekly income was 25*l*. 15*s*. 1*d*.; 8*s*. 10½*d*. per family, or 1*s*. 7½*d*. per head. A number of these were weavers, from whose income if we deduct 2*s*. for expenses connected with their labour, 2*s*. 6*d*. for house rent, 3*d*. for direct taxes, and 7*d*. for fuel, we shall have

---

* This includes the parish allowance, when any such allowance was made.
† This deduction appears to be too great.

342   *Mr. Henderson's Report*

3*s.* 6¼*d.* left for clothing and feeding 5·48 individuals, or about 8*d.* per head per week, or a little more than 1*d.* a day.

" In several instances I investigated the quantity and price of provision on which the poor lived; but have only preserved one case that I can entirely depend upon—it is that of one Ann Ducket, a weaver, and five children. The mother earns by weaving, 4*s.* 6*d.* per week; and the parish to which she belongs allows her 4*s.* a week, making in all 8*s.* 6*d.* per week. She lives with her mother and brother; so that she only pays part of the rental of a house, or 1*s.* 6*d.* a week, and 5½*d.* for coals. She stated that she purchased weekly a score of potatoes, at 4*d.* a score, 1*s.* 6*d.* worth of coarse flour, 7*d.* worth of milk, 7*d.* worth of oatbread, 6*d.* worth of meal, 7*d.* worth of bacon, 3*d.* worth of coffee, 1½*d.* of sugar, and 3*d.* worth of treacle; the whole amounting to 6*s.* 8*d.*, leaving 1*s.* 10*d.* for expenses connected with her labour and clothing. According to this statement, each individual would have for his or her daily support, not quite half a pound of potatoes, a half-penny worth of wheat bread, three ounces of milk, one-sixth of an oat cake, an ounce and a half of oatmeal, two-fifths of an ounce of bacon, the same of treacle, and a similar portion of sugar and coffee, which would be about a pound of food for each individual per day, eight ounces of which would be potatoes."

This statement proves the necessity of relief; but it ought, at the same time, to caution overseers against the danger of perpetuating such wretchedness by a system of bounties in the shape of parish allowances. Hand-loom weaving, in its coarser branches, is completely superseded as a profitable employment, and ought to be abandoned with all possible dispatch. It is gratifying to observe, that the number of weavers is diminishing (though in various degrees) in all the large towns; that few young persons there are now brought up to weaving, few new looms made, and nothing is more common than to see a solitary weaver working amidst vacant looms, which have been deserted for other occupations.

The townships in almost all the parishes in Lancashire, maintain their poor separately, having overseers appointed under 12 and 13 Car. II. cap. 12.; the number of these parishes and townships is about 466, and in 1830-31 there were 202 select vestries, and 228 assistant overseers appointed In many of the large towns, select vestries have produced a more intelligent and vigilant administration of the poor-laws, and checked the corrupt practices to which closer modes of management are liable. It is to be regretted, that those best qualified are often unwilling to undertake the office of vestrymen, which, in some instances, lessens the efficiency of these vestries. In country townships, the select vestries are likewise beneficial, though their effects are not so decided : in townships, not having a regular assistant overseer, there is usually a salary, varying from 7*l.* to 30*l.* a year, annexed to the office of overseer, and the same person continues in office for a number of years; and where there are no select vestries, committees of eight or ten rate-payers frequently manage the parochial business : this system of management has long been extensively established in the county with good effect, being an evident approximation, though without the sanction of law, to the administration by select vestries and assistant overseers.

The magistrates interfere little with questions of relief in Lancashire, and usually decline to order relief at home when the overseers offer admission to the workhouse. Some complaints, however, on this head have reached the commission in the answers to the queries; and a few places might be mentioned where the overseers are occasionally thwarted in correct plans of management by the notions which some magistrates entertain, and act upon with respect to relief, especially in their not allowing distinctions to be made on the score of misconduct. The tone of applicants for relief varies much at different places, and is most clamorous and menacing where appeals are listened to most readily. The following extracts from the answers of an eminent magistrate of the county will record his opinion on this point. " I have observed, with much regret, the practice of hearing applications for relief which prevails at some petty sessions. Instead of considering them as appeals from the overseer's judgment, the application is entertained as of course, the overseer appears as an advocate against the pauper, and the decision is final. This course puts all parties out of their proper place, and is inconsistent either with justice or economy. But I do not see how it can be remedied, except by a better understanding of what is really for the good of the poor, a mistaken kindness for whom induces the magistrates to undertake this labour. The objection to a change would be, that it is not safe to trust the poor to the mercy of overseers; no doubt, the present system has a tendency to set these officers in opposition to the poor ; but, if a change were judiciously and gradually made, I think they would merit increased confidence."

These instances, however, are exceptions from the general line of conduct pursued by the magistrates : they have not in any place sanctioned a fixed scale of relief, or attempted to control the parochial authorities, in the free exercise of their judgment in the first instance as to the amount to be granted.

The aggregate expenditure of the county of Lancaster in relief, will bear a satisfactory comparison with other parts of the kingdom, subject to the poor-laws. This will appear by referring to the best test of the extent of pauperism, viz. the proportion which the sum expended on the poor bears to the number of the population. In the year ending 25th March, 1831, the amount of the expenditure of this county in relief was 293,226*l.*; the population 1,336,854: so that the proportion for each individual would be 4*s.* 4½*d.*, being smaller than in any other county in England or Wales.

In Cumberland, the English county where the proportion was least with the exception of Lancashire, the expenditure was 46,166*l.*, population 169,681, being 5*s.* 5¼*d.* a head. The average expenditure throughout England and throughout Wales was as follows:

	Population, 1831.	Expenditure in relief to the Poor. £.	Rate per head. s. d.
England	13,089,338	6,509,466	9 11¼
Wales	805,236	289,422	7 2¼

The following table shows the expenditure in relief to the poor at various towns in Lancashire, during the year ended March 25th, 1832; the amounts have been calculated from the parochial accounts, deducting payments for county, highway, church-rates, and all other items, not appertaining to the relief of the poor. The sums paid on account of paupers resident out of the parish have been deducted, and the sums paid to paupers belonging to other parishes, but residing within the parish, have been added to the expenditure of every parish; this appearing to be the proper mode of ascertaining the expenditure on the pauper inhabitants of each place. The valuation made in 1829 to the county rate is also given, as it is in general in close approximation to the present annual value of the property assessed.

	Population, 1831.	Sums expended for the relief of the Poor. £.	Rate per head. s. d.	Valuation to the County-rate, 1829. £.
Liverpool	165,175	35,633	4 3¼	751,156
Manchester	142,026	40,555	5 8½	371,749
Preston	33,112	8,232	4 11½	80,984
Oldham	32,381	3,763	2 3¾	54,798
Wigan	20,774	4,293	4 1½	38,435
Warrington	16,018	5,531	6 10¾	48,070
Lancaster	12,613	3,620	5 8¾	30,715
Burnley	7,551	2,319	6 1½	15,879
Habergham Eaves	5,817	1,036	3 6½	14,390
Garstang	924	452	9 9¼	2,744

In this commercial and manufacturing county the condition of the towns is more important than the condition of the rural districts; and, indeed, the country districts, in the greatest portion of the county, are more affected by commercial than by agricultural vicissitudes. I therefore propose to limit this communication to a notice of the administration of the poor-laws in the towns above enumerated.

LIVERPOOL.

LIVERPOOL affords a striking example of the operation of a select vestry under Mr. Sturges Bourne's act, in reducing the parochial expenditure : the result may be shown by a comparison of the year ending March, 1821, the last before the establishment of a select vestry, with the year ending March, 1831 :

Population of Liverpool.	Expenditure on the Poor.	Proportion per Head.
1820-21 ...118,972	£46,357.	7s. 9½d.
1830-31....165,175	34,524	4 2

Thus an actual diminution of expenditure, to the extent of 11,833*l.*, has been effected, notwithstanding an increase of the population in the proportion of one-third ; so that the saving might be estimated at 15,000*l.* a year more, making a total saving of 27,000*l.* a year.

In contending with the practical difficulties of pauperism, it is encouraging to observe that an improved system of management has frequently produced a vast change in a short space of time : the establishment of a select vestry at Liverpool appears to have produced its full effect in about three years, as will appear from the following tables, the first showing the diminution of the number of paupers ; the latter, which shows the decrease in expenditure, has been continued to the parochial year 1831, ended 25th March, 1832 :

	Select Vestry.		
	1820-21.	1821-22. 1822-23.	1823-24.
Average number of cases relieved out of the work-house	3222 ..	2433 .. 1719	.. 1435
Average number of in-mates in the workhouse	1492 ..	342 .. 1142	.. 1009

Expenditure of the Parish of Liverpool on the Poor in the Workhouse, including all the Expenses of that Establishment, and on the Poor out of the Workhouse, including all the Expenses of the Overseer's department.

Years.	Poor in Workhouse.	Poor out of Workhouse.	Total.
1820-21..	£13,527	... £27,103	.... £40,620
1821-22....	12,160	... 19,494	 31,650
1822-23....	8,434	... 14,310	 22,744
1823-24....	8,153	... 12,566	 20,769
1824-25....	9,979	... 12,069	 22,045
1825-26....	9,145	... 11,814	 20,969
1826-27....	11,513	... 11,296	 22,809
1827-28....	11,257	... 11,122	 22,379
1828-29....	10,259	... 10,034	 20,293
1829-30....	11,359	... 11,793	 23,152
1830-31....	14,288	... 13,906	 28,194
1831-32....	13,790	... 14,922	 28,712

This change was brought about by a thorough investigation of all the cases on the parish books: the parties receiving relief were examined, and the circumstances under which they first became chargeable were carefully scrutinized, by which means numerous impositions were detected, and the parish was enabled to reduce or withdraw many of the allowances. Great exertions were also made to provide work for able-bodied paupers: the vestry at one time contracted to fill up part of an old stone-quarry, and make a road over it; at another to cultivate by spade labour a large tract of ground called the Rector's Fields; and at another time to level, for the sum of 1000*l.*, a large rock near the workhouse, on the site of which the infirmary has since been built. Thus they set to work all able-bodied applicants for relief, and also turned all able-bodied men out of the workhouse, paying them one shilling a day to provide themselves, and exacting a good day's work in return. Many under this system, who had been for years in the workhouse, quitted it, and eventually found employment for themselves elsewhere.

The permanent usefulness of the select vestry, consisting in their vigilance and intelligence in administering relief, it may be well to state a few details of their proceedings in this department.

The select vestry is divided into five boards, each of four members; one of these boards sits in rotation every week day, except Tuesday, at nine or ten A.M., and the business usually lasts till one P.M. A salaried secretary constantly attends, and takes a principal share in conducting the business. This preserves uniformity in the management of all the boards, and on changing the select vestry the parish still has the benefit of the secretary's experience and knowledge of the cases on the books.

On a first application for relief, if entertained at all, the name and address of the applicant are taken down on a card, which is delivered to the visitor, a salaried officer, in order that he may ascertain the nature of the case at the abode of the party, the visitor makes a written report to the select vestry, on which, and on a subsequent examination of the party, relief is granted or refused. In cases of urgent necessity, a few shillings are sometimes ordered before visitation, and the visitor has always a discretionary power to relieve when he visits, but the general rule is for the vestry to decide on the propriety of relief.

When the distress is of a temporary nature, the pauper is required to appear once a week before the board. No excuse, except sickness, proved by a medical certificate, is admitted; the party is urged by the board, when it seems practicable, to seek other means of support, and when this is not done within a reasonable time, the relief is diminished or stopped. When the case presents no prospect of early improvement, a card or ticket is given for relief during a definite period of three or six months, according to circumstances, and the sum granted is paid weekly on presenting the card at the pay-office. When the period has elapsed, another visitation and examination takes place before another card is granted; the cards in cases apparently hopeless used to be perpetual, but are now subject to annual revision, and the members of the select vestry frequently act as visitors in such cases.

During my attendance at one of the boards, 250 cases were disposed of in three hours. The secretary takes the leading part in interrogating the applicants, and in fixing the amount of relief, but the select vestrymen present were also active, referring to the books, filling up pay-orders, and visitation cards, and occasionally deciding on the necessity or on the amount of the relief. It appeared to me that every case was fairly considered, and in most instances my judgment concurred with the decisions : a few may be cited as specimens to enable others to judge of their propriety; it should be observed that cases of refusal have been chiefly selected.

A healthy-looking young woman applied for relief, saying she was starving; the board having ascertained that she belonged to Liverpool offered to take her into the workhouse; she would not go in, and relief was refused. A man applied for relief, saying he had landed that morning from Dublin, and wished to go to London; he was told the parish had no money for travellers. A woman who came three weeks before from Rochdale, in a state of pregnancy, and had been delivered in Liverpool of a child, since dead, applied for assistance to go back to Rochdale—relief was refused; it was suspected she had come to Liverpool, in order to fix the parish with the child. A woman brought four children, saying that their parents both died of the cholera a few days before, and that she was their aunt, and willing to take them, if the parish would allow her 2s. a week for each child; she was told it was too much, the workhouse was mentioned, and she agreed to take 5s. a week, and to endeavour to get the eldest, a boy, to sea—ordered to be visited, and if her account should prove correct, 5s. a week to be allowed. A boy about sixteen, formerly in the workhouse, had been working at brickmaking during the summer : that employment failing, he now applied for an order to return to the workhouse—granted. Relief applied for on behalf of a woman lying in, whose husband had gone up the country. It appearing on inquiry that he left her immediately before her confinement, relief was refused; it is a common device for the husband to abscond in such cases, and endeavour to cast the burthen of the wife's confinement on the parish. A pensioner's wife applied for relief, her husband having deserted her; she was admitted to the workhouse, and steps taken to stop her husband's pension. A woman applied for relief who had been in the workhouse before; on being offered re-admission, she readily accepted it. An old woman came for relief; on being offered an order for the workhouse, she refused it angrily, and went away, saying, she could go there at any time, they could not deny her *that.* A man seventy years of age applied for an order for himself and his wife to go into the workhouse—granted. A young good-looking widow, who had one child by her husband, and an illegitimate child since his death, applied for relief; the board offered to take her and both the children into the workhouse, if she would make over to the parish 2*s.* a week which she received from the putative father of the natural child; she refused to assent to this, but wished the parish to take the lawful child, and leave her the bastard. The board would not consent to this arrangement, and she went away. A woman with one child, who used to get her living as a laundress, applied in consequence of getting no work, as the cholera prevented strangers coming to the town this summer—ordered 2*s.* a week for a few weeks. A man employed as a watchman applied for relief; he had lost his wife and several relations, who died of cholera in his house, and had a surgeon's certificate that the bedding had been destroyed by his orders; he was left with a large family—1*l.* ordered; he had received 1*l.* 10*s.* from another source. The wife of a Scotch sailor applied for relief; refused, and told, if relieved, she should be passed to Scotland. A woman residing as the tenant in a house worth 30*l.* a year, was refused relief, the rule being not to grant it to occupiers of a house above 10*l.* annual value. A woman with three young children applied for assistance to follow her husband, a stone-mason, to New York; she said she could obtain a passage for 25*s.* each person, and could raise 2*l.*, if the parish would allow her 3*l.* to pay the remainder. The woman was in great poverty, and it was clearly the interest of the parish to grant her request, and get rid of the family; but the unfavourable accounts from New York, the uncertainty of the woman as to her husband's situation, and the miserable prospects of such a family during the voyage at this season, induced the board to refuse the application, and to grant a weekly allowance to the family.

No regular relief is given to able-bodied men having families, when fully employed; in casualties, as in the case of the watchman, they are sometimes assisted; no rents are ever paid by the parish, and no applications for rent ever granted, though no doubt the relief given may frequently be applied in payment of rent.

The class of persons last admitted to the select vestry consists of the Irish applying to be relieved and passed to Dublin. No person who has not seen them could have a notion of the crowds which sometimes besiege the parish office for this purpose, or of the poverty and wretchedness which they generally exhibit. Yet there is no doubt that many of these applicants are able to pay for their passage, but choose to make the experiment of applying for a passage at the expense of the county: husbands send their wives and families to beg a passage; men trust their clothes and money to a companion, and present themselves in apparent destitution; others conceal their money in their cravats or stockings. In dealing with these cases there is nothing but the applicant's story and appearance to guide the board, and accurate discrimination is impossible; several impositions were detected while the assistant-commissioner was present. A woman with a large family said she had not seen her husband for ten months, but a boy, her son, said he had seen his father the same day. A man came with a wife and four orphans, as he stated, but they proved to be his children by a former wife; he had been reaping, and was told he must pay for the passage of himself and family. Young and healthy persons applying were refused almost as a matter of course, but in cases of infirmity and helplessness they were almost always passed; the general rule was, to refuse applications of a doubtful nature, as in cases of real necessity the same parties usually present themselves again on a future day.

Since steam-navigation has increased the facility of intercourse with Ireland, Liverpool and the county in general have been grievously burthened with Irish paupers. The difficulty which the select vestry have had to contend with from this source, and the temper and spirit in which they have acted, appear from the annual Report, April, 1824, which states, that " the lower order of Irish, tempted by the facility of communication, and the prospect of obtaining employment in the manufacturing districts, resort to Liverpool with their wives and children in overwhelming numbers. It is impossible to behold such a mass of misery and wretchedness without feelings of compassion, and yet to administer relief indiscriminately is only to hold out encouragement to others, and ultimately to increase the evil. An immediate removal of new comers back again to their own country, though sanctioned by the law, might be considered a harsh proceeding, and has never been resorted to: after a fruitless journey, therefore, into the interior, the same unfortunate individuals return, in the course of a few weeks, in a still more deplorable condition, and again become chargeable to the parish or the county. It is no exaggeration to state, that of the casual poor who obtain temporary relief, two-thirds are composed of this description."

Though the select vestry felt the necessity of abridging relief on this head, and made every effort to retrench it as far as appeared consistent with humanity, still the numbers of Irish passed by the parish, exclusive of those passed from other parts of the county, and England, were, in ten months of the year 1824-25, 2262; in 1826-27, 2254; in 1827-28, 1547.

The proceedings of the select vestry show that the workhouse is frequently used as a test of the real necessities of applicants for relief; and that while some, who pretend to be starving, refuse, others, really in want, solicit admission, and those who had been inmates before apply to enter it again: as it is the largest establishment of the kind in the kingdom, and generally considered to be well regulated, a few details may be admissible.

When visited in September, 1832, it contained 1715 inmates, and can accommodate in winter, 1750. The present governor has had the management about twenty-eight years: on his appointment in 1804, there were 800 inmates; no separation of the sexes, only five weaving-looms, and no other employment for the paupers beyond the necessary business of the house. The door-keepers were paupers, who frequently took bribes for admission, and the house was altogether in a most disorderly state. The governor procured a paid doorkeeper, separated the sexes as completely as the nature of the building would permit, except in cases of married people, who had small apartments allotted to them; he also exacted from each person able to work, a reasonable portion of labour daily, for which purpose dry picking of oakum was introduced: this is a tedious and irksome process of manual labour, by which junk, old shipping-ropes cut into pieces a few inches long, is untwisted, the yarns separated and reduced to shreds by the hand and fingers, and by rubbing against the apron worn by the picker: there is nothing unwholesome or straining in this employment, but it is tiresome, and various attempts were made to evade it: one mode tried was by boiling the junk in water, after which it is easily pulled into shreds, but the ropes lose their efficacy to resist water, and consequently the oakum is unfit for caulking, its destined use. The introduction of labour thinned the house very much: it was sometimes difficult to procure a sufficient supply of junk, which was generally obtained from Plymouth; when the supply was known to be scanty, paupers flocked in; but the sight of a load of junk before the door would deter them for a length of time.

The children, nine years of age, are taught to weave, and their time is divided between school and the looms; under this system they thrive better, and the instruction they get in weaving promotes their being apprenticed. The choice of the children is complied with as far as possible in apprenticing them; some are bound to tradesmen, tailors, shoemakers, &c., some go to sea, but the largest proportion, until recently, went to cotton factories, where most of them were bound to persons of respectability ; on leaving the workhouse, they are told to send information if they are not well treated. It is easy to ascertain how those fare who were apprenticed in Liverpool, and the others are visited by some of the overseers usually every year, but at all events once in the course of two years. The apprenticing and visitation of the children is occasionally adverted to in the Reports of the select vestry *. Instances not unfrequently occur of individuals who have served their time with credit, calling at the workhouse or at the select vestry, and stating that they are able to earn a comfortable subsistence.

It has been the practice to encourage children of poor persons living in town to come to the workhouse for employment : they continue to live with their parents, and receive 1*s.* a week until they are initiated in weaving, then 1*s.* 6*d.* a week is allowed, and after two years they have their diet in the workhouse in addition. These children have the same school instruction as the children in the house, and are usually between fifty and sixty in number. As hand-loom weaving has ceased to be a profitable employment, attempts are now making to give the industry of the children a more useful direction by teaching them common trades, but this improvement has not yet made much progress.

The inmates of the workhouse were formerly allowed to go out every Thursday afternoon; this permission led to many irregularities, the paupers frequently returning drunk, and begging or otherwise misconducting themselves in the streets to the scandal of the establishment. They also used to go out on Sundays to church, but a chapel has been built within the workhouse; and a regulation was adopted in 1831, which restricted the liberty of leaving the house to the first Thursday afternoon in every month, except in the case of paupers upwards of sixty years of age, who are still permitted to go out every Thursday. The Catholics go out to chapel at eight every Sunday morning, and return at ten. Thus, one condition of entering this workhouse is submission to constant confinement, except for a few hours every month.

The rooms are well ventilated, floors kept clean, and sprinkled daily with chloride of lime, and the walls frequently whitewashed. Although the cholera has been so prevalent in Liverpool, only nine cases occurred up to Sept. 6, 1832, in this establishment; four of these proved fatal, one being the case of a pauper who,

---

* See Reports, 1827, 1829, 1830.

before his admission, had been employed as a bearer of the litter in which cholera patients were carried to the hospital.

The governor lays great stress on classification generally, and on a complete separation of the sexes; there are lock-wards for males and for females in this establishment, and the governor thinks them essential to prevent the most depraved inmates corrupting or annoying decent and orderly paupers: in the small houses, in which two or three married couples live together, those of congenial habits and character are placed together.

When the workhouse was visited, some of the boys and girls were busy weaving, but the greater part of them were in a spacious school-room under the chapel; their general appearance was satisfactory: the oakum-shop was almost filled by men seated on benches and picking oakum. The hours of work are from six in the morning to six in the evening in summer, and from eight until four in winter, allowing half an hour for breakfast, and one hour for dinner; persons eighty years of age and upwards are exempted from any labour, but from all under that age and in health, a task is required in proportion to their ability and strength; those who, from age or infirmity, have a limited task, are allowed to choose their own time for performing it, and used formerly to pick the oakum in their own rooms; but owing to the risk of fire, this practice has been discontinued, and all this work must now be done in the shop. A full measure of employment is exacted from the able-bodied. the object being to discourage laziness, and, as the governor expressed it. to " work them out." The consequence is, that not more than twenty of the inmates were able-bodied men. The aged people appeared the most cheerful inmates: the avowed principle of management is to make them and the young most comfortable. The women were all employed, chiefly in sewing. attending to the young children, acting as nurses. and performing household offices.

About 200 of the inmates were in the house for the second or third time. Applications to the select vestry for re-admission to the workhouse are not in general granted, until a character of the applicant is obtained from the governor; and paupers on leaving the house frequently express a hope to the governor that he will give them a character if they should require to come in again.

A general appearance of order and discipline prevails throughout the establishment. The governor, who is a steady systematic man. stated that 1000 or 1800 paupers were as easily managed as 500. He has two salaried clerks, a schoolmaster. and two weavers acting as overlookers, who receive salaries; and the governor's wife has two paid female assistants; the rest of the establishment is conducted by paupers selected from the inmates.

A fever hospital, a detached building, for 140 patients, is supported by the parish, within the walls, and forms part of the workhouse establishment; the diet, wine, &c. for the patients, materially increase the general expenditure; female paupers act as nurses, and having some privileges in consequence, are usually desirous to be so employed. The total weekly cost, including provisions, clothing, and all the expense of the establishment was last year, 3*s.* 2*d.* per head; but as there was an extraordinary item of 1426*l.* for buildings, perhaps 3*s.* may be considered a fair estimate, *communibus annis.* The weekly cost for provisions and clothing was 2*s.* 2½*d.* per head.

The following tables show the fluctuation and employments of the population in the workhouse :—

On the 25th of March, 1831, there were in the house . 1696
During the year ending 25th of March, 1832, admitted . 2962

4678

During the year, Discharged . . 2540
Dead . . . 477*

3017

Remaining in the house 25th of March, 1832 . 1661

Ages of the inmates:		
Under 15 years	.	589
15 to 40	. .	242
40 to 50	. .	135
above 50	. .	695

1661

Aged, infirm, and sick, not able to work	437
Aged and infirm employed . .	426
Able-bodied under sixty years of age employed (males 67, females 142) } .	209
Children employed	159
„ not employed . . .	430

1661

Of this number, 639 were males and 1022 females, the average

* The Fever Hospital accounts for this mortality.

2 A

number in the house throughout the year was 1648, being about 1 per cent. on the population of the town.

There is a surgeon with a salary of 300*l.* a year, to attend the poor in the workhouse; the parish subscribes 500 guineas annually to the dispensaries, through which medical attendance is given to the paupers out of the house.

As magisterial interference is extremely rare, the decision on the propriety of relief rests almost entirely with the select vestry. The allowances are extremely moderate, and not made on any fixed scale; though, in some degree, they are regulated by the cost of clothing and maintenance in the workhouse. Those who complain that the relief granted is insufficient are frequently taken into the workhouse.

The management would probably be improved by more visitation of the poor. It is impossible for a single visiter to do justice to so large a parish as Liverpool: cases of hardship probably occur where relief is refused without visitation, and relief may sometimes be given too sparingly for want of information, which more frequent visits would supply. Though the administration is vigilant and economical, it may be doubted whether the advantage of the poorer classes would be promoted by any relaxation: under the present system their habits are generally industrious, and their wages sufficient to secure their independence and comfort. Workmen, who have trades, seldom fail to obtain employment and good wages; the usual wages of common labourers are 3*s.* a day. Of the multitude resorting to Liverpool for work, some submit to receive lower wages, but these cases are exceptions; it is also true, that there is much distress among this class for want of employment; this, however much it may be regretted, seems unavoidable in a town peculiarly liable to an influx of labourers from Ireland; indeed, the natives of that country compose, at a moderate estimate, one-half of the common labourers in Liverpool. If the parish was to take charge of all those unemployed at any given time, it is probable that the super-abundance of labour would be equally great in a few months afterwards.

It is contrary to the habits and character of sailors to spunge on the parish whilst they are fit for active service; even after that period, the number chargeable is comparatively small. Owing, however, to the casualties incident to a sea-faring life, their families often fall on the parish for support. When their families are relieved during their absence at sea, the 32d section of Mr. S. Bourne's act is enforced as far as is practicable, and the money advanced is repaid by the ship-owners out of the wages of the seamen.

Instances sometimes occur of sailors coming forward voluntarily, and repaying the money advanced. Settlement by apprenticeship opens a wide door to litigation, from uncertainty as to the place of the last forty days' residence under indentures: this objection is peculiarly strong in cases of apprentices in merchant-ships, who, from the nature of their service, are constantly sailing from port to port; and when, in the old age of the party, or perhaps after his death, the question of settlement arises, it is involved in a degree of obscurity, which is seldom cleared up without incurring the expenses of an appeal.

In 1823 a resolution was passed by the general vestry to assess the owners of small tenements, according to the 19th section of Mr. Sturges Bourne's act. The number of houses of which the rentals were between 6*l.* and 20*l.* a year, was very great in Liverpool, and the amount of rates levied from them exceedingly small, no fewer than 18,000 assessments being annually discharged by the parish as incapable of being enforced. The owners were accordingly rated, and called on to show cause why the rates were not paid: they attended, and 14,532 cases were investigated, at the rate of 300 or 400 daily; but not one party in 100 would admit his property to be within the act. They declared, almost universally, that the letting was for a year or longer, with rent reserved quarterly; in short, notwithstanding the quantity of property of the value within the act, the experiment scarcely produced enough to pay for the notices issued on the occasion.

Application was made to parliament in 1831, for a local act, which was originally intended to apply to all tenements under 15*l.* a year rental; but meeting with much opposition, it was limited to tenements rated at 12*l.* a year. By this act (1 Wm. IV. cap. xxi.), the owners are made liable to the payment of the rates, where the premises are rated or assessed at a yearly value not exceeding 12*l.* By thus making the assessment, and not the rent, the test of liability, all fraud or collusion as to the amount of rent is obviated. The act empowers the overseers to compound with the landlords, and requires them to accept two-thirds of the rate, where tendered within three months, in full for the whole rate. There is a clause making the occupiers of the premises liable to the rates, and their goods to distress to the extent of rent due to the owners, with a power of deducting the amount from their rent. Under this small tenement act many of the cottage owners compounded for two-thirds of the rates, and 4230*l.* was collected last year, and paid into the parish coffers last year, which sum would otherwise have been almost wholly lost to the parish. The number of receipts given on the payment of rates, for the seven preceding years, was about 10,000; in the last year the number was about 14,000, an increase chiefly attributable to the small tenement act. In fact, the rates are now better paid in Liverpool, on houses under 12*l.* rental, than on those above 12*l.* and under 20*l.*

It seems just that the owners of this species of property should have considerable indulgence in compounding for the rates, to compensate for the peculiar liability imposed on them. It would be more convenient for the parish to make the tenant primarily liable, and the landlord responsible on his default; but this course would have an injurious effect on the contracts between landlord and tenant, from the uncertain position in which the former would stand with reference to the rates. The changes of ownership to which this species of property is peculiarly subject, and other difficulties which may occur with reference to the owners, seem to render it expedient that the rates should be made a charge on the land, limiting the arrear chargeable to a period of two or three years.

The expenditure on the poor in Liverpool in the year 1831-32, amounted to 35,633*l.* 3*s.* 7*d.*, which would require a poor-rate of 1*s.* 4*d.* in the pound on the rack-rent; the rates actually laid were 1*s.* 2*d.* for the poor, 5*d.* for the county, and 2*d.* for the church,—all together 1*s.* 9*d.*; but the rate for the poor was deficient to the extent of 2*d.* in the pound.

OLDHAM.

THE affairs of the poor at Oldham have long been well managed, and the inhabitants have never been degraded by extensive pauperism. Previously to Mr. Sturges Bourne's Act, a species of select vestry, consisting of a committee of seventeen rate-payers, acting with the churchwardens and overseers, conducted the township business; so that at Easter 1820, when the act was adopted, the change was little more than nominal.

There is an assistant overseer, with a salary of 100*l.* a year. The members of the select vestry, carefully chosen from different parts of the township, usually perform personally the duty of visiting the poor at their abodes; by which means they are able to exercise on the cases relieved an exact discrimination, to which the excellent condition of the township is mainly to be ascribed. After providing for the aged, sick, widows with families, and other usual dependants on parochial aid, the hand-loom weavers require the principal attention; they are said to be reluctant to apply for relief, but are generally compelled to come when they have three or four children under the age (ten years) at which they can generally find employment in the cotton mills. The select vestry has taken great pains to shift these weavers to more profitable occupations. Situations have been procured for many of them in the power-loom factories, their families having been maintained by the township whilst they were learning to work at the power-looms, which requires about a fortnight. Thus their number has been diminished, as the power-looms, of which there are now several thousands in Oldham, increased in number; and there is reason to expect that hand-loom weaving of a coarse description will be gradually extinguished at Oldham. These weavers here are considered an orderly and industrious class; their contributions to Friendly Societies are frequently paid by the township, and they meet with more favour than the hatters, also a numerous body, probably about a thousand, and often burthensome; their wages average 1*l.* per week, but the demand for their labour is irregular, and many of them, being improvident and intemperate, are reduced to great distress. There are many machine-makers, and probably seven hundred colliers at Oldham, but they never apply for relief when employed, as is generally the case.

No regular or permanent relief is afforded to any able-bodied men except weavers; but occasional relief is frequently given, without setting the applicants to work, in the expectation that they will find themselves employment; if they continue burthensome, they are set to work on the roads. About twenty able-bodied men out of work were receiving relief in October, 1832. No application for relief is entertained, if the earnings amount to 2*s.* a head for each member of the family: it is not, however, a matter of course to make up the deficiency when the earnings are less.

The magistrates seldom interfere with the decisions of the select vestry; and never order relief at home, in cases where admission is offered to the workhouse. On the day I attended the petty sessions at Oldham, there was no case of appeal from the decision of any overseer or vestry in the district.

The workhouse is an old building, and usually contains about 130 inmates, more weavers than any other class; there are also hatters, colliers, and others. A retired soldier, with a salary of 22*l.* a year, acts as governor, and is useful to the parish in arious other matters connected with the management of the poor.

All the inmates who are able to work are employed, either at looms in the house, in cultivating the garden, on the roads, or in the cotton factories; and, in the last case, the manufacturers pay the wages to the township.

None but the aged or sick are allowed tea, coffee, tobacco, or snuff. The house, though homely, is clean; and the people seem content with the provisions, which are supplied by tender. They are allowed to go out when their work is done, on asking leave, and the governor said that bad consequences seldom followed the indulgence.

There is a complete separation of the sexes, except in cases of old married people, who are allowed to live together: young married persons are separated. There is great difference in the practice of workhouses, as to married persons. At Manchester, husband and wife are invariably separated; and a case occurred, where an old man of eighty, a tinker, who, though in great distress, turned back from the house, when he found that he must be separated from his wife, an old woman of seventy. He was afterwards, however, compelled by want to take refuge in the house, and died there, after remaining some time, according to the rule, deprived of his wife's society. On the other hand, in the workhouse at Wigan, there are three married couples, who have had seven children, begotten and born in the workhouse: at Liverpool all married couples live together, with the exception of a man and his wife, who were both inmates of the workhouse when single, and left it for the purpose of being married; after a few weeks they both returned to the workhouse, where they still are, but have not been allowed to live together. The whole expense of the workhouse, including provisions, clothing, and the expense of the establishment, is 2s. 5d. a week for each inmate.

The township is at little charge from bastardy, because the mother usually keeps the child; and when no money is received from the putative father, nothing is paid to her, unless she is in a condition to require relief as a pauper; which is seldom the case, as it is considered that a woman ought to maintain herself and one child, and no allowance is made to a widow with one child. This practice has been adopted in several other populous places, as will appear from the following items from the overseer's accounts for 1831-32.

	Received from fathers of illegitimate children.	Paid to mothers of illegitimate children.
Wigan	£194 4 9	£190 4 9
Salford	575 8 11	586 14 0

At Ormskirk and North Meols the same course is pursued: natural affection prevents the mother's parting with her child, in order that it may be maintained by the parish; though the law, which does not recognize any relationship, leaves her at liberty so to do, on paying the amount of the order upon her, which is seldom in this county sufficient to maintain the child. In Oldham, the common orders are 2*s.* for the first, 1*s.* 9*d.* for a second, and 1*s.* 6*d.* for a third child, which sums are imposed both on the fathers and on the mothers. The sums ordered were formerly larger, but were reduced in 1821, with a view to lessen the number of defaults in payment and imprisonment of the putative fathers.

A list of the parties receiving relief, with the rate of relief, is occasionally printed and published with the overseer's account. The last publication was in July, 1830. A similar list is published annually at Warrington, Prescot, Garstang, Padiham, and other places; and the practice has been found beneficial in regulating the amount of allowance, detecting impositions, and preventing improper applications; it is also a check on the amount of payments made to the paupers, who are sure to complain when set down for a larger sum than they have actually received.

The general vestry rejected a proposal to adopt the nineteenth section of Mr. Sturges Bourne's Act. The rates are in many instances not collected from small tenements: in a few cases the landlords, by agreement with the tenants, pay the rates; on the whole the collection is extremely good, not more than seven per cent. of the whole rate ultimately remaining uncollected. A complete collection has an importance beyond the sum brought into the parish chest; for in proportion as the pressure of the poor-rate descends lower in the scale of society, it will be found that those who distribute it, "having an eye to those who pay," as the Oldham overseer said, are more economical; and the poor are less ready to resort to a fund, to which their neighbours and equals are contributors. At Ormskirk, the ultimate deficiency does not exceed 1 per cent.; and I am convinced that the collection is a strong check on pauperism, from which that town is remarkably exempt.

The tendency of the population to resort to and accumulate in towns is peculiarly strong in this county; and, consequently, almost every large town contains a large proportion of poor with country settlements. When such persons become chargeable, the usual course is to apprize the overseer of the place of settlement; who, if the liability is clear, gives a direction to the overseer where the pauper is, to relieve him as one of his own poor, and under takes to pay the sum so advanced. This system is unquestion ably open to abuse, and some check by visitation is requisite; but, on the whole, it operates beneficially to the country townships. By mutual candour and fair dealing between the overseers, litigation and removals are diminished, the poor are less harassed, and probably less burthensome, as they are generally better able to earn a living where they remain. It has been proposed that the magistrates should have power to enforce these arrangements, which seem to rest on the honour of the parties. The following items from the accounts of several towns will give some notion of the relative situation of the towns and country parishes, in the balance of these accounts, and may assist in estimating the effect as between manufacturing towns and country parishes, of making residence confer a settlement.

	Paid by the Town for its own Poor in other Parishes.			Received by the Town for the Poor of other Parishes.			Balance in favour of the Town.		
Oldham	£153	5	0	£274	12	1	£121	7	1
Manchester	1640	10	0	3410	6	6	1769	16	6
Salford	326	10	10	690	13	11	364	3	1
Wigan	414	9	11	1120	14	1	706	4	2
Liverpool	1214	9	1	1792	7	2	577	18	1
Preston	387	8	7	616	9	0	229	0	5
	4136	13	5	7905	2	9	3768	9	4

Lancaster, owing to the depressed condition of its manufactures and trade, is an exception to the general rule, paying 549*l*. 15*s*. 3*d*. for its own poor in other townships, and disbursing 425*l*. 19*s*. 4*d*. for the poor of other townships in Lancaster. The sound condition of Oldham is not attributable to uninterrupted prosperity. In the year 1826, in consequence of the failure of Saddleworth bank, the accidental burning of the Priory Mills, and many of the factories ceasing to work, a large portion of the population was thrown out of employment and reduced to want. The poor-rates were doubled, and the select vestry made great efforts to meet the evil, sometimes meeting at twelve o'clock in the day and sitting until three or four o'clock the following morning, and it was remarked that the relief administered by the select vestry was far more efficient than the subscription funds sent from London, and distributed through other hands. A well-organized system of relief has peculiar value in fluctuations such as these, to which manufacturing towns are extremely liable. The expenditure of the township was gradually reduced to its usual limits, as the difficulties of the times were surmounted. The poor-rate, last year, was 2*s*. in the pound, on a valuation of three-fourths of the rack-rent.

MANCHESTER.

SINCE the year 1790, the affairs of the poor at Manchester have been conducted under a Local Act, obtained for the purposes of building a poor-house and increasing the number of overseers in proportion to an increasing population. Three churchwardens and ten sidesmen are appointed under this act to manage all parochial affairs ; and it is highly creditable to the public spirit of the town, that the most respectable merchants, manufacturers and ' tradesmen, willingly serve these useful, though troublesome offices. The senior churchwarden, so far as his office regards the poor, attends to the assessment and collection of the rates, and the second superintends the workhouse. The senior sidesman attends to the removals ; the second, to the bastardy department ; and the eight others manage the administration of relief.

The town is divided into four districts ; two sidesmen, and a visiting overseer with a salary, are appointed to each district, and form a board, which sits once every week, to dispense relief. The system· of visitation at the abodes of the poor, so indispensable to a right disposal of cases in large towns, is brought to great perfection here ; relief is never refused without visitation, and each visiting overseer, having a limited district, acquires an accurate knowledge of the condition of the poor : his written reports on the cases visited are preserved, and often referred to with advantage after a lapse of years ; it is part of his duty to be present at the board sitting for relief, and to assist in regulating the amount.

The cases of applicants for relief are carefully considered at the boards, and disposed of, as it appeared to me, with discrimination and liberality. Hand-loom weavers constitute the extraordinary burthen on the township ; those employed on work of a common description usually make out a case for relief when they have three or more children under ten years of age ; printed forms are used for the purpose of ascertaining from their employers the amount of their earnings, and their character for industry ; and after inquiring into their means of subsistence, the deficiency is usually made up to 2*s.* a head for each member of the family. It rarely happens that relief is given to other persons in health and full employment ; but many receive relief on the ground of being unable to find employment, and often without being set to work. In fact, there is great want of employment for persons past the prime of life ; one effect of recent inventions in machinery has been, to increase the demand for the labour of young persons, and to diminish the demand for the labour of persons past the prime of life. Incessant activity is required to follow the speed of the machinery, and strength is of secondary importance ; the workman, in many departments, loses his value as soon as his sight begins to fail, or his hand to lose its steadiness ; the consequence is, that many operatives between forty and fifty years of age are superannuated, and unfit for the work to

which they have been accustomed; and there is little chance of
persons at that period of life, getting employment in the factories.
Young persons, especially females, readily get employment, and at
the age of sixteen or eighteen, young men and women are frequently in the receipt of as large wages as they can expect to earn
at any period of their lives: thus they have a fair opportunity of
making provision for after life; but this premature independence
too often induces them to quit their parents' houses, that they
may be more at liberty to follow their own inclinations.

The important portion of the population engaged in the factories is independent of parochial aid. The following is a statement of the number and wages of the people in the employ of
Messrs. Birley, Hornby, and Kirk, made out in January, 1832,
and not materially varied up to the subsequent October, when I
visited the factory:

AVERAGE WAGES OF PERSONS EMPLOYED.

	Spinners.			Weavers.	
	£	s.	d.	s.	d.
Men	1	0	6	— 15	1¾
Women . . .	0	11	3½	— 9	7¼
Children . . .	0	5	10	— 5	4¼

	Number employed.	Average Wages of the whole number.
		s. d.
Men .	379	. . . 18 4
Women	563	. . . 10 5
Children	634	
Total . .	1576	

On my expressing a wish to see all the people at work, Mr.
H. Birley conducted me through every room in the building: and
I may be allowed, in passing, to attest the general cheerful and
healthful appearance of the people employed, and to pay a just
tribute to the regard shown for their comfort in many of the arrangements in this splendid establishment.

Mr. Foster, the police magistrate, every Wednesday hears appeals from the board, and the overseers are perfectly satisfied with
the control thus exercised. About thirty cases were disposed of
by him on the day I attended. In one instance, a mechanic,
earning 1*l.* 8*s.* weekly, was brought up to shew cause why an
order should not be made upon him to maintain his father; he
did not object to make an allowance, but contended that the
township should contribute, being strongly impressed with a notion
that the support of his father was a burthen which the township
ought to share, and for that reason he was dissatisfied with the
result by which he was ordered to pay 4*s.* a week. The in-

fluence of the poor-laws on the ties of nature is, I apprehend, often overrated; this case illustrates their usual effect. The proportion which the expenditure bears to the population, is larger in Manchester than in Wigan, Preston, and many other manufacturing towns; this, in a great degree, arises from the different practice adopted with reference to the unsettled Irish poor, as will appear from the following comparative account.

	Population in 1831.	Cases relieved in one week, 1827. English.	Irish.	Irish cases in one week, 1831.
Manchester . .	108,017 .	1821 .	264 .	554
Stockport . .	21,726 .	304 .	9 .	5
Macclesfield . .	17,746 .	290 .	— .	0
Warrington . .	13,570 .	327 .	6 .	6
Oldham . . .	21,662 .	467 .	1 .	0
Spotland (part of Rochdale) . .	20,000 .	600 .	4 .	1
Wigan . . .	17,716 .	421 .	6 .	7
Ashton-under-Lyne	9,222 .	420 .	1 .	20
Preston . . .	24,575 .	585 .	15 .	—
Blackburn . .	21,940 .	339 .	30 .	—
Great and Little Bolton	31,295 .	$\left\{\begin{matrix}1150\\187\end{matrix}\right\}$.	$\left\{\begin{matrix}46\\1\end{matrix}\right\}$.	20
Bury . . .	10,583 .	140 .	— .	1

Thus in one week, in 1827, out of the population of 108,017, the number of Irish cases relieved in Manchester was 264, whereas in the other principal manufacturing townships collectively, out of a population of 210,053, the total number of Irish cases relieved was 119; and whilst the number of Irish cases in Manchester, as compared with the English cases, was in a proportion exceeding one to seven, the average of the other townships in the aggregate was only in the proportion of one to forty-four. These facts were stated in a representation made in 1827, by the churchwardens and sidesmen of Manchester to the magistrates, pointing out the increasing burthen from Irish paupers, and suggesting the expediency of discouraging their applications for relief. This representation, however, has not been pressed on the magistrates, by applications for removals; which, if made, would be granted: the general rule adopted by the magistrates, and acquiesced in by the township, is to relieve the Irish who have been twelve years resident in Manchester, and not to remove them unless they bear bad characters; occasional relief is also given to a considerable extent, to those who have been resident for shorter periods.

The proportion of Irish cases to English cases has been

increasing of late years, as will appear by comparing the number relieved in one week:

Year.	One week's cases. English.	Irish.
1827	1821	264
1831	2022	554

The amount granted in relief to the Irish poor without settlements, in 1831-32, was 3498*l.* 3*s.* 10½*d.*

These facts shew the inroads of Irish pauperism; a grievance likely to continue as long as want of employment and extreme poverty drive the natives of Ireland into a country where those evils exist in a minor degree. It is true, that since the law facilitated the removal of the Irish receiving relief, many towns, by removing or threatening to remove all who receive relief, have almost entirely prevented applications from the Irish, and parochial aid is seldom extended to them except in sickness: thus in Wigan, where about 2,000 of the inhabitants are Irish, not 30*l.* is expended annually in relief to them. It must, however, be borne in mind, that this saving is purchased by severe privations, and the alternative must, in many cases, have a very harsh operation, especially as the removal, almost invariably, is made to Dublin, though the parties may be natives of the remotest parts of Ireland.

The work-house is professedly and in fact a poor-house; an asylum for the aged, infirm poor, and children. The house is spacious, and the rooms, bedding, &c., in admirable order, the inmates able to work weave, and the children are taught to read and head pins; there is a chapel within the walls, and a chaplain, with a salary. There is a surgeon also, with 100*l.* a year; a most useful appointment, as he visits and attends the poor out of the house. The average weekly expense per head for provisions and clothing is 2*s.* 9*d.*, but the expenses of so complete an establishment are necessarily heavy, and the total cost per head per annum was 13*l.* 3*s.* 3*d.* The establishment, therefore, though well conducted, does not appear to answer the ends of economy with reference to the inmates; and with reference to the out-door poor, as admission is rather a matter of favour, little use can be made of the workhouse as an alternative to repel improper applications for relief.

The effect of the poor-laws, regarded as a national charity, may be seen to advantage at Manchester; the quantity of distress and suffering alleviated is extremely great; and it is a satisfactory part of the management that many poor widows with families, aged, and infirm persons are encouraged and aided in their schemes for keeping shops, &c., which turn their industry to the best account.

The 19th section of Mr. Sturges Bourne's act has been adopted here with good effect ; but it has been found expedient to make abatements to the landlords, to the extent of nearly half the rates. At Preston, the same provision was adopted in 1821, but its effect is frequently avoided by leases for a year : on the whole, I am certain that a general enactment making landlords liable for the rates of small houses would be generally useful and acceptable throughout this country ; 10*l.* annual value of the houses would be a proper limit of such liability in towns, and 6*l.* in country places.

The following summary of the expenditure out of the poor rate in Manchester, in the year 1831-32, was furnished by Mr. Gardiner, the directing overseer :

EXPENDITURE, 1831-32.	£.	*s.*	*d.*	£.	*s.*	*d.*
Poor out of the workhouse .	21,814	5	5·			
Deduct received from pensioners, &c.	1,189	10	2			
				20,624	15	3
Poorhouse . . .	7,915	4	6			
Deduct received for sundries .	277	2	7½			
				7,638	1	10½
Vagrancy				450	16	0
Miscellaneous, overseers and collector's salaries, &c. . .	16,958	0	10			
Deduct county-rates, constables, &c.	10,037	5	1			
				6,920	15	6
Loss by bastardy				725	3	5
Loss by out-township poor . . .				1,913	3	7
Expenditure on the poor .				38,272	15	10½
A rate of 3*s.* per £. raises about .	45,000	0	0			
Deduct one-sixth for county-rates, &c.	7,500	0	0			
	37,500	0	0			

So that the total expense of relief to the poor is 2*s.* 6½*d.* in the pound, on an assessment of about three-fourths of the rack-rent ; deducting one-fourth on that account, leaves the expense at 1*s.* 11*d.* in the pound on rack-rent.

WIGAN.

A PROPOSAL to adopt a select vestry at Wigan was rejected, apparently with reason, for the present management answers well. One overseer is appointed every year, and there are three assistant overseers who have held their offices during the last 16 years, one of them is governor of the workhouse, another collector : the dispensation of relief is left to the assistant overseer, and a committee is appointed to examine the accounts every month. Complaints by applicants for relief to the mayor of Wigan are rare, and he usually interferes by way of recommendation to the overseer. On the 21st September, 1832, the number of paupers was as follows: In the workhouse, 130; cases relieved out of the house, 370; of the latter upwards of 200 were aged persons, the remainder consisted of cripples, widows with families, and weavers and spinners, with three or more young children. Weavers and spinners are the only able-bodied men who receive relief; those who have voluntarily thrown themselves out of work are never assisted by the parish. There is much distress in the town, and an overseer assured me that 1000 small houses, which he had recently visited, were so barely and miserably provided with bedding, &c., that the value of the whole furniture would not exceed 1000*l.* The poorer classes here subsist chiefly on oatmeal porridge, buttermilk, potatoes, a little bread, and occasionally a little bacon. Lamentable as this state of things is, the remedy I apprehend ought not to be sought in increasing the poor-rates, which already press heavily on the rate-payers; they were last year nominally 4*s.* in the pound, probably equivalent to 2*s.* 9*d.*; economy is here a matter of necessity. The management, though strict, being fair and judicious, is not unpopular with the poor; and the rate-payers have much reason to be satisfied with the collector and governor of the workhouse, who last year had a vote of thanks from the committee of accounts.

PRESTON.

SINCE 1821, with the interruption of a single year, Preston has had a select vestry, with general good effect: owing to the apathy of the principal rate-payers, the management has now (1832) fallen in part into improper hands, and is rapidly deteriorating. The publication of the names of persons receiving relief has been discontinued, the discipline of the workhouse relaxed, and the scale of allowance occasionally increased, though the cheapness of articles of food at present does not warrant such a change. One of the overseers has complained of the responsibility which the law imposes on him for the acts of the select vestry, over which he has no control. I happened to attend a meeting of the rate-payers, where one of the persons present and clamorous during the proceedings was, as I was informed, a pauper, who had thrown himself out of work on a reduction of his wages from 1*l.* to 18*s.* a week, and became a pensioner of the parish. Several other cases were cited, where workmen on trifling disputes had quitted their employers, and were taken into the pay of the parish.

In one instance, a man threw up work at which he was earning 1*l.* a week, on account of a dispute as to 3*d.* a week in rent: whatever may be the merits of the dispute, a man must be destitute of the spirit of independence, who can thus throw his family on the parish ; and it is only by a gross abuse that the parish funds can be made applicable to support him in such a case. The interests of the rate-payers, and the general condition of the poor must both suffer from this system. The management prior to the present year appears to have been fair and considerate towards the poor, whose necessities were relieved, though pauperism was checked. The general condition of the labouring classes in Preston, notwithstanding the difficulties under which the hand-loom weavers are struggling, is better than in most towns in the county. There are two assistant overseers who visit the poor : owing to the care bestowed on ascertaining the facts in disputed settlements, the expense of litigation during the last three years was under 36*l.*

LANCASTER.

At Lancaster the overseers, with the aid of an experienced assistant with a salary, conduct the affairs of the poor ; the expenditure bears the same proportion to the population as at Manchester, but the proportion of paupers is greater, owing to the less flourishing state of this city : the management is economical, and the parish authorities have no wish to lessen the control of the magistrates, which I, therefore, conclude to be sparingly exercised. In the year 1831-32, the rate was 2*s.* 6*d.* in the pound on the rack-rent.

The sum of 140*l.* was lately received in one year by the township, in fines of 10*l.* from persons refusing to take parish apprentices : this reluctance is to be regretted, though, I apprehend, it is often well founded. In a workhouse of a populous borough I found the children not put to any work ; and though they were said to be taught by a pauper, such instruction was probably little more than nominal, for the boys were lolling about the yard, and the place pointed out as the school-room was inadequate and unfit for the purpose. Children, thus shut up in ignorance and idleness, and exposed to the moral contamination of a workhouse, are almost necessarily unfit for the duties required from them as apprentices ; all labour is an intolerable hardship, their masters objects of aversion, and they rarely acquire habits of industry in after life. If the public undertakes to bring up children, it surely becomes a duty to provide the means of moral and religious instruction, and to lay the foundation of those habits, which are essential to make them useful members of society.

The practice in some towns pursued systematically is, to bind the parish apprentices into out-townships, in order to shift the settlement, so that the binding parish may be rid of them. When I inquired of the assistant overseer at the borough above referred to, how the apprentices turned out after they were bound, his answer was, " We have nothing to do with them afterwards." Though these observations are introduced here, I disclaim applying them in any degree to Lancaster.

BURNLEY.

BURNLEY, in 1826, suffered much from the failure of a bank, which caused many of the cotton factories to stop working, and threw a large portion of the population on the poor-rates; the town has not yet recovered from the effects of this calamity, and want of capital is one cause why power-looms have not been introduced to a greater extent: there are now seven or eight power-loom factories. The hand-loom weavers are very numerous, they weave coarse calicoes, and are not able to earn more than 5s. a week. There is a select vestry, and though the scale of allowance, 1s. 6d. a head, is small, they are kind, and perhaps in some cases too easy with the applicants. A stout young man applied for relief whilst I was present: it appeared he was a weaver with a wife and four children, who had been sent at considerable expense by the parish to work at a colliery at a distance: the wages he received there at first were 18s. a week, but were afterwards lowered to 15s., and although he could not earn above 5s. at Burnley, he brought his family back, and presented himself at the vestry : after some reproof he was ordered 5s., a pair of looms, and a house belonging to the parish : it ought, however, to be stated that fear of the cholera, which had broken out among the colliers, was the cause assigned by the man for his return. The prospect for this part of this country is melancholy, if hand-loom weavers, with youth, strength, and opportunities of gainful employment, reject the means of independence, and are suffered to remain burthensome to the public. Their former occupation is gone for ever, and it is only by exerting themselves in new walks of life that they can reasonably expect to be raised from their present abject condition.

Pauperism is extensive here, and the condition of those receiving relief wretched. The poor-rates last year were equivalent to 4s. 6d. in the pound on the rack-rent; it is usual here to make the paupers contribute to the poor-rate, by stopping the rate out of the relief, but the payment not being *bonâ fide*, cannot answer any good purpose. Owing to the smaller proportion of hand-loom weavers, and a larger proportion of power-loom factories, the adjacent township of Habergham Eaves is in a prosperous condition.

WARRINGTON.

AT Warrington the expenditure is large in proportion to the population, the number of hand-loom weavers is inconsiderable, and they are the only able-bodied persons, in full employment, who receive relief; fustian cutters, owing to the irregular demand for their labour, are occasionally burthensome.

In consequence of several factories being destroyed by fire, the township suffered much a few years since, the work-people being thrown on the poor-rates for support: but at present the general condition of the town is flourishing, and I am at a loss to account for the amount of the expenditure. The present management is by overseers annually appointed, two salaried assistant overseers, and a committee. Probably a select vestry would operate beneficially in reducing the rates, which were last year equivalent to 3*s.* 4*d.* in the pound on the rack-rent. There was last year a deficiency of 28 per cent. on the collection of the rates, 19 per cent. being lost from poor persons being excused. The landlords in some instances voluntarily pay the rates: but many of the small houses are owned by persons who derive the principal part of their income from that species of property. There is no doubt that an enactment, making the landlords liable for the rates, would operate beneficially: though it may be fairly presumed that the enormous deficiency here might be lessened by bestowing more pains on the collection.

GARSTANG.

ONE of the principal rate-payers in Garstang stated that a select vestry had been the salvation of that place. It appears that, prior to the year 1821, there was a paid overseer, to whom the management of the poor was left. He was a respectable man, but had not sufficient firmness to resist improper applications, or check the progress of pauperism. The consequence was, that the rates in 1820-21, amounted to 6*s.* 6*d.* in the pound on the rack-rent, a burthen which threatened ruin to many of the rate-payers. In June, 1821, a select vestry was formed; and although they had to clear off a debt of 300*l.* they speedily effected a great reduction of the rates. The cases were all investigated respectively, and the relief adjusted by judgment of the vestry. The expenditure which, according to the parliamentary returns, was 720*l.* in 1819-20, was

2 B

reduced to 347*l.* in 1822-23, and to 216*l.* in 1828-29. It was
fortunate that the management was thus brought into a sound
condition, as the town was visited a few years afterwards by great
distress; first, from the temporary stoppage, in September, 1829,
and finally, from the failure, in November, 1830, of some long-
established and extensive calico printers, who had employed about
600 persons belonging to this and two or three adjacent townships.
Had this disaster occurred before the expenditure was retrenched,
and an improved system adopted, the result must have been overwhelming both to the poor and the rate-payers; whereas, under
the select vestry, it was met by a rate of 3*s.* 3*d.* in the years
1830-31, 1831-32.

Catteral, where the print-works were situated, suffered still
more severely; and although they have a select vestry and assistant overseer, the rates last year amounted to 5*s.* in the pound, on
a valuation said to be above the rack-rent. This burthen is
severely felt by the farmers, the population now being chiefly
agricultural. This calamity would have been much more grievous,
had not the population in these places and in Kirkland, an
adjacent township, adapted itself in a remarkable degree to the
vicissitude, by migrating in search of employment. Money was
advanced by the vestries to the printers to go in search of employment, and their families were supported in their absence, and when
situations were procured by them, their goods and families were
carted at the expense of the township to Blackburn, Preston, or
Burnley. These exertions are highly meritorious, and their effect
in relieving the township will partly appear from the population
returns :

	1821.	1831.	Decrease.
Catteral	704	457	247
Kirkland	511	458	53
Garstang	936	929	7
	2151	1844	307

The decrease is imperfectly shown here, since at Garstang the
population was about 1100 before the failure, and does not now
exceed 850.

The practice in bastardy cases is extremely fluctuating and
unsettled. A magistrate in this neighbourhood recommends, in
his answers, a uniform low rate of allowance, without regard to
the means or station of the father; but at Garstang, as at many
other places, the allowances vary from 1*s.* 3*d.* to 4*s.* a week, although a child may be maintained for 3*s.* a week. If the putative

fathers do not pay in some places, the overseers are required by the magistrate to pay the whole allowance, on the ground that they should not have let the man escape, though it is often out of their power to detain him, as the personal demand, which is an indispensable preliminary to taking out a warrant for his apprehension, always affords an opportunity to abscond; at other places nothing is paid to the mother, except in cases of necessity. The Learned Chairman of the Preston Sessions, in one of his answers, says, " The overseers are too apt to consider the mother entitled to the full amount of the order, though not paid by the man. I always caution them against this, and order them in such cases to relieve the child with 1s. a week, or what necessity may require;" and accordingly at Preston and many other places 1s. a week is usually given by the parish in such cases. Two orders were made here on the same day, one for 4s. a week for the child of G. S., the father being a schoolmaster, another for 4s. a week on D., a man-servant, at twelve guineas a year wages; one of these orders was paid in full the first year, 8l. was paid the second year, and it has since been reduced to 2s. 6d. weekly; in the other case, the fathers of the parties arranged that 2s. a week should be paid. The magistrates no doubt imposed these sums with a view to the peculiar circumstances of each case, probably regarding the father in the first case as a greater moral delinquent, considering his station and office, and probably looking to some aggravation in the man's conduct in the latter case; the law, however, merely contemplates an indemnity to the parish, and if the parish officers were allowed to fix the amount of the indemnity the scale would almost always be low. Overseers state that the fathers in general are not unwilling to pay according to their ability, but large orders drive them to abscond and produce vagrancy.

The extent of bastardy depends chiefly on the standard of moral feeling on the subject, and the most marked variations exist between parishes when the practice is lightly regarded, and those where it is stigmatized; the remedy therefore must be sought in improving the tone of general opinion on the subject. As a subordinate means of repressing the practice, a frequent and strict collection of the sums imposed on the putative father has considerable effect.

At Garstang last year regular relief was given to five able-bodied men ; four being weavers with families, at Wigan; and the other a calico-printer, a widower, with two children; occasional relief was given to eleven able-bodied men, most of whom had been calico printers : they were relieved without setting them to work. Labourers' wages here average 2s. a day, in summer, and 1s. 6d. in winter; and they maintain their families decently on

9 ~~~s~~, herrings, bacon, and oatbread; very little wheaten
d.

/have the honour to remain,
My Lords and Gentlemen,
Your obedient faithful servant,
GILBERT HENDERSON.
Temple, Dec. 21, 1832.

CAMBRIDGE.

MY LORDS AND GENTLEMEN,
In compliance with Lord Melbourne's desire, I submit to
you the following examples of good and bad management, as the
most instructive which fell under my view as assistant poor-law
commissioner.
I have the honour to be,
My Lords and Gentlemen,
Your obedient humble servant,
JOHN W. COWELL.
London, Feb. 25, 1833.
19, *Chester-street, Grosvenor Place.*

ROYSTON.

ONE of the first places that attracted my attention was Royston;
and it appeared to me that so much was to be learned there, that
I visited it twice, the first time in company with Mr. Bishop, the
second time with Mr. Senior.

The population of this place, a town and parish, partly in
Cambridgeshire, partly in Herts, has increased since the year
1821, from 1474 to 1757. The business carried on is such as
naturally belongs to a town in a large agricultural district. But
as the acreage of the whole parish is only 300, the *interest* is
not farming, strictly so called.

The population has received an augmentation of one-fifth in
the course of the last ten years. This increment, Mr. Docwra, the
permanent overseer, states as consisting chiefly of out-parishioners
who are not permitted to gain a settlement in the parish, but have
been gradually brought into it as substitutes for native parish-
oners.

These out-parishioners, having no claim on the rates, and nothing to depend upon but character and ability, are invariably
honest, industrious, and orderly. But Mr. Docwra states, that

the class of able-bodied native labourers, for whom it has been found necessary to substitute the out-parishioners, would be as good labourers as the others if not dependent on the parish. The inhabitants in general object to employ them, owing to their bad habits and character; and they are supported by the parish in idleness, in cottages and the workhouse.

Mr. Warren, a builder and carpenter, frequently employs as many as fifty men at a time; and at moments when he is known to be in want of hands, and is giving work to men who daily come four, five, and six miles, Mr. Docwra has offered him able-bodied men on the parish. But Mr. Warren's answer always is, " I won't have your men; they want more looking after than I can afford;" and in reply to Mr. Docwra's observation that he would have to pay more to the rates if he did not take the men, Mr. Warren has said, that he preferred doing so to taking the work of the parish labourers with the trouble of looking after them. Mr. Docwra has frequently received similar answers from other townsmen engaged in business, particularly from Mr. Smith, a large seedsman, to whom he applied only a few days before I was at Royston. Mr. Smith said he had work for four men, and wanted them, but would have nothing to do with parishioners. Mr. Docwra, a few days before my last visit, sent John James, an able-bodied labourer, who applied for work, to a·Mr. Luke, a farmer, who employed him in taking in a rick. The work is easy, but, after being two hours at it, James complained that he was not strong enough. Mr. Luke said he did not like to keep a grumbler, and desired to have him changed. Mr. Docwra desired R. Reed, another able-bodied applicant for work, to take James's place. Reed remonstrated against being employed, but at last went away to the job, muttering against the hardship of being employed, since the other man was as able to do the work as he was, and he might have as well have been indulged in idleness as James.

Mr. Docwra attributed the bad character and conduct of the native population to the countenance and support which the magistrates afford to the complaints of paupers, against which he declared all resistance on the part of the overseers to be vain; and he accounted for the good conduct of the ex-parishioners by the fact of their having no power to apply to the magistrates, and being in consequence solely dependent on character for employment.

The poor-rate increases. The county rates, &c., have been deducted from the following list, which comprehends only the annual amounts strictly expended on the poor.

	£.	s.	d.
1826.	693	13	9
1827.	584	4	4
1828.	752	18	6
1829.	891	18	4
1830.	938	3	10
1831.	973	9	8

Royston having so small an acreage as 300, and the chief inhabitants being engaged in occupations subordinate to agriculture, and not in agriculture itself, and consequently having no motive to throw on the parson and the shopkeepers the wages of other people's labourers, they have constantly refused to sanction the "allowance system," and have rejected the following scale formally forwarded to the vestry.

County of Cambridge.

The Churchwardens and Overseers of the Poor are requested to regulate the incomes of such persons who may apply to them for relief or employment according to the price of bread, namely—

A single woman .... the price of three quartern loaves per week.
A single man .... Ditto   four   do.
A man and his wife ...... Ditto   seven   do.
Ditto   and 1 child..... Ditto   eight   do.
Ditto   and 2 children .. Ditto   nine   do.
Ditto   and 3 ditto ..... Ditto   eleven   do.
Man, wife, 4 children, and upwards, at the price of two quartern loaves per head, per week.

It will be necessary to add to the above income in all cases of sickness or other kind of distress, and particularly of such persons or families who deserve encouragement by their good behaviour, whom Parish Officers should mark both by commendation and reward.

By order of the magistrates assembled at the Shire-Hall, Cambridge, December 15, 1821.

Robert Gee, *Clerk to the Magistrates.*

The vestry has had many struggles with the neighbouring magistracy, on the subject of the allowance system, and had Royston, instead of 300, possessed an acreage of 6000, as there would then have been many farmers in the vestry, the allowance system might have flourished as vigorously in that as in the surrounding parishes. But the shopkeepers and agricultural tradesmen, who constitute the whole vestry,—in order to protect themselves against the magistrates, as we were informed,—adopted Mr. S. Bourne's Act, and have strenuously resisted the keeping up of a large standing army of paupers for the benefit of the landlords, and farmers of neighbouring parishes, who in spring, harvest, and fine weather, would take them off the rates at 6d. and

1*s.* a day, and send them back again in shoals in winter and bad weather.

An irregular skirmish had been kept up for several years between the neighbouring authorities, endeavouring to enforce obedience to a scale, and the inhabitants of Royston declining it. At last, however, the opposing parties came to a regular action, in which victory seems to have declared for the inhabitants of Royston. Mr. Bishop and I directed an account of this transaction to be forwarded to the Poor Law Commission, and the following is an extract from the letter received by the Commission from the assistant-overseer, the names of the magistrates being omitted :—

" Gentlemen—Being particularly requested by Mr. Bishop and Mr. Cowell to state to you in full the particulars relative to what has taken place between this parish and the magistrates, within the last two or three years, with respect to making up the labourers' wages, with a copy of the minutes from the select vestry book, on that subject, the following is a copy of the 7th August, 1829 :—

" ' The overseers laid before the vestry an application of John James for an allowance to make up his wages, and stated he is employed by Mr. Charles Cautherly, and receives upwards of 10*s.* per week as a day labourer, and that John James applied to the overseers for an allowance of 1*s.* 8*d.* per week, to make up his wages to 11*s.* 8*d.* The overseers state that they have been summoned by Mr. A. B., a magistrate in this county, at the suit of John James, to appear before him on Monday next, to answer his complaint. The vestry took into consideration, that the clerk of the peace for the county of Cambridge had, by direction of the court of quarter sessions, issued a circular letter to all the parish officers in the county, one of which to that part of this parish which lies in Cambridgeshire, was laid before this meeting, in which the practice of making up wages out of the poor-rate is reprobated as impolitic and pernicious, and they considered that if the system of making up wages was adopted in this case, it would apply to the other labourers of the parish, and would entail upon the poor-rate a charge which could not be borne, and they considered that an order for making up wages, if made by the said A. B., would be illegal, and they directed that the overseers should decline to make any payment under it, and that any proceedings instituted to force obedience to such an order, should be defended by the parish officers at the expense of this parish, out of the poor-rate.'

" In the above case the man James not having applied, in the first instance, to the vestry, as the law requires, the magistrate found that he could not make an order ; and being talked to by a gentleman of the vestry, upon the consequences likely to ensue by adopting such a system, it was dropped for that time.

· " On the 6th of April, 1831, John James and Joseph Wood again applied to the petty sessions (James having been refused relief by the vestry). After the usual questions of the number of their children, and the amount of their earnings, they were informed that it was not sufficient, giving me at the time a verbal order to make up their wages to a certain sum ; but not thinkiug myself at liberty to comply without again mentioning it to the vestry, I put it off till it met, when it was unanimously objected to. A few days after, the overseers received a summons to appear at Mr. C. D.'s at **** on the following Monday, to show cause why relief should not be given. The vestry was again convened upon the occasion, who considered it illegal to make up wages to labourers in full employ, and gave instructions to the overseers to refuse obedience to any order made by the magistrates for enforcing such claims, and that the overseers be defended at the expense of the parish.

" The distance to **** being eight miles, I was desired to write the following letter to Mr. C. D. :—

" Sir—The overseers of Royston have received a summons to appear before you and other magistrates at ****, on Monday next, on the complaint of Joseph Wood and John James. I beg leave to inform you that, as one of the overseers is ill, and confined at his house, and cannot go to ****, if you would allow the matter to be heard before you at the petty sessions at Royston, on Wednesday next, being two days after, it would be an accommodation to the overseers; and as to the men who apply, it would be also less trouble to them. If you will inform me by the bearer that you will let the case be heard at Royston on Wednesday, I will inform the men that they need not attend at ****, but that they must on Wednesday.

" I am, Sir,

" Your very respectful and obedient servant,

" GAM. DOCWRA, *Vestry Clerk.*

" To which I received the following answer :—

" ****, *Saturday afternoon.*

" Sir—I cannot make the alteration you request to be made as to the time of hearing the cases for which the overseers of Royston are summoned to appear at my house on Monday next, on my own authority alone. It would require the concurrence of the other magistrates who have signed the summons to such an alteration before it can be made; and it may be doubtful whether Wednesday will suit the convenience of them all to attend at Royston. It is now half-past two o'clock, and I have not an opportunity of consulting with them on the subject. Had the communication been made at an earlier day, perhaps the arrangement you request might have been made.

" I am, Sir, your faithful servant,

" C. D.

"On Monday, the 18th, I accompanied one of the overseers, who had just entered upon his office, to ****, where we met Mr. A. B., Mr. C. D., and Mr. E. F., magistrates for this county. After hearing the respective cases some time, I was ordered to leave the room, with James and Wood, when, as the overseer informed me, they tried first to persuade, by appealing to his feelings, then to intimidate, by pointing out the consequences upon his refusal of complying with their order; but he was proof against both, and informed them that, as he was but just come into office, the duties of which he was not much acquainted with, consequently he could not think of acting contrary to the wish of the vestry, and that if they thought proper to make an order, he was under the necessity to say he must refuse complying with it. Upon which they gave him until Wednesday to consider of it, telling him that, if he did not comply by that time, they would certainly give an order, and enforce it,—the men having an order to meet them again on the Wednesday, at Royston; but by some unaccountable cause, the men did not appear, to the joy apparently of the magistrates and overseer; since which time they have not tried to enforce it.

" I am, gentlemen,

" Your obedient humble servant,

" GAMALIEL DOCWRA,

" Assistant Overseer."

To the Poor Law Commissioners.

The following case affords matter for much reflection. A retired labourer, residing at * * *, having some land and other property, had a daughter, who, about the year 1805, gained a settlement in ——— parish, by living there in service one year. Since 1822, she lived with her father, and was supported by him, being confined to the house by infirmity. In the year 1832, she applied for relief to * * * parish, at the instigation, it is believed, of a neighbouring magistrate, who told her father that he was very much to blame for keeping her at his own expense, and that he had better inquire as to her settlement.

The parish officers of * * * relieved her, and immediately applied to the same magistrate, and another neighbouring magistrate, for an order of removal to ——————. This was granted, but, as was foreseen, could not be executed in consequence of her illness, and was accordingly suspended by the same magistrates, at the same time and day, on which it was made. The * * * officers commenced allowing her (or really her father) 3s. a week, and required ——— to reimburse them. Even the officer who brought the order to ———, exclaimed against the shamefulness of the transaction. ——— offered 2s. 6d., which the father agreed to take, and it was paid till the daughter's death.

The magistrates in this neighbourhood are said to have an objection to piece-work. Docwra the overseer's evidence is,—" If I tender piece-work, the magistrates say,—You must pay the unmarried men on the same terms as you do the married; we will not allow you to pay them differently."

But if you don't tender piece-work, will they allow you to pay the married and single differently?—" Certainly; their objection applies to piece-work."

What advantage would the labourers reap from honesty, sobriety, frugality, orderly conduct, when those of them who, from natural and uncontrollable propensity, take to saving, or those whom chance has visited with the misfortune of a legacy, are refused, not relief (for that they do not want), but *work*.

The following instances struck Mr. Senior and myself so forcibly, when we heard of them at Royston last November, that we afterwards requested our informants to furnish them in writing, and they are now given as we received them:—

" Sir,—At the request of Mr. Wedd, of this place, I forward a case which has occurred on a small farm of mine in this neighbourhood, relative to the poor-laws. And have the honour to be,

" Sir,

" Your most obedient servant,

" W. W. NASH."

N. W. Senior, Esq.
Poor Law Commission.

" Mr. Nash, of Royston, is proprietor and occupier of a farm containing 150 acres, situate a mile and a half from his residence, and in about equal proportions in the parishes of Barhway and Reed, in the county of Hertford. It is what is usually called an outfield farm, being at the extremity of these parishes, and nearly equidistant from Royston, Therfield, Reed, Barhway, and Barley. Mr. Nash employed six men (to whom he gives throughout the year, 12s. a week), two boys, and six horses. In 1829, Mr.

Clarke, the overseer of Reed (a respectable man, who occupies half the parish, and has generally managed all its public concerns), told Mr. Nash he could no longer collect the money for poor-rates, without resorting to coercive measures, which he would not do; and that the unemployed poor must be apportioned among the occupiers of land, in proportion to their respective quantities; and that he (Mr. Nash) must take two more men. All Mr. Nash's labourers had been some years in his service, and were steady, industrious men, and he regretted the necessity of parting with any of them. The two men displaced were those who came last into his service (and for that reason only.) One was a parishioner of Royston, an excellent workman at any kind of work. He lived near Mr. Nash's house (a great convenience), and his wife superintended a small school Mrs. Nash had established for the benefit of her poor neighbours. The other was John Watford, a parishioner of Barley, a steady, industrious, trustworthy, single man, *who, by long and rigid economy, had saved about* 100*l.* Of the two men sent in their stead, one was a married man, with a family, sickly and not much inclined to work; the other a single man, addicted to drinking. On being dismissed, Watford applied in vain to the farmers of Barley for employment. *It was well known that he had saved money, and could not come upon the parish, although any of them would willingly have taken him had it been otherwise.* Watford has a brother also, who, like himself, *has saved money;* and though he has a family, and has been laid aside from work for six years, has received no assistance from the parish. After living a few months without being able to get any work, he bought a cart and two horses, and has ever since obtained a precarious subsistence, by carrying corn to London for one of the Cambridge merchants; but just now the current of corn is northward, and he has nothing to do, and *at any time he would gladly have exchanged his employment for that of day labour, if he could have obtained work.* No reflection is intended on the overseers of Barley; they only do what all others are expected to do; though the young men point at Watford, and *call him a fool,* for not spending his money at a public-house, as they do, adding, that then he would get work."

———

" Since Mr. Senior was at Royston last week, another instance has occurred on this farm, illustrative of the working of the poor-laws. John Warren, an inhabitant of Therfield, has been house-keeper there for nine years. A few weeks ago, the bailiff told Mr. Nash he could not find employment for so many men. Mr. Nash desired him to dismiss a bankwayman, who happened to have misconducted himself. The bailiff's wife shortly afterwards told Mr. Nash that, if he pleased, John Warren would like to go, as he had a large family, and the justices (the magistrates of the Royston division) would give him as much or more, without work, as he earned, and he should avoid the dirty walks from Therfield this winter. Mr. Nash (who is a proprietor, but not an occupier in Therfield) has accordingly discharged him, and he will no doubt, next week, add 12s. or 15s. to the enormous eleemosynary payments made in this disorganized and demoralized parish, by the natural and inevitable operation of the poor-laws. Previous to 1814, there were there no unemployed poor, and they were remarkable for their industrious and orderly conduct, and all was satisfactory, liberal, and remunerative : now a large portion of the poor have no work, and many lands lie unploughed, covered with thistles, and spreading their seeds with every wind for miles around ; and it is said the largest and most wealthy owner and occupier has seen his men steal his corn out of the barns, but would not prosecute, alleging that he must keep them, and that they would live on less if they had the trouble of carrying it away, than if he was to thrash and carry it to Hertford, and bring the produce back to them in money. One of the largest barns on this gentleman's farm has been pulled down piecemeal by the poor, and carried away for fuel. The only probable amelioration of the system may be, perhaps, in appointing itinerant stipendiaries, who should execute the duties of both magistrate and overseer. It is unjust to compel a large occupier, whose business requires more personal attention than that of other men, to give his time and exertion gratuitously to a disgusting public duty,—the only reward of which is either a broken head, or the chance of being burnt in his bed."

Royston, January 29th, 1833.

" Dear Sir,

" I write in answer to your inquiry into the case alluded to in the return to your queries from Royston parish, of refusal of employment to labourers on account of their having legacies bequeathed to them. There are obvious motives for disinclination to state particulars, which might be considered to reflect on persons who have no opportunity of giving their own explanations as to their execution of the poor-laws. The facts of the case, divested of reference to the locality of its occurrence, are the following :—

" An individual who had risen from poverty, and accumulated considerable personal property, bequeathed legacies to a number of labourers, his relations. Circumstances delayed for several months the collecting in the testator's estate. The overseer's deputy of one parish, in which some of the legatees were labourers, urged to the agent of the executors the payment, *on the ground that it would benefit the parishioners, as when the legacies were paid they would not find employment for the legatees, because they would have property of their own.*

" The legatees afterwards applied for money on account of their legacies. *It was then stated that some of them, who lived in a different parish, had been refused employment, because they were entitled to property.*

" An occupier of land in another parish near this place told me, to-day, that in his parish they refused employment to labourers who had money left them. He said that he held 320 acres of light land of the value of 18*s.* an acre, subject to tithes. He pays 74*l.* tithe composition, and 100*l.* for poor-rates, and is compelled to employ fourteen men and six boys, and requires the labour of only ten men and three boys. His extra labour at 10*s.* a week (which is the current rate for men), and half as much for boys, is 130*l.* He pays, in addition, surveyors and churchwarden's rates. There are sometimes from fifteen to twenty labourers employed in useless public work, besides boys. It is not surprising that, in such circumstances, the occupiers should refuse to employ labourers who have any property.

" Another occupier stated yesterday that he held 165 acres of land, of which half was pasture. He was compelled to employ twelve men and boys, and his farm required the labour of only five. He is about to give notice that he will quit. Every useless labourer is calculated to add 5*s.* an acre to the rent of a farm of 100 acres.

" The improvement in agricultural implements, the cultivation of artificial grasses, improved roads, and greater skill and agricultural knowledge, enable an occupier to cultivate his land with less labour. All these would be sources of profit, but they are all counteracted and made causes of additional perplexity by the redundant population, which the system of the poor-laws has augmented.

" It is common for young agricultural labourers to say, that they are treated worse as single men, than they would be as married men, and that they shall marry to better their conditions in this respect.

" I remain, dear Sir,
" Yours very respectfully,
(Signed) " J. P. WEDD."

N. W. Senior, Esq.
Poor Law Commission.

The following letter was received by Mr. Senior, and communicated to me as I was concluding my remarks on Royston.— Assuming the accuracy of the facts, it shows what may be the consequences of well-meant interference.

Royston, February 21st, 1833.

" Sir,—The inclosed order affords a melancholy illustration of the pernicious working of the poor laws. Robert Reed has a wife and five children, his wife had been convicted in a penalty for stealing turnips and turnip-tops to send to London for sale; and before she paid the penalty, she was apprehended on two other informations for stealing more of the same articles on subsequent days.

" One of the Cambridgeshire magistrates committed her to jail for six months. Immediately after her commitment, the husband applied to the overseers to provide a woman to take care of his children; the overseers offered to provide a woman for that purpose free of expense to the husband and without his finding her either board or lodging. The husband immediately went to the magistrates of Hertfordshire, in which county he was settled, who called up the overseers; they represented that they had offered to find a woman to take care of the children in the husband's house free of expense to him; the magistrates, however, said they thought some one of the husband's relations the most proper for this purpose, and they required the overseers to pay money to the husband to enable him to procure a substitute for his wife in the case of the children, and they made the inclosed order for 11s. per week. The husband had been receiving 9s. per week from the parish for work, before his wife went to jail, and the ground of the application was (as correctly stated in the order) the imprisonment of the wife.

" The husband had lost his character, and was therefore refused employment by the farmers.

" The effects of the present system as shewn by the inclosed order, are;

" That prosecution for crime is made doubly burdensome, as not only the expense of it is great, but also all the consequences of it are to be made good to the family of the offender out of the poor's rate, and thus a prospect of perfect impunity to crime is held out to the poor.

" I have the honour to remain, Sir,
" Your most obedient servant,
" GAM. DOCWRA,
" Vestry clerk of the parish of
Royston, Herts."

To N. W. Senior, Esq.,
  Poor Law Commission.

Herts ⎱ *To the Churchwardens and Overseers of the Poor of the*
to wit ⎰ *Parish of Royston, in the said County.*

Whereas Robert Reed, of the parish of Royston, in the said county, hath made oath before the Rev. Thos. Sisson, the Rev. Henry Morrice, and the Rev. J. Lafont, three of his Majesty's justices of the peace for the said county, that he the said Robert Reed is very poor and impotent, and not able to support himself and family of five children by his labour, and that he the said Robert Reed did on Friday last appear at the Select Vestry, for the purpose of obtaining relief, but that the Select Vestry did not assemble on that day which had been appointed for their meeting.

And whereas two of the overseers of the poor of the said parish have appeared before us, to shew cause why relief should not be given to the said Robert Reed, and having not shewn any sufficient cause.

And whereas it appears to us, that the wife of the said Robert Reed is now confined in the House of Correction at Cambridge, and that he is put to considerable expense in providing a person to look after his said five children ; We do therefore *order* the churchwardens and overseers of the poor of the said parish, or such of them to whom these presents shall come, to pay unto the said Robert Reed, the sum of eleven shillings weekly and every week, for and towards the support and maintenance of himself and family, for one month from the day of the date hereof.

Given under our hands and seal this twentieth day of February, in the year of our Lord one thousand eight hundred and thirty-three.

THOMAS SISSON,
JOHN LAFONT,
HENRY MORRICE.

GREAT SHELFORD, CAMBRIDGESHIRE.

POPULATION.

1801	.	570		1821	.	718
1811	.	593		1831	.	812

This parish consists of 2000 acres, of which 500 are waste, and 1500 cultivated. There are 75 able-bodied agricultural labourers' families, and as, according to the calculations of my informant, Mr. ——, 45 are all that are necessary for a thorough cultivation of the soil, there is a surplus of 30 families. Mr. —— owns in fee 500 of the whole 1500 cultivable acres, and farms them himself. He pays 10s. an acre poor-rate = 250l. per annum. In addition, though he only requires for his farm the regular labour of 16 men, yet he constantly employs 20 or 21. The wages of these supernumerary men amount in money to 150l. per annum, and he calculates the value of the return yielded by their superfluous labour at 50l. per annum. Consequently, we must consider that another sum of 100l. is added to his poor-rate, which makes it amount altogether to 350l. per annum. But taking his rates at only 10s. per acre, as he estimates the rent of his land under present circumstances to be still worth more than 1l. per annum per acre, and knows that the rent of the remaining 1000 acres is as valuable as that of his own 500; he considers the fee-simple of the parish to be actually worth the sum of 45,000l.

We asked him what he thought it would be worth, if the poor-rates were moderate: he rated it at 60,000l. We then inquired what he thought was likely to be its value in ten years. He threw up his hands in despair, and refused to make any estimate; and indeed seemed to think, if the progress of pauperism continued, the whole beneficial interest would by that time be confiscated.

We endeavoured to find what remedies he contemplated. The only one seemed to be a labour-rate: we remarked, that as the population was already excessive, and rapidly increasing, a labour-rate, by fixing that population to the soil, might increase or at least perpetuate the evil. He admitted the truth of this remark, but urged, that a labour-rate was the only mode *of making the tithe-owner bear his fair share.*

We suggested that the only effectual cure was to make relief less agreeable than wages. To which he replied that, if that were attempted, the paupers would soon make it disagreeable to be a resident; and mentioned a fire by which, some months before, the barns of the tithe lessee had been destroyed by an incendiary well known, but yet protected by the sympathy of his fellows.

The following minutes of our subsequent conversation throw some light on the causes which produced and perpetuate the local congestion under which Great Shelford is suffering.

How came this parish to be so over-peopled? You say there is no surplus population in the neighbourhood, and that the whole number of acres in the county, divided by the whole number of labourers' families, gives only three families to every hundred acres, according to Lord Hardwicke's returns?—It arose about 40 years ago, when several little shopkeepers gave settlements to servants, and as the poor were well attended to by my father and the other occupants and owners in the parish, none would ever quit it, and they have gone on increasing, till they have become what they are now, idle, dissolute, good for nothing, and the real masters of the parish.

Can you do nothing to get rid of some of them ; cannot you get the overseers of neighbouring parishes to help you, or the farmers who want hands?—No, our men won't quit the parish, they will not go even five miles off to Cambridge. The other day I said to a man who was receiving 12*s.* a week for his family, an able-bodied young man, " They want a hand at the oil-mills, and the wages are 12*s.* a week, go and do a little work there." He answered, that he would not, unless the parish gave him 2*s.* a week, besides the wages he was to earn.

Was that done?—Yes.

You bribed the man by 2*s.* to go and earn 12*s.*?—Yes; it was a bribe, but we saved 10*s.* a week.

And are all your men of this character?—Yes, more or less, the whole of them. They know they have a right on the parish, and must be maintained; they will hardly do any thing for themselves. Some time ago I offered a man who works for me, and is a good man enough, with a large family, an acre rent free. I said, You have a large family coming on, and if an acre will be of any service to you for a garden, and to keep a pig or two, you are welcome to it. But he would not take it.

Why, what did he say?—He said, Thank'ye, sir, I should like it; but I should not like to give up my privilege on the parish. I said, Why, if you have an acre rent free, you must not expect the parish to allow you what it does now. Then he said, he would rather not have it.

Do you think he felt any gratitude to you?—No: I dare say he thought it was as broad as it was long.

So that an act, for which in France, or Switzerland, or Germany, a man would have gained the love and respect of all the neighbourhood, created mistrust instead of gratitude.—Gratitude! I am not aware that they ever feel grateful for any thing. Whenever they are ill, they send their basins here for soup, or any other little delicacy they may want; and not to me only, but the other gentlemen and farmers are just as willing as I am; and we go to visit and assist them, but they never seem grateful, or behave better. They think every thing is their right.

Is bastardy pretty much the same in your parish as in the rest of the county?—Yes—very bad. There are two women who have four children each, and each by three different fathers. The order on the father varies from 1*s.* 6*d.* to 3*s.* 6*d.*, according to his circumstances. *But the women extort money by threatening to swear the child first to one, then to another.*

2 c

Have you much experience in land and agriculture in this county?—A great deal. Besides my own 500 acres here, I farm 900 more in the adjoining parish; altogether I farm 1400 acres.

What should you say a farmer is compelled to spend in wages of labour per annum, upon each acre, taking them one with another, woodland, pasture, arable?—My expenditure averages about 1*l.* 5*s.* per acre, in wages, for the whole of my 1400 acres; and all the farmers that I know throughout the county must lay out as much—some more.

What is the general character of the agricultural labouring population about these parts; is it in general as bad as that of your labourers?—Much the same everywhere.

ELY

Is divided into two parishes; of which Trinity contains 4325, while the total population is 6189.

The amount of rates 3970*l.*, and of charities about 1200*l.* per annum.

The bench of magistrates meets once a year at Michaelmas, and calls before them all the overseers, and says to this effect: " We have considered the price of things, and shall recommend 1*s.* 6*d.* for a child, &c. We shall make orders according to this scale, and we think it may save trouble to you and ourselves to tell you so at once." Mr. Bishop and I examined eight or ten persons, being overseers and vestrymen. They described themselves as having no chance whatever against a pauper before a magistrate; declared unanimously that they were disgusted with applying to magistrates in any case, however flagrant; and as finding it, by experience, to be the best way to settle as well as they could with a pauper claimant, without permitting him to summon them.

They pay the parish paupers every Wednesday, from six to nine o'clock in the evening, who are so turbulent and violent, that they are obliged to have a constable always present for their personal protection. Relief is independent of character, and they make no inquiry as to whether the wants of the applicants are real or simulated; guiding themselves, in giving or withholding relief, in every particular case, by their conjectures as to the probability of the magistrates ordering it or not.

In short, the whole picture of Ely is nothing but a second edition of Royston, with this feature in aggravation, viz. that they have not been able to keep out the allowance-system; for it is an extensively agricultural parish; the estimate of the annual value of the real property is 30,000*l.*; and the farmers form a large portion of the vestry.

The following was given us as a specimen of the way in which applications were made and disposed of.

" I want my money."

" How much have you earned ?"—" Four shillings."

" How many children have you ?"—" Six."

" Well, here are six eighteen pences for you."

We inquired what, if the man had said he earned nothing, instead of 4*s.*, they should have given him.—13*s.* instead of 9*s.* We inquired if they could assign any reason why the man earned or acknowledged earning 4*s.*—None.

Publishing the names of paupers is rather detrimental than otherwise. Those who are not receiving relief, read the names of those who are, and come immediately and apply for "their money;" and if they do not receive it, abuse the overseers, and say they will have them up before their betters.

There is quite work enough in the parish for all the population ; the labour of which, however, under the system above described, is insufficient, and recourse is had to ex-parishioners, whose wages are half as much again as those of the native population, owing to their superior conduct, accounted for by their having no dependence except on character and ability.

A pauper named Sutton returned to the parish with his wife and child, having been away some time, and applied for relief and clothes for himself and family. The overseers, suspecting that he possessed clothes, managed to get him and his wife out of the room, keeping his little girl in, and then asked the child where her Sunday frock was. She answered, that it was locked up in a box at Cambridge with other things. Here the mother came in to call the girl out, but the overseers would not let her go, whereupon the father Sutton came in with a bludgeon, and seized the child by the arm. The overseers held her, but the father pulling her so as to hurt her, they let her go, and he took her out and beat her violently. He then returned, demanding relief, which they refused. He abused them dreadfully, threatening to rip up one, burn the town, &c. and behaved with such violence that they were compelled to have him handcuffed and his legs tied, and he was wheeled in a barrow to the magistrate, where they charged him with assault. The magistrate asked whether they could swear they were in bodily fear of Sutton, and they replying that they were not, he dismissed the charge, *and ordered Sutton relief.*

A proprietor possessing nearly the whole of a parish at some distance from Ely, has, we were told, hired a farm in Ely, which he manages by a bailiff; he sends his own parishioners to work on it. To these persons his bailiff gives settlements in Ely, by hiring, and at the end of the year they are turned off upon Trinity parish in Ely, and their places supplied by a fresh immigration from the mother parish. The proprietor may have had very different motives from those attributed to him by our examinants, and this circumstance is not mentioned for the purpose of casting any reflection on him (we do not know his name, nor what account of the transaction he himself might give,) but in order to point out the temptations which " settlement by hiring and service " throws in the way of persons even of station and education. In the case of Great Shelford, narrated above, are not the landowners, who daily see their property slowly but surely passing away from them, under a strong temptation to save themselves from ruin, by hiring a couple of farms for seven years in two distinct parishes, and bribing their supernumerary families to take service there? And this is clearly possible by the existing law.

BINGHAM, NOTTS.

AFTER such spectacles as are afforded by Royston, Great Shelford, and Ely, and the painful reflections which they suggest, it is pleasing to turn the eye to Bingham, in Nottinghamshire. There the energy and good sense, the wise and enlarged benevolence of one man, has redeemed his parish from a state of demoralisation as great and inveterate as any that I have described above; and his example, extending to Southwell, to Derby, to Uley in Gloucestershire, besides the great benefits which it has conferred on all those places, serves to show that there is a remedy within our reach for pauperism—the great plague-spot upon the English social system.

The annual value of the real property of Bingham, as assessed in 1815, was 7498*l*. The increase of the population has been as follows :—

1801	.	1082	1821	.	1574
1811	.	1326	1831	.	1738

That portion of the poor-rates expended on the poor has been as follows :—

1816 to 17	£1231
1817 to 18	1206
1818 to 19	984*
1819 to 20	711
1820 to 21	510
1821 to 22	338
1822 to 23	228
1823 to 24	365
1824 to 25	431

* New system began this year.

1825 to 26	£356
1826 to 27	345
1827 to 28	360
1828 to 29	334
1829 to 30	388
1830 to 31	370
1831 to 32 .	449

The Rev. Mr. Lowe became the incumbent of this parish in the year 1814; he is a magistrate, and resides on his living. He found it in a terrible state. In the year 1817 there were more than 40 inmates in the workhouse, 78 receiving constant weekly pay out of it, and for the twelve weeks ending the 27th of June that year, I counted the number of roundsmen in the parish books, and found it amount to 103.

The state of morals was that which invariably accompanies this manner of administering the poor-laws. The labourers were turbulent, idle, dissolute, profuse—scarcely a night passed without mischief, and in the two years preceding 1818, seven men of the parish were transported for felonies. The poor, to use the words of my examinants, Mr. Lowe and Deane the overseer, were completely masters.

In 1818-19, Mr. Lowe undertook to remedy this state of things. Being satisfied that it proceeded entirely from the operation of the poor-laws, and that there was no cause, independent of their influence, to prevent his parishioners from being happy, honest, and industrious; and knowing that it was impossible to refuse relief according to the practice and custom of the country, he devised means for rendering relief itself so irksome and disagreeable, that none would consent to receive it who could possibly do without it, while at the same time it should come in the shape of comfort and consolation to those whom every benevolent man would wish to succour—the old, infirm, idiots, and cripples.

For this purpose he placed in the workhouse a steady, cooltempered man, who was procured from a distance, and was not known in the parish, as master, refused all relief in kind or money, and sent every applicant and his family at once into the workhouse. The fare is meat three times a week, soup twice, pudding once, milk porridge five times.

Surely no man who says that he cannot maintain himself, wife, and children by the sweat of his brow—who declares that he is starving,—who applies for charity, has a right to complain of being placed in a clean and comfortable house, of having a good bed to sleep on, and such fare every day as I have described above; and had Mr. Lowe stopped here, matters would not have been much mended. But the applicant who entered the work-

house " *on the plea that he was starving for want of work ;*" was
taken at his word, and told that these luxuries and benefits
could only be given by the parish *against work*, and in addition,
that a certain regular routine was established, to which all the
inmates must conform. The man goes to one side of the house,
the wife to the other, and the children into the school-room.
Separation is steadily enforced. Their own clothes are taken off,
and the uniform of the workhouse put on. No beer, tobacco,
or snuff is allowed. Regular hours kept, or meals forfeited.
Every one must appear in a state of personal cleanliness. No
access to bed-rooms during the day. No communication with
friends out of doors. Breaking stones in the yard by the grate,
as large a quantity required every day as an able-bodied labourer
is enabled to break.

What is there in all this of which an applicant for a portion of
the property of others, *on the ground that he is starving*, has
any right to complain? He has a better house over his head;
better clothes on his back; better and more palatable food to eat;
better medical advice. than nine-tenths of the peasantry of Germany, France, Switzerland, and Italy, and he is not required to
do harder work. But the monotony, the restraint, the want of
stimulants, the regularity of hours, are irksome to the pretended
pauper. He bethinks himself of liberty and work, and work he
will find, if there is a job undone in the parish or neighbourhood
within a day's walk. No man stood this discipline for three weeks.
After a struggle which lasted a few months, the paupers of Bingham gave the matter up. The inmates of the workhouse dropped
from forty-five to twelve, who were all either old, idiots, or infirm, and to whom a workhouse is really a place of comfort.
The number of persons relieved out of the workhouse dropped
from seventy-eight to twenty-seven. The weekly pay from 6*l.*
to 1*l.* 16*s.* to pensioners, all of whom are old and blind, or crippled. These are permitted to live with their relations, as such
instances of relieving out of the workhouse produce no mischief.

Wages rose to twelve shillings a week, winter and summer, all
the year through; the labourer husbanded his resources, took a
pride and pleasure in his cottage, and resumed his rank in the
scale of moral being.

The effect of this system is far more important in a moral
point of view, than in a pecuniary or an economical one. The
conduct and habits of the population of Bingham, according to the representations of Mr. Lowe and Deane, and by the
consent of the neighbourhood, is now as different from what it
was fifteen years ago as can be conceived; no crimes, no mis-
deeds, no disturbances.

The same system was afterwards, in the year 1821, introduced with the same results at Southwell, twelve miles distant, by Captain Nicholls; and since Captain Nicholls's departure in 1823, has been kept up by the bench of magistrates of that place. The Rev. Mr. Becher published an account of it in his well-known pamphlet entitled " The Antipauper System," where, however, the simplicity of Mr. Lowe's principle is mingled with some extraneous matter. That principle is merely to render " the gaining a livelihood by relief more irksome than gaining a livelihood by labour." Relief becomes in consequence an object of aversion, and labour of desire. A well-regulated workhouse was the engine employed by Mr. Lowe for carrying this principle into practice, and it is the fittest instrument for the purpose. But though " the tendering relief on such terms as render it an object of aversion and not of desire to the applicants," is all that is necessary for the abolition of pauperism, Mr. Lowe assisted this measure by another equally simple and equally efficacious: *he rated all cottages, and steadily and perseveringly enforced the payments.* The sums were trifling, but the poor took a pride in finding that they, as well as their richer neighbours, contributed to parish burdens; their motives to save, and their jealousy of each other, speedily led them to take an interest in the expenditure of those funds to which they contributed. Deane, the overseer, told me that since cottages had been rated, the poor contributors were excessively jealous of those who received relief in cases where it was not fairly required. They never object to relief being granted in cases which, in their opinion, require it; but, wherever they think he has been imposed upon, some one or other generally comes and gives him notice. Only the week before I was at Bingham, Deane, on applying for a rate to a cottager, a woman, received it accompanied with the following warning : " I say, I shan't pay any more rates if my money is thrown away.— I hear that idle fellow Jack —— had 5*s.* from the parish some weeks ago, because he said his child was ill: I shan't pay my money to such like."

I have already exceeded the limits prescribed by Lord Melbourne, but I hope to be permitted to add a few notices respecting the Bastardy Laws.

BASTARDY LAWS.

The theory of a law—the text of a law is nothing. The practice of the law is the real law. It is according to *the practice* that men shape their actions, and according to nothing else.

The *practice* of the English law respecting bastardy is shortly this :—

Whenever a woman is pregnant of a bastard child which the overseer apprehends may become chargeable on the parish, or whenever a woman applies for relief for her bastard after having given birth to it, the overseer has power to compel her to declare on oath the father, and then to compel him to pay the parish the amount of whatever order of maintenance the magistrate may make upon him. The sole *object* of this legislation is to *save expense to the parish.* The *effect* of it is, as might have been foreseen, to promote bastardy ; to make want of chastity on the woman's part the shortest road to obtaining either a husband or a competent maintenance ; and to encourage extortion and perjury. It would be impossible for the heart of man or demon to devise a more effective instrument for extinguishing every noble feeling in the female heart—for blighting the sweetest domestic affections, and for degrading the males and females of that portion of the community connected with the receipt of parish relief,— than this truly diabolical institution.

In the first place, I appeal to the experience of all overseers in rural districts, whether the instances of marriages taking place among the labouring classes, without previous pregnancy, are not so very rare as to constitute no exception to the general assertion, that " pregnancy precedes marriage."

In the second place, I ask, whether marriages are not, in most instances, brought about by the threat, which the woman holds out to the man of swearing the child to him if he does not marry her; and whether the power afforded to the man of suggesting to the woman that she may place him in this predicament is not the infallible topic of seduction and persuasion which he employs in the rare instances which require persuasion?

In the third place, I appeal to every assistant-overseer who has been any time in office, whether he has not, in his own experience, *known* of several instances of perjury and extortion on the part of women in his own parish, and *heard* of many more.

I proceed to give miscellaneous instances.

DOWNHAM MARKET, NORFOLK.

Order on the father, 2s., *but depends upon the circumstances.* The overseers stated as follows :—

" A woman refused to declare the father of the child of which she was pregnant. They threatened her with imprisonment if she persevered in her contumacy, whereupon she declared she would swear the child to one of them. This she proceeded to do. She appeared before the magistrate, and had the name of the overseer actually inserted in the order, but when the oath was tendered to her, relented.

SWAFFHAM, NORFOLK.

A woman in a neighbouring parish had five illegitimate child_ ren, for which she was allowed 10*s.* per week, and 6*s.* for herself. Finding herself pregnant for the sixth time, she employed a man to go round to various persons with whom she might or might not have had connexion, to acquaint each of them separately with the fact of her pregnancy, and of her intention of swearing the child to him unless he consented to send her a sum of money, when she would engage to swear it to some one else. Her demands for this hush-money ranged as high as 10*l.* in some instances. The first man to whom her ambassador applied, gave him 10*l.* The ambassador returned, and represented to his employer that the man had laughed at her threat, but had sent her half-a_ crown, out of which he thought she ought to give him 1*s.* 6*d.* for his trouble. To this she consented; so he benefited 9*l.* 19*s.*, and she 1*s.* by this first negotiation. She carried on this course with several persons with various success, and at last swore the child to a man who resisted, and on his appeal succeeded in getting the order on him quashed. The case was tried at Swaffham, where the above circumstances came to light in court.

This woman was never punished. She gave birth to her child, was allowed 2*s.* for it by the parish, and is now in the receipt of 18*s.* per week, the produce of successful bastardy adventures.

My informant in this and the following instance was Mr. Sewell, clerk to the magistrates at Swaffham.

A woman of Swaffham was reproached by the magistrate, Mr. Young, with the burdens she had brought upon the parish, upon the occasion of her appearing before him to present the parish with her seventh bastard. She replied, " I am not going to be disappointed in my company with men to save the parish." This woman now receives 14*s.* a week for her seven bastards, being 2*s.* a head for each. Mr. Sewell informed me that had she been a widow with seven legitimate children, she would not have received so much by 4*s.* or 5*s.* a week according to their scale of allowance to widows. A bastard child is thus about 25 per cent. more valuable to a parent than a legitimate one. The pre_ mium upon want of chastity, perjury, and extortion, is here very obvious; and Mr. Sewell informed me that it is considered a good speculation to marry a woman who can bring a fortune of one or two bastards to her husband. Mr. Sewell had never known in the course of his experience but two women punished for having illegitimate children. The profligacy in this neighbourhood is very great.

WISBEACH.

I witnessed the following case at the petty-session. A girl about eighteen, with a bastard child, was brought before the bench under the following circumstances. The real father was stated to be a married man, the driver of a coach, who had promised to allow the girl 4*s.* a week if she would swear the child to another man and not to him. This she had done, when the coachman had immediately abandoned her, and the putative father, a pedlar, could not be found. Consequently she was now a burden on the parish, which allowed her 2*s.* a week, and as she could not maintain herself on this, she would not quit the workhouse, whereupon the overseer brought her up before the bench to have her committed to prison. The girl did not deny, nor admit any part of the above story, nor did the magistrates enquire into it. They told her that if she did not quit the workhouse within a fortnight, and the overseer brought her up again, they would commit her for three months. The girl said she had no where to go to, having no father or mother,—that she could not leave her child under a year, so as to get her livelihood, and had besides no shoes and stockings, having borrowed those she had on to come to the bench. The overseer promised her two pair of stockings and a pair of shoes if she would quit the house in a fortnight; and this bribe, reinforced by the threat of the magistrates, induced her to promise that she would go.

ROYSTON.

Informant Mr. Dockwra; order, 2*s.,—varies according to the circumstances of the father.*

Many girls have got as much as 20*l.* or 30*l.* from different young men not to swear children to them; has heard young men jeering one another in this way,—" Ah, you had to come down with a 5*l.* note, or otherwise she would have sworn it to you." Some girls pretend to be pregnant when they are not so, to extort money.

A girl, to extort money, swore a child to the clergyman's son, of which he proved himself not to be the father.

One woman named Smith, has three children by three different fathers. She has never been punished, and the parish allows her

6*s.* per week. Women are very rarely punished ; has only known one or two instances in his memory of the parish. Bastardy very common.

HOLBEACH, LINCOLNSHIRE.

Informants, the overseer and master of the workhouse.

Many illegitimate children; ten or twelve every year; bastards increasing; order from 1*s.* to 2*s.* 6*d.* and above,—*depends on the circumstances of the father.*

An unmarried girl, upon leaving the workhouse after her fourth confinement, said to the master, " Well, if I have the good luck to have another child, I shall draw a good sum from the parish, and with what I can earn myself, shall be better off than any married woman in the parish;" and the master added, that she had met with the good luck she hoped for, as she told him, a short time before I was at Holbeach, that she was five months gone with child.

I asked him what she had for each child?—He answered 2*s.*; and that women in that neighbourhood could easily earn 5*s.* a week all the year through. Thus she will have 15*s.* a week.

BASFORD, NOTTINGHAM.

Population, 6325, the centre of the stocking manufactory.

Informant, William Caddick, has been permanent overseer for twenty years.

" Order on father, 2*s.*,—*depends on circumstances of father.* If overseer says the father is rich, and apply for a larger order, magistrates never refuse ; always give the mothers all that the parish receives from the fathers ; thinks this makes women fix on rich fathers ; knows many instances of perjury,—sometimes can prove them. A case occurred yesterday. A girl, who had had two bastard children, was pregnant of a third, and swore it to a young man in easy circumstances. He appealed to the quarter-sessions, which yesterday decided in his favour. The child was thrown on the parish; the man proving, by several witnesses, that the girl had said among her friends, that she had fixed upon him because he was rich, and the real father too poor to allow her anything; and likewise that, after having sworn the child to him, she was unacquainted with him by sight, and mistook his brother for him in the presence of several persons. This girl had not been punished for her two previous bastards. It is proverbial among girls and women, that they would rather their children were all bastards,

—has *often* heard girls and women say *that.* There must be something wrong in the magistrates ordering a woman 2*s.* for a bastard, when, if a poor family applies for relief, they direct the overseer to make up the earnings on the scale of 1*s.* 3*d.* for each child; so that the poor man's children are worse off, we consider, than the bastards. A girl with three bastards will live better than a man working coarse stockings; *she* will get 6*s.* for her bastards, and earn 2*s.* or 3*s.* besides,—*he* will only be able to earn, after clearing his expenses (viz. rent of frame, needles, seaming, &c.), 6*s.* per week. A widow with a legitimate child is never allowed more than 1*s.* 6*d.*, sometimes less, and sometimes nothing,—depends upon her earnings; but a woman with bastards is *sure* of 2*s.* a week for each;—yes, even if she were earning 20*s.* a week. During twenty years he has been in office, magistrates would never punish a woman for having a bastard, though he has frequently applied for it. Bastardy is very much increasing in Basford: believes that one-third of all the number applying to the parish, old and young, are bastards."

ST. MARY'S PARISH, NOTTINGHAM.

Population, 39,500.

Mr. Barnet, assistant overseer, informant.

Annual average of bastard births, 70·4; and annual removals of pregnant women, 100.

As the bastardy account is very heavy in this parish, amounting, upon an average, to 730*l.* per annum, on which the parish loses about 250*l.*, and sometimes more than 300*l.*, Mr. Barnet about four years ago introduced a new method of proceeding. The usual one is for the woman to swear the child before birth, which course the women always prefer themselves. He determined never to permit a child to be sworn till after birth, for the purpose of saving the 3*l.* or 4*l.* expense, incurred in getting at and securing the father before birth, as he found this outlay fall mainly upon the parish. Since he has acted on this plan, he has been surprised at finding women continually naming and swearing their children to different fathers from those whom they named and wished to swear against before birth; and in these cases is convinced that they really name the true fathers after birth, and were ready to swear falsely before birth. The continual recurrence of this fact makes a strong impression upon him, and he accounts for it as follows:—Various motives influence them before birth; they wish to swear the child to a rich father, or to extort money; they wish to spare the real father if they like him, and fix on another; they take a spite against some one, and rush to the overseer, and make him an instrument of vengeance in their hands; but after birth,—when they are ill,—can extort nóthing—have no hope of vengeance —and are serious from the dangers they have just passed, their minds are more open to the action of good principles, and they lose, besides, all hope of the overseer aiding them in marrying, if they fix upon an ex-parishioner, as the child, by being born, is already settled. He considers that this change has greatly diminished perjury; though, if generally introduced, it would still leave overseers open to the temptation of encouraging perjury, as they always wish women to fix on rich fathers, as the parish is thereby better secured.

The order on the father varies according to his circumstances, and the parish always gives the mother all they get. This, Mr. Barnet is aware, operates as a direct premium on perjury. He has seen many instances where he has felt no conviction that the woman selected the right man, and knows of many instances of perjury. A young man courted a girl, aged seventeen, with intent to marry her; but they quarrelled. He was a journeyman, honest, industrious, and likely to do well. She came to the overseer, and wanted to swear a child to this young man. The overseer sent for him: he declared he had never had illicit connexion with her—had never suspected she was capable of incontinency, believing her above it, and would not credit that she was unchaste. However, she turned out to be with child, and, after much cross-examination, admitted that she had never had connexion with this young man; and said that she had fixed upon him as the father, because she knew he was honest and industrious, and thought they would force him to marry her. Hitherto, if the father failed to pay, the parish allowed the mothers 2*s.* for each bastard. They allowed widows but 1*s.* 6*d.* for legitimate children, and have just lowered the allowance of the bastard's mother to the same sum; but still, whenever the father does pay, the harlot is better off than the honest woman.

Nine out of ten of the orders of removal which the parish receives are cases of bastardy. Mr. Barnet knows whole families in the town which are bastards, from generation to generation. He has observed that magistrates generally favour the mothers of bastards in their complaints against overseers.

BINGHAM.

Bastardy flourished in this parish in the usual way up to the year 1818. The practice was the same here as elsewhere, and the effects of course the same.

In 1818, Mr. Lowe introduced a change marked by the wisdom which characterises his other proceedings.

For the seven years ending 1818, the average annual number of bastard births in Bingham was six; and the average annual number of marriages was thirteen and two-thirds. For the seven years ending 1824, the average annual number of bastard births was under two, and that of marriages ten.

Dean, the overseer's, account is as follows:—Twelve years ago we introduced this custom: when a woman came, saying she was with child, she was taken before the magistrate in the usual way; the sessions made the order on the father in the usual way. Then we told her she must get the money from the father herself, as we should never trouble him; and that if she became chargeable to us, we should send her to the house of correction, *and all women are invariably so sent.* Before this we used to have five or six bastards born every year; now we have under two. These are still sworn and affiliated in the usual way; there is no change in that respect; but if the mother applies for relief, we enforce the law, and send her to prison. So the mothers now never think of applying to the parish, but arrange with the fathers as well as they can, and maintain the children as well as they can. There are no bastards on the parish books now but *one;* and this is a particular case, where the mother was ill-treated by the father. For nearly the first three years after the first example was made, there was not one bastard birth in the parish (except in the case of a woman who was an idiot); neither has there been any instance whatever, for the last twelve years, of any woman *ever* having a *second* bastard child. Before this change there were many,—one woman had five; but at that time this parish paid as others do now, 2*s.* for every bastard, whether the money was obtained from the father or not.

This method of dealing with bastardy sweeps away the motive to perjury—the power of extorting money—deprives the woman of the hope of getting a husband, or large weekly allowances by incontinency, and the man of the most powerful topic for effecting seduction; and turns the moral sense of the poor into the right channel.

All laws regarding bastardy, which contemplate the slightest punishment on the man, have the inherent defect of encouraging what they aim at repressing. Such laws must give the woman power, either directly or indirectly, over the man; he will use that fact as a motive to induce her to yield; and she will yield because she knows she shall be able to effect his punishment if he deceives her.

The man may in all cases be as guilty as the woman; and it may seem hard or unjust to punish *her,* the weaker and more helpless of the two, and to suffer *him* to go unpunished; but the object of penal law is to *repress crime,* and not to punish it. Punishment is a means to an end; the end is the *prevention of crime;* and a punishment which operates to *encourage* instead of to *prevent* crime (as is the case in bastardy when the father is punished), frustrates the very object which alone can justify one human being In inflicting pain on another.

It may safely be affirmed, that the virtue of female chastity does not exist among the lower orders of England, except to a certain extent among domestic female servants, who know that they hold their situations by that tenure, and are more prudent in consequence. Among the residue, all evidence goes to prove that it is a nonentity. A daughter grows up; she learns what her mother was; she sees what her sisters and neighbours are; finds that nobody thinks the worse of them, and that nothing is expected of herself, and that there is a short road to marriage or a mainte- nance. The English law has abolished female chastity, self-respect, proper pride, and all the charities of domestic life, derived from and connected with its existence. It has destroyed, likewise, the beneficial influence which this virtue in women reflects on the character of men. If it is considered desirable to restore it, the way is easy, and sure, and short. It is only necessary to enact that it shall be unlawful for parishes to give relief to a mother for a bastard, without sending her to prison for three or six months, and to deprive parishes of all claim on the father. By acting on a somewhat similar principle, Mr. Whately, of Cookham, Berks, has reduced the annual bastardy births of his parish from fifteen to one.

CUMBERLAND.
CITY OF CARLISLE.

My Lords and Gentlemen,

In compliance with your letter of the 5th December, I forward extracts from my report on Carlisle. These will show the good effects that result from the administration being con- fided to an elected select body, with paid officers to act under it. They likewise point out a desirable change in the laws respecting the collection of the rates; and they give instances of abuses in granting an allowance to the mothers of illegitimate children: lastly, they describe a mode of farming the poor which seems peculiar to a part of the county of Cumberland.

I have the honour to be,
My Lords and Gentlemen,
Your very obedient Servant,
*
J. W. PRINGLE.

IN submitting the following Report on the management of the poor in the city of Carlisle, I shall at the same time bring forward observations made in parishes in the adjoining districts, where they appear to come in illustration of any material point.

The city of Carlisle is divided into two parishes, each of them includes also a considerable agricultural district. The total population by the last census is 20,006. These parishes are divided into sixteen townships; but they have in several cases united for the management of their poor, as will be seen by the following table, showing the population of the districts, and the rate per £. when reduced to what is stated to be the rack-rent.

	Population.	Rate per £.	
		s.	*d.*
Parish of St. Mary's.—District within the liberties. five Townships	5071	1	4
Caldewgate, Township	5104	3	3
Rickergate ditto	1448	1	4
Parish of St. Cuthbert.—District within, or English Street Township	3773	2	0
District without, 8 Townships	4610	1	5

In Caldewgate a workhouse has lately been built, which tends temporarily to raise the rates.

The management of the poor in these districts is nearly the same; the difference in rates must arise chiefly from the nature of the population in each.

St. Mary's Within is so far remarkable, that in three years from the period of the establishment of a select vestry, which took place in 1820, the rates were reduced from 6s. 6d. to 2s. 6d. in the pound. This was partly accomplished by establishing a system of accounts, which are examined and closed at each meeting of the vestry; by discontinuing relief to workmen, and making a careful investigation previous to granting it to others; and appointing an efficient person to the situation of assistant overseer and master of the workhouse, which is in good order, both as regards the house and the accounts. The person filling these two offices had previously been a pay-serjeant in the army.

The work going on in the house was teazing hair; 2 lbs. to 4 lbs. to be done as a task daily by each pauper; the value of the work one penny per lb.

I may adduce Whitehaven as a similar instance of the good effects of the management being placed in the hands of an efficient committee, elected by the rate payers, with paid officers to act under it. The rates there, in 1822, when the Select Vestry was established, amounted to 4420l., and are now brought down to 2000l.

The establishment of Select Vestries in rural and small townships is merely nominal, inasmuch as there does not exist either means or often disposition to make them efficient.

To recur, however, to St. Mary's, Carlisle. The payment of the rent of houses for paupers was at the same time discontinued in this district, and is almost so in the others. In St. Cuthbert's Within, 20*l.* is still paid on this account. The rents of these houses is from 2*l.* to 3*l.* 10*s.* each.

When rents were generally paid, it was found that the better orders of the working classes had difficulty in getting houses, the landlords giving the preference to those tenants who were receiving parochial relief.

The mode of collecting the rates, adopted in St. Mary's Within, appears to be worthy of remark.

The overseers, after calling twice on those rated, and demanding payment, give to the vestry, together with the money received, a list of the defaulters.

The assistant overseer then obtains from the magistrates one summons for the whole, and all who cannot show sufficient cause for being excused, are then made to pay.

By this means, arrears are never allowed, nor the collection of a new rate authorized until the previous one is settled.

It is in the power, however, of an overseer to prevent the working of this system; for the vestry have no authority to compel him to account for his collection by a given time, nor to make him furnish a list of defaulters.

The advantages of a law, giving the vestry such authority over the overseer, was strongly urged, and the necessity for such a power was exemplified in the proceedings of a select vestry, which I attended, in an adjoining parish, Haytown. The overseer there paid in 9*l.* " on account," but refused to furnish a list of those who had not paid, repeating, " they are good men, and will pay." In the large parish of Aldstone, another case bearing on this point was mentioned to me; in the preceding year two assistant-overseers, at salaries of 40*l.* each, had been appointed, chiefly for the collection of the rates, which had been done from absolute necessity, as, previously, the yearly overseers would only collect and pay the money when they chose. The parish also had no security, and one overseer went off last year to America with above 100*l.*

There are three poor-houses in Carlisle; they appear all to be well managed. The expense per head, for maintenance only, is 1*s.* 7*d.* or 1*s.* 8*d.* weekly.

The diet—milk porridge for breakfast and supper; meat and broth, with barley-bread, for dinner. The very old have white bread, and tea. The diet appears to be ample. The same cost for maintenance I found to be very general in the poor-houses of the neighbouring rural parishes.

At Arthuret, and Aldstone, the only places where they were fed by contract, the sum was 1s. 6d. per head weekly, and children under one year not charged for. At Penrith the expense is 2s.; and at Milinthorpe, where there is a united poor-house for sixteen townships, 2s. 5d.

The latter sum being so much above the average of those in the neighbourhood was, I understood, owing to the interference of a gentleman of large property near it, who insisted on the pauper having many additional comforts.

The general observation made by the farmers and small proprietors was, however, that even in those houses, where the average price was only 1s. 6d. per head, the inmates were living not only better than many labourers, but even than small farmers, who were paying rates.

In Kendal they had six couple in the house, each with two to four children; one couple had been there five years, during which period two children had been born.

In this house the cost of maintenance is 2s. 10¼d., per head, or, after deducting the earnings, 1s. 11¾d. These earnings arise from the weaving of coarse articles by hand-looms, a trade which is still taught the children, although worse than useless to them in after life; inasmuch as it unfits them for husbandry labour, and hand-loom weaving is almost driven out of the market by machinery. The younger children, too, continue to be employed in making cards for the teasing of wool, a work hurtful to the eyes, and long since superseded by machinery, by which it is done both better and cheaper.

In Haytown poor-house was a couple, the man lame and the woman nearly blind, who had married in that state as paupers, and now had four children. They had been during the whole period on parish relief, and had been taken into the house about twelve months, where they had a room to themselves.

The children in the poor-houses of Carlisle are all taught reading and writing, and a few also arithmetic.

The boys are apprenticed out at thirteen or fourteen, and 2l. to 5l. given as a premium.

The girls get into service about the same age: there is a difficulty in finding places for the children, particularly the girls. In St. Cuthbert's, five girls above thirteen were in the house. Both boys and girls turn out fairly.

Amongst the children there were nearly as many who had been deserted by their parents, as bastards and orphans. Of the thirty-six children in the poor-house of St. Mary's, thirteen were bastards; and twelve deserted by their parents. The children in the house are better clad, fed and taught than those of the same class out of it, and therefore encouragement arises to desert them.

The number on out-relief in Carlisle is very considerable, as may be observed by the published lists, from which the following is taken, namely,

In St. Mary's within the Liberties, those on regular pensions, amounting to 48

In S. Mary's without the Liberties   74

St. Cuthbert's within, ditto . . . 53

The assistant overseer of St. Cuthbert's Without having died a few days previous, and the lists not being printed, I could not ascertain the exact number, but comparing the amount of poor-rates, it may be taken at the same . 53

And in the small townships . . 30

Total . . 258

The number receiving casual relief was stated to be throughout the year about the same . . . 258

But during the four winter months, there are double that number. Spread the relief given to these extra 258 during four months, over the whole year, and it is equal to an addition of paupers amounting to . . 86

By adding the number of paupers in the workhouses 183

And the mothers of illegitimate children . . . 80

The total will be 865

which, compared with the amount of poor's-rate, 4986*l.*, gives about 2*s.* per week for each pauper, the officers' salaries, and the house expenses being included.

The population being 20,000, the proportion is nearly one pauper in twenty-three; but it must be remarked that these returns do not contain all the persons actually in receipt of parish assistance, who are resident in Carlisle, a great proportion of the weavers being non-parishioners, and having an allowance from their own parishes; but since it is not generally paid through the overseers of this city, the number cannot be easily ascertained.

In referring to the printed lists, it will be observed, that out of sixty illegitimate children, the allowance from the father is only recovered for twelve; five of the women on this list have also each two children. Punishment for bastardy appears to be very rarely inflicted, indeed only when the overseer makes such an application. Bastardy, and the litigation it causes, is referred to in this neighbourhood, in assigning reasons for the increase of the poor-rates. It seems not unusual for the daughters of the small

2 D 2

farmers, or statesmen, as they are here called, (men farming their own property,) to have bastard children, and to come to the parish for an allowance.

It cannot be expected that the overseer will apply for the punishment of people in this station of life.

The following extract is from a letter written by the overseer of the parish of ————

" We at this time, in our parish, are supporting two bastard children whose mothers have landed property of their own, and would not marry the fathers of their children.

" 'The daughters of some farmers, and even land-owners, have bastard children. These farmers and land-owners keep their daughters and children with them, and regularly keep back their poor-rate to meet the parish allowance for their daughters' bastards. We have no doubt the same grievance exists in many other parishes."

I could adduce many townships where one or more cases of farmers' daughters receiving such an allowance had occurred, but shall prefer giving an extract from the letter of a clergyman of a parish more than twenty miles from that to which the above refers :—

" A very different description of women have, of late years, become the mothers of bastard children ; formerly it was confined to the daughters of cottagers, and girls employed in farm husbandry : but of late very respectable farmers' daughters have been in that situation, and applied to have their offspring taken care of by the parish. As one plan to remedy the evil, the magistrates should impose a larger sum on the mother ; although this would not put an end to bastardy, the parish would not be so much burthened by this numerous description of mothers, as they would, in many instances, be kept at the expense of her parents, who, from their mode of management, are often too frequently to blame."

In another parish, the clergyman said, that in one year, to seven legitimate children he had baptized nine bastards ; they were almost all of them, however, the children of women at service out of the parish, removed there to lie in. One from Suffolk, at a great expense.

It was an observation frequently made, that the custom of hiring farm servants to live in the house leads frequently to these connexions ; and that the certainty of an allowance of money to the mother, either from the father or from the parish, encourages, it ; whilst in the south, the contrary system leads to improvident early marriages.

A mode of farming the poor is common in the townships to the north and east of Carlisle, which, since it is, I believe, peculiar to this part of the country, I shall here notice, namely, to contract with a person for a fixed sum, who undertakes to satisfy all claims of the paupers belonging to the township.

The township of Belbank, of which the population is 485, is farmed in this manner for the sum of 42*l.*; and Trough, population 169, for 32*l.* yearly. There is no poor-house belonging to these townships.

Brampton, of which the population is 3330, is farmed for the sum of 656*l.* It has a poor-house, in which were 30 inmates, who appeared to be taken care of as well as in the generality of poor-houses ; indeed they were rather cleaner, and looked better, than was usually found in the small poor-houses.

The contract is offered by public advertisement, and the lowest tender is accepted, if the person making it be approved of at the general meeting of the rate payers called together for that object. The person taking the contract has the use of the poor-house and ground attached, where there is such an establishment ; if not, he takes the paupers whom he cannot satisfy with a small payment, into his own house. They are generally small farmers' men, who, in many cases, sit down to their meals with the paupers.

This custom will cease to appear extraordinary, when it is stated to be usual for the farmer and his labourers to dine at the same table : and to give further proof of the different state of this part of the kingdom as compared with the south, I found the perpetual curate of a parish lodging and boarding in the house of one of these contractors.

The prevalence of this system of farming will be sufficient to indicate that magisterial authority, in ordering relief, is very seldom exercised. As far as I could ascertain, the paupers, generally, both on out-relief and in the poor-houses, in the townships thus farmed, were as well taken care of as in those conducted on the common system.

The rates where it has been adopted are kept down as compared to the adjoining townships.

The other advantages stated to result, are the saving vestry meetings and trouble to overseers ; the rendering almost all accounts unnecessary ; the making the paupers sensible that their claims will be rigidly inquired into, and resisted, unless strong and just.

As far as able-bodied and bastardy cases are concerned, there appears no objection to this system of farming. But it must be much feared that the old and infirm, who are unable to urge their claims, will often in consequence suffer.

HADDINGTONSHIRE.

My Lords and Gentlemen,

In compliance with your letter of the 5th of December, I have selected the Report of the parish of Dirleton, as it illustrates the opposite effects of the assessing and non-assessing system. I have the honour to be,

My Lords and Gentlemen,

Your obedient Servant,

Temple.   E. Carleton Tufnell.

DIRLETON,

Agricultural parish, Population 1384.

This is one of the most interesting parishes I have visited, as it presents one of the very few instances that Scotland affords of the abolition of assessments. I have, consequently, thought it expedient to give a short history of its condition previous to that event.

Before the year 1804, the poor of Dirleton were entirely supported by the Church collections, and the interest of a small sum that had been left to their use. In fact, the money arising from these sources was occasionally beyond the demand for it, insomuch that the session found themselves at times in the possession of a residue, which they distributed among the poor of neighbouring parishes, a thing now, I believe, unheard of in any part of Scotland.

The two unfavourable seasons that preceded 1804, caused a much greater application to be made to the poor's funds than before; and in this year the heritors and kirk session, unable to meet the demand by the ordinary sources of income, instead of enlarging their donations, introduced an assessment, which at first only amounted to 20*l.* The rate at which they increased, and their whole progress from beginning to end, will be seen in the annexed table.

£.		£.	s.
1804 20		1814 94	10
1806 30		1816 105	
1807 60		1818 105	
1809 40		1820 105	
1812 105		1822 73	10

It will be perceived that in the last year of their existence, they amounted to 73*l.* 10*s.* a considerable decrease on former years, which, however, was not owing to any diminution of the poor, but solely to a decrease in the price of provisions, which took place in that year. The truth of this will be shown by reference to " Cleland's Statistics," which give the corn prices in Scotland for a series of years.

It is to be observed, that the year after the assessments were begun, the difficulties that had caused their introduction ceased, but an increased demand for relief had been created by this procedure, and could not be kept down, consequently, the rates went on increasing, till they had reached five times their original amount.

In the mean time the condition of the poor, so far from being improved from the sums spent on them, was rapidly deteriorating. " We are prepared to state, on the authority of the father of the session, who has administered under both systems, that to his knowledge and belief, there has been decidedly more discomfort and discontent among the objects of parochial aid since the introduction of assessments than formerly existed. In point of fact, it was notorious that a work of mischief was going forward. We felt convinced that the wants of the poor increased in the direct ratio to the augmentation of the means of supplying them. We saw an exasperated state of feeling bursting forth from high-raised and disappointed expectations, where formerly there would have been nothing but sentiments of gratitude *." In this state of things every moral means were taken to allay the evil, a parochial library of religious books for gratuitous circulation was set on foot, a friendly society was established, as also a savings' bank, and both were attended with the greatest success.

All these measures, however, though doubtless they had their utility, failed of the desired end, and it was determined to take some more effectual course. A meeting of the heritors and tenants was called, and after some deliberation, they decided on the bold step of at once abolishing assessments. At the same time they agreed to increase considerably their church donations, without which the change could not have been so rapidly made; this, with an intimation from the pulpit of the new arrangements, caused an instantaneous augmentation in the collections, which have ever since supplied the place of assessments.

---

* This is an extract from a book published by the Rev. Mr. Stark, the minister at Dirleton, entitled, " Considerations addressed to the Heritors and Kirk-Sessions of Scotland," from which part of this account is taken. To his untiring perseverance and excellent management, Dirleton is chiefly indebted for the improvement that has taken place in the condition of its poor.

The change excited considerable clamour among the poor, who thought themselves robbed of their rights; and the minister, the Rev. Mr. Stark, who was the principal adviser of the measure, had to bear much odium on that account; it was, however, persisted in, and the result is given in the adjoining table.

Comparative Statement of the Receipts and Disbursements to the Poor in the Parish of Dirleton for the years 1821 and 1831 respectively.

1821.	Dr.	£.	s.	d.	1821.	Cr.	£.	s.	d.
1821.									
Jan. 1. Balance		1	0	6	Paid to the poor on the roll	124	5	0	
Assessment received		97	18	6	Paid legacies, per deed	2	10	0	
Collections ditto		21	8	4	Casual poor and house-rents	11	16	0	
Int. of mortified money		44	13	0	Paid for coals	4	14	1	
Mort. cloth money		2	11	8	Paid for educating poor scholars	7	1	3	
					Paid for book to ditto	1	0	0	
					Paid Clerk's salary	5	0	0	
					Paid Beadle's ditto, and fees	3	6	10	
					Paid Presbytery and Synod's dues	1	3	0	
					1821.				
					Dec. 31, Balance in hand	6	15	10	
Total of Poor Funds		167	12	0		£167	12	0	

1831.	Dr.	£.	s.	d.	1831.	Cr.	£.	s.	d.
1831.					Paid to the Poor on the Roll,				
Jan. 1. Balance		35	9	11	including three Lunatics	114	16	0	
Collections		106	19	9½	Paid Legacies	2	10	0	
Mort cloth money		4	0	8	Casual Poor and house rents	20	3	0¼	
Paupers' effects sold		2	9	10	For coals	13	5	8	
Int. of money		44	0	0	For educating poor scholars	6	1	6	
					For books for ditto	1	0	0	
					Clerk's salary	5	0	0	
					Beadle's ditto	3	0	4	
					Presbytery and Synod's dues	1	3	0	
					Incidental	0	11	0	
					1831.				
					Dec. 31. Balance in hand	25	8	11	
Total of Poor's Fund		£193	0	2½		£193	0	2½	

Comparison between the years 1821 and 1831.

Years.	Population.	No. of Paupers	Lunatics.	Collections. £. s. d.	Assessments. £.
1821.	1315	36	1	21 8 4	100
1831.	1384	26	3	106 19 9½	none.

The chief point to observe in this table is the diminution of paupers from thirty-six in 1821, to twenty-six in 1831, though the population has simultaneously increased. Still, however, this result of the non-assessing system is less favourable than it would otherwise appear, as 1831 happened to be a year of peculiar hardship to the parish, owing to a great deal of sickness among the poor. At the present moment the expenditure is considerably reduced, and the accounts of this year will exhibit the advantages of the present system of management in a greatly more favourable light. The increase of the church collections from 21*l.* to 106*l.* is also very remarkable.

	Population.	Number of Poor.	Amount of Assessments.	Church Collections.	No. of Persons to one Pauper.
			£.	£. *s.*	
Dirleton ...	1384	26	none.	106 19	53 $\frac{24}{100}$
Haddington.	5883	153	850	44	38 $\frac{44}{100}$
Tranent	3620	90	400	13	40 $\frac{22}{100}$

The annexed table is given in order to contrast the condition of Dirleton with that of the two neighbouring parishes of Haddington and Tranent. The effect, however, of the non-assessing system cannot at present be fairly seen, nor is it likely to be, so long as the places in the vicinity persist in following the ancient practice of assessment. The present success of it has been obtained under every adverse circumstance, under all the difficulties of a new project, without the assistance or countenance of any neighbouring parishes, and with all the effects of their evil example to contend with. What might be the result in Dirleton, were it supported by the practice of its neighbours, can only be conjectured; as it is, I was assured, that an improved moral change has already been wrought in the habits of the population. The diminution of paupers has been mentioned; the friendly society, which before the abolition of assessments numbered eighty-six members, has increased to one hundred and twenty; though the times have been at least as hard since; there are far fewer applications for relief, less clamour and discontent among the poor, and greatly diminished trouble in managing them. The result would have been more marked, had a similar treatment been adopted with the neighbouring poor.

It may possibly be objected that the table of expenses for the years 1821 and 1831 proves little in favour of the new system, since subtracting in each year the sums paid for lunatics who cannot strictly be termed paupers, as no management can either increase or diminish their numbers, the money expended in 1821 for the regular and casual poor amounted to 133*l.* 1*s.*, and in 1831, to 115*l.* 3*s.*, a diminution of only 17*l.* 18*s.* It has been already stated that 1831 was a year of unusual difficulty, owing to the prevalence of disease, and this explains why the saving has not been greater; the result this year will be very different. But the excellence of the non-assessing system must not be judged of from this test. It is not to save the pockets of the rich, but the principles and morals of the poor, that this system is introduced; its invariable effect is to diminish the poor-rates, but this is of infinitely minor importance in comparison with the moral change it produces in the habits of the poorer classes. This change has been begun and is in progress in Dirle-ton; and though the expenses were even increased by the new management, the inhabitant would think it a cheap purchase, when the return is the increased industry and morality of the labourers. I have not met with more than one parish in Scotland, where the assessments could be felt as a real burthen; the expenses and other evils of English pauperism are at present only in prospect. Therefore, the saving of money can never be an object with those who either oppose the introduction or desire the extinction of assessments in this part of the kingdom. In Dirle-ton, many persons now give voluntarily, more than they formerly were compelled to pay legally, towards the support of the poor, others again give less, and some little or nothing. But the minister was by no means desirous that each person should give in proportion to his wealth, as the apportioning to each heritor his due share of what was required would have the semblance of compulsion, and in fact would differ little from an actual assessment, and this the poor are quick enough to find out. As it is, they see that the donations are purely voluntary, and consequently are less eager to press their claims on a fund, whose existence depends on the kindness of their superiors, and receive relief less as a matter of right, than as the effect of the consideration and benevolence of the givers.

APPENDIX.

INSTRUCTIONS.

THE Central Commissioners are directed by His Majesty's Commission
to make a diligent and full inquiry into the practical operation of the
laws for the relief of the poor in England and Wales, and into the
manner in which those laws are administered, and to report whether
any, and what, alterations, amendments, or improvements may be
beneficially made in the said laws, or in the manner of administering
them ; and how the same may be best carried into effect.

This extensive inquiry may be conveniently divided into four heads :—

I. The form in which parochial relief is given.

II. The persons to whom it is given.

III. The persons by whom it is awarded.

IV. The persons at whose expense it is given.

It is probable that this inquiry will suggest considerable alterations
in the existing law ; and it is also probable that those alterations may
be facilitated by some further measures, such as—

V. Affording facilities for emigration.

VI. Facilitating the occupation, and even the acquisition of land by
labourers.

VII. Removing the tax on servants, so far as it is found to interfere
with their residence under their employers' roof.

VIII. Improving the rural police.

On these points there is already much information before the public,
and much more may be expected from the replies to the queries circulated by the commissioners. Those replies must, however, in general,
be imperfect, from the absence of details and vouchers as to matters of
fact, and of reasons where opinions are stated. There is no comparison
between the information afforded by them to the central commissioners,
and that which could be obtained if it were in their power to sift the
facts and the opinions contained in the different replies by the inspection of documents and cross-examination of witnesses ; if they could
ascertain the state of the poor by personal inquiry among them, and
the administration of the poor-laws, by being present at vestries and
at the sessions of magistrates.

As the constitution of the Central Board renders it impossible that these offices can be adequately performed by them in person, it is proposed that they should be executed by assistant commissioners.

The duty of an assistant commissioner will be, to proceed to the district, which will be indicated to him by the Board, taking with him whatever replies may have been returned from that district, and sets of blank queries for distribution. He will also be furnished with letters from the Home Department, which he can direct and deliver as he may find it expedient, requesting assistance in his inquiries.

He will communicate with the clergy, magistrates, and parish officers, deliver the printed queries to those who have not received them, and arrange the times and places of meeting at which the replies already given, or to be given, are to be explained, and the parish books and other vouchers produced.

The inspection of these documents will enable him to judge of the correctness of the replies, and probably offer him subjects of further inquiry. An investigation into all the circumstances connected with a single entry may give him a better insight into the actual management of a parish than could have been derived from any voluntary statements. He will endeavour, as far as possible, to be present at vestry meetings, and at the petty sessions of magistrates.

He will keep a full daily journal of his proceedings, and give to the Central Board, at least once a week, a sketch of his proceedings. The commissioners wish to leave it in the discretion of each assistant commissioner, either to make one final report at the termination of his labours, or distinct reports, from time to time, as soon as he has sufficient materials, but they would much prefer the latter course where it is practicable.

The urgency of the questions submitted to the Central Commissioners is such, that it is highly desirable that they should make their report to his Majesty before the commencement of the next session of parliament. And as the reports which they will receive from the assistant commissioners may be expected to form the most valuable part of their materials, it is important that they should all be received before the end of *November*. A much larger district has been assigned to each assistant commissioner than would have been expedient, if it had not been necessary to reduce, as far as it may be practicable, the number of their reports, and the expenses of the commission. It will be impossible, therefore, that each assistant commissioner should make a full, or even a cursory inquiry into the circumstances of each parish within his district, or even, in those parishes which he selects for observation, into all the subjects of inquiry which will be pointed out. He must use his own discretion as to the places which appear to be most deserving of investigation, and as to the points of inquiry which may be most successfully investigated in each particular parish: dwelling principally on those facts from which some general inference may be drawn, and which form the rule rather than the exception. And as it is understood that, although his time, like that of the other commissioners, is to be afforded gratuitously, his expenses are to be borne by the public, he will endeavour so to arrange his proceedings, as to render those expenses as moderate as may be consistent with the full performance of his duties.

Such is the outline of the general duties of an assistant commissioner.

The following instructions are intended to point out the specific points of inquiry which appear to the commissioners to be the most material. They have been arranged, as far as it was practicable, under the heads into which the subject has already been divided. But it has been found impossible to keep the first and second heads distinct.

I. THE FORM IN WHICH RELIEF IS GIVEN.

The form in which relief is given must be either in kind or in money.

1. *Relief in Kind.*

Relief, when given in kind, is generally given in a parochial or incorporated poorhouse, workhouse, or house of industry ; or by affording medical assistance, or lodging, or land.

The assistant commissioner will inquire whether the parish, which is the subject of his inquiries, possesses or has the use of a workhouse, poorhouse, or house of industry, either confined to its own poor, or in common with any other parish or parishes.

Where the parish possesses or has the use of such an establishment, he will endeavour to obtain answers, as full and as particular as possible, to Questions 12, 13, 14, 15, 16, 17, 18, 19, and 20, of the town queries. He will also inquire whether the house possesses any garden or farm, and the use to which it is applied ; and whether any school is attached to it, or any place where children are kept apart from its other inmates, and their religious and moral education attended to. He will endeavour to ascertain whether any means are adopted to prevent residence in the house from being an object of desire or indifference to the able-bodied poor, either by forced employment, restrictions on leaving it, separation of the sexes, prohibition of fermented liquors and tobacco, or by any other expedients, and the success of those measures. If no such measures are adopted, he will inquire into the causes and the consequences of their omission ; and whether there is any and what class of persons who actually oppose, or may be expected to oppose, their introduction or enforcement. If such an establishment has been recently made, or enlarged, or discontinued, he will ascertain what have been the results : he will compare the condition of those parishes which do, and those which do not, give relief out of the house : he will inquire into the management and effects of incorporated or hundred houses, as compared with parochial establishments, and ascertain whether, in any cases in which workhouses would be desirable, the smallness of the parish forms the obstacle to their being established ; and whether the rate-payers are acquainted with the conditions under which parishes can now unite to form workhouses, or would be likely to avail themselves of any additional facilities that might be given for forming united workhouses, or houses of industry, to the expense of which parishes might contribute in proportion to the number of paupers they might severally send to them: and he will collect facts and opinions as to the practicability and expediency of an enactment prohibiting, with any and what exceptions, relief to the able-bodied out of the workhouse or poorhouse in any parish possessing, or having the use of, such an establishment.

Where relief is given, by affording medical attendance, he will inquire whether that relief is confined to the inmates of the workhouse, or is extended to any, and what, other class of persons, and what has been the average yearly expense of supplying it during the last three years. If a contract is made with the medical attendant, whether that contract includes the paupers, either casual or resident, who have settlements elsewhere; and, if it does not include them, what is the difference between the sums charged for their treatment, and those charged for the treatment of the settled paupers.

Where relief is given, by providing lodging, he will inquire whether this is effected by means of houses belonging to the parish, or by payment of rent on the pauper's behalf: and, where the latter practice exists, he will inquire into its effects on the rent of the apartments or cottages inhabited by the poor.

The remarks respecting relief in land will be found in page 424.

2. *Relief in Money.*

The questions concerning relief in money are so mixed up with those which respect the relief of the able-bodied, that it will be advisable to consider them under that head.

II. THE PERSONS TO WHOM RELIEF IS GIVEN.

The persons to whom relief is given may be divided into the impotent and the able-bodied.

1. *The Impotent.*

Under this head are comprised all those who are prevented by disease of body or mind, by old age, or by infancy, from earning a part or the whole of their subsistence. The natural fund for the support of the legitimate children of the able-bodied is their parents' earnings. Parochial relief, when afforded to them, is afforded virtually to their parents. It is to be considered, therefore, under the head of relief to the able-bodied.

The impotent may, therefore, be divided into the diseased, the aged, and orphan and deserted children: to whom may be added, as the law is now administered, bastards; since the putative father, though he may be forced to contribute towards their support, never possesses the full rights or is subject to the full obligations of a father, and more frequently avoids both. The assistant commissioner will inquire what provision is made for lunatics and idiots; and into the amount and the degree of relief afforded to the diseased and the aged, and to orphan children; and particularly how far the clause of the 48d of *Elizabeth*, which directs the grandfather and father, grandmother and mother, and children of every poor, old, blind, lame, and impotent person, or other poor person not able to work, to be assessed to the support of every such poor person, is put in force ; and, if not put in force, what are the obstacles to its enforcement. He will inquire into the treatment of children deserted by their father; and how far that crime appears to be encouraged by the father's reliance on their being maintained, in his absence, by the parish.

He will ascertain the practice of the parish in the apprenticing of poor children ; inquiring to what class of persons they are apprenticed, and whether such persons take them voluntarily or by compulsion ; and, if the latter, according to what principle they are distributed : whether any, and what care is taken to see that they are well treated and taught ; and whether there are any grounds for supposing that a power to bind for less than seven years would be expedient.

He will consider the law and practice concerning bastardy as one of the most important subjects submitted to his investigation. The bastardy laws appear to produce effects very different from what may have been supposed to have been the objects of their institution. The sum charged on the father appears to have been intended merely as an indemnification to the parish. It often operates, however, as a punishment to the father, a pecuniary reward to the mother, and a means by which the woman obtains a husband, and her parish rids itself of a parishioner. It appears that the sum varies from 1*s.* to 2*s.* 6*d.* a week in country-places, and 5*s.* in towns ; that it is frequently sufficient to repay the woman for the loss which her misconduct would otherwise have occasioned to her ; and if she have more than one bastard, to be a source of emolument. The commissioner will endeavour to ascertain the practice of each parish in bastardy cases, and its effects on the morals of the inhabitants, both male and female, and on the increase of population; and to collect opinions in answer to the Questions 2, 3, and 4, of Queries No. 2.

And with reference to the degree in which the public provision for sickness and old age interferes with the exercise of prudence, he will inquire whether the parish has any savings bank, or friendly or benefit societies, to which the labourers are contributors ; and the average amount of each labourer's annual contribution: and if that amount appears to be increasing or diminishing, he will endeavour to ascertain the causes of such increase or diminution. And he will collect facts and opinions as to the expediency and practicability of, any further legislative measures for the promotion or regulation of such institutions.

2. *The Able-bodied.*

The able-bodied may be divided into the single and the married; and, again, as a cross division, into the employed and the unemployed : and the employed may be divided into those employed on account of the parish, and those employed by individuals.

The practice with respect to the relief of the able-bodied varies much in different parishes. In some, it is absolutely refused; in others, it is confined to the married; in others, to those who have one or more children. In some, it is given only in kind; in others, in money.

When given in money, it is generally effected in one of the five following modes :—

1st, By the parish giving to those who profess to be without employment a daily or weekly sum, without requiring from the applicants any work at all. The commissioners have heard of unemployed ablebodied young men receiving 2s. 6d. a week from the parish, on condition of their giving no further trouble.

2d, By the parish employing and paying the applicants for relief.

3d, By the parish paying the occupiers of property, to employ the applicants for relief, at a rate of wages fixed by the parish, and depending not on the services, but on the wants, of the applicants; the employer being repaid all that he advances beyond a certain sum. This is the roundsman, or billet, or ticket system. On this plan the pauper receives in general a ticket from the overseer, directing him to apply to a given farmer, and to work for him a day at a certain sum; generally, about 1s. if a single man; 1s. 3d. if married, without a family; 1s. 6d. if he have a wife and one child; and so on. The value of his services is charged by the parish to the farmer, at a sum sometimes as low as 2d. a day; and all that the farmer has paid beyond that estimated value is repaid to him out of the rates.

4th, By an agreement among the rate-payers, that each of them shall employ and pay out of his own money a certain number of labourers, in proportion not to his real demand for labour, but according to his rental, or to his contribution to the rates, or to the number of horses that he keeps for tillage, or to the number of acres that he occupies, or according to some other scale. Where such an agreement exists, it is generally enforced by an additional rate imposed, by general consent, on those who do not employ their full proportion. This may be called the labour-rate system.

5th, By the parish allowing to the labourers who are employed by individuals, relief in aid of their wages. In some places this is given only occasionally, or to meet occasional wants; to buy, for instance, a coat or a pair of shoes, or to pay the rent of a cottage. In other places, it is considered that a certain weekly sum, or more frequently the value of a certain quantity of flour or bread, is to be received by each member of a family. The amount of a man's earnings (those of his wife and children are seldom inquired into) is ascertained, or at least professed, or attempted, to be ascertained ; and the deficiency, if any, paid by the parish. In other places no such inquiry is made after there are a given number of children, beginning sometimes at one, sometimes at two, sometimes at three, and sometimes at four ; but a certain sum, or the price of a given quantity of flour or bread, is given to the father for each child above the specified number, whatever may be the amount of his earnings. The word "allowance" is sometimes used as comprehending all parochial relief afforded to those who are employed by individuals at the average wages of the district. But sometimes this term is confined to the relief which a person so employed obtains on account of his children : any relief which he may obtain on his own account being termed " payment of wages out of rates."

It will be the duty of the assistant commissioner to ascertain how far any one or more of these practices may prevail, or may have prevailed, in a parish. Where relief is given to able-bodied persons absolutely unemployed, he will inquire whether the parish adopts this system merely to save trouble, or to save expense, either because a person when in employment requires a more costly diet, or because the value of his labour would not be equal to the cost of tools and materials. Where labour is professed to be required in return for relief, he will inquire into the nature of the employment, whether it is paid for by the day or by the piece, the amount of payment for a given amount of labour, the variation of payment according to age, sex, celibacy, or number of children, the superintendence by which the amount of labour exerted is ascertained, and the value of the produce after deducting the expense of tools and materials. And he will compare the amount of work done, and of money received, by persons so employed by the parish, with the work which would have been exacted from the same persons, and the wages which would have been paid to them, if they had been employed by individuals. Places have been mentioned, where a man with a wife might have the choice of receiving 6*s.* a week from the parish for doing nothing, or 7*s.* 6*d.* from the parish for almost nominal work, from eight in the morning till three in the afternoon, or 9*s.* from a farmer for hard work during the regular hours of labour.

The assistant commissioner will endeavour to ascertain the time at which the relief of the able-bodied originated in any parish ; whether it is increasing, stationary, or diminishing, or has ceased ; and the causes and results of its origin, increase, continuance, diminution, or termination. Whether it arose in consequence of any sudden increase in the price of the necessaries of life, or any sudden diminution of the demand for labour, or any sudden increase in the number of labourers, or a desire to reduce the wages of men single, or with small families, or to throw on those who employ few labourers a part of the wages of those employed by others, or the interference of magistrates or imitation of neighbouring parishes. He will also inquire into its effects on the industry, habits and character of the labourer, the increase of population, the rate of wages, the profits of farming, the increase or diminution of farming capital, and the rent and improvement of land. He will particularly inquire into the effects of the labour-rate system on grass lands, and on small farms, particularly when farmed by their proprietors, and on shopkeepers, and the owners of tithes, and others having a small demand for labour. And he will endeavour to ascertain whether any or all of these effects have occasioned such a rate of wages, or such a deficiency of profitable employment in proportion to the existing population, as to occasion any, and what, difficulty in its discontinuance; and by what class of persons,

2 E

and by what means its discontinuance is likely to be opposed. Where the difficulty appears to arise from a local redundancy of population, he will carefully distinguish between those cases of redundant population in which there are more labourers than could be profitably employed at the existing prices of produce, although the labourers were intelligent and industrious, and the farmers wealthy, and those in which the redundancy is occasioned either by the want of capital among the farmers, or by the indolence or unskilful habits of the labourers. Where the redundancy is of the former description, he will endeavour to ascertain how far it has been occasioned by the stimulus applied to population by the relief of the able-bodied; and for that purpose inquire into the frequency of marriages where the husband at the time, or shortly before or after the time, of the marriage, was in the receipt of parish relief, and into the proportion of the number of such marriages to those of independent labourers; and compare the average age of marriage among paupers and among independent labourers. And, with a view to ascertain the effects of the relief of the able-bodied on the character of the labourers, he will inquire as to any difference in character between those who have and those who have not settlements in the parish. He will, of course, give particular attention to those cases in which the practice has been diminished or discontinued; to the class of persons by whom, and the means by which, such diminution or discontinuance has been effected; and to the class of persons by whom, and the means by which, that diminution or discontinuance has been resisted; and to the effects of such diminution or discontinuance on the industry, habits and character of the labourer, the increase of population, the rate of wages, the profits of farming, the increase or diminution of agricultural capital, and the rent and improvement of land; and he will particularly inquire whether such diminution or discontinuance has in any, and what, degree been effected by executing, as nearly as possible, that part of the 43d of *Elizabeth* which directs the parish officers " to set to work the children of all such whose parents shall not be thought able to keep and maintain them," by feeding and employing such children, and refusing all other relief to the father.

III. THE PERSONS BY WHOM RELIEF IS AWARDED.

The persons by whom relief is awarded are—
1. The overseers.
2. The vestry, either general or select, or their officers other than the overseers.
3. The magistrates.

1. *Overseers.*

In most parishes the overseers are annual officers, compelled to serve in rotation. It appears probable that such agents will be prevented by their other avocations from giving the time necessary to the vigilant and effectual performance of their duties; that neither diligence nor zeal are to be expected from persons on whom a disagreeable and unpaid office has been forced ; and that, even when zealous and diligent, they will often fail from want of experience and skill. To these sources of mal-administration may be added the danger of the parochial fund being misapplied, either in the way of actual embezzlement, or, what is more frequent, through partiality and favouritism to the relations, friends, dependants, customers, or debtors of the overseer, or through the desire of general popularity, or through the fear of general unpopularity, or of the hostility of particular individuals. The evils arising from the want of zeal, diligence and experience, have been attempted to be remedied by the appointment of permanent assistant overseers with a salary : the degree in which this attempt has been successful is an important subject of investigation.

The assistant commissioner will inquire what have been the professions or trades of the overseers in the parish during the last ten years, the periods at which they came into office, and their usual period of service. Where an assistant overseer has been appointed, he will inquire as to the effects, and where one has been discontinued, into the causes and consequences of such discontinuance. He will inquire how far the overseers or assistant overseers are competent judges of the work exacted from the paupers employed by the parish, particularly when that work consists, as is generally the case, of work on the road. He will inquire whether they unite to the office of overseer that of stone warden, or way warden, or surveyor of the roads ; and if they do not, into the obstacles to the union of those offices with that of overseer, and into the inconveniences which arise from their separation. He will inquire into the mode in which the accounts of the parish are kept, audited and published ; and he will collect facts and opinions as to the propriety of their being kept under distinct, and what, heads of expenditure ; as to their being balanced and audited at more frequent, and what, periods ; by whom they should be audited, and whether any advantage would arise from their being periodically printed, with the names of those who have been relieved, the amount, and the grounds of relief, and as to the possibility of enforcing such measures by enactment. He will endeavour to ascertain in each parish how far the parochial funds appear to have been profusely or improperly applied, in consequence of all or any of the causes of mal-administration which have been adverted to. He will compare, on these points, the state of towns with that of villages, and of small with that of large parishes ; and will collect facts and opinions as to the effects that might be expected from the union or the subdivision of parishes, and from any change in the selection, and time of service, of unpaid and of salaried overseers.

2. *Vestries.*

So far as magistrates do not interfere, the superintendence of a parish devolves principally on the vestry. The assistant-commissioner will ascertain in each parish whether the vestry is open or select, either under the 59th George III., cap. 12 (commonly called Mr. Sturges Bourne's Act), or any local Act. He will inquire into its periods of

2 E 2

meeting, the number of persons who usually attend, and their professions and trades; inquiring particularly how many of them are employers of labourers, landlords of cottages, or keepers of shops frequented by the poor; and how many of them, being farmers, farm their own property, or hold under leases, or from year to year, or at will. He will inquire what degree of authority or influence they exert over the parish officers. Where a select vestry has been established, he will ascertain what have been its effects; and where one has been discontinued, into the causes and consequences of its discontinuance. He will collect facts and opinions as to the practicability and the probable effects of allowing a landlord, though not rated, to vote in the vestry, in person or by proxy; and if so allowed, what influence should be given to his vote, compared with that of the tenant, and how far that influence ought to depend on the amount of his property. Recollecting that, in the few cases mentioned in the parliamentary evidence of extensive reforms effected in country parishes, those reforms generally appear to have been effected by the clergyman, he will particularly inquire in each parish what part the clergyman takes in the proceedings of the vestry. And with reference to the twenty-fifth question of Queries, No. 2., he will endeavour to ascertain whether, if the decision of the vestry, or select vestry, in matters of relief were made final, the vestry would be more likely to err by general profuseness, or by general niggardliness, or by partiality arising from any of the causes which have been pointed out as likely to occasion it to occur on the part of overseers.

3. *Magistrates.*

Great difference appears to exist in the degree in which magistrates in different districts interfere with the management of the poor. In some places they appear to act as if the property of the rate-payers were an unlimited fund, to be drawn upon by the magistrates as the stewards for the paupers; in others, they appear to consider the overseers, or the vestry, as the proper distributers of parochial charity, and interfere, if at all, only in favour of the impotent. It is probable that something between these two lines of conduct is the usual course, leaning towards the former in the worst administered rural districts, and towards the latter in the towns and the more prosperous parts of the country. This is a subject requiring the particular attention of the assistant-commissioner. Where he finds much interference, he will inquire whether the magistrates, who are most active or ready in such interference, are or are not resident within the parish in whose concerns they interfere, or within what distance; whether they contribute to its rates, and attend its vestries; whether any and what profit arises to their clerks from summonses and orders. Where there are, or have been, select vestries, he will inquire how far the magistrates make orders for relief, without its having been previously proved on oath that application 'ias been made to the vestry, and relief refused. He will inquire generally, whether they pay any and what attention to the character of the applicant, and the causes of his distress. He will compare the parishes in which the interference of magistrates is frequent, with those in which it is sparingly exercised, as to the comparative industry, habits, and character of the labourers, the increase of population, the rate of wages, the profits of farming, the increase or diminution of agricultural capital, and the rent and improvement of land. He will collect facts and opinions as to the practicability and expediency of exonerating the magistrates, wholly or partially, from their jurisdiction with respect to relief; and as to the means by which any enactment for that purpose could be made effectual; and he will endeavour to collect facts and opinions as to the practicability and expediency of appointing and paying persons having, for that special purpose, magisterial authority, subject to a strict superintendence, and removable in case of unfitness, and either itinerant or stationary, to perform, in the administration of the poor-laws, all or some part of the duties now imposed on the local magistracy.

IV. THE PERSONS AT WHOSE EXPENSE RELIEF IS GIVEN.

The persons at whose expense parochial relief is afforded, are those rated to the poor in the parish or township from which the pauper is entitled to relief, either by settlement or as a casual pauper. This subject may be considered under two heads—

1. The mode in which the rate is assessed and collected.
2. The means by which a person, being an object of relief, acquires a claim to relief from a given parish or township.

1. *Assessment and Collection.*

The assistant commissioner will inquire in each parish whether the assessment is considered as fair; and if complained of as unfair, what would be the expense of enforcing a new assessment; and he will collect opinions as to the means of reducing that expense. He will inquire whether there are any, and what, houses or lands exempted from assessment, or from which the sums assessed are not actually collected. In some parishes every tenement is rated, and the payment is uniformly enforced; and it appears, from the evidence already before the Commissioners, that in such places the poor act as checks upon one another, and that improper application for relief is often prevented by the unpopularity of the attempt to increase a burthen in which all immediately participate, and is often rendered unsuccessful by being denounced to the parochial officers. In other places the rates are collected from the poor only when non-parishioners; a practice which not only abandons the advantage of making the labouring class feel the pressure of the rate, but adds one more to the numerous impediments opposed by the law of settlement to the free circulation of labour. It must be added, that in many places, particularly in the neighbourhood of towns, and where rents are paid by the parish, a class of persons has arisen who speculate in cottages, and in letting apartments to the poor; and, since it has been discovered that the poor are willing and able to pay high rents for small portions of land, speculation will probably take that direction also, and persons will be found to purchase a field or two, to be divided into slips, and let to labourers. The practice of exempting small tenements from rates is very favourable to both these speculations, as it enables the proprietor to increase the rent by the amount of rate remitted, and to be the owner of houses and lands, and yet escape the principal burthens to which such property is subjected.

The assistant commissioner will inquire in each parish what persons are the occupiers and owners of those properties which are not assessed to the poor-rate, or from which the rates are not actually collected. What is their ability and rank in life; and whether they are members of the vestry, or have any means of influencing its decisions; and how far, and with what effect, the 19th section of Mr. Sturges Bourne's Act, which enables the proprietors of certain dwellings to be rated, has been acted on; and he will collect facts and opinions as to the propriety of an enactment, making it imperative with respect to tenements not exceeding a given, and what, annual value, or occupied by a given number or class of persons, to charge the proprietors either instead of the occupiers, or, which probably would be better, on their default of payment.

2. A person acquires a claim to relief from a given parish, either as a casual pauper, or as having a settlement in that parish.

1st, Casual Paupers.—The assistant commissioner will inquire in each parish what has been the expense of casual paupers during the last three years: what proportion it has borne to that of the settled paupers: how much of that expense has been recovered from other parishes, and what proportion has been incurred on account of Scotch or Irish poor; and whether there are any and what number of casual paupers who have become virtually settled in the parish, from their having no known place of settlement to which they might be removed.

2dly, Settled paupers.—The possibility of acquiring, and consequently of losing a settlement by hiring and service, apprenticeship, renting and purchasing a tenement, and serving a parish office, appears often to occasion transactions, into which men have entered with very different views, to produce important and unforeseen effects on their own welfare, and on that of others; and it also occasions acts to be forborne or done, in order to prevent or to produce consequences which have no natural connexion with those acts. It appears, from the replies to question 5, (Queries, No. 2.) that the fear of giving a settlement by hiring and service has a tendency to prevent steady employment; the labourer, in those cases in which he might otherwise have been hired for an indefinite period, or by the year, being hired for fifty-one weeks, and the service, if renewed, being renewed after a week's interval—an interval generally spent in idleness and dissipation. Cases have also been mentioned, where a person has hired for a year those among the labourers settled in his parish, whom he most wished to get rid of, and settled them in some other parish, by keeping them there during the last forty days of the year, and then dismissing them. Where the rents of cottages are paid by the parish, the landlords of cottages have taken apprentices for the express purpose of giving them settlements, in order that they might in time become their tenants. Threats have been held out in other places, that if cottages were rated, the rents should be raised to 10*l.* a year (of course collusively), and the parish punished by their being let to out-parishioners.

On the other hand, it has been urged that, if all these modes of acquiring a settlement are abolished, villages may be seriously injured by the return, in old age and infirmity, of those who have left them in youth and vigour; and that the paupers may suffer, by being removed from their acquired friends, to places in which they have become strangers.

Settlement by residence has been proposed as an answer to these objections; but this again might perhaps be made the source of much fraud and oppression. There are country parishes in which every cottage has been pulled down, so that all the work is done by labourers who are legally resident in some adjoining parish.

The assistant commissioner will endeavour to ascertain the amount and nature of the inconveniences arising from each of the existing modes of acquiring a settlement; and inquire into the probable consequences, both immediate and ultimate, of abolishing any one or more of them, and substituting any, and what, other sources of settlement in their room. And he will particularly inquire, in each parish, what number of Irish or Scotch adults, or young children of Irish or Scotch fathers, have acquired settlements there within the last five years, and under what heads of settlement.

The four other subjects to which allusion has been made,—emigration, the acquisition of land by labourers, taxation on domestic servants, and rural police, though not strictly within the province of the commissioners, are too much connected with it to be left out of their consideration. Emigration, indeed, and amendment of the poor-laws, must, for any useful purpose, be united. To attempt to diminish population by removing a portion of the people, and yet leaving in full force the most powerful machinery that ever was applied to their increase, is to attempt to exhaust, by continual pumping, the waters of a perpetual fountain. And, at the same time, it appears essential to any material change in the poor-laws, that the local superabundance created or perpetuated by those laws should be drawn off.

V. EMIGRATION.

The assistant commissioner will therefore pay particular attention to emigration. He will endeavour to ascertain all the facts connected with every case in which an emigration has been effected, and its influence on the rates of the parish, and on the wages and character of the remaining labourers. He will inquire what sort of persons were sent out, and how many, and of what character, and within what period, have returned. Where no such attempt has been made, he will ascertain whether the omission is to be attributed to the absence of a redundant population, (and if so, how that absence is to be accounted for,) or to any, and what, difficulties or objections on the part of the rate-payers or of the labourers. And he will collect facts and opinions as to the propriety of an enactment enabling any, and what, majority, in number and value, of the rate-payers, with or without the concurrence of any, and what, majority, in number and value, of the proprietors, to raise money for emigration, in what, if any definite proportion to the rental or rates, and as to the period within which such money should be repaid, and the portion, if any, which should be paid by the proprietors.

VI. ACQUISITION OF LAND BY LABOURERS.

The evidence already before the commissioners shows that the occupation of land by labourers is rapidly increasing. The assistant commissioner will inquire, in each parish, into the mode in which this is effected, and into its results. For these purposes he will inquire whether the lessors are the landowners, the farmers, or the parish officers; distinguishing, in the case of landowners, between the cases in which the lessors are the principal landowners, and those in which they are small proprietors. Whether any, and what, selection is made of the occupiers, and what terms, as to rent, period of enjoyment, abstinence from requiring relief, or conduct, are imposed on them. What quantity is allotted to each occupier, and on what principle. What assistance they receive in manuring, working, or seed. How long the practice has existed, and with what effects, as to the welfare and conduct of the labourers, and amount of rates. And he will endeavour to collect facts and opinions as to the average quantity of land which a labourer can beneficially occupy, without withdrawing him from ordinary labour, and as to the expediency of any enactments either to facilitate the practice, or to guard against the danger of its creating a cottier population resembling that of Ireland. He will inquire as to the existence of any lands now positively or comparatively useless, which may be applied to this purpose; carefully distinguishing between that land which, though commonly called *waste*, is very far from being *wasted*, but is now turned to its best account as sheepwalk, and that which is really unproductive, or less productive than it might be made by a judicious and profitable application of labour. He will also inquire whether the actual ownership of land by labourers or small proprietors is less common than formerly, and whether that is to be attributed to the pressure of poor-rates, the obligation imposed on an applicant for relief of parting with his property, the stamp duties on alienation, or the expense of making a title. And with reference to the last point, he will inquire whether small proprietors are more usual in any, and in what degree, among copyholders than among freeholders.

VII. TAXATION ON DOMESTIC SERVANTS.

It has been supposed that the residence of farming labourers with their employers has been diminished by the tax on domestic servants;

a tax to which the farmer' exposes himself, if he allows the labourers residing under his roof to perform menial offices. The assistant commissioner will inquire whether this supposition is well founded, and whether there is any reason to believe that exempting from the tax all labourers principally employed in agriculture, though occasionally performing menial offices, would tend to make them more frequently resident under their employers' roofs.

VIII. RURAL POLICE.

The last point which has been adverted to is rural police. The assistant commissioner will inquire in each parish into the ordinary and extraordinary means which it possesses of enforcing public order. The number of constables or tything-men, their general character and remuneration, and the number of yeomanry and special constables, who might be depended upon on any emergency. And he will collect facts and opinions as to the propriety of any, and what, legislative measures on this subject. He will also inquire whether there have been any riots, disturbances, or fires, within the last two years, and endeavour to ascertain their causes, the effects which have resulted or may be expected to result from them, and the nature and success of the measures by which they were resisted, prevented, or punished.

A brief and imperfect outline has now been given of the specific points of inquiry respecting the practical operation of the laws for the relief of the poor, and the manner in which those laws are administered. But there are two general inquiries, to which each specific inquiry may be made subservient. One is, the great question how far the law which throws on the owners of property the duty of providing the subsistence, and superintending the conduct of the poor, has really effected its object;—how far the proprietors of land and capital appear to have had the power and the will to create, or increase, or render secure, the prosperity and morality of those who live by the wages of labour. It has been supposed that it was to the 43d of *Elizabeth*, and to the superintendence which it forced the richer to exercise over the poorer, that we owed the industry, the orderly habits, and the adequation of their numbers to the demand for labour, which within the memory of man distinguished the English labourers; and that the idleness, profligacy and improvidence, which now debase the character and increase the numbers of the population of many of the south-eastern districts, are owing to the changes, partly by statute, and partly by practice, to which that law has been subjected. On the other hand, it has been maintained, that it is the natural tendency of public relief, however purely and wisely administered, to become a substitute, and a very bad substitute, for private charity on the part of the rich, and industry and forethought on the part of the poor; that the pure or wise administration of that relief is the exception, not the rule; that it has more frequently been used as an engine to reduce the wages of labour, or to shift their burthen from the employer, or to gratify the love of power or of popularity; that where real humanity has been the motive of interference, it has been so little assisted by knowledge or diligence, as to produce, or aggravate, or perpetuate, the misery which it was intended to relieve; and that the system appeared to work well only while balanced by an almost arbitrary power of removal, and the dread of the workhouse, and while the range of magisterial interference was closely limited.

The other general question is, how far the evils of the present system, or rather of the law which allows, or at least does not prevent, the existence in every parish of every different system of abuse, are diminishing, stationary, or increasing. There can be no doubt that any change in the poor-laws, or in the manner of administering them, if great enough to be extensively beneficial, must be attended with immediate local suffering. If, however, the present evils, oppressive as they are, appear to be diminishing, or even to be stationary, it may be more prudent to endure them, than to encounter the certain inconvenience, and the probable hazard, of any extensive alteration. But if the conclusions drawn in the House of Commons' Report, of 1817, be correct,—if it be true, that " unless some efficacious check be interposed, the amount of the assessment will continue, as it has done, to increase, until, at a period more or less remote, according to the progress the evil has already made in different places, it shall have absorbed the profits of the property on which the rate may have been assessed, producing thereby the neglect and ruin of the land, and the waste or removal of other property, to the utter subversion of that happy order of society so long upheld in these kingdoms;"—if the progress of the evil, even during the short period that has elapsed since that Report was made, may be traced in the diminished cultivation and value of the land; the diminution of industry, forethought, and natural affection among the labourers; the conversion of wages from a matter of contract into a matter of right, and of charity itself into a source of discord, and even of hostility; in the accelerated increase of every form of profligacy; in fires, riots, and organised and almost treasonable robbery and devastation;—if such be the representation which the Commissioners have to make to his Majesty; they cannot append to it a suggestion of mere palliative amendments.

COPIES OF THE QUERIES CIRCULATED BY THE COMMISSIONERS.

Queries for Rural Districts.—No. I.

1. Name and county of your parish or township?
2. Number of acres in your parish or township?
3. How much common? How much woodland? How much arable? How much pasture?
4. Number of labourers sufficient for the proper cultivation of the land?

5. Number of agricultural labourers in your parish?

6. Number of labourers generally out of employment, and how maintained in summer and in winter?

7. Weekly wages, with and without beer or cider, in summer and in winter?

8. Whether labourers are apportioned amongst the occupiers according to the extent of occupation, acreage rent, or number of horses employed?

9. Whether any distinction is made in wages paid by their employers to married and single men when employed by individuals?

10. Whether any and what allowance is made from the poor's rate on account of large families, and if so, at what number of children does it begin?

11. Whether the system of roundsmen is practised, or has been practised?

12. Is any work done for individuals, and partly paid for by the parish?

13. What class of persons are generally the owners of cottages?

14. The rent of cottages?

15. Whether gardens to the cottages?

16. Whether any land let to labourers: if so, the quantity to each, and at what rent?

17. What are your rates per pound by the year, at rack-rent, or how estimated?

18. Have they increased or diminished during the last year, compared with the preceding?

19. Have you a select vestry and assistant overseer, and what has been the effect?

20. Have you a workhouse? state the number, age, and sex of its inmates.

21. What number of individuals received relief last week, not being in the workhouse?

22. What can women, and children under sixteen, earn per week, in summer, in winter, and harvest; and how employed?

23. How many non-parishioners have you in general, distinguishing Irish and Scotch?

Queries for Rural Districts.—No. II.

1. Are there many or few landowners in your parish; and are the farms large or small?

2. What is the allowance received by a woman for a bastard? and does it generally repay her, or more than repay her, the expense of keeping it? and is the existing law for the punishment of the mother whose bastard child becomes chargeable often executed for the first or for the second offence?

3. What number of bastards have been chargeable to your parish, and what has been the expence occasioned by them during each of the last five years? and how much of that expence has been recovered from the putative fathers? and how much from the mothers?

4. Can you suggest any, and what, change in the laws respecting bastardy?

5. Do the labourers in your neighbourhood change their services more frequently than formerly? and how do you account for that circumstance?

6. Are there many cases in your parish where the labourer owns his cottage?

7. What class of persons are the usual owners of cottages?

8. Are cottages frequently exempted from rates? and is their rent often paid by the parish?

9. Is the industry of the labourers in your neighbourhood supposed to be increasing or diminishing; that is, are your labourers supposed to be better or worse workmen than they formerly were?

10. Have you any, and what, employment for women and children?

11. Is piece-work general in your neighbourhood?

12. What in the whole might an *average* labourer, obtaining an *average* amount of employment both in day-work and piece-work, expect to earn in the year, including harvest work and the value of all his other advantages and means of living, except parish relief?

You will observe, that this question refers to an *average* labourer obtaining an *average* amount of employment, not to the best labourer in constant employment.

13. What in the whole might his wife and four children, aged 14, 11, 8, and 5 years respectively, (the eldest a boy,) expect to earn in the year? obtaining, as in the former case, an average amount of employment.

14. Could the family subsist on these earnings? and if so, on what food?

15. Could it lay by anything? and how much?

16. Is there any, and what, difference between the wages paid by the employer to the married and unmarried, when employed by individuals?

17. Have you any, and how many, able-bodied labourers in the employment of individuals receiving allowance or regular relief from your parish on their own account or on that of their families?

18. Is that relief or allowance generally given in consequence of the advice or order of the magistrates? or under the opinion that the magistrates would make an order for it, if application were made to them?

19. Is any, and what, attention paid to the character of the applicant, or to the causes of his distress?

20. Is relief or allowance given according to any, and what scale?

21. Can you state the particulars of any attempt which has been made in your neighbourhood to discontinue the system (after it has once prevailed) of giving to able-bodied labourers in the employ of individuals parish allowance on their own account, or on that of their families?

22. What do you think would be the effects, both immediate and ultimate, of an enactment forbidding such allowance, and thus throwing wholly on parish employment all those whose earnings could not fully support themselves and their families?

23. Would it be advisable that the parish, instead of giving allowance to the father, should take charge of, employ, and feed his children during the day? and if such a practice has prevailed, has it increased or diminished the number of able-bodied applicants for relief?

24. What do you think would be the effect of an enactment enabling parishes to tax themselves in order to facilitate emigration?

25. What do you think would be the effect, immediate and ultimate, of making the decision of the vestry or select vestry in matters of relief final?

26. If an appeal from the vestry or select vestry shall continue, what do you think would be the effect, immediate and ultimate, of restoring the law as it stood before the stat. 36 Geo. III. cap. 23, was passed, so that, in any parish having a workhouse or poorhouse, the magistrates should not have the power of ordering relief to be given to persons who should refuse to enter the workhouse or poorhouse?

27. Do you know of any cases in which the clause of Mr. Sturges Bourne's Act (59 Geo. III. cap. 12, § 29), enabling relief to be made by way of loan, has been acted on?

28. Is the amount of agricultural capital in your neighbourhood increasing, or diminishing? And do you attribute such increase or diminution to any cause connected with the administration of the poor laws?

29. Can you suggest any improvement in the mode of keeping and auditing and publishing parish accounts?

30. Can you suggest any, and what, alteration in the settlement laws, for the purpose either of extending the market for labour, or interfering less with contracts, or diminishing fraud or litigation?

31. Do you think it would be advisable to afford greater facilities than now exist, either for the union or for the subdivision of parishes or townships, for any purpose connected with the management of parochial affairs?

32. Can you give the Commissioners any information respecting the causes and consequences of the agricultural riots and burning of 1830 and 1831?

33. What is the name and county of the parish, township, or district to which your answers refer?

Town Queries.—No. III.

1. Have you a local act for the management of the Poor? what is its date, and what have been its effects?

2. In whom does it invest the power of distributing relief?

3. In what other respect do its provisions differ from the general law of the land?

4. Do you think any of its provisions might be advantageously applied to parishes in general?

5. Are the concerns of the parish managed by any boards or committees appointed by the vestry?

6. Have you had any experience of a select vestry under Mr. Sturges Bourne's Act, 59 Geo. III. cap. 12? and for what period? what have been its effects?

7. How many overseers have you? of what class of persons are they? are they usually tradesmen, or men engaged in business?

8. Do they often serve in successive years?

9. Have you any assistant or paid overseer, or other salaried officer, to assist those who administer parish relief?

10. Is your parish for any purposes divided into wards or districts, with parish officers resident in each?

11. Do you think it would be advisable to afford greater facilities than now exist, either for the union, or, on the other hand, for the subdivision, of parishes or townships, for any purposes connected with the management of parochial affairs?

12. Have you a workhouse in your parish? state the number, age, and sex of its inmates, and, as far as you can ascertain them, their former occupations.

13. Are all or any, and which, of the paupers in the workhouse employed, and on what description of work?

14. What has been the profit or loss to the parish during the last year, in consequence of their having been so employed?

15. Is any, and what, distinction made in fare or treatment between the aged and impotent, and the able-bodied inmates of the workhouse? and is the allowance of food to the latter proportioned to the work done?

16. Is there a separation of the male from the female inmates in your workhouse?

17. Do you farm any, and how many, of your poor? and at what rate per head? and since when? and what has been its effect?

18. What is the expense of the poor in the workhouse per head per week, including the expense of the establishment?

19. What is the average expense per head per year, including all the expense of the establishment?

20. Have you any and what improvements to suggest in the management of workhouses?

21. How do you provide for your infant poor?

22. State the numbers, ages, sexes, and description, and, as far as you can ascertain them, the present or former occupations, of the poor relieved out of the workhouse?

23. Are the overseers or other persons who distribute relief to the out-poor acquainted with the persons of the out-paupers?

24. Is there any visitation of the poor at their houses? or what other means are taken to ascertain the real necessities of the applicants for relief?

25. Are there any means taken to ascertain whether the aged poor applying for relief have children able to maintain them?

26. Are any means taken to ascertain whether persons claiming relief on account of temporary want of employment have voluntarily thrown themselves out of work, or have previously received wages sufficient to enable them to make provision against the stoppage of work? and, in apportioning relief, is any, and what, attention paid to the character of the applicant, or the causes of his distress?

27. Is allowance or regular relief out of the workhouse given by your parish to any able-bodied mechanics, manufacturers, labourers, or

servants? state the number, and, as far as you can, the actual or former occupations, of the persons to whom such relief is given?

28. Is that relief or allowance given in consequence of the advice or order of the magistrate? or under the opinion that the magistrates would make an order if application were made to them?

29. Is it given according to any, and what, scale? Is it given to any persons wholly employed by individuals, on the ground that their wages are insufficient to maintain their children?

30. To how many able-bodied men (parishioners) has occasional relief been given during the last year? and have the numbers so relieved exceeded or fallen short of the annual average?

31. Have you any, and what, mode of employing able-bodied paupers out of the workhouse?

32. Is relief ever, and under what circumstances, given to able-bodied applicants, without setting them to work?

33. Have you any, and what, employment for women and children?

34. What are the classes of manufacturers, workmen, or labourers in your parish whom you believe to be most subject to distress?

35. What in the whole might an average man of each of these classes, obtaining an average amount of employment in day-work and piece or job work, expect to earn in the whole year, including all his advantages and means of living, except parish relief?

N. B. You will observe, that this question refers to an average man, obtaining an average amount of employment, not to the best workman in constant employment.

36. What in the whole might his wife and four children, aged 14, 11, 8, and 5 years respectively, (the eldest a boy,) expect to earn in a year, obtaining, as in the former case, an average amount of employment?

37. Could the family subsist on these earnings, and if so, on what food?

38. Could it lay by anything? and how much?

39. What proportion of the labouring poor in your parish do you believe to be non-parishioners? What proportion of these are Irish or Scotch?

40. Are your payments on account of casual poor considerable?

41. Can you state the particulars of any attempt which has been made in your neighbourhood to discontinue the system (after it has once prevailed) of giving parish allowance to able-bodied men in the employ of individuals, or to the families of such men?

42. What do you think would be the effects, both immediate and ultimate, of an enactment forbidding such allowance, and thus throwing wholly on parish employment all those whose earnings could not fully support themselves and their families?

43. Would it be advisable that the parish, instead of giving allowance to the father, should take charge of, employ, and feed his children during the day? and if such a practice has prevailed, has it increased or diminished the number of able-bodied applicants for relief?

44. What do you think would be the effect of an enactment enabling parishes to tax themselves in order to facilitate emigration?

45. What do you think would be the effect, immediate and ultima of making the decision of the vestry or select vestry in matters of reli final?

46. If an appeal from the vestry or select vestry shall continue, wh do you think would be the effect, immediate and ultimate, of restorin the law as it stood before the stat. 36 Geo. III. cap. 23, was p so that, in any parish having a workhouse or poorhouse, the magistrat should not have the power of ordering relief to be given to persons w should refuse to enter the workhouse or poorhouse?

47. Are there many small houses or cottages in your parish?

48. What class of persons are the usual proprietors of them?

49. Are these dwellings in any case exempted from rates?

50. Are the landlords rated in respect of houses below any, and wh rent?

51. Do they compound, or are they rated on the same terms as occupiers of other houses?

52. Where the occupiers are rated in respect of small houses or co tages, are the rates usually paid?

53. What is the usual per-centage of the whole rate imposed on yo parish which is not ultimately collected?

54. How does the deficiency arise?

55. What is the allowance received by a woman for a bastard, an does it generally repay her, or more than repay her, the expense keeping it? and is the existing law for the punishment of the moth whose bastard child becomes chargeable often executed for the first for the second offence?

56. What number of bastards have been chargeable to your parish and what has been the expense occasioned by them during each of th last five years? and how much of that expense has been recovere from the putative fathers? and how much from the mothers?

57. Can you suggest any, and what, change in the laws respectin bastardy?

58. Can you suggest any, and what, improvement in the settleme laws?

59. What has been the expense annually in the last three years removing paupers? What expense in the same three years has arise annually from litigation respecting settlements?

60. Is there any provision for auditing your parish accounts? a they published, or rendered accessible and intelligible to the p rishioners?

61. Can you suggest any improvement in the mode of keeping an auditing and publishing such accounts?

62. What is the name and county of the city, town, parish, or tow ship to which your answers refer?

London: W. CLOWES, Stamford Street.

Lightning Source UK Ltd.
Milton Keynes UK
UKHW010302220119
335963UK00013B/1050/P